T0214194

Lecture Notes in Computer Science   12543

Founding Editors

Gerhard Goos
Karlsruhe Institute of Technology, Karlsruhe, Germany
Juris Hartmanis
Cornell University, Ithaca, NY, USA

Editorial Board Members

Elisa Bertino
Purdue University, West Lafayette, IN, USA
Wen Gao
Peking University, Beijing, China
Bernhard Steffen
TU Dortmund University, Dortmund, Germany
Gerhard Woeginger
RWTH Aachen, Aachen, Germany
Moti Yung
Columbia University, New York, NY, USA

More information about this subseries at http://www.springer.com/series/7408

Valentina Casola · Alessandra De Benedictis ·
Massimiliano Rak (Eds.)

Testing Software and Systems

32nd IFIP WG 6.1 International Conference, ICTSS 2020
Naples, Italy, December 9–11, 2020
Proceedings

 Springer

Editors
Valentina Casola (iD)
University of Naples Federico II
Naples, Italy

Alessandra De Benedictis (iD)
University of Naples Federico II
Naples, Italy

Massimiliano Rak (iD)
University of Campania "Luigi Vanvitelli"
Aversa, Italy

ISSN 0302-9743   ISSN 1611-3349   (electronic)
Lecture Notes in Computer Science
ISBN 978-3-030-64880-0   ISBN 978-3-030-64881-7   (eBook)
https://doi.org/10.1007/978-3-030-64881-7

LNCS Sublibrary: SL2 – Programming and Software Engineering

© IFIP International Federation for Information Processing 2020
This work is subject to copyright. All rights are reserved by the Publisher, whether the whole or part of the material is concerned, specifically the rights of translation, reprinting, reuse of illustrations, recitation, broadcasting, reproduction on microfilms or in any other physical way, and transmission or information storage and retrieval, electronic adaptation, computer software, or by similar or dissimilar methodology now known or hereafter developed.
The use of general descriptive names, registered names, trademarks, service marks, etc. in this publication does not imply, even in the absence of a specific statement, that such names are exempt from the relevant protective laws and regulations and therefore free for general use.
The publisher, the authors and the editors are safe to assume that the advice and information in this book are believed to be true and accurate at the date of publication. Neither the publisher nor the authors or the editors give a warranty, expressed or implied, with respect to the material contained herein or for any errors or omissions that may have been made. The publisher remains neutral with regard to jurisdictional claims in published maps and institutional affiliations.

This Springer imprint is published by the registered company Springer Nature Switzerland AG
The registered company address is: Gewerbestrasse 11, 6330 Cham, Switzerland

Preface

This volume contains the proceedings of the 32nd IFIP International Conference on Testing Software and Systems (ICTSS 2020). IFIP-ICTSS has become a traditional event of the WG 6.1 of the International Federation for Information Processing (IFIP). The conference was supposed to be in Napoli, Italy, during December 9–11, 2020, but, due to the COVID-19 pandemic, it was held online, as a virtual conference.

ICTSS is a series of international conferences addressing conceptual, theoretical, and practical problems of testing software systems, including communication protocols, services, distributed platforms, middleware, embedded, cyber-physical systems, and security infrastructures. It is a forum for researchers, developers, testers, and users from industry to review, discuss, and learn about new approaches, concepts, theories, methodologies, tools, and experiences in the field of testing of software and systems.

IFIP-ICTSS 2020 received 43 submissions. Each paper was reviewed in a single-blind process by three reviewers on average and discussed by the Program Committee. After a careful selection process, the Program Committee accepted 17 regular papers and 4 short papers. The papers cover a large range of subjects such as test-case generation, testing in relation with artificial intelligence, proof and verification techniques, security, performance, as well as empirical studies. In particular, in the 32nd conference edition, a large space was given to security testing models and techniques.

IFIP-ICTSS 2020 also hosted an industrial event with the participation of big and small enterprises, discussing about their vision and practical experiences on software and security testing, with the aim to encourage interactions and exchanges between the scientific and industrial communities interested in testing.

We would like to thank the Steering Committee for their advice and support in the organization of the conference. Many thanks to the Program Committee members, as well as to the additional reviewers, for their careful reviews and participation in the discussions during the paper selection. The process of reviewing and selecting the papers was significantly simplified through the use of EasyChair. We would also like to thank IFIP for their continuous support of the conference series, as well as Springer for having published this volume.

We would like to thank the CERICT Organizing Committee, particularly Marco Guarino, Michele Salza, and Tiziana Cibelli for their support in the preparation of the conference, as well as in financial and organizational aspects. We kindly thank Silvio Stefanucci, the conference webmaster.

Finally, we are very grateful to the scientific sponsors of the conference: the University of Naples Federico II, the University of Campania Luigi Vanvitelli, and the University of Sannio. Their support strongly contributed to the success of this event.

On behalf of the IFIP-ICTSS organizers, we hope that you find the proceedings useful, interesting, and challenging.

December 2020

Valentina Casola
Alessandra De Benedictis
Massimiliano Rak

Organization

General Chairs

Valentina Casola — University of Naples Federico II, Italy
Massimiliano Rak — University of Campania Luigi Vanvitelli, Italy

Program Committee Chair

Alessandra De Benedictis — University of Naples Federico II, Italy

Steering Committee

Inmaculada Medina Bulo — University of Càdiz, Spain
Ana Cavalli — Télécom SudParis, France
Christophe Gaston — CEA List, France
Rob Hierons — The University of Sheffield, UK
Nikolai Kosmatov — CEA List, France
Pascale Le Gall — CentraleSupélec, France
Francisco Palomo Lozano — University of Càdiz, Spain
Mercedes Merayo — Universidad Complutense de Madrid, Spain
Andreas Ulrich — Siemens AG, Germany
Husnu Yenigun — Sabanci University, Turkey
Nina Yevtushenko — Tomsk State University, Russia

Program Committee

Rui Abreu — INESC-ID/IST, University of Lisbon, Portugal
Bernhard K. Aichernig — TU Graz, Austria
Antonia Bertolino — ISTI-CNR, Italy
Valentina Casola — University of Naples Federico II, Italy
Ana Rosa Cavalli — Télécom SudParis, France
Xiao Chen — Monash University, Australia
David Clark — University College London, UK
Giovanni Cozzolino — University of Naples Federico II, Italy
Alessandra De Benedictis — University of Naples Federico II, Italy
Pedro Delgado-Pérez — University of Càdiz, Spain
Sergio Di Martino — University of Naples Federico II, Italy
Khaled El-Fakih — American University of Sharjah, UAE
Ylies Falcone — Université Grenoble Alpes, France
Anna Rita Fasolino — University of Naples Federico II, Italy
Jun Gao — University of Luxembourg, Luxembourg
Angelo Gargantini — University of Bergamo, Italy

Christophe Gaston   CEA, France
Juergen Grossmann   Fraunhofer, Germany
Roland Groz   Grenoble INP, LIG, France
Rob Hierons   The University of Sheffield, UK
Teruo Higashino   Osaka University, Japan
Thierry Jéron   Inria, France
Ferhat Khendek   Concordia University, Canada
Pingfan Kong   University of Luxembourg, Luxembourg
Nikolai Kosmatov   CEA List, France
Moez Krichen   ReDCAD Research Unit, Tunisia
Natalia Kushik   Télécom SudParis, France
Pascale Le Gall   CentraleSupélec, France
Kui Liu   Nanjing University of Aeronautics and Astronautics,
                           China
Luis Llana   Universidad Complutense de Madrid, Spain
Delphine Longuet   Université Paris-Sud, LRI, France
Jorge Lopez   Airbus Defense and Space, France
Radu Mateescu   Inria, France
Inmaculada Medina-Bulo   University of Càdiz, Spain
Mercedes Merayo   Universidad Complutense de Madrid, Spain
Roberto Nardone   Mediterranean University of Reggio Calabria, Italy
Roberto Natella   University of Naples Federico II, Italy
Manuel Núñez   Universidad Complutense de Madrid, Spain
Mike Papadakis   University of Luxembourg, Luxembourg
Antonio Pecchia   University of Sannio, Italy
Jan Peleska   TZI, Universtät Bremen, Germany
Roberto Pietrantuono   University of Naples Federico II, Italy
Massimiliano Rak   University of Campania Luigi Vanvitelli, Italy
Antoine Rollet   LaBRI, Bordeaux INP, CNRS, University of Bordeaux,
                           France
Stefano Russo   University of Naples Federico II, Italy
Sébastien Salva   LIMOS, France
Sergio Segura   University of Seville, Spain
Hasan Sozer   Ozyegin University, Turkey
Daniel Sundmark   Mälardalen University, Sweden
Kenji Suzuki   Kennisbron Co., Ltd, Japan
Masaki Suzuki   KDDI Research, Inc., Japan
Porfirio Tramontana   University of Naples Federico II, Italy
Andreas Ulrich   Siemens AG, Germany
Umberto Villano   University of Sannio, Italy
Burkhart Wolff   Université Paris-Sud, France
Franz Wotawa   TU Graz, Austria
Hüsnü Yenigün   Sabanci University, Turkey
Nina Yevtushenko   Institute for System Programming, RAS, Russia
Fatiha Zaidi   Université Paris-Sud, France

Workshop Chair

Roberto Nardone   Mediterranean University of Reggio Calabria, Italy

Publicity Chair

Umberto Villano   University of Sannio, Italy

Additional Reviewers

Nicola Amatucci   Francesco Moscato
Christian Esposito   Giovanni Salzillo
Massimo Ficco   Luigi Libero Lucio Starace
Salah Ghamizi   Salvatore Venticinque
Daniele Granata   Vincenzo Norman Vitale
Alessio Merlo

Contents

Model-Based Testing

Using Model Learning for the Generation of Mock Components

Sébastien Salva[✉] and Elliott Blot[✉]

LIMOS CNRS UMR 6158, Clermont Auvergne University, Aubière, France
sebastien.salva@uca.fr, eblot@isima.fr

Abstract. Mocking objects is a common technique that substitutes parts of a program to simplify the test case development, to increase test coverage or to speed up performance. Today, mocks are almost exclusively used with object oriented programs. But mocks could offer the same benefits with communicating systems to make them more reliable. This paper proposes a model-based approach to help developers generate mocks for this kind of system, i.e. systems made up of components interacting with each other by data networks and whose communications can be monitored. The approach combines model learning to infer models from event logs, quality metric measurements to help chose the components that may be replaced by mocks, and mock generation and execution algorithms to reduce the mock development time. The approach has been implemented as a tool chain with which we performed experimentations to evaluate its benefits in terms of usability and efficiency.

Keywords: Mock · Model learning · Quality metrics · Communicating systems

1 Introduction

A technique commonly used in the context of crafting tests for software applications consists of replacing a software component (typically a class) with a test-specific version called *mock*, which behaves in a predefined and controlled way, while satisfying some behaviours of the original. Mocks are often used by developers to make test development easier or to increase test coverage. Mocks may indeed be used to simplify the dependencies that make testing difficult (e.g., infrastructure or environment related dependencies [3,21]). Besides, mocks are used to increase test efficiency by replacing slow-to-access components. This paper addresses the generation of mocks for communicating systems and proposes a model-based mock generation. When reviewing the literature, it is particularly noticeable that mocks are often developed for testing object oriented-programs and are usually written by hands, although some papers have focused on the automatic generation of mocks.

© IFIP International Federation for Information Processing 2020
Published by Springer Nature Switzerland AG 2020
V. Casola et al. (Eds.): ICTSS 2020, LNCS 12543, pp. 3–19, 2020.
https://doi.org/10.1007/978-3-030-64881-7_1

Related Work: The idea of simulating real components (most of the time objects in the literature) with mocks for testing is not new in software engineering. The notion of mock object originates from the paper of Mackinnon et al. [14] and has then been continuously investigated, e.g., in [3,10,11,21]. Some of these works pointed out the distinctions between mocks and other related terms such as stub or fake. In this paper, we will use the term mock to denote a component that mimics an original component and whose behaviours can be verified by tests to ensure that it is invoked as expected by the components being tested.

A few works related to mock generation have been proposed afterwards. Saff et al. [16] proposed to automatically replace some objects instantiated within test cases by mocks to speed up the test execution or to isolate other objects to make the bug detection easier. The mock generation is performed by instrumenting Java classes to record both method calls and responses in transcripts. These ones are used as specifications of mock objects. Tillmann and Schulte proposed to generate mocks by means of a symbolic analysis of .NET codes [24]. These mocks represent variables, which can be given to a robustness test generator for producing unexpected but admissible input values. Galler et al. generate mocks from Design by Contract specifications, which allow developers to establish the semantics of objects with pre-, post-conditions and invariants [12]. These conditions and invariants are used as specifications of mocks. Alshahwan et al. also proposed the mock generation from method post-conditions but also from test coverage measurements [2].

Apart from some guides or good practices dealing with Web service mocking, we did not find any attempt to mock other kinds of components in the literature, yet the need for replacing components by mocks for testing other kinds of systems under test (SUT) continues. Like object oriented-programs, the use of mocks for testing communicating systems could help experiment in isolation some components having dependencies that make testing difficult. Using mocks could also help increase test coverage. After our literature review, we believe that these four main obstacles currently prevent the use of mocks for testing communicating systems:

- the lack of specification. If no component specification is provided, it becomes long and difficult to develop interoperable mocks;
- the difficulty in maintaining mocks when SUT is updated;
- the difficulty of choosing the *mockable* components that is, those that may be replaced by mocks;
- the lack of tools to help generate mock components.

Contributions: This paper addresses these obstacles and proposes an approach for helping developers in: the analysis of a communicating system to classify its components; the choice of mockable components; and the mock generation. In our context, the mock components can be used for several purposes, e.g., for increasing test coverage, for security testing, or for testing new systems made up of reusable components during the development activity. To reach these purposes, our approach combines model learning, quality metrics evaluation and mock generation. Model learning is used to infer models, which encode the behaviours of every component of a communicating system and its architecture. On these models, we evaluate 6 quality metrics mostly related to Auditability, Testability and Dependability. These metrics allow to classify components into 4 categories: "Mock", "Test", "Test in Isolation" and "Code Review". We finally propose model-based algorithms to help generate and execute mocks.

This approach has been implemented as a tool chain available in [18]. We performed a preliminary experimentation on a home automation system composed of smart devices to assess its benefits in terms of usability and efficiency.

Paper Organisation: Section 2 recalls some preliminary definitions and notations. Section 3 presents our approach: we give an overview of our model learning algorithm called CkTail; We define quality metrics and show how to classify components with them; we introduce the mock generation and execution algorithms. The next section introduces an empirical evaluation. Section 5 summarises our contributions and draws some perspectives for future work.

2   Preliminaries

We express the behaviours of communicating components with Input Output Labelled Transition Systems. This model is defined in terms of states and transitions labelled by input or output actions, taken from a general action set $\mathcal{L}$, which expresses what happens.

Definition 1 (IOLTS). *An Input Output Labelled Transition System (IOLTS) is a 4-tuple $\langle Q, q0, \Sigma, \rightarrow \rangle$ where:*

- *Q is a finite set of states; $q0$ is the initial state;*
- *$\Sigma \subseteq \mathcal{L}$ is the finite set of actions. $\Sigma_I \subseteq \Sigma$ is the finite set of input actions, $\Sigma_O \subseteq \Sigma$ is the finite set of output actions, with $\Sigma_O \cap \Sigma_I = \emptyset$;*
- *$\rightarrow \subseteq Q \times \Sigma \times Q$ is a finite set of transitions.*

We also define the following notations: $(q_1, a, q_2) \in \rightarrow \Leftrightarrow_{def} q_1 \xrightarrow{a} q_2; q \xrightarrow{a} \Leftrightarrow_{def} \exists q_2 \in Q : q \xrightarrow{a} q_2$. Furthermore, to better match the functioning of communicating systems, an action has the form $a(\alpha)$ with a a label and α an assignment of parameters in P, with P the set of parameter assignments. For example, the action $switch\,(from := c_1, to := c_2, cmd := on)$ is made up of the label "switch" followed by parameter assignments expressing the components involved in the communication and the switch command. We use the following notations on action sequences. The concatenation of two action sequences $\sigma_1, \sigma_2 \in \mathcal{L}^*$ is denoted $\sigma_1.\sigma_2$. ϵ denotes the empty sequence. A run $q_0 a_1(\alpha_1) q_1 \ldots q_n$ of the IOLTS $\mathcal{L}$ is an alternate sequence of states and actions starting from the initial state q_0. A trace is a finite sequence of actions in $\mathcal{L}^*$.

The dependencies among the components of a communicating system are captured with a Directed Acyclic Graph (DAG), where component identifiers are labelled on vertices.

Definition 2 (Directed Acyclic Graph). *A DAG Dg is a 2-tuple $\langle V_{Dg}, E_{Dg} \rangle$ where V is the finite set of vertices and E the finite set of edges. λ denotes a labelling function mapping each vertex $v \in V$ to a label $\lambda(v)$*

3 A Model-Based Mock Generation Approach

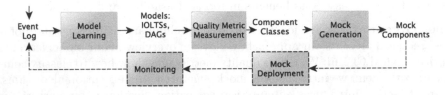

Fig. 1. Approach overview

Our approach is structured into 3 main steps, illustrated in Fig. 1. A model learning technique is firstly applied to a given event log collected from a system denoted SUT. For every component c_1 of SUT, it generates one IOLTS $\mathscr{L}(c_1)$ expressing the behaviours of c_1 along with one dependency graph $Dg(c_1)$ expressing how c_1 interacts with some other components of SUT. The second step computes quality metrics on these models, and assists the developer in the component classification under the categories: "Mock", "Test", "Test in Isolation", "Code Review". Once the mockable components are identified, the third step helps the developer in the mock generation by means of the IOLTSs produced previously. It is worth noting that mocks often increase test coverage along with the generation of more logs, which may be later used to generate more precise IOLTSs and re-evaluate metrics. This cycle may help produce mocks that better simulate real components. These steps are detailed in the following.

3.1 Model Generation

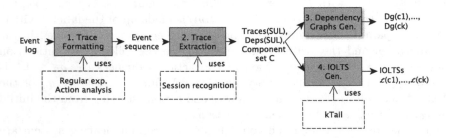

Fig. 2. Model learning with the CkTail approach

We proposed a model learning approach called Communicating system kTail, shortened CkTail, to learn models of communicating systems from event logs. We summarise here the functioning of CkTail but we refer to [17] for the technical details. The CkTail's algorithms rely on some assumptions, which are required to interpret the communications among the components of SUT in event logs. These are given below:

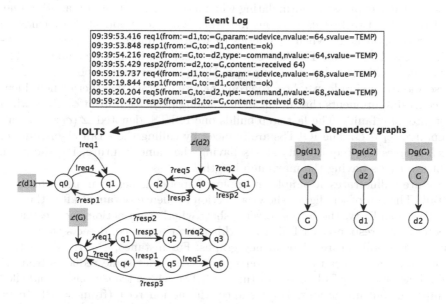

Fig. 3. Example of model generation with CkTail

- **A1 Event log:** we consider the components of SUT as black-boxes whose communications can be monitored. Event logs are collected in a synchronous environment. Furthermore, the messages include timestamps given by a global clock for ordering them. We consider having one event log;
- **A2 Message content:** components produce messages that include parameter assignments allowing to identify the source and the destination of every message. Other parameter assignments may be used to encode data. Besides, a message is either identified as a request or a response;
- **A3 Component collaboration:** the components of SUT can run in parallel and communicate with each other. But, they have to follow this strict behaviour: they cannot run multiple instances; requests are processed by a component on a first-come, first served basis. Besides, every response is associated with the last request w.r.t. the request-response exchange pattern.

The assumption A3 helps segment an event log into sessions, i.e. temporary message interchanges among components forming some behaviours of SUT from one of its initial states to one of its final states.

Figure 2 illustrates the 4 steps of CkTail. The event log is firstly formatted into a sequence of actions of the form $a(\alpha)$ with a a label and α some parameter assignments, by using tools or regular expressions. The second step relies on A3 to recognise sessions in the action sequence and to extract traces. In the meantime, this step detects dependencies among the components of SUT. It returns the trace set $Traces(\text{SUT})$, the set of components C and the set $Deps(\text{SUT})$, which gathers component dependencies under the form of component lists $c_1 \ldots c_k$. We have defined the notion of component dependency by means of three expressions formulating when a component relies on another one. Intuitively, the two first expressions illustrate that a component c_1 depends on another component c_2 when c_1 queries c_2 with a request or by means of successive nested requests. The last expression deals with data dependency. The third step builds one dependency graph $Dg(c_1)$ for every component $c_1 \in C$. These show in a simple way how the components interact together or help identify central components that might have a strong negative impact on SUT when they integrate faults. The last step builds one IOLTS, denoted $\mathscr{L}(c_1)$ for every component $c_1 \in C$. The IOLTSs are reduced by calling the kTail algorithm [4], which merges the (equivalent) states having the same k-future, i.e. the same event sequences having the maximum length k.

Figure 3 illustrates a simple example of model generation performed by CkTail. The top of the figure shows an action sequence obtained after the first step. For simplicity, the labels directly show whether an action encodes either a request or a response. CkTail covers this action sequence, detects three components and builds three dependency graphs. For instance, $Dg(d1)$ shows that $d1$ depends on G because the action sequence includes some requests from $d1$ to G. Thereafter, CkTail generates three IOLTSs whose transitions are labelled by input or output actions. For instance, the action req1 (from := d1, to := G, ...) has been doubled with an output !req1 and an input ?req1. The former is labelled on the transition $q_0 \rightarrow q_1$ of $\mathscr{L}(D1)$ to express the sending of the request by $d1$; the latter is labelled on the transition $q_0 \rightarrow q_1$ of $\mathscr{L}(G)$ to express that G expects to receive the input ?req1.

3.2   Quality Attribute Evaluation

Some quality attributes can now be automatically evaluated for all the components of SUT. By means of these attributes, we propose to classify the components into 4 categories "Mock", "Testable", "Testable in Isolation", "Code Review", to help developers dress their test plan. To select relevant quality attributes, we firstly studied the papers dealing with the use of mocks for testing, e.g., [2,3,10–12,16,21–23]. In particular, we took back the conclusions of the recent surveys of Spadini et al. [21,22], which intuitively report that developers often use mocks to replace the components that are difficult to interpret, complex, not testable, or those that are called by others (e.g., external components like Web services). Then, we studied some papers related to Testability [7–9,19] and Dependability [5,20]. We finally selected 6 attributes, which, when used together, help classify a component into the previous categories. We kept the attributes dedicated to:

Table 1. Classification of a component in component categories w.r.t. quality attributes. X stands for "is member of". X, X+, X++ denote 3 levels of interest.

Quality metrics						Component categories			
Acc^f	Und^f	$InDeps^f$	$OutDeps^f$	Obs^f	$Cont^f$	Mock	Test in isolation	Test	Code review
0	≥0	≥0	≥0	≥0	≥0				X
≥0	weak	≥0	≥0	≥0	≥0				X
>0	strong	0	0	strong	weak		X		X
>0	strong	>0	>0	weak	weak	X			X
>0	strong	>0	0	strong	weak	X+	X		X
>0	strong	0	>0	strong	weak	X++		X	X
>0	strong	>0	>0	strong	weak	X		X	X
>0	strong	>0	0	weak	strong	X+	X		X
>0	strong	0	>0	weak	strong			X	X
>0	strong	>0	>0	weak	strong	X		X	X
>0	strong	>0	>0	strong	strong	X+		X++	
>0	strong	0	>0	strong	strong			X++	
>0	strong	>0	0	strong	strong	X++	X++		
>0	strong	0	0	strong	strong		X++		
>0	strong	0	0	weak	strong	X			X
>0	strong	0	0	weak	weak				X

- evaluating the degree to which a component of SUT is understandable and reachable through PO or PCO (point of control and observation). We consider Understandability and Accessibility;
- selecting the components that can be tested. Testability often refers to two other attributes called Observability and Controllability;
  identifying the dependencies among components. We distinguish between dependent and dependee components. Intuitively, the former depend on other components; the latter are required by other components. With regard to these two kinds of components, we consider In- and Out-Dependability.

Quality attribute measurement is usually performed on specifications with metrics. But in the present work, we have models inferred by a model learning technique. They generalise what we observed about SUT, but may expose more behaviours than those possible (over-approximation) or may ignore behaviours that can occur (under-approximation). As a consequence, we shall talk about *fuzzy* metrics in the remainder of the paper. We hence measure quality with the 6-tuple $\langle Acc^f, Und^f, InDeps^f, OutDeps^f, Obs^f, Cont^f \rangle$. This notion of fuzzy metric, albeit unusual, reinforces the fact that the quality measurement may evolve as we gather more data by testing SUT and updating the models.

Table 1 summarises our literature study and our interpretations of the relationships of a component with the four component categories studied in the paper with respect to quality metric measurements. We use the imprecise terms "weak" "strong" to express two levels of range of values whose definition is left to the user's knowledge on SUT. For instance, the range weak <0.5 and strong ≥0.5 is a possible solution, but not suitable for any system. The relations expressed in Table 1 are discussed per category below.

Mock Category: Table 1 brings out two kinds of mockable components:

- accessible and dependee components, which could be replaced by mocks to deeper test how dependent components interacts with them. When Observability or Controllability of a dependee component are weak, the developer has to assess how the lack of Testability may impede the testing result interpretations. Furthermore, if a dependee component is also a dependant one, the mock may be more difficult to devise;
- accessible, uncontrollable and dependent only components are also good candidates because such components cannot be experimented with tests although they trigger interactions with other components. Mocking out those components should allow to deeper test SUT. As previously, the developer needs to consider Observability and in-Dependability to assess the difficulty of replacing these components with mocks.

Test, Test in Isolation Categories: a testable component has to expose both Observability and Controllability. Out-Dependability (with $OutDeps^f > 0$) is here used to make the distinction between the categories Test and Test in isolation. In Table 1, the level of interest is the lowest when a component exposes weak Observability or Controllability. Here, the developer needs to assess whether testing should be conducted.

Code Review Category: Table 1 shows that many kinds of components belong to this category. These components either are unreachable or have unreadable behaviours, or they are not testable (weak Obs^f or weak $Cont^f$).

We now define the fuzzy quality metrics in the remainder of this section. The metrics for Understandability and Observability are taken from the papers [7–9,19] and adapted to our models. The metrics for Accessibility, Dependability and Controllability are revisited to take into account some specificities of communicating systems.

Component Understandability evaluates how much component information can be interpreted and recognised [1,15]. In our context, this attribute mainly depends on the clearness/interpretation of the actions. As these are made up of parameter assignments, we say that Understandability depends on how assignments are interpretable, which we evaluate with the boolean expression isReadable. For instance, the latter may be implemented to call tools for detecting whether parameter values are encrypted. Given a component $c_1 \in C$, the metric which assesses the Understandability of c_1 is given below. The more $Und^f(c_1)$ is close to 1, the more interpretable the IOLTS $\mathscr{L}(c_1)$ is.

$$- Und(a(\alpha)) =_{def} 0 \leq \frac{\sum\limits_{(x:=v) \in \alpha} isReadable(x := v)}{|\alpha|} \leq 1$$

$$- Und^f(c_1) =_{def} 0 \leq \frac{\sum\limits_{a(\alpha) \in \Sigma} Und(a(\alpha))}{|\Sigma|} \leq 1$$

Component Accessibility is usually expressed through the accesses of Points of Control and Observations (PCO). Several PCO may be required to bring a full access to a communicating system. Accessibility may be hampered by diverse restrictions applied on the component interfaces e.g., security policies, or by the nature of the protocols used. We evaluate the ability to interact with a component $c_1 \in C$ through its interfaces with:

$$0 \leq Acc^f(c_1) =_{def} \frac{\text{\# interfaces of } c_1 \text{interconnected with reachable PCO}}{\text{\# interfaces of } c_1} \leq 1$$

Component Dependability helps better understand the architecture of a component-based system, and may also be used to evaluate or refine other attributes, e.g., Reusability [5,13,20]. The metric given below relies upon the DAGs generated by CkTail from which the sets of dependent and dependee components can be extracted. This separation offers the advantage of defining two metrics $OutDeps^f$ and $InDeps^f$, which help better evaluate if a component is mockable. The degree to which a component requires other components for functioning is measured by $OutDeps^f$. $InDeps^f$ defines the degree to which a component is needed by other ones. The closer to 1 $OutDeps^f(c_1)$ and $InDeps^f(c_1)$ are, the more important c_1 is in the architecture of SUT and its functioning.

$$- \ OutDeps^f(c_1) =_{def} 0 \leq \frac{|\{\lambda(v) \mid v \in V(Dg(c1))\} \setminus \{c_1\}|}{|C|-1} \leq 1$$

$$- \ InDeps^f(c_1) =_{def} 0 \leq \frac{|\{\lambda(v_1) \mid v_1 \rightarrow v_2 \in \bigcup_{c \in C} E_{Dg(c)} \wedge \lambda(v_2) = c_1\} \setminus \{c_1\}|}{|C|-1}$$
$$\leq 1$$

Component Observability evaluates how *the specified inputs affect the outputs* [9]. For a component c_1 modelled with the IOLTS $\mathscr{L}(c_1) = \langle Q, q0, \Sigma, \rightarrow \rangle$, Observability is measured with:

$$- \ out(a_1(\alpha_1)) =_{def} \bigcup_{q_1 \xrightarrow{a_1(\alpha_1)} q_2} \{a(\alpha) \in \Sigma_O \mid q_2 \xrightarrow{a(\alpha)}\}$$

$-$

$$Obs(u_1(\alpha_1)) =_{def} \begin{cases} 1 \text{ iff } \forall a_2(\alpha_2) \in \Sigma_I \neq a_1(\alpha_1) : out(a_2(\alpha_2)) \cap out(a_1(\alpha_1)) \\ = \emptyset \wedge out(a_1(\alpha_1)) \neq \emptyset \\ 0 \text{ otherwise} \end{cases}$$

$$- \ 0 \leq Obs^f(c_1) \leq 1 =_{def} \sum_{a_1(\alpha_1) \in \Sigma_I} \frac{Obs(a_1(\alpha_1))}{|\Sigma_I|}$$

Component Controllability refers to the capability of a component to reach one of its internal state by means of a specified input that forces it to give a desired output. We denote the metric that evaluates how a component c_1 can be directly controlled through queries sent to its interfaces with $ContD(c_1)$. This metric depends on the Accessibility of c_1. But, when some interfaces are not accessible, we propose another way to measure the capability of controlling c_1 by considering interactions through a chain of components calling each other. In this case, we define another metric denoted $ContI$. The Controllability of c_1 is measured with $Cont^f(c_1)$, which evaluates the best way to control c_1, either directly or through a chain of components.

Definition 3 (Component Controllability). *Let* $a_1(\alpha_1) \in \Sigma_O$ *be an output action of* $\mathscr{L}(c_1) = \langle Q, q0, \Sigma, \rightarrow \rangle$, *and* $\mathscr{L}(c_2) = \langle Q', q0', \Sigma', \rightarrow' \rangle$ *such that* $\Sigma_I' \cap \Sigma_I = \Sigma_O' \cap \Sigma_O = \emptyset$.

- $in(q_0, \mathscr{L}(c_1)) =_{def} \emptyset$
- $in(q_1, \mathscr{L}(c_1)) =_{def} \{a(\alpha) \in \Sigma_I \mid q_2 \xrightarrow{a(\alpha)} q_1\} \cup \{a(\alpha) \in in(q_2, \mathscr{L}(c_1)) \mid a_2(\alpha_2) \in \Sigma_O \wedge q_2 \xrightarrow{a_2(\alpha_2)} q_1\}$
- $in(a_1(\alpha_1), \mathscr{L}(c_1)) = \displaystyle\bigcup_{q_1 \xrightarrow{a_1(\alpha_1)} q_2 \in \rightarrow} in(q_1, \mathscr{L}(c_1))$

- $Cont(a_1(\alpha_1), \mathscr{L}(c_1)) = \begin{cases} 1 \text{ iff } \forall a_2(\alpha_2) \in \Sigma_O \neq a_1(\alpha_1): \\ \quad in(a_2(\alpha_2), \mathscr{L}(c_1)) \cap in(a_1(\alpha_1), \mathscr{L}(c_1)) = \emptyset \\ \quad \wedge in(a_1(\alpha_1), \mathscr{L}(c_1)) \neq \emptyset \\ 0 \text{ otherwise} \end{cases}$

- $0 \leq ContD(c_1) \leq 1 = \displaystyle\sum_{a_1(\alpha_1) \in \Sigma_O} \frac{Cont(a_1(\alpha_1), \mathscr{L}(c_1))}{|\Sigma_O|} * Acc^f(c_1)$

- $0 \leq ContI(c_1, c_k c_{k-1} \ldots c_1) \leq 1 = \displaystyle\sum_{a_1(\alpha_1) \in \Sigma_O} \frac{Cont(a_1(\alpha_1), \mathscr{L}(c_k) \parallel \cdots \parallel \mathscr{L}(c_1))}{|\Sigma_O|} *$

  $Acc^f(c_k)$
- $0 \leq Cont^f(c_1) \leq 1 = max(\{ContI(c_1, c_k c_{k-1} \ldots c_1) \mid Dg(c_k) = (V, E) \wedge c_k \rightarrow c_{k-1} \rightarrow \cdots \rightarrow c_1 \in E^*\} \cup \{ContD(c_1)\})$

3.3   Mock Generation and Execution

In reference to [14, 22], we recall that developing a mock comes down to creating a component that mimics the behaviours of another real component (H1). A mocks should be easily created, easily set up, and directly queriable (H2). In the tests, the developer has to specify how the mock ought to be exercised (H3). Besides, a mock can be handled by tests to verify that it runs as expected (H4). If the mock is not exercised as expected, it should return an error so that tests fail (H5). With regard to these requirements and to take advantage of the models inferred previously, we have designed a mock for communicating systems as a *Mock runner*, which is responsible for running behaviours encoded in a *Mock model*.

For a component $c_1 \in C$, a Mock model is a specialised IOLTS $\mathscr{L}$ that expresses some behaviours used to simulate c_1 (H1). It is specialised in the sense that every action $a(\alpha)$ has to include new assignments of the parameters *weight*, *repetition*, *delay*, so that it may be used as a mock specification by the Mock runner. The parameter *weight*, which is initialised to 0, will be used to better cover the outgoing transitions of an indeterministic state q, instead of randomly firing one of the transitions of q. The parameter *repetition* will be used to repeat the sending of an output action a large number of times without altering the readability of $\mathcal{L}$. The parameter *delay* expresses a legal period of inactivity, and will be used to detect quiescent states. With an output action, *delay* expresses a waiting time before the sending of the action. With an input action, it sets the period of time after which the action cannot be received any-more.

Definition 4 (Mock model). *A Mock model for $c_1 \in C$ is an IOLTS $\langle Q, q0, \Sigma, \rightarrow \rangle$ such that Q is the finite set of states, q_0 is the initial state, $\rightarrow$ is the transition relation, $Q_t \subseteq Q$ is the non empty set of terminal states, Σ is the action set of the form $a(\alpha)$ such that α is composed of the assignments of the parameters weight, repetition and delay. $weight(a(\alpha)) = w$, $repetition(a(\alpha)) = r$, $delay(a(\alpha)) = d$ denote these parameter assignments.*

Component	Acc^J	Und^J	$InDeps^J$	$OutDeps^J$	Obs^J	$Cont^J$	Mock
d1	1	1	1/2	1/2	1	0	X+
d2	1	1	1/2	1/2	1	1	X+
G	1	1	1/2	1/2	0	0	X

(a) Quality metrics

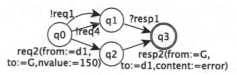

(b) Example of Mock model for d1

Fig. 4. Quality metrics and Mock model example for the system of Fig. 3

A Mock model $\mathcal{L}$ for c_1 may be written from scratch, but we strongly recommend to derive it from the IOLTS $\mathcal{L}(c1)$ (H2). For instance, for conformance testing, $\mathcal{L}$ might correspond to $\mathcal{L}(c1)$ whose some paths are pruned. Mocks are also used with other testing types. With robustness testing, a Mock model might be automatically generated by injecting faults in $\mathcal{L}(c1)$, e.g., transition removal, transition duplication, action alteration, etc. With security testing, the Mock model might be automatically generated from $\mathcal{L}(c1)$ by injecting sequences of transitions expressing attack scenarios. If we take back our example of Fig. 3, the quality metrics given in Fig. 4a reveal that d1 and d2 are good candidates as mockable components. Figure 4b shows a mock example for d1. This IOLTS was written by hands from the IOTS $\mathcal{L}(d1)$ of Fig. 3. It aims at experimenting G with unexpected and high temperature values.

Algorithm 1: Mock Runner

---

input : IOLTS $\mathscr{L} = \langle Q, q0, \Sigma, \rightarrow \rangle$

1 **repeat**

2   Take $a(\alpha)$ in inputFifoqueue;

3   **if** $q_0 \xrightarrow{a(\alpha)}$ **then**

4   Take $t = q_0 \xrightarrow{?a(\alpha)} q_1 \in \rightarrow$ such that $weight(?a(\alpha))$ is the smallest;

5         $weight(?a(\alpha))$++;

6         $treatInstance(q_0?a(\alpha)q_1, now())$;

7   **else**

8   Log(Error);

9   **if** $\exists !a(\alpha) \in \Sigma_O : q_0 \xrightarrow{!a(\alpha)}$ **then**

10   Take $t = q_0 \xrightarrow{!a(\alpha)} q_1 \in \rightarrow$ such that $weight(t)$ is the smallest;

11         $weight(t)$++; $r \leftarrow q_0$;

12   **for** $i \leftarrow 1$ to $repetition(!a(\alpha))$ **do**

13   send $a(\alpha)$; wait $delay(!a(\alpha))$);

14             $r \leftarrow r.!a(\alpha).q_1$;

15         $treatInstance(r, now())$;

16 **Procedure** $treatInstance(r, time)$ **is**

17   **while** $not\ expires(r)$ **do**

18   Log(r); $q \leftarrow$ last state of r;

19   **if** $Receipt\ a(\alpha)\ and\ q \xrightarrow{?a(\alpha)} and\ (now()\text{-}time) < delay(?a(\alpha))$ **then**

20   Take $q \xrightarrow{?a(\alpha)} q_1 \in \rightarrow$ such that $weight(?a(\alpha))$ is the smallest;

21             $weight(?a(\alpha))$++;

22             $r \leftarrow r.?a(\alpha).q_1$;

23             $time \leftarrow now()$;

24   **else**

25   add $a(\alpha)$ to inputFifoqueue;

26   **if** $\exists !a(\alpha) \in \Sigma^O : q \xrightarrow{!a(\alpha)} and\ (now()\text{-}time) > delay(!a(\alpha))$ **then**

27   Take $q \xrightarrow{!a(\alpha)} q_1 \in \rightarrow$ such that $weight(!a(\alpha))$ is the smallest;

28             $weight(a(\alpha))$++;

29   **for** $i \leftarrow 1$ to $repetition(!a(\alpha))$ **do**

30   send $a(\alpha)$; wait $delay(!a(\alpha))$);

31                 $r \leftarrow r.!a(\alpha).q_1$;

32             $time \leftarrow now()$;

33   Log(r);

A Mock runner is a generic piece of software in the sense that its design and implementation depend on the type of system considered. For instance, it may be implemented as a Web service for HTTP components. The Mock runner is implemented by Algorithm 1. It takes as input a Mock model $\mathscr{L}$, which specifies the mock behaviours (H3). Then, it creates instances, i.e. concrete executions by following the paths of $\mathscr{L}$ from its initial state. We chose to create one instance at a time to make the test results more easily interpretable (H2). As a consequence, if an incoming action is received but cannot be consumed in the current instance, it is stored in "inputFifoqueue" for being processed later. The Mock runner starts an instance by either processing an incoming action in inputFifoqueue (line 3) or by sending an action if an output action may be fired from the initial state of $\mathscr{L}$ (line 8). In both cases, if the initial state is not deterministic, the Mock runner chooses the transition whose action includes the smallest weight. Then, the weight of this action is increased so that another transition will be fired later. In line 9, if the Mock runner receives an unexpected action, it inserts an error in its log, so that the test, which handles the Mock runner, may fail (H5).

The Mock runner creates an instance given under the form of the couple $(r, time)$ with r a run of $\mathscr{L}$ and $time$ the current time returned by the clock of the Mock runner. This last parameter is used to compute waiting times before sending actions or time delays during which the Mock runner allows the receipt of input actions. When the Mock runner creates an instance that starts with an output action (line 12), it sends it as many times as it is specified by the parameter repetition. The run r is updated accordingly.

Once a new run is created, the Mock runner calls the procedure $treatInstance$ to process a run $q_0 a_0(\alpha_0) \ldots q$ until it expires. For simplicity, the run expiration (line 17) is not detailed in the procedure. We say that a run $q_0 a_0(\alpha_0) \ldots q$ expires if either $q \in Q_t$ is a terminal state, or q is a quiescent state ($\forall q \xrightarrow{a(\alpha)} q_2 : a(\alpha) \in \Sigma^I \wedge now() - time > delay(a(\alpha)))$). The procedure logs every run update (lines 18,33) so that the mock behaviours can be verified by tests (H4). The remaining of the procedure is very similar to Algorithm 1: it either waits for the receipt of an action $a(\alpha)$, or sends an output action if an output action may be fired from the state q. The procedure updates the run r and $time$ for every received or sent action.

4   Preliminary Evaluation

Our approach is implemented as a prototype tool chain, which gathers the model learning tool CkTail, a tool to compute quality metrics on IOLTSs and DAGs, along with two Mock runners [18]. The first is implemented as a Java Web service that can be deployed on Web servers. The second Mock runner is implemented as a C++ Web service that can be installed on some embedded boards (Arduino compatibles). The latter can replace real devices more easily as these boards can be placed anywhere, but their memory and computing capabilities are limited. At the moment, both Mock runners are implemented with a slightly simplified version of the algorithm proposed in Sect. 3.3 as they take IOLTS paths as inputs, given under the form of rules. However, both Mock runners offer the capability to execute on demand some robustness tests (addition or removal of messages, injection of unexpected values in HTTP verbs and contents) and some security tests (injection of denial-of-service (DoS) or Cross-site scripting (XSS) attacks). This prototype tool chain was employed to begin evaluating the usability of our approach through the questions given below. The study has been conducted on a real home automation system. We firstly monitored it during 5 min and collected an event log of 240 HTTP messages involving 12 components. From the event log, we generated 12 IOLTSs along with 12 DAGS and evaluated quality metrics. Table 2 provides the IOLTS sizes, 4 quality measures ($Acc^f = Und^f = 1$ for all the components) and the recommendations given by Table 1.

Table 2. Model sizes, quality metrics and category relationships automatically generated for our case study

Component	# transitions	$InDeps^f$	$OutDeps^f$	Obs^f	$Cont^f$	Mock	Test	Test in isolation
Light Meter	4	0	1/11	1	0	X++	X	
Weather Web serv	2	1/11	0	1	1	X++		X++
Switch A	3	1/11	0	0	1	X+		X
Switch B	7	1/11	1/11	0	0	X		
Heatpump Th.1	3	0	1/11	1	0	X++	X	
Heatpump Th.2	5	0	1/11	1	0	X++	X	
Heatpump Th.3	4	0	1/11	1	0	X++	X	
Heatpump Th.4	7	1/11	1/11	0	1	X	X	
Heatpump Th.5	11	1/11	2/11	0	1/4	X		
Heatpump Th.6	11	1/11	2/11	0	1/4	X		
Client	72	3/11	1/11	1/2	1/36	X		
Gateway	136	8/11	6/11	2/25	3/62	X		

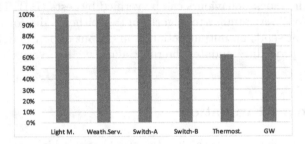

Fig. 5. Proportion of valid traces of the mocks

Does the Mock Generation from Models Allow to Save Time?

This question investigates how our tool chain is time efficient in comparison to manual coding. The experiment was carried out by 24 fourth year Computer Science students. Most of them have good skills in the development and test of Web applications and all of them attended a course on Internet of Thing implementation. We asked them to develop one mock as a Java service by using the Mockito framework, and another mock as a C++ service, for every component of SUT. These mocks had to simulate real components only. We separated the event log into 12 files (one file per component) and gave every file to a group of two students. On average, the students took less than 30 min for implementing the Java mock and 60 min for the C++ mock for the small components. The mocks of the gateway required more than 60 min and 120 min respectively. The total time is around 5 h 30 min for the Java mocks and 11 h for the C++ versions. Although some studies concluded that considering students for experiments is not controversial [6], we might still consider that experts could do it for half the time, that is 2 h 45 min and 5 h 30 min With our tool chain, it required 1 h 30 min to generate all the mocks (30 min to format the event log, 10 min to generate models, the remaining time to write rules). Hence, we are convinced that the tool brings greater efficiency.

Can the Generated Mocks Replace Real Devices? Can They Be Used for Testing? What Are the Observed Limitations?

To investigate these questions, we replaced the 6 most mockable components given in Table 2 along with the gateway by their mocks (Java and C++ mocks) in three phases: 1) substitution of the components one after another; 2) substitution of the 6 components; 3) substitution of all the components (gateway included). In the meantime, we monitored SUT to collect event logs during 5 min We firstly observed that mocks communicated as expected with the other components (no crash or hang of SUT). Then, we measured the proportion of valid traces of every mock, that is the proportion of traces of a mock accepted by the IOLTS of its real device. The bar graph of Fig. 5 illustrates the proportion of valid traces for the 7 components. We obverse that the mocks of the basic devices (light meter, switch, weather forecast service) behave as expected and can completely replace real devices. The mocks of the other components provided between 62% and 72% of valid traces. After inspection, we observed that these mocks, which simulate more complex components, received messages composed of unexpected values, e.g., temperate orders, and replied with error messages. These results confirm that the precision of the IOLTSs used to build mocks is important. Here, the IOLTSs are under-approximated (they exclude correct behaviours).

Besides replicating a real device, a mock aims to be called by a test case to set and verify expectations on interactions with a given component under test. We implemented the Mock runners with these purposes in mind. The Mock runners are services whose methods can be called from test cases. The mock initialisation is carried out by a method taking a rule set as a parameter. Besides, a test case can have access to the 10 last messages received or sent by the mock to verify its behaviour. We successfully wrote security test cases with the 6 previous mocks to check whether the gateway is vulnerable to some DoS or XSS attacks. In these test cases, the mocks are initialised with rules extracted from IOLTSs, and are then called to inject predefined attacks in these rules. We observed in this experiment that the gateway was vulnerable to the receipt of multiple long messages provoking slowdowns and finally unresponsiveness.

This study has also revealed several limitations that need to be investigated in the future. Although the Java Mock runner accepts large rule files and can replace complex components, the second Mock runner only supports rule files having up to 40 actions on account of the memory limitations of the board. In general, mocks are also implemented to speed up the testing stage. The Java Mock runner can indeed be used to quicker provide HTTP responses, but not the second Mock runner. Our current mock implementation does not support data flow management, which is another strong limitation. The data flow of the mocks do not follow any distribution and do not meet any temporal pattern. For instance, the mock of the light meter periodically sends luminance measurements, which are arbitrarily chosen. The data flow exposes unexpected peaks and falls, which corresponds to an incorrect behaviour for this kind of component.

5   Conclusion

We have proposed a model-based mock generation approach, which combines model learning, quality metrics evaluation and mock generation to assist developers in the test of communicating systems. Given an event log, model learning allows to get models, which can be automatically analysed with quality metrics to help classify every component of a communicating system and choose the best candidates for mocking out. The models are also used to ease the mock generation. As future work, we firstly plan to evaluate our approach on further kinds of systems, e.g., Web service compositions. We also intend to consider further quality metrics to refine the range of levels of interest for the mockable components. As suggested in our evaluation, we need to improve the Mock runner algorithms so that mocks might provide consistent data-flows, e.g., by following predefined distributions or temporal patterns.

References

1. Al-Qutaish, R.: Quality models in software engineering literature: an analytical and comparative study. J. Am. Sci. **6**, 166–175 (2010)
2. Alshahwan, N., Jia, Y., Lakhotia, K., Fraser, G., Shuler, D., Tonella, P.: AUTO-MOCK: automated synthesis of a mock environment for test case generation. In: Harman, M., Muccini, H., Schulte, W., Xie, T. (eds.) Practical Software Testing: Tool Automation and Human Factors, no. 10111 in Dagstuhl Seminar Proceedings, Schloss Dagstuhl - Leibniz-Zentrum fuer Informatik, Germany, Dagstuhl, Germany (2010). http://drops.dagstuhl.de/opus/volltexte/2010/2618
3. Arcuri, A., Fraser, G., Just, R.: Private API access and functional mocking in automated unit test generation. In: 2017 IEEE International Conference on Software Testing, Verification and Validation (ICST), pp. 126–137 (2017)
4. Biermann, A., Feldman, J.: On the synthesis of finite-state machines from samples of their behavior. IEEE Trans. Comput. **C-21**(6), 592–597 (972). https://doi.org/10.1109/TC.1972.5009015
5. Caliebe, P., Herpel, T., German, R.: Dependency-based test case selection and prioritization in embedded systems. In: 2012 IEEE Fifth International Conference on Software Testing, Verification and Validation, pp. 731–735 (2012)
6. Daun, M., Hübscher, C., Weyer, T.: Controlled experiments with student participants in software engineering: preliminary results from a systematic mapping study. CoRR abs/1708.04662 (2017)
7. Drira, K., Azéma, P., de Saqui Sannes, P.: Testability analysis in communicating systems. Comput. Netw. **36**(5), 671–693 (2001). https://doi.org/10.1016/S1389-1286(01)00183-9. http://www.sciencedirect.com/science/article/pii/S1389128601001839. Theme Issue: The Economics of Networking
8. Dssouli, R., Karoui, K., Petrenko, A., Rafiq, O.: Towards testable communication software. In: Cavalli, A., Budkowski, S. (eds.) Protocol Test Systems VIII. ITI-FIP, pp. 237–251. Springer, Boston, MA (1996). https://doi.org/10.1007/978-0-387-34988-6_15
9. Freedman, R.S.: Testability of software components. IEEE Trans. Softw. Eng. **17**(6), 553–564 (1991). https://doi.org/10.1109/32.87281

10. Freeman, S., Mackinnon, T., Pryce, N., Walnes, J.: Mock roles, not objects. In: Companion to the 19th Annual ACM SIGPLAN Conference on Object-Oriented Programming Systems, Languages, and Applications, OOPSLA 2004, New York, NY, USA, pp. 236-246. Association for Computing Machinery (2004). https://doi.org/10.1145/1028664.1028765

11. Freeman, S., Pryce, N.: Growing Object-Oriented Software, Guided by Tests, 1st edn. Addison-Wesley Professional, Boston (2009)

12. Galler, S.J., Maller, A., Wotawa, F.: Automatically extracting mock object behavior from design by contract; specification for test data generation. In: Proceedings of the 5th Workshop on Automation of Software Test, May 2010

13. Gui, G., Scott, P.: Measuring software component reusability by coupling and cohesion metrics. J. Comput. 4, 797–805 (2009). https://doi.org/10.4304/jcp.4.9.797-805

14. Mackinnon, T., Freeman, S., Craig, P.: Endo-Testing: Unit Testing with Mock Objects, pp. 287–301. Addison-Wesley Longman Publishing Co., Inc., Boston (2001)

15. Nazir, M., Khan, R.A., Mustafa, K.: A metrics based model for understandability quantification. CoRR abs/1004.4463 (2010). http://arxiv.org/abs/1004.4463

16. Saff, D., Artzi, S., Perkins, J.H., Ernst, M.D.: Automatic test factoring for Java. In: Proceedings of the 20th IEEE/ACM International Conference on Automated Software Engineering, ASE 2005, New York, NY, USA, pp. 114–123. Association for Computing Machinery (2005). https://doi.org/10.1145/1101908.1101927

17. Salva, S., Blot, E.: CkTail: model learning of communicating systems. In: Proceedings of the 15th International Conference on Evaluation of Novel Approaches to Software Engineering, ENASE 2020, Prague, CZECH REPUBLIC, 5–6 May 2020 (2020)

18. Salva, S.: Using model learning for the generation of mock components, companion site. https://perso.limos.fr/~sesalva/tools/mockgen/

19. Salva, S., Fouchal, H., Bloch, S.: Metrics for timed systems testing. In: 4th International Conference on Distributed Systems (OPODIS), Paris, France, December 2000

20. Sharma, A., Grover, P.S., Kumar, R.: Dependency analysis for component-based software systems. SIGSOFT Softw. Eng. Notes 34(4), 1-6 (2009). https://doi.org/10.1145/1543405.1543424

21. Spadini, D., Aniche, M., Bruntink, M., Bacchelli, A.: Mock objects for testing Java systems. Empirical Softw. Engg. 24(3), 1461–1498 (2019). https://doi.org/10.1007/s10664-018-9663-0

22. Spadini, D., Aniche, M.F., Bruntink, M., Bacchelli, A.: To mock or not to mock? An empirical study on mocking practices. In: 2017 IEEE/ACM 14th International Conference on Mining Software Repositories (MSR), pp. 402–412 (2017)

23. Succi, G., Marchesi, M. (eds.): Extreme Programming Examined. Addison Wesley Longman Publishing Co., Inc., Boston (2001)

24. Tillmann, N., Schulte, W.: Mock-object generation with behavior. In: 21st IEEE/ACM International Conference on Automated Software Engineering (ASE 2006), pp. 365–368 (2006)

Interrogating Virtual Agents: In Quest of Security Vulnerabilities

Josip Bozic and Franz Wotawa(✉)

Institute of Software Technology, Graz University of Technology, 8010 Graz, Austria
{jbozic,wotawa}@ist.tugraz.at

Abstract. Chatbots, i.e., systems that communicate in natural language, have been of increasing importance over the last few years. These virtual agents provide specific services or products to clients on a 24/7 basis. Chatbots provide a simple and intuitive interface, i.e., natural language processing, which makes them increasingly attractive for various applications. In fact, chatbots are used as substitutes for repetitive tasks or user inquiries that can be automated. However, these advantages always are accompanied with concerns, e.g., whether security and privacy can be assured. These concerns become more and more important, because in contrast to simple requests, more sophisticated chatbots are able to utilize personalized services to users. In such cases, sensitive user data are processed and exchanged. Hence, such systems become natural targets for cyber-attacks with unforeseen consequences. For this reason, assuring information security of chatbots is an important challenge in practice. In this paper, we contribute to this challenge and introduce an automated security testing approach for chatbots. The presented framework is able to generate and run tests in order to detect intrinsic software weaknesses leading to the XSS vulnerability. We assume a vulnerability to be triggered when obtaining critical information from or crashing the virtual agent, regardless of its purpose. We discuss the underlying basic foundations and demonstrate the testing approach using several real-world chatbots.

Keywords: Security testing · Model-based testing · Chatbots · Web applications

1 Introduction

In 1966, Joseph Weizenbaum invented the very first program that communicates with users in natural language [39]. Such systems, called chatbots [29], usually provide information about services and goods from a specific domain. However, since such systems offer many opportunities [25], they are becoming increasingly popular on the global market [4,13]. Chatbots are usually deployed in form of virtual assistants, either as stand-alone applications or are integrated into websites in form of chat widgets. In such way, they are easily accessible, and

© IFIP International Federation for Information Processing 2020
Published by Springer Nature Switzerland AG 2020
V. Casola et al. (Eds.): ICTSS 2020, LNCS 12543, pp. 20–34, 2020.
https://doi.org/10.1007/978-3-030-64881-7_2

also easy to interact with. Since they provide consistent answers in real-time, they save time and effort for clients to obtain requested information. In fact, due to such advantages, they might become even more popular than classical web applications [17].

Chatbots are developed further to respond to more specific customers' demands. Virtual assistants are considered in more sensitive domains like medicine [21,26], fintech [16], and banking [22]. Besides the usual natural language processing (NLP) layer, such chatbots apply more complex techniques from AI. They rely on a knowledge base and collect private data from user interactions and also learn from them. For such systems, ensuring information security becomes of uttermost importance. Requirements like confidentiality of user data, however, are challenged by the fact that chatbots rely on the common web infrastructure. In fact, since chatbots often come in form of web applications, they inherit their vulnerabilities as well [18]. Subsequently, cyber-attacks that target web vulnerabilities like cross-site scripting (XSS) [34] can be also executed against chatbots. Even more, this vulnerability motivates further malicious attempts, like denial-of-service (DDoS) attacks [6] or content spoofing [5].

Until now, proposed approaches usually test functional correctness of NLP systems. Such works apply different dialogue strategies by generating either valid [20,38] or invalid [35] language inputs. Subsequently, correctness functions are applied in order to evaluate the chatbot's behavior with regard to correct language output. Unfortunately, there is little work that puts focus on security issues.

Lots of research has been conducted for testing of web applications. Such works focus either on strengthening the detection mechanisms against attacks [28,30] or take the role of the attacker [19,27,31]. The latter case is covered, among others, by approaches from the area of model-based testing [24]. In this technique, test cases are automatically generated from a model of the system under test (SUT) or the attack itself. In addition to that, security testing can be combined with other techniques, like combinatorial testing (CT) [36], fuzzing [23] or model-checking [33].

This paper builds upon our previous work in [18], which contains an initial discussion about a security testing problem for chatbots. The motivation behind this work is to address the previously mentioned issues. Therefore, we introduce a framework that tests chatbot implementations for reflected XSS vulnerabilities in an automated manner. Subsequently, the approach is evaluated against several real-world applications, thereby discussing the obtained empirical results. We also want to note that, to our knowledge, this is the first paper where chatbots are successfully tested for security vulnerabilities.

The paper is structured as follows. Section 2 introduces the testing approach for chatbots. Section 2.1 and Sect. 2.2 discuss the underlying test generation and execution techniques, respectively. Then, Sect. 3 discusses the results from several real-world applications. Section 4 discusses related work and Sect. 5 concludes the work.

2   Approach Overview

NLP systems are usually implemented to fulfill a specific purpose. This means that they expect user inputs to fit pre-defined communication patterns. However, the question arises how the system behaves when confronted with unexpected, even malicious inputs. Since user communication is difficult to predict, the chatbot must withstand a broad scope of possible inputs. In order to function correctly, the chatbot must be resistant at least against common cyber-attacks. Therefore, a testing framework must be able to successfully test chatbots, regardless of their purpose.

Cyber-attacks against web applications represent an issue since the dawn of these systems. In fact, persistent vulnerabilities in web applications [10] motivate malicious users to abuse their weaknesses. XSS, for example, is triggered by injecting malicious JavaScript code into HTML elements. This attack usually targets user input fields of a website, where a user interacts with a website in a textual manner. Subsequently, in case that the attack was successful, a malicious code is executed at the side of the user.

In this paper, we introduce a testing approach for the detection of XSS in chatbots. This testing problem can be divided into three separate tasks, which represent integral parts of a testing framework implementation:

1. Test case generation
2. Test oracle definition
3. Test case execution

In the following sections, we will elaborate every task in detail and explain their role in the overall testing framework.

2.1   Test Case Generation

In order to trigger a vulnerability, user inputs must be defined in a way so that they contain executable JavaScript code. Each of such inputs, called attack vectors, represents a concrete test case. Unfortunately, the problem with XSS represents the fact that no standardized structure exists for such inputs. Actually, this can be considered the main reason for the difficulty to effectively defend against it. However, some mandatory information is always needed in order to execute the XSS code. In this paper, the test generation resembles the technique from our previous paper [19]. We define a small formal grammar that contains information about XSS, which is used to construct executable attack vectors. For this case, we relied on the official HTML specification [8], our experience and external sources (e.g. [14,15]). The attack grammar is built from finite sets of terminal and nonterminal symbols in the standard BNF. Every row in the grammar consists of a rule, which includes a left-hand side (LHS) and right-hand side (RHS). Each LHS consists of a single symbol, whereas the RHS contains an indefinite number of symbols. As common in BNF grammars, each rule defines when the LHS can be rewritten to its RHS. The resulting attack grammar in BNF is defined in the following way.

```
<pre>::= >
<opening>::= < <html> <content> >
<html>::= input | IFRAME | SCRIPT | A | img
<content>::= _ <attribute> = <value>
<attribute>::= type | value | <div/onmouseover | SRC |
    a | HREF | _ | title
<value>::= j_a_v_a_s_c_r_i_p_t_:a_l_e_r_t_%28_1_%29 |
    "text" | '' | 'alert(1)' | "javascript:alert('XSS
    ');" | ">" | "http://www.google.com" |
    j_a_v_a_s_c_r_i_p_t_:a_l_e_r_t_%28_1_%29 | "/" |
    _=" | "onerror='prompt(1)'"
<middle>::= alert(1) | XSS
<closing>::= </A> | XSS | </IFRAME> | </SCRIPT> | _
<post>::= ''
```

Attack grammar for test generation

As can be seen, JavaScript code is put into a formal representation of terminal and nonterminal symbols. The symbols themselves are defined so that they act as building blocks for attack vectors. Whereas concrete code is defined as terminals, the following elements are defined as nonterminals.

- pre: Sometimes symbols can be put in front of the actual script. This can lead to a filter bypass where the following script is executed in the aftermath.
- opening: This placeholder contains a HTML opening tag, which contains a set of HTML tags, attributes and values.
- html: This HTML tag contains statements or point to an external code. These can embed client side scripts, images, inline frames, hyperlinks and input fields in websites.
- content: This element contains an attribute-value pair in HTML and an equal symbol in between.
- attribute: HTML attributes include, among others, the type of input elements, initial values, location, title about an element.
- value: The placeholder for the actual payload that is meant to be executed. It can have multiple forms, depending on the intention of the attack.
- middle: The content of this element is eventually placed between the opening and closing tags. It contains either a window object or simple text.
- closing: Closing HTML tags are usually placed at the end of the input, thereby making it a valid JavaScript code. However, this element can be omitted altogether, thereby confusing the target system.
- post: In rear of the code one or multiple symbols can be inserted. SUTs might behave differently when encountering these symbols.

As already mentioned, XSS lacks a standard specification, which means that its attack vectors can come in different flavors. For this reason, we want to generate a test set that covers a wide scope of possible XSS appearances. In fact, the attack grammar provides enough information for the generation of such test cases. For example, let's consider five different cases of possible XSS structures.

```
<ex1>::=<<html><content><content><content>><closing>
<ex2>::=<<html><content>><closing>␣<<html><content>
      <content>><closing>␣<<html><content>␣<post>
<ex3>::=<<html><content>><middle><closing>
<ex4>::=<pre><middle>␣<opening><closing>
<ex5>::=<<html><content><content><content>>
```

Every case can be defined as an expression <ex> that consists of a set of attack grammar symbols. In fact, these expressions act as a guideline for the generation of attack vectors. We define them according to our experience and available information from the aforementioned sources. Every sequence of elements in an expression defines the order of nonterminals, which will be converted into corresponding terminals. The subsequently generated concatenation of terminals in one sequence represents an attack vector. Test cases are generated with a modified version of Grammar-Solver [7]. Grammar-Solver reads an expression and searches for corresponding nonterminals in the attack grammar. Every occurrence of a LHS symbol is rewritten by symbols of the RHS of the grammar. In fact, in every run, only one terminal is picked from the RHS for an element of an expression. Then the solver switches to the next element and repeats the process. Basically, the implementation generates attack vectors in a pairwise manner. It produces a cross product of unique combinations of terminals for every attack vector. However, even with a small grammar such as ours, the number of combinations would be too exhaustive for some of the <ex>'s. In order to avoid a combinatorial explosion, we restrict the number of terminal symbols on the RHS for certain expressions (like <ex2>). Even with a subset of the grammar, we generate a sufficient number of attack vectors. Figure 1 depicts the overall test case generation approach.

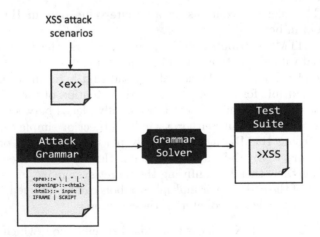

Fig. 1. Attack grammar-driven test case generation

Let's demonstrate the approach on an example. We want to generate attack vectors from the fourth expression, `<ex4>`. This expression consists of four non-terminals at the RHS and one space terminal in between. Now Grammar-Solver recursively starts at the first element, `<pre>`, and searches further in the parse tree of the nonterminal. The next element, `<middle>`, contains two terminals. After the space symbol, `<opening>` is traversed further, thereby encountering additional nonterminals `<html>` and `<content>`. The final element represents a HTML closing tag, `<closing>`. In the first run, the first terminals from the bottom of the parse tree of every nonterminal are selected, respectively. After the selection process is done, the concatenated terminals comprise the attack vector:

```
>alert(1) <input type=j a v a s c r i p t :a l e r t %28 1 %29></A>
```

The generated output represents one instance of possible values from the attack grammar. Subsequently, a different combination of values results in different attack vectors. The test generation process terminates once all combinations of terminals from the grammar are exhausted. The final output of this technique represents a unique test set for every `<ex>`.

2.2   Test Oracle and Execution

After the test set is generated from the grammar, the test execution process can be initiated. The generated attack vectors are submitted against a virtual agent in an automated manner. In this approach, a vulnerability is triggered by obtaining critical information from or breaking down the virtual agent. The shape of the expected information from a chatbot is defined in the test oracle in [19]. The typical attack vector for reflected XSS contains code that is meant to be executed on side of the client. In case of a secured application, intern security mechanisms will prevent this from happening. However, since XSS requires that its script is processed unaffected, potential input filters must be bypassed. For this reason, the attack grammar generates attack vectors with diverse input elements. By doing so, we hope to increase the likelihood that some attack vector avoids filtering mechanisms.

At the beginning of the execution process of a test case, the initial state of the SUT is processed and memorized. Then, individual attack vectors are submitted and the corresponding response is recorded. The behavior of the SUT is compared to its initial state by checking its output against the test oracle. Usually the reflected code from the SUT resembles the code from the attack vector. Actually, if the response code matches the input code, we conclude that a XSS vulnerability is triggered. On the other hand, if the submitted attack vector is filtered, the HTTP response contains an encoded input. In this case, no code will be executed, thus the attack was ineffective. Figure 2 depicts the communication flow with a filtered attack vector.

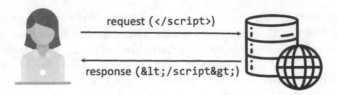

Fig. 2. Attack scenario for XSS over HTTP (Icons made by Freepik and Smashicons from www.flaticon.com, respectively.)

The virtual agent itself is either set up locally or accessed online over common HTTP. For every attack vector, a HTTP request is generated and sent to a SUT. As already mentioned in Sect. 2, the main targets for XSS represent user input fields. In case that the chatbot comprises static HTML content, we rely on HttpClient [1] for interaction purposes. On the other hand, Selenium WebDriver [12] is used as the API for testing of dynamic web elements. For this reason, we set up the standalone Selenium server v.3.141.59. The attacked chatbot replies with a HTTP response, which eventually contains an executable code. This response is parsed and its extracted content is automatically checked against the test oracle. Finally, a test verdict is given. Figure 3 depicts the entire test execution process.

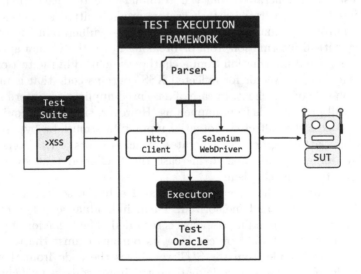

Fig. 3. Test case execution for chatbots

If a vulnerability is triggered, we conclude that the test case was successful. Otherwise, the attack vector was ineffective, thus returning a failing verdict. In fact, a test case consists of one such execution between the testing framework and chatbot. Afterwards, the execution switches to the next attack vector. The entire process is repeated until the very last test case has not been executed.

3 Evaluation

Chatbots are programs that simulate human-like interaction based on a set of NLP rules. In this paper, we do not test its ability to engage in complex communication or its understanding capabilities of natural language. Also, we don't test its memory functions with regard to correctness of stored information. In our quest, we confront the virtual agent aggressively with malicious inputs in order to extract useful information. In this case, useful information represents reflected code that is retrieved from the SUT. As demanded by the test oracle in Sect. 2.2, this information indicates that a security vulnerability is encountered in the application. For every expression, a different number of test cases is generated. In total, we generated an amount of 21355 attack vectors. For <ex1> we obtained 1458 inputs, 10368 for <ex2>, 4400 for <ex3>, again 4400 for <ex4> and 729 for <ex5>. The testing framework generates test cases on-the-fly by assigning attack vectors to HTTP requests. We tested a set of four different SUTs for reflected XSS vulnerabilities in an automated manner. The tested chatbots include the following ones:

- Aztekium Bot [2]: This educational chatbot provides information from different topics, including technical issues and lexical items. Therefore, it differs from other chatbots since its purpose is not to pretend to be human. It supports multiple languages and does not use a database.
- Jeeney [9]: This virtual agent adapts a more private approach to every user. By doing so, it learns from their interactions. It relies on the N.R. Research Engine[1], which allows the chatbot to endeavor in more complex communication. Also, it conducts a more complex analysis of provided user information.
- *SUT3*: Primarily, this chatbot is meant for entertaining purposes. However, this interactive agent can be used to practice writing skills in English as well. It should be noted that this chatbot is no longer being updated since 2002.
- *SUT4*: This system represents an open source chatbot platform. Chatbots can be implemented and customized in this platform for multiple purposes. Each system encompasses an object database, which can be reused and manipulated further. The supplement AI engine enables the chatbot to remember information from interaction with a user. In contrast to the other tested SUTs that were tested online, this chatbot was set up locally at the Apache Tomcat server, v.9.0.10.

Table 1 depicts all testing results. Every chatbot (SUT) is tested with test suites from individual expressions (TS). The total number of successful test cases (#success) counts attack vectors that were successful in triggering XSS. The number of failed test cases (#fail) depicts the number when no vulnerability was

---

[1] Neural Reliquary. http://www.jeeney.com/nr.html, accessed: 28.08.2020.

triggered. In general, chatbots behave differently when confronted with attack vectors from individual test suites. However, in certain cases they react in a similar manner. We will elaborate our observations and interpret the outcome of every SUT separately.

Table 1. Test results for XSS in chatbots

SUT	TS	$\#success$	$\#fail$
Aztekium Bot	<ex1>	1,458	0
	<ex2>	10,368	0
	<ex3>	4,312	88
	<ex4>	4,342	58
	<ex5>	729	0
Jeeney	<ex1>	1458	0
	<ex2>	10,368	0
	<ex3>	4,350	50
	<ex4>	4,350	50
	<ex5>	672	57
SUT3	<ex1>	0	1,458
	<ex2>	0	10,368
	<ex3>	2,383	2,017
	<ex4>	0	4,400
	<ex5>	674	55
SUT4	<ex1>	1,458	0
	<ex2>	10,368	0
	<ex3>	4,350	50
	<ex4>	4,350	50
	<ex5>	672	57

Aztekium Bot: This chatbot was very receptive to XSS detection attempts. In fact, all attack vectors from <ex1> and <ex2> were successful. However, a sanitation mechanism was encountered for <ex3> when a textual non-HTML input was at the end of the attack vector. The same can be said with <ex4> but only in cases when no closing tag exists. Without the last HTML element, the attack vector succeeds. Unfortunately, we encountered a possibly false positive issue for img elements: The input should be rejected when a textual data was present between HTML elements. However, this was not the case. The rest of the image elements were successful for <ex5>. Basically, this makes this chatbot receptive to all HTML tags.

Jeeney: This virtual agent did behave in the most curious way when being security tested. It did not filter attack vectors even in case that a closing HTML element was present, as in <ex1>. However, we encountered a discrepancy when we manually tested successfully flagged script elements with a browser. To our surprise, none of these HTML tags was triggered in the browser. But this filter is mitigated in <ex2> by injecting a script inside an iframe element. The hidden tag is not detected and is subsequently executed. We encountered a similar scenario in <ex3> with img elements. A aforegoing text in attack vectors seems to prevent the img from triggering. Although flagged as successful by the testing framework, no image tag was executed in the browser. For <ex3>, <ex4> and <ex5> all malformed attack vectors are rejected by the chatbot. However, plane img elements were triggered in the chatbot for <ex5>. In general, we were able to trigger iframe and input elements in all cases where they occurred.

SUT3: In contrast to other SUTs, this bot demonstrated the most distinctive behavior. Relative simple attack vectors resulted in XSS, whereas more complex inputs didn't. It resisted all attempts from <ex1> and <ex2>. The reason therefore is that the chatbot filters the last <closing> element in case that it comprises a non-HTML text. For <ex3> we were able to trigger input and iframe but just in cases where the input was properly closed by a HTML element. However, script was filtered even in properly closed inputs. Attack vectors from <ex4> were utterly rejected due to aforegoing <pre> element. On the other hand, the img element generally triggered a defect for <ex5> but was dismissed in cases of bad structure (like missing attributes). In general, this chatbot is the most equipped with serious input validation mechanisms.

SUT4: The bots from this multi-purpose chat platform are very receptive to XSS attempts. In fact, all input, iframe and script elements from <ex1> and <ex2> are subject to XSS. There were some cases in <ex3>, where attack vectors were rejected due to malformed inputs. This was only the case when an attribute was missing inside HTML tags. Even more interesting is the fact that aforegoing pre element from <ex4> succeeds to cover the XSS attempt. However, we did detect some false positives with the test oracle with <ex5>: A malformed img element is flagged as successful although it might not be triggered by the system.

The proposed testing framework succeeded to trigger security leaks in every chatbot. In general, a security leak indicates an implementation flaw or oversight. Unfortunately, the tested SUTs lack the ability to defend themselves against relatively simple XSS attempts. We assume that such behavior is caused either by a lack of sufficient security awareness or expertise. By triggering XSS from test cases from different expressions, we also get some insight about causes of the issue. For example, the omission or insertion of certain symbols in attack vectors can change the reaction of a SUT. The post-analysis of the results reveals that XSS can be triggered when specific elements occur in an attack vector. In fact, this observation affirms the claim of combinatorial test generation, where vulnerabilities are triggered by some critical combination of its components (e.g. [36]). The observed chatbot behavior also indicates that XSS inputs, in order to be triggered, must have a structure. On the one hand, some SUTs reject inputs due to an unexpected element in the attack vector. On the other hand, these chatbots process the XSS code in case of its absence nevertheless. Since the chatbot does not expect cyber-attacks, it fails to recognize the malicious XSS content of the received input. This means that the attack vector is treated like harmless JavaScript code. Although reflected XSS does not necessarily represent a harmful vulnerability, the inability to cover it can still lead to more devastating attacks, like unauthorized server access, etc.

However, despite positive results we must consider the occurrence of some false positives. Test oracles represent a distinct problem in software testing and XSS is no exception. Also, the discrepancy between results from methods that test static and dynamic web content must be considered, respectively. HttpClient offers the advantage to bypass a web browser by relying on its *headless* approach. On the other hand, Selenium WebDriver emulates a browser and therefore relies on its infrastructure and content filters. Therefore, this matter affects the results to a certain degree as well.

Regardless of this open issue, we want to emphasize the positive sides of the approach. The testing framework successfully triggers security vulnerabilities in chatbots and provides some clues about its root causes. Because of these facts, we consider the presented approach as a good starting point for future endeavors.

4   Related Work

To our knowledge, almost no works exist that focus on security issues in chatbots. However, vulnerabilities do represent a real issue in these systems, which need to be addressed. Until then, the current state-of-the-art leaves them vulnerable to exploitation attempts in the future. The current research focus in chatbots lies either in testing of functional aspects and usability [20,35,38] or non-functional properties [32]. In the former case, understanding of language and context in NLP systems is tested. On the other hand, the latter work measures a chatbot's NLP capabilities by applying load testing. In both cases, input parameters are evaluated by relying on correctness and performance functions. However, these functions stand in stark contrast to test oracles from the domain of security testing.

On the other hand, several approaches exist that test for XSS in web applications. These include, among others, the following works.

The authors of [27] introduce a mutation-based XSS testing approach that exploits intrinsic security leaks in web browsers. In this approach, malicious attack vectors are stored in their "harmless form" in HTML markups. In fact, the attack vector is mutated by the browser during the generic rendering of a website. This happens because the browser accesses the markup and decodes the content in order to parse it into a DOM structure. By doing so, the attack vector is unintentionally mutated into an executable form. The mXSS attack vector is assigned to a innerHTML property, thereby executing the malicious code. The attack is demonstrated on several scenarios against web applications and mitigation mechanisms. This attack is so destructive because the attack evolves during a pre-processing stage. In such way, the attack vector escapes potential detection mechanisms. In our approach, we don't primarily target the browser, since HttpClient bypasses the browser altogether. Also, we don't apply mutations on a specific attack vector but generate them in a combinatorial manner.

A security testing methodology for online business services is presented in [37]. The work focuses on authentication protocols for Multi-Party Web Applications (MPWAs) and subsequent web vulnerabilities. The authors analyze attack strategies for known vulnerabilities, including XSS, and subsequently abbreviate reproducible, i.e. application-independent, representations. These attack patterns represent general attack scenarios for testing against specific attacks. We share this work's intention in defining reproducible, black-box testing guidelines for XSS. However, our work generates concrete test cases with an intern test generation technique.

The approach in [36] introduces a combinatorial testing approach for analyzing XSS vulnerabilities. The authors define a combinatorial input model for test case generation, which are subsequently executed. Then, an automated fault-localization technique analyses the structure of every successful attack vector. Eventually, suspicious XSS-inducing combinations of parameter values are detected. Afterwards, such a combination is added to a new input model. From this model, new attack vectors are generated in a combinatorial manner. In fact, these constitute refined test cases with regard to the initial model. Similar to our approach, this work applies combinatorial test generation. However, the structure and values of attack vectors differs from this approach.

The authors of [31] introduce a unit testing approach for testing against XSS. Unit tests are generated automatically, i.e. each unit test represents a XSS test case. In order to generate attack vectors, they define an attack grammar. The grammar is subdivided into several input types, like URI resources, CSS specifications, HTML events and JavaScript code. Subsequently, attack vectors are generated by relying on sentences for each sub-grammar. Similar to our testing approach, this paper also defines a structure for XSS attack vectors. The resulting attack grammar is used in combination with sentences, that resemble our grammar and expressions, respectively. However, in contrast to their approach, we discuss a black-box testing technique, which does not have insights into the source code of a SUT.

A general overview about XSS is given in [34], whereas popular security tools for XSS testing include OWASP ZAP [11] and Burp Suite [3]. Whereas the former relies on fuzzing for automated testing, the latter represents a manual testing tool.

5   Conclusion and Future Work

In this paper, we address security issues in the increasingly important field of NLP systems. For this sake, we introduce a security testing approach for the detection of a harmful vulnerability in chatbots, namely XSS. A grammar-based test case generation technique is presented that generates malicious inputs for this purpose. Subsequently, these attack vectors are automatically executed by a testing framework. The presented approach is evaluated on four real-world chatbots with promising empirical results. The approach confirms that XSS is encountered in every of the tested chatbots. Basically, this observation reaffirms our claim that vulnerabilities do present a real issue in chatbots.

In order to test chatbots, we relied on just a small attack grammar. Additional elements can be added to the grammar easily. In such way, different test suites will be generated. Also, custom expressions will contribute to the test case diversity as well. However, in order to define such grammar, some manual effort and expert knowledge is needed. Also, it should be noted that our approach is meant for testing purposes only. A real security breach exploitation, for example a data theft, has yet to be proven.

With this paper, we hope to raise awareness about the importance of security testing for chatbots. In fact, we claim that these issues will represent an important topic in the future. For this reason, security testing should be incorporated into the chatbot development cycle and used for regression testing as well. In the future, we plan to extend the testing framework in order to detect additional vulnerability types in chatbots [10].

Acknowledgments. The research presented in the paper has been funded in part by the Austrian Research Promotion Agency (FFG) under grant 865248 (Securing Web Technologies with Combinatorial Interaction Testing - SecWIT). We want to express our gratitude to the owners of the tested chatbots for giving us the opportunity and permission to use their systems for research purposes. Also, we want to thank the anonymous reviewers for their constructive feedback, which was addressed in the paper.

References

1. Apache HttpComponents - HttpClient. https://hc.apache.org/httpcomponents-client-ga/. Accessed 06 Sept 2018
2. Aztekium Bot. http://aztekium.pl/bot. Accessed 27 Aug 2020
3. Burp Suite. http://portswigger.net/burp/. Accessed 27 Aug 2020
4. Chatbot Report 2019: Global Trends and Analysis. https://chatbotsmagazine.com/chatbot-report-2019-global-trends-and-analysis-a487afec05b. Accessed 05 Aug 2020
5. Content Spoofing Software Attack. https://owasp.org/www-community/attacks/Content_Spoofing. Accessed 08 Aug 2020
6. DDoS attacks through XSS. https://www.incibe-cert.es/en/blog/ddos-attacks-through-xss. Accessed 05 Aug 2020
7. Grammar-solver. https://github.com/bd21/Grammar-Solver. Accessed 13 July 2018
8. HTML Tutorial. https://www.w3schools.com/html/. Accessed 13 July 2018
9. Jeeney AI. http://www.jeeney.com. Accessed 27 Aug 2020
10. OWASP Top Ten Web Application Security Risks. https://www.owasp.org/index.php/Category:OWASP_Top_Ten_Project. Accessed 10 Aug 2020
11. OWASP ZAP Zed Attack Proxy. https://owasp.org/www-project-zap/. Accessed 27 Aug 2020
12. Selenium. https://www.selenium.dev. Accessed 10 Aug 2020

13. Top 12 Chatbots Trends and Statistics to Follow in 2020. https://aalavai.com/post/top-12-chatbots-trends-and-statistics-to-follow-in-2020. Accessed 05 Aug 2020

14. XSS Filter Bypass List. https://gist.github.com/rvrsh3ll/09a8b933291f9f98e8ec. Accessed 11 Aug 2020

15. XSS Filter Evasion Cheat Sheet. https://www.owasp.org/index.php/XSS_Filter_Evasion_Cheat_Sheet. Accessed 13 July 2018

16. Altinok, D.: An ontology-based dialogue management system for banking and finance dialogue systems. In: Proceedings of the the First Financial Narrative Processing Workshop (FNP 2018)@LREC'18 (2018)

17. Beriault-Poirier, A., Prom Tep, S., Sénécal, S.: Putting chatbots to the test: does the user experience score higher with chatbots than websites? In: Ahram, T., Karwowski, W., Taiar, R. (eds.) IHSED 2018. AISC, vol. 876, pp. 204–212. Springer, Cham (2019). https://doi.org/10.1007/978-3-030-02053-8_32

18. Bozic, J., Wotawa, F.: Security testing for chatbots. In: Medina-Bulo, I., Merayo, M.G., Hierons, R. (eds.) ICTSS 2018. LNCS, vol. 11146, pp. 33–38. Springer, Cham (2018). https://doi.org/10.1007/978-3-319-99927-2_3

19. Bozic, J., Wotawa, F.: Planning-based security testing of web applications with attack grammars. Softw. Qual. J. 28(1), 307–334 (2020). https://doi.org/10.1007/s11219-019-09469-y

20. Bravo-Santos, S., Guerra, E., de Lara, J.: Testing chatbots with CHARM. In: Shepperd, M., Brito e Abreu, F., Rodrigues da Silva, A., Pérez-Castillo, R. (eds.) QUATIC 2020. CCIS, vol. 1266, pp. 426–438. Springer, Cham (2020). https://doi.org/10.1007/978-3-030-58793-2_34

21. Chung, K., Park, R.C.: Chatbot-based heathcare service with a knowledge base for cloud computing. Clust. Comput. 22(1), 1925–1937 (2018). https://doi.org/10.1007/s10586-018-2334-5

22. Doherty, D., Curran, K.: Chatbots for online banking services. In: Web Intelligence, vol. 17, Issue 4 (2019)

23. Duchene, F., Rawat, S., Richier, J.L., Groz, R.: KameleonFuzz : the day Darwin drove my XSS Fuzzer! In: Proceedings of the 1st European workshop on Web Application Security Research (WASR 2013) (2013)

24. Felderer, M., Zech, P., Breu, R., Büchler, M., Pretschner, A.: Model-based security testing: a taxonomy and systematic classification. Softw. Test. Verif. Reliab. 26(2), 119–148 (2016)

25. Følstad, A., Brandtzæg, P.B.: Chatbots and the new world of HCI. ACM Interact. 24(4), 38–42 (2017)

26. Gabarron, E., Larbi, D., Denecke, K., Årsand, E.: What do we know about the use of chatbots for public health? In: Studies in Health Technology and Informatics (2020)

27. Heiderich, M., Schwenk, J., Frosch, T., Magazinius, J., Yang, E.Z.: mXSS Attacks: attacking well-secured web-applications by using innerHTML mutations. In: Proceedings of the 2013 ACM SIGSAC Conference on Computer & Communications Security (CCS 2013) (2013)

28. Lin, A.W., Barceló, P.: String solving with word equations and transducers: towards a logic for analysing mutation XSS. In: Proceedings of the 43rd Annual ACM SIGPLAN-SIGACT Symposium on Principles of Programming Languages (POPL 2016) (2016)

29. Mauldin, M.L.: ChatterBots, TinyMuds and the turing test: entering the Loebner prize competition. In: AAAI 1994 Proceedings of the Twelfth National Conference on Artificial Intelligence, vol. 1, pp. 16–21 (1994)

30. Mereani, F.A., Howe, J.M.: Detecting cross-site scripting attacks using machine learning. In: Hassanien, A.E., Tolba, M.F., Elhoseny, M., Mostafa, M. (eds.) AMLTA 2018. AISC, vol. 723, pp. 200–210. Springer, Cham (2018). https://doi.org/10.1007/978-3-319-74690-6_20

31. Mohammadi, M., Chu, B., Lipford, H.R.: Detecting cross-site scripting vulnerabilities through automated unit testing. In: Proceedings of the 2017 IEEE International Conference on Software Quality, Reliability and Security (QRS 2017), pp. 364–373 (2017)

32. Okanović, D., Beck, S., Merz, L., Zorn, C., Merino, L., van Hoorn, A., Beck, F.: Can a chatbot support software engineers with load testing? Approach and experiences. In: Proceedings of the 11th ACM/SPEC International Conference on Performance Engineering (ICPE 2020) (2020)

33. Peroli, M., De Meo, F., Viganò, L., Guardini, D.: MobSTer: a model-based security testing framework for web applications. Softw. Test. Verif. Reliab. **28**(8), e1685 (2018)

34. Rodríguez, G.E., Torres, J.G., Flores, P., Benavides, D.E.: Cross-site scripting (XSS) attacks and mitigation: a survey. Comput. Netw. **166**, 106960 (2020)

35. Ruane, E., Faure, T., Smith, R., Bean, D., Carson-Berndsen, J., Ventresque, A.: BoTest: a framework to test the quality of conversational agents using divergent input examples. In: Proceedings of the 23rd International Conference on Intelligent User Interfaces Companion (IUI 2018 Companion) (2018)

36. Simos, D.E., Kleine, K., Ghandehari, L.S.G., Garn, B., Lei, Yu.: A combinatorial approach to analyzing cross-site scripting (XSS) vulnerabilities in web application security testing. In: Wotawa, F., Nica, M., Kushik, N. (eds.) ICTSS 2016. LNCS, vol. 9976, pp. 70–85. Springer, Cham (2016). https://doi.org/10.1007/978-3-319-47443-4_5

37. Sudhodanan, A., Armando, A., Carbone, R., Compagna, L.: Attack patterns for black-box security testing of multi-party web applications. In: Proceedings of the 23rd Network and Distributed System Security Symposium (NDSS 2016) (2016)

38. Vasconcelos, M., Candello, H., Pinhanez, C., dos Santos, T.: Bottester: testing conversational systems with simulated users. In: IHC 2017: Proceedings of the XVI Brazilian Symposium on Human Factors in Computing Systems (2017)

39. Weizenbaum, J.: ELIZA-a computer program for the study of natural language communication between man and machine. Commun. ACM **9**(1), 36–45 (1966)

Giving a Model-Based Testing Language a Formal Semantics via Partial MAX-SAT

Bernhard K. Aichernig[1] and Christian Burghard[1,2]

[1] Institute of Software Technology, Graz University of Technology, Graz, Austria
{aichernig,burghard}@ist.tugraz.at
[2] AVL List GmbH, Graz, Austria
christian.burghard@avl.com

Abstract. Domain-specific Languages (DSLs) are widely used in model-based testing to make the benefits of modeling available to test engineers while avoiding the problem of excessive learning effort. Complex DSLs benefit from a formal definition of their semantics for model processing as well as consistency checking. A formal semantics can be established by mapping the model domain to a well-known formalism. In this paper, we present an industrial use case which includes a mapping from domain-specific models to Moore Machines, based on a Partial MAX-SAT problem, encoding a predicative semantics for the model-to-model mapping. We show how Partial MAX-SAT solves the frame problem for a non-trivial DSL in which the non-effect on variables cannot be determined statically. We evaluated the performance of our model-transformation algorithm based on models from our industrial use case.

Keywords: Partial moore machines · Model transformation · Consistency checking · Formal semantics · Frame problem · Partial MAX-SAT

1 Introduction

Model-based Testing (MBT) has emerged as a widely adopted practice for the verification of industrial systems [20,22,27]. Following this development, the AVL List GmbH is testing its portfolio of automotive measurement devices via an MBT approach based on a textual domain-specific modeling language called MDML. In our previous work [8,9], we designed the MDML language and modeling environment to provide our test engineers with an intuitively understandable model-based testing tool.

In a more recent development stage, we incorporated a model transformation from MDML models to Partial Moore Machines as the initial step of our model-based testing toolchain. This transformation to a well-defined formalism provides MDML with an operational semantics. In the current version of our toolchain, it is largely based on a *Partial MAX-SAT* (PMSAT) problem, encoding predicative

© IFIP International Federation for Information Processing 2020
Published by Springer Nature Switzerland AG 2020
V. Casola et al. (Eds.): ICTSS 2020, LNCS 12543, pp. 35–51, 2020.
https://doi.org/10.1007/978-3-030-64881-7_3

```
1   public statevar Mode {Standby, Measure} = Standby;
2   private statevar Timer {Off, On} = Off;
3   input Action {STBY, SMES, STIM};
4
5   given Mode = Standby {
6     when Action = SMES then Mode -> Measure;
7   }
8   given Mode = Measure {
9     when Action = STBY then Mode -> Standby;
10    given Timer = On when 15 sec elapsed then Mode -> last;
11  }
12  when Action = STIM then Timer -> On;
13  when Mode -> Standby then Timer -> Off;
14  fallback {
15    when Action = any then DoNothing;
16  }
```

Listing 1.1. Example MDML model

semantics. We chose a SAT-based implementation for our model transformation to cope with the potentially complex interplay of specialized language features.

Before giving formal definitions, we briefly describe the syntax and semantics of MDML informally by the example model in Listing 1.1, which we will use for explanatory purposes throughout this work. Each MDML model starts with the definition of one or more *state variables* (Lines 1–2), including their name, value domain, initial value and a `public` or `private` classifier which indicates if the value of this variable is visible to an outside observer. This is followed by the definition of at least one `input` channel (Line 3), defining one or more input symbols through which the system can be controlled from the outside. The rest of the model consists of a hierarchy of rules, defining changes to state variables dependent on the current state variable values and the received input.

Beyond this basic structure, MDML incorporates several specialized language features which facilitate the modeling of specific behaviors or allow for a very concise model representation, e.g. `last`-*transitions* (Listing 1.1, Line 10), *secondary actions* (Line 13) or `fallback` *blocks* (Lines 14–16), all of which will be explained over the course of this work. These special features complicate the semantic evaluation of MDML models and, as our model-based testing toolchain evolved, the need for a more explicit model representation arose. A graph-based representation of the modeled state machine - e.g. in the form of a Moore Machine, would have a beneficial impact on further stages of our MBT toolchain, e.g. test case generation [23], visualization [7] and tracing. A Partial Moore Machine generated from the MDML model in Listing 1.1 can be seen in Fig. 1.

The semantics of MDML state machine models as collections of state variables makes them subject to the *frame problem* - i.e. the problem of reasoning about system variables which are implicitly assumed to remain unchanged during an operation. The use of PMSAT is dictated by specific MDML language constructs - the aforementioned *secondary actions* - which significantly complicate a purely SAT-based solution of the frame problem. Lines 9 and 10 in Listing 1.1, for example, each specify a transition from Mode = Measure to Mode = Standby. However, the secondary action in Line 13 states that, whenever the Mode changes to Standby, the Timer must change to Off. This is a condition on the post-state

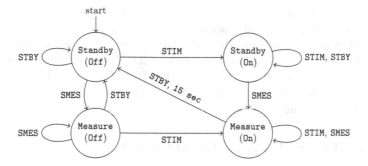

Fig. 1. Partial Moore Machine representation of the system represented in Listing 1.1. The values of `private` state variables, which are not part of the output, are displayed in brackets.

of a transition, depending on another property of the post-state. In Fig. 1, the result can be seen as the two transitions labeled STBY which are not loops.

To the best of our knowledge, we are the first to provide a formal semantics to a domain-specific language via Partial MAX-SAT. Especially our treatment of the frame problem seems to be novel. We also contribute some experiences on the industrial use of a PMSAT-based model transformation. Defining an operational semantics for a front-end modeling language also has the effect of closely relating model transformation to consistency checking. We show how, through a small alteration, our model transformation setup can be used to uncover semantic inconsistencies within MDML models.

The rest of this paper is structured as follows: Section 2 introduces some necessary preliminaries, Sect. 3 outlines the syntax of the MDML language and Sect. 4 defines a formal semantics based on those syntax elements. Sections 5 and 6 explain how a model transformation and a consistency check can be implemented using this formal semantics. Section 7 presents the results of a runtime evaluation as well as our experience with the implementation. Finally, Sect. 8 discusses related work and Sect. 9 concludes the paper.

2 Preliminaries

2.1 Measurement Device Modeling Language

The *Measurement Device Modeling Language* (MDML) was developed in close cooperation with AVL's test engineers to efficiently model the firmware state machines of measurement devices. The taxonomy of Utting et al. [27] classifies MDML as a *state-based* notation, which means that it specifies a system as a collection of variables, representing a snapshot of the internal state of the system, plus some operations that modify those variables through pre- and postconditions. The syntax of MDML allows for many degrees of freedom in the encoding of a specific state machine behavior and each engineer is able to develop a modeling style that suits his or her individual needs. After the test models have been established, we automatically generate test cases from them using various mutation-based, structural and random coverage metrics [8]. These test cases are then converted to C# code and deployed to our test automation system. However, the aforementioned syntactic freedom of MDML is paid for by an increased difficulty in model processing. Although MDML is an effective input language, it would benefit from a more explicit model representation for all further uses in the model-based testing toolchain.

2.2   SAT, MAX-SAT and Partial MAX-SAT

A *Boolean satisfiability* (SAT) *problem* inquires, if a given Boolean formula can be fulfilled. While SAT problems are NP-complete, a series of algorithms and implementations ("SAT solvers") have been developed which can solve such problems in a (relatively) efficient and highly scalable manner [4]. When run on a Boolean formula $f(b_1, \ldots, b_n)$ on the variables b_1 to b_n, a SAT solver either returns a solution $S : [1, n] \to \mathbb{B}$, or the message UNSAT if f is not satisfiable. SAT solvers usually require formulas to be given in *conjunctive normal form* (CNF), i.e. as a conjunction of clauses, each consisting of a disjunctions of Boolean literals. However, any Boolean formula can be rewritten to CNF. The *MAX-SAT* problem is related to SAT. Here, the solver tries to maximize the number of satisfied clauses in a given CNF-formula. A further variant of the MAX-SAT problem is called *Partial MAX-SAT* (PMSAT) [10]. Here, the clauses are partitioned into a set of *hard* clauses (Φ_{SAT}^H), which must be satisfied in any case, and a set of *soft* clauses (Φ_{SAT}^S), of which a maximum number must be satisfied. Both MAX-SAT and PMSAT can be viewed as optimization problems with a cost function equal to the number of unfulfilled (soft) clauses.

2.3   Moore Machines

Definition 1 (Moore Machine). *A Moore Machine is a tuple* $\langle Q, q_0, I, O, \delta, \lambda \rangle$ *with a finite set of states Q, an initial state $q_0 \in Q$, a set of input symbols I, a set of output symbols O, a transition function $\delta : Q \times I \to Q$ and an output function $\lambda : Q \to O$.*

Definition 2 (Partial Moore Machine). *A Partial Moore Machine (PMM) is a generalization of a Moore Machine with a partial function $\delta : Q \times I \nrightarrow Q$.*

2.4   Frame Problem

The frame problem is a rather old problem that was first formulated by McCarthy and Hayes in a discussion of philosophical aspects of AI [17]. It is the problem of expressing the assumption in First-Order-Logic, that all system variables, which are not explicitly stated to be changed during an operation, remain unchanged. In classical specification methods, such as Z [25], VDM [13] and B [1], the set of changed variables for a given operation is known at the time of specification. Such a partial variable assignment can easily be transformed into a total assignment by assigning all remaining variables their current value. In this way, the frame problem can be solved on a syntactic level. The Unified Theory of Programming (UTP) [2,11] makes this transformation from partial to total assignments explicit. Separation Logic [21] leverages this a-priori knowledge in order to reason about programs with a high number of state-defining variables.

3 MDML Syntax

The syntax of MDML is given by the following production rules:

$$
\begin{aligned}
Model &::= V_S^+ \; C^+ \; Root_M \; Root_F^? \\
V_S &::= (\textbf{public} \mid \textbf{private}) \; \textbf{statevar} \; ID_v \; \{D_v\} \; \text{=} \; \iota_v; \\
D_v &::= x \; (, \; x)^* \\
x &::= ID \\
\iota_v &::= x \\
C &::= \textbf{input} \; ID_c \; \{I_c\}; \\
I_c &::= x \; (, \; x)^* \\
Root_M &::= Node^+ \\
Node &::= G \mid W \mid T \\
G &::= \textbf{given} \; Rule_G \; (\textbf{and} \; Rule_G)^* \; (Node \mid \{Node^+\}) \\
Rule_G &::= ID_v \; ((\; \text{=} \; \mid \; \text{!=} \;) \; x \mid \textbf{not}^? \; \textbf{in} \; \{x \; (, \; x)^*\}) \\
W &::= \textbf{when} \; Rule_W \; (\textbf{or} \; Rule_W)^* \; (Node \mid \{Node^+\}) \\
Rule_W &::= Action_I \mid \tau \mid Action_S \\
Action_I &::= ID_c \; ((\; \text{=} \; \mid \; \text{!=} \;) \; x \mid \; \text{=} \; \textbf{any} \mid \textbf{not}^? \; \textbf{in} \; \{x \; (, \; x)^*\}) \\
\tau &::= INT \; (\textbf{ms} \mid \textbf{sec} \mid \textbf{min}) \; \textbf{elapsed} \\
Action_S &::= ID_v \; \text{->} \; x \\
T &::= \textbf{then} \; Rule_T \; (\textbf{and} \; Rule_T)^*; \\
Rule_T &::= ID_v \; \text{->} \; x \mid ID_v \; \text{->} \; \textbf{last} \mid \textbf{DoNothing} \\
Root_F &::= \textbf{fallback} \; \{Node^+\}
\end{aligned}
$$

In the above grammar, ID maps to an identifier terminal and INT to an integer terminal. In the rest of this paper, we will re-use some of the non-terminal symbols to denote the set of all their instantiations within a given syntactically correct MDML model - i.e. the set of all *state variables* V_S, the set of all *input channels* C, the set of all **given** statements G, the set of all **when** statements W, the set of all **then** statements T and the set $Node$ for the union of the latter three. In contrast, we use D_v as the set of domain values and ι_v as the initial value for a given state variable v, as well as I_c as the set of input values for a given input channel c. Let I_τ be the set of all instantiations of τ and let $RNode = Node \cup \{Root_M, Root_F\}$. With $\mathcal{P}$ signifying the powerset, we define the function $children : RNode \rightarrow \mathcal{P}(Node)$ which maps a non-terminal instantiation to the set of all instantiations of $Node$ on the right side of its production rule. We also define $parent : Node \rightarrow RNode$ as the inverse of $children$ and $ancestors :$ $Node \rightarrow \mathcal{P}(RNode)$ as the transitive closure of $parent$. We illustrate all three functions on Lines 14–16 of Listing 1.1:

$children(\text{when Action = any then DoNothing;}) = \{(\text{then DoNothing;})\}$

$parent(\text{when Action = any then DoNothing;}) = Root_F$

$ancestors(\text{then DoNothing}) = \{Root_F, (\text{when Action = any} \dots)\}$

Using these functions, we formulate the additional syntactic rule that for each **then** statement $t \in T$, $ancestors(t)$ must contain exactly one **when** statement from W. There are also some type restrictions to be considered. For a given state variable $v \in \mathcal{V}_S$, ι_v must be an element of D_v and for each occurrence of ID_v on the right side of a production rule together with an x, x must be an element of D_v. We also define all different D_v to be disjoint sets of state variable values, even if shared value IDs occur. For each input channel $c \in C$, each occurrence of ID_c together with an x on the right side of a production rule, x must be a member of I_c. All I_c are pairwise disjoint the same way as all D_v.

4   MDML Semantics

With a clearly defined syntax in place, we now define a formal semantics for MDML. By mapping MDML models to Partial Moore Machines (PMMs), we first establish an operational semantics. This mapping, in turn, relies upon a Boolean predicative semantics.

4.1   Operational Semantics

Let $\mathcal{V} = \{v_1, \dots, v_n\}$ be the set of all model variables, including but not limited to $\mathcal{V}_S$. Further, let $D_\times = D_{v_1} \times \cdots \times D_{v_n}$ and $D_\cup = D_{v_1} \cup \cdots \cup D_{v_n}$. Let $public : \mathcal{V} \rightarrow \mathbb{B}$ be $true$, iff the argument is an element of $\mathcal{V}_S$ and declared **public**. Let $\mathcal{V}_P = \{v_{P1}, \dots, v_{Pm}\} = \{v \in \mathcal{V}_S \mid public(v)\}$ and let $D_{P\times}$ be defined analogous to $D_\times$, on $\mathcal{V}_P$, instead of $\mathcal{V}_S$. We define the semantics of MDML models by mapping them to PMMs in the following way:

$$Q \subseteq D_\times \tag{1}$$

$$q_0 =_{df} [\iota_{v_1}, \dots, \iota_{v_n}] \tag{2}$$

$$I =_{df} I_\tau \cup \bigcup_{c \in C} I_c \tag{3}$$

$$O \subseteq D_{P\times} \tag{4}$$

$$\lambda(q) =_{df} [eval(q, v_{P1}), \dots, eval(q, v_{Pm})] \tag{5}$$

Other than externally triggered transitions, MDML also supports time-triggered transitions (see Listing 1.1, Line 10). Rather than giving MDML a full-fledged Timed-Automata semantics, we simply treat time triggers (I_τ) in the same way as external inputs, in the sense of "the external controller lets time pass" (see Eq. 3). This abstraction is not without its shortcomings but it is sufficient for our MBT purposes. As shown by Eq. 1, the state space of the PMM is a subset of the space of possible valuations for the variables in $\mathcal{V}$. We define $eval : D_\times \times \mathcal{V} \to D_\cup$ to retrieve the value of a given variable in a given state. Finally, we define the transition function δ, based on the predicate $transition : D_\times \times I \times D_\times \to \mathbb{B}$:

$$\forall q \in Q, i \in I, q' \in D_\times : \delta(q,i) = q' \wedge q' \in Q \Leftrightarrow transition(q,i,q') \qquad (6)$$

The remainder of this section will be dedicated to defining $transition(q,i,q')$ based on the contents of a given MDML model. We first break it down into its individual semantic components and finally relate them to the syntactic elements of MDML.

4.2 Predicative Semantics

The *transition* predicate is dependent on the *primary action* predicate pa, the *secondary action* predicate sa, the *history* predicate $hist$ and the *framing* predicate fra:

$$transition\,(q,i,q') \Leftrightarrow pa(q,i,q') \wedge sa(q,i,q') \wedge hist\,(q,q') \wedge fra(q,i,q') \qquad (7)$$

For all Boolean predicates introduced in this and the next section, we assume an implicit dependence on q, i, and q'. In these definitions, we use $\underline{v}$ and $\underline{v}'$ as a shorthand for the assignment of $v \in \mathcal{V}$ in q and q', respectively.

Primary Action. A primary action is the immediate response of the state machine to an external input or a time-trigger (see *Action$_I$* and τ in the grammar definition, as well as Lines 6, 9, 10, 12 and 15 in Listing 1.1), encoded in the rule hierarchy of the MDML model. This hierarchy is composed of **given** statements, encoding conditions on q, **when** statements, encoding conditions on i and **then** statements, encoding conditions on q'. A **then** statement is *enabled* if the conditions of all its superordinate **given** statements evaluate to *true* and it is *triggered* if the condition of its superordinate **when** statement evaluates to *true*. A predicative definition of "enabled" and "triggered" will follow in Sect. 4.3. Let $T_P \subseteq T$ be the set of **then** statements which are both enabled and triggered. In a well-formed MDML model, the set of primary actions T_P has either zero or one elements. In the case of zero elements, the MDML model does not specify a transition for the specific pair of pre-state and input. In this case, we define $transition(q,i,q') =_{df} false$ and $\delta(q,i)$ remains undefined. If T_P contains more than one element, the MDML model is malformed and an inconsistency error is reported. For all further considerations, we assume $T_P = \{t_P\}$.

$$pa(q,i,q') =_{df} upd(t_P) \qquad (8)$$

The *update* predicate $upd : T \to \mathbb{B}$ encodes the effect of a **then** statement on q' and will also be defined in Sect. 4.3.

Secondary Action. A secondary action is a value change of a variable v which is conditioned on a value change of a different variable v_w, as exemplified by Listing 1.1, Line 13. The effect is akin to that of a *change-trigger* in UML [19]. Secondary actions are encoded as **when** statements with a trigger rule of the form $Action_S ::= ID_{v_w}$ **->** x_w. Let $T_S \subseteq T \times Action_S$ be the set of pairs of all enabled **then** statements and rules of their superordinate **when** statements of the form $Action_S$. We also restrict T_S to those pairs which share the same root node as t_P. The secondary action predicate is given as:

$$sa(q, i, q') =_{df} \bigwedge_{\langle (ID_{v_w} -> x_w), t \rangle \in T_S} \left(\left(\underline{v_w} \neq x_w \wedge \underline{v'_w} = x_w \right) \rightarrow upd(t) \right) \tag{9}$$

As can be seen from the above definition, the updates of each **then** statement t are performed if v_w simultaneously changes from a value other than x_w to x_w.

History Variable Maintenance. MDML offers a language construct called **last-transition** (see Listing 1.1, Line 10), where a state variable is reset to its most recent previous value. This cannot be accomplished without adding additional model variables on a semantic level. Let $\mathcal{V}_H \subseteq \mathcal{V}_S$ be the set of all state variables v for which a **then** rule $Rule_T ::= ID_v$ **->** **last** exists. We define a new set of state variables called *history* variables $\mathcal{H}$, which are bijectively associated with the variables in $\mathcal{V}_H$. For each $v \in \mathcal{V}_H$, we have an associated $h_v \in \mathcal{H}$ with $D_v = D_{h_v}$ and $\iota_v = \iota_{h_v}$. We can now complete the definition of the set of model variables as $\mathcal{V} = \mathcal{V}_S \cup \mathcal{H}$. The variables in $\mathcal{H}$ will be used to store the previous value of their counterparts in $\mathcal{V}_H$. This is accomplished by the history maintenance predicate:

$$hist(q, q') =_{df} \bigwedge_{v \in \mathcal{V}_H} \left(\left(\underline{v'} = \underline{v} \rightarrow \underline{h'_v} = \underline{h_v} \right) \wedge \left(\underline{v'} \neq \underline{v} \rightarrow \underline{h'_v} = \underline{v} \right) \right) \tag{10}$$

Framing. The predicates defined above clearly define $\underline{v'}$ for some $v \in \mathcal{V}_S$ and leave it undefined for others. If the $\underline{v'}$ is not defined by either the primary or the secondary action, it shall remain unchanged:

$$fra(q, i, q') =_{df} \bigwedge_{v \in \mathcal{V}_S} \neg def(v) \rightarrow \underline{v'} = \underline{v} \tag{11}$$

$$def(v) =_{df} \exists x \in D_v : pa(q, i, q') \wedge sa(q, i, q') \vdash \underline{v'} = x \tag{12}$$

The helper predicate $def : \mathcal{V}_S \rightarrow \mathbb{B}$ evaluates to *true* iff a unique value for $\underline{v'}$ can be formally deduced (expressed by the symbol $\vdash$) from the primary and/or secondary action predicates. The effect of the framing predicate can be observed in Listing 1.1, Lines 5–7, where transitions from states with $\underline{\text{Mode}} = \text{Standby}$ to $\underline{\text{Mode}}' = \text{Measure}$ are specified. These transitions exist regardless of the value of $\underline{\text{Timer}}$ and trigger no secondary actions. Therefore, the framing predicate will cause $\underline{\text{Timer}}' = \underline{\text{Timer}}$ for each resulting transition. This results in the two transitions in Fig. 1 which are labeled SMES and are not self-transitions.

4.3 Rule Hierarchy

As previously stated, we express the semantics of **given** and **when** statements via the predicates en ("enables") and tr ("triggers"), which are defined on the syntactic elements of the rule hierarchy:

$$
\begin{aligned}
en(Root_M) &\Leftrightarrow_{df} & true \\
en(G) &\Leftrightarrow_{df} & en(parent(G)) \wedge en(Rule_{G1}) \\
& & \wedge \cdots \wedge en(Rule_{Gk}) \\
en(ID_v \texttt{ = } x) &\Leftrightarrow_{df} & \underline{v} = x \\
en(ID_v \texttt{ != } x) &\Leftrightarrow_{df} & \underline{v} \neq x \\
en(ID_v \texttt{ in } \{x_1, \ldots, x_k\}) &\Leftrightarrow_{df} & \underline{v} \in \{x_1 \ldots, x_k\} \\
en(ID_v \texttt{ not in } \{x_1, \ldots, x_k\}) &\Leftrightarrow_{df} & \underline{v} \notin \{x_1 \ldots, x_k\} \\
en(W) &\Leftrightarrow_{df} & en(parent(W)) \\
en(T) &\Leftrightarrow_{df} & en(parent(T)) \\
en(Root_F) &\Leftrightarrow_{df} & \nexists\, t \in T_P : Root_M \in ancestors(t)
\end{aligned}
$$

The main root of the rule hierarchy ($Root_M$) is enabled by default. Each **given** statement inherits the enabledness of its parent and imposes its own conditions ($Rule_G$) on q in the form of equality, inequality and set exclusion and inclusion of state variable values $\underline{v}$ in q. Both **when** and **then** statements inherit enabledness from their parent statements. The **when** statements in Lines 12 and 13 of Listing 1.1, for example, are direct children of $Root_M$ and always enabled while those in Lines 6, 9 and 10 are conditioned upon the value of the state variable Mode in q. We complete the definition of en by examining the semantics of the **fallback** root $Root_F$, which is enabled when the main rule hierarchy specifies no primary action. The **fallback** mechanism was designed to provide the users of MDML with an easy way to incorporate "exception handling" in their models or make their models input-complete. Secondary actions ($Action_S$) do not rely upon this predicate and evaluate to *false*. The semantics of **when** statements is encoded in the predicate tr:

$$
\begin{aligned}
tr(Root_M) &\Leftrightarrow_{df} & false \\
tr(Root_F) &\Leftrightarrow_{df} & false \\
tr(G) &\Leftrightarrow_{df} & tr(parent(G)) \\
tr(W) &\Leftrightarrow_{df} & tr(Rule_{W1}) \vee \quad \vee tr(Rule_{Wk}) \\
tr(ID_c \texttt{ = } x) &\Leftrightarrow_{df} & i = x \\
tr(ID_c \texttt{ != } x) &\Leftrightarrow_{df} & i \in I_c \setminus \{x\} \\
tr(ID_c \texttt{ in } \{x_1, \ldots, x_n\}) &\Leftrightarrow_{df} & i \in \{x_1, \ldots, x_k\} \\
tr(ID_c \texttt{ not in } \{x_1, \ldots, x_n\}) &\Leftrightarrow_{df} & i \in I_c \setminus \{x_1, \ldots, x_k\}
\end{aligned}
$$

$$tr(ID_c \;\texttt{=}\; \texttt{any}) \qquad\qquad \Leftrightarrow_{df} \qquad\qquad i \in I_c$$

$$tr(\tau) \qquad\qquad \Leftrightarrow_{df} \qquad\qquad i = \tau$$

$$tr(Action_S) \qquad\qquad \Leftrightarrow_{df} \qquad\qquad false$$

$$tr(T) \qquad\qquad \Leftrightarrow_{df} \qquad\qquad tr(parent(T))$$

Unlike the value of *en*, *tr* starts out as *false* on both roots. If the current input i satisfies a trigger rule $Rule_W$ of a **when** statement, the statement gets triggered. Here, $Rule_W$ can again be based on equality or inequality, as well as set inclusion and exclusion relative to the input alphabet I_c of a given input channel c. However, since i is not guaranteed to be an element of I_c, the conditions are formulated in a type-safe manner. Alternatively, primary actions can be triggered by time triggers τ. Analogous to *en*, **given** and **then** statements inherit the *tr* value of their parent node. The effect of a **then** statement on q' is encoded by the update predicate *upd*:

$$upd(T) \qquad\qquad \Leftrightarrow_{df} \qquad upd(Rule_{T1}) \wedge \cdots \wedge upd(Rule_{Tk})$$

$$upd(ID_v \;\texttt{->}\; x) \qquad\qquad \Leftrightarrow_{df} \qquad \underline{v}' = x$$

$$upd(ID_v \;\texttt{->}\; \texttt{last}) \qquad\qquad \Leftrightarrow_{df} \qquad \underline{v}' = \underline{h_v}$$

$$upd(\texttt{DoNothing}) \qquad\qquad \Leftrightarrow_{df} \qquad \bigwedge_{v \in V_S} \underline{v}' = \underline{v}$$

The most common case of $Rule_T$ is the assignment of $\underline{v}'$ to a specific value x. Alternatively, the rule $\texttt{DoNothing}$ encodes a self-transition $(\delta(q, i) = q)$ and $ID_v \;\texttt{->}\; \texttt{last}$ causes $\underline{v}'$ to assume the value that was held prior to $\underline{v}$.

5   Model Transformation

To transform a given MDML model into a PMM, we first obtain I and q_0 directly from the model. We then perform a closure on Q under δ for all $i \in I$. To do that, we state the *transformation problem* as obtaining a post-state q' for a given pre-state q and input i according to Eq. 6. The transformation problem is a *Constraint Satisfaction Problem* (CSP), which we encode as a PMSAT problem and solve with an appropriate solver. We do, however perform a pre-filtering step by computing T_P and T_S via imperative algorithms and therefore exclude all irrelevant model elements from the CSP. This was done to further both performance and ease of implementation.

5.1   PMSAT-Encoding of the Transformation Problem

The assignments of the MDML model variables in both pre- and post-state become the variables of the CSP:

$$\mathcal{V}_{CSP} = \bigcup_{v \in \mathcal{V}} \{\underline{v}, \underline{v}'\} \qquad\qquad (13)$$

There are multiple ways to encode a CSP into SAT. For the transformation problem, we follow the *direct encoding* method described by Walsh [28]. The encoding of CSP variables with multi-value domains into Boolean SAT variables is accomplished by:

$$\mathcal{V}_{SAT} = \{b_{\underline{v}x} \in \mathbb{B} \mid \underline{v} \in \mathcal{V}_{CSP} \wedge x \in D_v \wedge (b_{\underline{v}x} = true \Leftrightarrow \underline{v} = x)\} \tag{14}$$

Although there are more concise encodings, the direct encoding was again chosen to ease implementation. The MDML model in Listing 1.1, for example, would produce eight Boolean variables, for `Mode=Standby`, `Mode=Measure`, `Timer=On` and `Timer=Off` in both q and q'. This encoding requires additional clauses to ensure that each CSP variable is assigned exactly one value. The valuation in the pre-state q is known a-priori and can be directly evaluated as $x = eval(q, v)$ and all Boolean variables encoding q can be set to a fixed value:

$$pre(q) = \bigwedge_{v \in \mathcal{V}} \left(\underline{v} = x \wedge \bigwedge_{\tilde{x} \in D_v \setminus \{x\}} \underline{v} \neq \tilde{x} \right) \tag{15}$$

The valuation in the post-state q is as of yet unknown and only restricted by the known variable domains.

$$post(q') = \bigwedge_{v \in \mathcal{V}} \left(\left(\bigvee_{x \in D_v} \underline{v}' = x \right) \wedge \bigwedge_{x_1 \in D_v, x_2 \in D_v \setminus \{x_1\}} (\underline{v}' = x_1 \rightarrow \underline{v}' \neq x_2) \right) \tag{16}$$

Leaving the conversion to CNF implicit, the full set of hard clauses for the PMSAT problem emerges as:

$$\Phi_{SAT}^H = pa(q, i, q') \wedge sa(q, i, q') \wedge hist\,(q, q') \wedge pre(q) \wedge post(q') \tag{17}$$

Up to this point, $fra(q, i, q')$ has not been represented in terms of a first-order logic formula. In CSP problems, framing axioms explicitly ensure that every variable change has a defined cause [14]. However, this would require us to establish an explicit cause-and-effect relationship between variable changes to ensure that each secondary action is directly or indirectly caused by the primary action. Otherwise, the solution might contain groups of secondary actions which are causing each other - i.e. forming causal loops. Instead of using framing axioms, we decided to formulate the transformation problem in PMSAT and model $fra(q, i, q')$ by means of soft clauses:

$$\Phi_{SAT}^S = \bigwedge_{v \in \mathcal{V}_S} \underline{v}' = \underline{v} \tag{18}$$

Theorem 1. *If the SAT problem Φ_{SAT}^H has a solution,[1] the solution to the PMSAT problem $\langle \Phi_{SAT}^H, \Phi_{SAT}^S \rangle$ satisfies transition (q, i, q').*

---

[1] Note that the reverse implication is trivially fulfilled, since PMSAT can only pick the optimum from all possible solutions of the underlying SAT problem.

Proof. The structure of the proof is as follows: First, we find a solution which minimizes the cost function of the PMSAT problem. Then, we confirm that this solution fulfills the framing predicate and is a valid solution to the SAT problem. Let $\mathcal{V}_d \subseteq \mathcal{V}_S$ be the set of all state variables which are uniquely defined, i.e. which are assigned the same value in all solutions of the pure SAT problem. Let $\mathcal{V}_f = \mathcal{V}_S \setminus \mathcal{V}_d$ be the set of all state variables which are not uniquely defined. Following Eq. 18, the cost function of the PMSAT problem can be re-formulated in the following way, intuitively showing the global minimum:

$$E(q') = c + \sum_{v \in \mathcal{V}_f} \begin{cases} 0 & \text{iff } \underline{v}' = \underline{v} \\ 1 & \textbf{otherwise} \end{cases} \tag{19}$$

Here, c is a constant value caused by the variables in $\mathcal{V}_d$. The post-state $q'_{\min}$ with $\forall v \in \mathcal{V}_f : \underline{v}' = \underline{v}$ yields the minimum cost value $E(q'_{\min}) = c$. We now examine the fulfillment of each predicate in Eqs. 7 and 17:

Primary Action: The primary action predicate references q' solely via the predicate *upd*, which either does not reference any given $\underline{v}'$ or restricts it to a single value. Therefore, all variables referenced by the primary action must be element of $\mathcal{V}_d$ and $q'_{\min}$ cannot falsify this predicate.

Secondary Action: The secondary action predicate references q' via the update predicate, as well as in the left-hand side of an implication. If a variable from $\mathcal{V}_d$ triggers a secondary action, all variables referenced by *upd* will be uniquely determined (see proof for primary action) and, in turn, be part of $\mathcal{V}_d$. The valuation of $\mathcal{V}_f$ in $q'_{\min}$, cannot trigger any secondary actions since $\underline{v}' = \underline{v}$ for all $v \in \mathcal{V}_f$. In other words, all variables in $\mathcal{V}_f$ trivially fulfill the predicate for $q'_{\min}$.

History: We assume that the assignment of all $h \in \mathcal{H}$ in $q'_{\min}$ satisfies the history predicate. All variables in $\mathcal{V}_S$ are either not referenced or referenced in the left-hand side of an implication and therefore cannot falsify the predicate.

Pre-state: The pre-state predicate does not reference q'.

Post-state: The post-state predicate establishes the domain for all $\underline{v}'$ but does not restrict them any further.

Framing: Let $\mathcal{V}_{dp} = \{v \in \mathcal{V}_S \mid \mathit{def}(v)\}$ and $\mathcal{V}_{fp} = \mathcal{V}_S \setminus \mathcal{V}_{dp}$. From the definition of *def* and $\mathcal{V}_d$, it follows that $\mathcal{V}_{dp} \subseteq \mathcal{V}_d$ and, consequently, $\mathcal{V}_f \subseteq \mathcal{V}_{fp}$. From the above proofs, it is evident that, if a given $\underline{v}'$ is not uniquely determined by the primary or secondary action, it also cannot be further determined by any other predicates. Therefore we get $\mathcal{V}_{fp} \subseteq \mathcal{V}_f$ and, consequently, $\mathcal{V}_{fp} = \mathcal{V}_f$. In $q'_{\min}$, we have $\underline{v}' = \underline{v}$ for all variables in $\mathcal{V}_f$, fulfilling the framing predicate.

With exception of the framing predicate, all other predicates are (either generally or specifically for $q'_{\min}$) independent of all variables in $\mathcal{V}_f$. Therefore $q'_{\min}$ must be a valid solution to the SAT problem. □

6   Consistency Check

In order to be transformed into a Partial Moore Machine (PMM), an MDML model needs to be *well-formed*. To define the notion of well-formedness, we exploit an important duality between model transformation and consistency checking: An MDML model is well-formed, iff the transformation into a PMM succeeds. Or in other words, each failure mode of the transformation corresponds to a possible type of model error. To avoid redundancies in our implementation, we directly check the consistency of MDML models by attempting a model transformation. Errors in the MDML model may take one of the following forms:

- Syntax errors are handled directly by the textual editor.
- Domain errors, e.g. when $c = x$ with $x \notin I_c$ are also handled by the editor.
- Explicit transformation errors, e.g. $|T_P| > 1$ are handled as software exceptions, thrown within the transformation algorithm.
- Contradictions within an MDML model can be discovered if $|T_P| = 1$ but $\nexists q' \in D_\times : transition\,(q, i, q')$. They will be the focus of this Section. Contradictions can be as obvious as then Mode -> Standby and Mode-> Measure, but also more subtle due to the involvement of secondary actions.
- Remaining gaps in the semantics definition - e.g. multiple time-triggered then statements enabled in the same pre-state - must be explicitly disallowed and prevented via dedicated consistency checking methods.

6.1   Inconsistency Detection via PMSAT

Assuming the transformation problem has no solution, despite having a unique primary action, we define the *checking problem* as detecting a set of model elements which causes the contradiction. The checking problem could be solved by computing an unsatisfiability core and removing any axiomatic clauses, e.g. from $pre(q)$, $post(q')$ or $hist\,(q, q')$. To avoid a further increase of requirements to the solver's capabilities, we instead formulate the checking problem again as a PMSAT problem. If a contradiction in the model prevents a solution of the transformation problem (Eq. 17), it is due to the presence of inconsistent *upd* predicates which only occur as part of *pa* and *sa*. To identify these contradictory predicates, we set up the checking problem $\langle \tilde{\Phi}^H_{SAT}, \tilde{\Phi}^S_{SAT} \rangle$ as a modified version of the transformation problem with *pa* and *sa* moved to the set of soft clauses:

$$\tilde{\Phi}^H_{SAT} = hist\,(q, q') \wedge pre(q) \wedge post(q') \tag{20}$$

$$\tilde{\Phi}^S_{SAT} = pa(q, i, q') \wedge sa(q, i, q') \tag{21}$$

In this way, the solver will remove the minimum number of clauses from *pa* and *sa* to produce a solution for q'. Each one of these unfulfilled clauses contains an update predicate (or part thereof) which contributes to the contradiction. By iterating through all solutions with the optimal cost value and backtracking the unfulfilled clauses of each solution to their syntactic element of origin, we obtain a set of update rules ($Rule_T$) which make the model inconsistent. These model elements are then marked as erroneous. Hence, we use PMSAT for debugging.

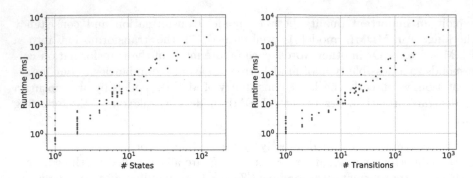

Fig. 2. Runtime evaluation of the model transformation with respect to the number of states $|Q|$ (left) and the number of transitions $|\delta|$ (right)

6.2 Warnings Against Dead Code and Redundancy

For the consistency checking of MDML models, we define an *error* as an aspect of the model which makes it unsuitable for further processing - e.g. test case generation. All other issues which do not fall under this category are classified as *warnings*. As such, we regard aspects of the MDML model which we believe may not reflect the intentions of the user, e.g. unreachable or redundant MDML statements. To identify such model elements, we relate the PMM, which was obtained through the model transformation, back to the original MDML model. The set of unreachable statements - i.e. dead code - can be obtained as $Node_U = \{n \in Node |\; \nexists\; q \in Q : en(q,n)\}$ while the set of redundant **given** statements is obtained as $G_R = \{g \in G \mid \nexists\; q \in Q : en(q, parent(g)) \wedge \neg en(q,g)\}$.

7 Evaluation

We have implemented the previously described model transformation and consistency checking mechanism as part of our MDML IDE, using the SAT4J solver [4]. We have analyzed the runtime of the model transformation on 87 MDML models, taking the median of 10 repetitions for each model. Figure 2 displays the runtime measurements with respect to the number of states ($|Q|$), as well as the number of transitions ($|\delta|$) of the individual MDML models. The runtime is polynomial with respect to both the number of states and transitions, as indicated by the linear-shaped distributions in both doubly-logarithmic plots.

8 Related Work

Our solution to the frame problem is similar to that of Answer Set Programming (ASP) [15]. The frame rule in ASP states that, if a property holds in the pre-state and it cannot be derived that the property does not hold in the post-state, then it is assumed that the property holds in the post-state.

Mapping a DSL to a Moore Machine-based semantics has been done before [3,5,24]. However, to the best of our knowledge, we are the first to define a predicative semantics of a DSL based on PMSAT. Biere et al. [6] have mapped the Bounded Model Checking problem to SAT. However, their technique is concerned with verifying temporal properties while we aim to check model consistency, unreachability, and redundancy. Hwong et al. [12] have designed and implemented a mapping from the textual *State Machine Language* to a process algebraic language called mCRL2 in order to verify the highly complex control software of one of the experiments at CERN. They then use Bounded Model Checking to detect live-locks and ensure *strong connectedness*. Löding and Peleska [16] present an operational semantics for their *Timed Moore Automata* formalism, which they use for livelock detection and SAT-based test case generation. Mechtaev et al. have devised a tool called DirectFix [18] for program repairs based on PMSAT or, more specifically, Partial MAX-SMT. Similarly to our approach, Tien et al. [26] use PMSAT to find contradictory constraints in SysML models.

9 Conclusion

We have defined a formal semantics for the pre-existing domain-specific modeling language MDML. We split the definition into an operational semantics, relating MDML models to Partial Moore Machines, and a predicative semantics, defining the relation between pre- and post-states of each transition. We have designed and implemented a model transformation from MDML models to PMMs, based on a Partial MAX-SAT problem. To the best of our knowledge, we are the first to show how PMSAT can be used to solve the frame problem when an approach based on pure SAT would significantly complicate the solution. However, we kept parts of the implementation imperative wherever the cost of a SAT-based implementation outweighed the benefits. We prioritized ease of implementation over performance, since the test models in our domain are rather small. In theory, we would be able to eliminate the need for PMSAT by excluding Secondary Actions from the language design. However, they considerably simplify the implementation of certain behaviors, resulting in shorter models. We have further established a duality between model transformation and consistency checking for MDML models, enabling us to turn the transformation into a consistency check with little effort. Our future work may encompass the automatic repair of contradictory MDML models, perhaps in a similar manner as DirectFix [18].

Acknowledgments. Research herein was partially funded by the Austrian Research Promotion Agency (FFG), program "ICT of the Future", project number 867535 Hybrid Domain-specific Language User eXperience (HybriDLUX).

References

1. Abrial, J.: The B-Book - Assigning Programs to Meanings. Cambridge University Press (1996). https://doi.org/10.1017/CBO9780511624162

2. Aichernig, B.K., He, J.: Refinement and test case generation in UTP. Electron. Notes Theor. Comput. Sci. **187**, 125–143 (2007). https://doi.org/10.1016/j.entcs.2006.08.048

3. Alenljung, T., Lennartson, B., Hosseini, M.N.: Sensor graphs for discrete event modeling applied to formal verification of PLCs. IEEE Trans. Control Syst. Technol. **20**(6), 1506–1521 (2012). https://doi.org/10.1109/TCST.2011.2168607

4. Berre, D.L., Parrain, A.: The Sat4j library, release 2.2. JSAT **7**(2–3), 59–6 (2010). https://satassociation.org/jsat/index.php/jsat/article/view/82

5. Beyak, L., Carette, J.: SAGA: a DSL for story management. In: Danvy, O., Shan, C. (eds.) Proceedings IFIP Working Conference on Domain-Specific Languages, DSL 2011, Bordeaux, France, 6–8 September 2011. EPTCS, vol. 66, pp. 48–67 (2011). https://doi.org/10.4204/EPTCS.66.3

6. Biere, A., Cimatti, A., Clarke, E.M., Strichman, O., Zhu, Y.: Bounded model checking. Adv. Comput. **58**, 117–148 (2003). https://doi.org/10.1016/S0065-2458(03)58003-2

7. Burghard, C., Berardinelli, L.: Visualizing multi-dimensional state spaces using selective abstraction. In: 2020 46th Euromicro Conference on Software Engineering and Advanced Applications (SEAA). IEEE (2020, accepted for publication)

8. Burghard, C.: Model-based testing of measurement devices using a domain-specific modelling language. Master's Thesis at Graz University of Technology (2018)

9. Burghard, C., Stieglbauer, G., Korošec, R.: Introducing MDML - a domain-specific modelling language for automotive measurement devices. In: CEUR Workshop Proceedings, vol. 1711, pp. 28–31 (2016)

10. Fu, Z., Malik, S.: On solving the partial MAX-SAT problem. In: Theory and Applications of Satisfiability Testing - SAT 2006, 9th International Conference, Seattle, WA, USA, 12–15 August 2006, Proceedings, pp. 252–265 (2006). https://doi.org/10.1007/11814948_25

11. Hoare, C.A.R., Jifeng, H.: Unifying Theories of Programming, vol. 14. Prentice Hall, Englewood Cliffs (1998)

12. Hwong, Y., Keiren, J.J.A., Kusters, V.J.J., Leemans, S.J.J., Willemse, T.A.C.: Formalising and analysing the control software of the compact muon solenoid experiment at the large hadron collider. Sci. Comput. Program. **78**(12), 2435–2452 (2013). https://doi.org/10.1016/j.scico.2012.11.009

13. Jones, C.B.: Systematic Software Development Using VDM. Prentice Hall International Series in Computer Science. Prentice Hall, Englewood Cliffs (1986)

14. Kaufmann, P., Kronegger, M., Pfandler, A., Seidl, M., Widl, M.: Global state checker: towards SAT-based reachability analysis of communicating state machines. In: Boulanger, F., Famelis, M., Ratiu, D. (eds.) Proceedings of the 10th International Workshop on Model Driven Engineering, Verification and Validation MoDeVVa 2013, Co-Located with 16th International Conference on Model Driven Engineering Languages and Systems (MoDELS 2013), Miami, Florida, USA, 1 October 2013. CEUR Workshop Proceedings, vol. 1069, pp. 31–40. CEUR-WS.org (2013). http://ceur-ws.org/Vol-1069/06-paper.pdf

15. Lifschitz, V.: What is answer set programming? In: Fox, D., Gomes, C.P. (eds.) Proceedings of the Twenty-Third AAAI Conference on Artificial Intelligence, AAAI 2008, Chicago, Illinois, USA, 13–17 July 2008, pp. 1594–1597. AAAI Press (2008). http://www.aaai.org/Library/AAAI/2008/aaai08-270.php

16. Löding, H., Peleska, J.: Timed Moore automata: test data generation and model checking. In: Third International Conference on Software Testing, Verification and Validation, ICST 2010, Paris, France, 7–9 April 2010, pp. 449–458. IEEE Computer Society (2010). https://doi.org/10.1109/ICST.2010.60

17. McCarthy, J., Hayes, P.J.: Some philosophical problems from the standpoint of artificial intelligence. In: Meltzer, B., Michie, D. (eds.) Machine Intelligence, pp. 463–502. Edinburgh University Press, Edinburgh (1969)
18. Mechtaev, S., Yi, J., Roychoudhury, A.: Directfix: looking for simple program repairs. In: Bertolino, A., Canfora, G., Elbaum, S.G. (eds.) 37th IEEE/ACM International Conference on Software Engineering, ICSE 2015, Florence, Italy, 16–24 May 2015, vol. 1, pp. 448–458. IEEE Computer Society (2015). https://doi.org/10.1109/ICSE.2015.63
19. Object Management Group: OMG Unified Modelling Language. version 2.5.1. Technical report, December 2017. https://www.omg.org/spec/UML/2.5.1/PDF
20. Peleska, J.: Industrial-strength model-based testing - state of the art and current challenges. In: Petrenko, A.K., Schlingloff, H. (eds.) Proceedings Eighth Workshop on Model-Based Testing, MBT 2013, Rome, Italy, 17th March 2013. EPTCS, vol. 111, pp. 3–28 (2013). https://doi.org/10.4204/EPTCS.111.1
21. Reynolds, J.C.: Separation logic: a logic for shared mutable data structures. In: 17th IEEE Symposium on Logic in Computer Science (LICS 2002), Copenhagen, Denmark, 22–25 July 2002, Proceedings, pp. 55–74. IEEE Computer Society (2002). https://doi.org/10.1109/LICS.2002.1029817
22. Sarma, M., Murthy, P.V.R., Jell, S., Ulrich, A.: Model-based testing in industry: a case study with two MBT tools. In: Zhu, H., Chan, W.K., Budnik, C.J., Kapfhammer, G.M. (eds.) The 5th Workshop on Automation of Software Test, AST 2010, Cape Town, South Africa, 3–4 May 2010, pp. 87–90. ACM (2010). https://doi.org/10.1145/1808266.1808279
23. Schlick, R., Herzner, W., Jöbstl, E.: Fault-based generation of test cases from UML-models – approach and some experiences. In: Flammini, F., Bologna, S., Vittorini, V. (eds.) SAFECOMP 2011. LNCS, vol. 6894, pp. 270–283. Springer, Heidelberg (2011). https://doi.org/10.1007/978-3-642-24270-0_20
24. Schuts, M., Hooman, J., Kurtev, I., Swagerman, D.: Reverse engineering of legacy software interfaces to a model-based approach. In: Ganzha, M., Maciaszek, L.A., Paprzycki, M. (eds.) Proceedings of the 2018 Federated Conference on Computer Science and Information Systems, FedCSIS 2018, Poznań, Poland, 9–12 eptember 2018. Annals of Computer Science and Information Systems, vol. 15, pp. 867–876 (2018). https://doi.org/10.15439/2018F64
25. Spivey, J.M.: Understanding Z : a specification language and its formal semantics. Ph.D. thesis, University of Oxford, UK (1985). http://ethos.bl.uk/OrderDetails. do?uin=uk.bl.ethos.371571
26. Tien, T.N., Nakajima, S., Thang, H.Q.: Modeling and debugging numerical constraints of cyber-physical systems design. In: Thang, H.Q., Thanh, B.N., Do, T.V., Bui, M., Hong, S.N. (eds.) 4th International Symposium on Information and Communication Technology, SoICT 2020, Danang, Viet Nam, 05–06 December 2013, pp. 251–260. ACM (2013). https://doi.org/10.1145/2542050.2542068
27. Utting, M., Pretschner, A., Legeard, D.. A taxonomy of model-based testing approaches. Softw. Test. Verif. Reliab. 22(5), 297–312 (2012). https://doi.org/10.1002/stvr.456
28. Walsh, T.: SAT v CSP. In: Dechter, R. (ed.) CP 2000. LNCS, vol. 1894, pp. 441–456. Springer, Heidelberg (2000). https://doi.org/10.1007/3-540-45349-0_32

Learning Abstracted Non-deterministic Finite State Machines

Andrea Pferscher$^{(\boxtimes)}$ and Bernhard K. Aichernig

Institute of Software Technology, Graz University of Technology, Graz, Austria
{apfersch,aichernig}@ist.tugraz.at

Abstract. Active automata learning gains increasing interest since it gives an insight into the behavior of a black-box system. A crucial drawback of the frequently used learning algorithms based on Angluin's L^* is that they become impractical if systems with a large input/output alphabet are learned. Previous work suggested to circumvent this problem by abstracting the input alphabet and the observed outputs. However, abstraction could introduce non-deterministic behavior. Already existing active automata learning algorithms for observable non-deterministic systems learn larger models if outputs are only observable after certain input/output sequences. In this paper, we introduce an abstraction scheme that merges akin states. Hence, we learn a more generic behavioral model of a black-box system. Furthermore, we evaluate our algorithm in a practical case study. In this case study, we learn the behavior of five different Message Queuing Telemetry Transport (MQTT) brokers interacting with multiple clients.

Keywords: Active automata learning · Model inference · Non-deterministic finite state machines · MQTT

1 Introduction

The origin of automata learning dates back to the seventies and eighties, when Gold [9] and Angluin [4] introduced algorithms to learn behavioral models of black-box systems. Later, in the seminal work of Peled et al. [17], automata learning proofed itself as a valuable tool to test black-box systems. Today automata learning reveals security vulnerabilities in TLS [20] or DTLS [8].

The applicability of automata learning, however, suffers from two main problems: (1) automata learning becomes infeasible for systems with a large input and output alphabet and (2) many systems behave non-deterministically, e.g. due to timed behavior or stochastic decisions. One promising solution for the first problem was proposed by Aarts et al. [2]. They presented an abstraction technique that introduces a more generic view on the system by creating an abstract and, therefore, smaller input and output alphabet. However, a too coarse view on the system creates non-determinism, which leads back to the second problem. In the literature, several work on learning-based testing [3,8,23] stress the problem of observing non-deterministic behavior during learning. However, we already find

© IFIP International Federation for Information Processing 2020
Published by Springer Nature Switzerland AG 2020
V. Casola et al. (Eds.): ICTSS 2020, LNCS 12543, pp. 52–69, 2020.
https://doi.org/10.1007/978-3-030-64881-7_4

learning algorithms [7,11,16] for observable non-deterministic reactive systems. To make them applicable, we have to provide an input and output alphabet that establishes observable non-determinism, i.e. systems where an input may lead to different states, but we can observe which state has been chosen.

In this paper, we propose an active learning algorithm for *observable non-deterministic finite state machines (ONFSMs)* that addresses both problems of active automata learning. The first problem is solved via a mapper that provides a more generic view on the system under test (SUT) via an abstract input/output alphabet. The non-deterministic behavior is handled by our learning algorithm for ONFSMs. We show that an abstracted input/output alphabet does not necessarily decrease the state space of a non-deterministic systems sufficiently. To overcome the state-space problem, we introduce a new abstraction technique that defines equivalence classes for outputs and merges akin states of the model.

We evaluated our proposed learning algorithm on the MQTT protocol, which is a publish/subscribe protocol that is frequently used in the Internet of Things (IoT). This protocol defines the communication between clients and a broker, where the broker manages the messages of the clients. Tappler et al. [23] showed that automata learning is an effective method to test the behavior of different MQTT brokers. However, in their work they only considered an interaction with one or two clients to keep the learning feasible. Furthermore, they stress that the non-deterministic behavior hampered the learning procedure. In this paper, we show that our algorithm for observable non-deterministic systems makes learning-based testing of the MQTT protocol in a multi-client setup feasible.

Our contribution comprises four aspects. (1) We analyze the challenges of learning an abstracted system that behaves non-deterministically. (2) We propose a new abstraction technique that manages these challenges. (3) We introduce a new active learning algorithm that integrates our proposed abstraction technique and, therefore, learns a more abstract model of a non-deterministic system. (4) We show the applicability of our algorithm in a case study and compare it to existing algorithms for deterministic finite state machines (FSMs).

Structure. Section 2 explains the modeling formalism and active automata learning. In Sect. 3, we introduce our learning algorithm including our novel abstraction technique. Our case study on five different MQTT brokers is presented in Sect. 4. Section 5 discusses related work. Finally, Sect. 6 concludes the paper.

2 Preliminaries

2.1 Finite State Machines

An *observable non-deterministic finite state machine (ONFSM)* is a 5-tuple $\mathcal{M} = \langle \Sigma_I, \Sigma_O, Q, q_0, h \rangle$ where Σ_I is the finite set of input symbols, Σ_O is the finite set of output symbols, Q is the finite set of states, q_0 is the initial state, and $h \subseteq Q \times \Sigma_I \times \Sigma_O \times Q$ is the transition relation.

We denote a transition in the ONFSM by $q \xrightarrow{i/o} q'$, where $(q, i, o, q') \in h$. The assumed ONFSMs are *input enabled*, i.e., there exists for every pair (q, i), where

$q \in Q$ and input $i \in \Sigma_I$, at least one output $o \in \Sigma_O$ and successor state $q' \in Q$. Further, we call the finite state machine *observable* if there exists for any triple (q, i, o) at most one q' such that (q, i, o, q') belongs to h. Hence, in fact, we have a state transition function $\delta : Q \times I \times O \rightarrow Q$, that maps a triplet (q, i, o) to a unique state q'. Note that learning algorithms, like the ones used in the tool **LearnLib** [10], commonly require deterministic systems. We define an FSM as deterministic if there exists for each input at most one output and succeeding state. In the literature, deterministic FSM are also known as Mealy machines.

Let $s \in (\Sigma_I \times \Sigma_O)^*$ be an input/outputs sequence, with the corresponding input projection $s_I \in \Sigma_I^*$ and output projection $s_O \in \Sigma_O^*$. We write ϵ for the empty sequence and $s \cdot s'$ for the concatenation of two sequences, where $s, s' \in (\Sigma_I \times \Sigma_O)^*$. We also define a single input/output pair $(i, o) \in (\Sigma_I \times \Sigma_O)$ as a sequence and, therefore, $s \cdot (i, o)$ is also defined. The function $pre(s)$ returns the prefixes of s, including the sequence s. Let $s^+ \in (\Sigma_I \times \Sigma_O)^+, s_I^+ \in \Sigma_I^+, s_O^+ \in \Sigma_O^+$ denote non-empty sequences. For convenience, we write $s \cdot (s_I^+, s_O^+)$, defining a sequence s that is concatenated with a sequence of input/output pairs.

2.2   Active Automata Learning

In active automata learning, we gain understanding about a system by actively questioning the SUT. Many active automata learning algorithms build on the seminal work of Angluin [4]. Her proposed algorithm (L^*) learns a deterministic finite automaton (DFA) that accepts a regular language. The learning procedure is based on the minimally adequate teacher (MAT) framework, which comprises a *teacher* and a *learner* component. The learner asks the teacher either a *membership query* or an *equivalence query*. The former one answers if a word is part of the language, whereas the second one checks if a hypothesis, i.e. a proposed DFA, represents the regular language. The equivalence query is either answered with *yes* or with a counterexample that shows an evidence to the non-conformance of the proposed hypothesis and the SUT. All the answers from the queries are saved in an *observation table*, which is then used to construct a hypothesis.

Angluin's L^* has been extended for different types of systems, including algorithms for Mealy machines [12,15,21]. In these algorithms for learning Mealy machines, membership queries are replaced by *output queries*. There, instead of asking whether a word is in the language, an input string is provided. The teacher executes this input string on the SUT and responds the observed output string. The observed outputs are then saved in the observation table.

The previously mentioned learning algorithms can only handle deterministic SUTs. Tackling the problem that systems behave non-deterministic due to various reasons, e.g. ignoring timed behavior, L^*-based learning algorithms [7,11,16] for ONFSMs were proposed. The algorithms for ONFSMs follow the idea of the Mealy machine learning algorithms, but instead of considering just one possible output for an input, all possible outputs are saved in the observation table.

One major drawback of the Angluin style algorithms is that they do not scale for a large input/output alphabet, since the number of required queries significantly grows with the increasing size of the used alphabet. To overcome this problem, Aarts et al. [2] proposed an abstraction technique that reduces the size of the used input/output alphabet of the learning algorithm. This abstraction technique introduces a mapper component that translates the communication between the learner and the SUT in both directions.

A mapper is an 8-tuple $\mathcal{A} = \langle \Sigma_I, \Sigma_O, R, r_0, \Sigma_I^{\mathcal{A}}, \Sigma_O^{\mathcal{A}}, \Delta, \nabla \rangle$, where Σ_I and Σ_O are the disjoint sets of concrete inputs and outputs, R is the set of mapper states, $r_0 \in R$ is the initial state, $\Sigma_I^{\mathcal{A}}$ and $\Sigma_O^{\mathcal{A}}$ are the finite disjoint sets of abstract inputs and outputs, $\Delta : R \times (\Sigma_I \cup \Sigma_O) \rightarrow R$ is the state transition function, and $\nabla : (R \times \Sigma_I \rightarrow \Sigma_I^{\mathcal{A}}) \cup (R \times \Sigma_O \rightarrow \Sigma_O^{\mathcal{A}})$ is the abstraction function. The mapper takes abstract inputs and translates them to concrete inputs, which can then be executed on the SUT. In return, the mapper observes concrete outputs from the SUT and returns the corresponding abstracted outputs to the learner. On each received input/output pair, the mapper updates its internal state.

A large input/output alphabet is not the only challenge that limits the feasibility of active automata learning. Berg et al. [5] state that the real bottleneck of active automata learning is the equivalence oracle since the presence of such an oracle is highly improbable. To make active learning practically applicable, tools like **LearnLib** [10] substitute the equivalence oracle by conformance testing.

3   Method

In this section, we describe our active learning algorithm for abstracted ONFSMs. Firstly, we introduce our basic learning setup. Secondly, we explain the two different levels of abstraction and, thirdly, we discuss the application of our abstraction mechanism on the learning algorithm.

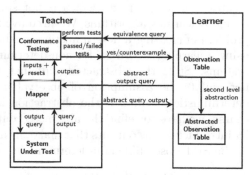

3.1   Learning Setup

Our proposed learning algorithm for ONFSMs is based on an Angluin-style active learning setup. For this, we define a *learner* that queries a

Fig. 1. Angluin's [4] traditional learning framework is extended by a mapper component and an abstracted observation table.

teacher. Figure 1 shows the components of our learning algorithm. The teacher comprises three components: (1) conformance testing, (2) a mapper and (3) the SUT. (1) The aim of conformance testing is to make the equivalence check feasible. For this, we assume that the learned model conforms to the SUT if a finite set of test cases passes. (2) The mapper is based on the idea of Aarts et al. [2], where the mapper translates a (possibly infinite) alphabet to a finite alphabet that is used by the learning algorithm to create an abstracted model. The difference to Aarts' proposed mapping concept is that we do not require an abstracted alphabet that assures that the learned model behaves deterministically. This gives us the possibility to create an even more abstract view on the SUT. (3) The SUT represents an interface, where concrete inputs can be executed and the corresponding concrete outputs can be observed by the mapper. This allows a black-box view on the SUT.

The difference to other active learning setups is that the learner uses an additional abstraction mechanism for the observation table. To avoid confusion between the abstraction done by the mapper and the abstraction of the observation table, we distinguish two levels of abstraction. We denote the abstraction by the mapper as first level abstraction and the abstraction of the observation table is denoted as second level abstraction.

3.2   First Level Abstraction

The first level abstraction comprises the mapper component of the teacher that translates abstract inputs to concrete inputs and concrete outputs to abstract outputs. The aim of mapping is to decrease the size of the alphabet to make the learning algorithm feasible. However, Aarts et al. [2] stress that a too abstract alphabet creates non-determinism, which is not suitable for many learning algorithms. We circumvent the problem of creating a deterministic alphabet by using a learning algorithm for non-deterministic systems. Still, the abstracted alphabet must not violate the assumption of observable non-deterministic outputs. If the abstraction is too coarse, we have to refine the abstracted outputs by introducing new outputs that make the model of the SUT observable non-deterministic.

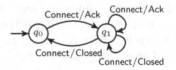

Fig. 2.   Abstracted   non-deterministic Mealy machine of the MQTT connection protocol

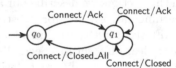

Fig. 3. The ONFSM of the MQTT connection protocol

Example 1 (Multi-client Connection Mapper). Our goal is to learn a model of an MQTT broker that interacts with several clients. For simplicity, here we only consider the connection procedure of the protocol. The clients can send a connection request to the broker. A client gets disconnected if the client is already connected. The concrete inputs are $\Sigma_I = \{\mathsf{Connect}(id)|id \in \mathbb{N}\}$ and the concrete outputs $\Sigma_O = \{\mathsf{Ack}(id), \mathsf{Closed}(id)|id \in \mathbb{N}\}$, where $id \in \mathbb{N}$ uniquely identifies a client by an integer. Therefore, the set of concrete inputs and outputs is infinite. To build a finite model of this connection protocol for multiple-clients, we have to define a mapper that abstracts the input/output alphabet. The mapper for this example has the abstracted inputs $\Sigma_I^{\mathcal{A}} = \{\mathsf{Connect}\}$ and abstracted outputs $\Sigma_O^{\mathcal{A}} = \{\mathsf{Ack}, \mathsf{Closed}\}$. The abstracted non-deterministic model is depicted in Fig. 2. We distinguish the states where no client (q_0) or more than one client (q_1) is connected. In the state where more than one client is connected, further clients can connect or disconnect. Since the Mealy machine in Fig. 2 is not observable

Table 1. Observation table of the multi-client connection protocol of Example 1.

$\Gamma \backslash E$	Connect
ϵ	Ack
(Connect, Ack)	Ack, Closed_All
(Connect, Ack)(Connect, Ack)	Ack, Closed
(Connect, Ack)(Connect, Closed_All)	Ack

Table 2. Abstracted observation table of Table 1.

$\Gamma \backslash E$	Connect
ϵ	Ack
(Connect, Ack)	Ack, Closed
(Connect, Ack)(Connect, Ack)	Ack, Closed
(Connect, Ack)(Connect, Closed_All)	Ack

non-deterministic, we have to refine the abstracted outputs to make the states distinguishable. For this, we add another abstract output Closed_All, capturing the observation when the last client gets disconnected, to Σ_O^A which makes the automaton observable non-deterministic. The refined model is depicted in Fig. 3.

3.3 Second Level Abstraction

The first level abstraction enables an abstracted view and supports the feasibility of the learning algorithm. However, due to the iterative state exploration of L^*, the first level abstraction might not be enough to keep the number of states low. To overcome this problem, we introduce a second level abstraction. The aim of this abstraction level is to decrease the state space by defining equivalent outputs. This is done by the definition of equivalence classes for outputs, which then replace the observations saved in the observation table. The mapping of the equivalence classes is a surjective function $\mu : \Sigma_O^A \to \Sigma_O^{A'}$ that maps an abstracted output of Σ_O^A to an equivalence class of $\Sigma_O^{A'}$.

Example 2 (Multi-Client Connection Equivalence Classes). Even though we abstracted the alphabet in Example 1, learning algorithms for ONFSMs, e.g. L_N [7], would learn a model similar to the one shown in Fig. 4. The problem is that these algorithms count the number of clients, and create a new state for each client. To avoid a large model, we want to merge akin states. For this, we define for the outputs $\Sigma_O^A = \{\text{Ack}, \text{Closed}, \text{Closed\_All}\}$ the following equivalence classes $\Sigma_O^{A'} = \{\text{Ack}, \text{Closed}\}$. The function μ for the second level abstraction of this example is defined as follows $\mu : \{\text{Ack}\} \to \text{Ack}, \{\text{Closed}, \text{Closed\_All}\} \to \text{Closed}$.

In our learning algorithm, the learner maintains an extended observation table. The classic observation table $\mathcal{T}$ is defined as a triplet $\langle \Gamma, E, T \rangle$, where $\Gamma \subset (\Sigma_I^A \times \Sigma_O^A)^*$ contains sequences of

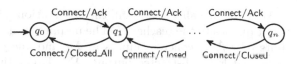

Fig. 4. Learned model of Example 1 without second level abstraction, which has $n+1$ states for n clients.

inputs and outputs, $E \subset \Sigma_I^{A+}$ is a suffixed closed set of input sequences, and T is a mapping $\Gamma \times E \to 2^{\Sigma_O^{A+}}$ containing first level abstract outputs of the power set of Σ_O^{A+}. The extension of the classical observation table $\mathcal{T}^{A'}$ is a 5-tuple

Algorithm 1. Learning algorithm using an abstracted observation table

Input: input alphabet Σ_I^A, equivalence class mapping μ, teacher Π	10: $\Gamma \leftarrow$ CompleteQueries($T^{A'}$)
Output: ONFSM $\mathcal{H}$	11: $\langle \Gamma, E, T \rangle \leftarrow$ FillTable($\langle \Gamma, E, T \rangle, \Pi$)
1: $\langle \Gamma, E, T \rangle \leftarrow$ InitTable(Σ_I^A)	12: $T^{A'} \leftarrow$ AbstractTable($\langle \Gamma, E, T \rangle, \mu$)
2: cex $\leftarrow \epsilon$	13: $E \leftarrow$ MakeConsistent($T^{A'}$)
3: **do**	14: $\langle \Gamma, E, T \rangle \leftarrow$ FillTable($\langle \Gamma, E, T \rangle, \Pi$)
4: $\langle \Gamma, E, T \rangle \leftarrow$ FillTable($\langle \Gamma, E, T \rangle, \Pi$)	15: $T^{A'} \leftarrow$ AbstractTable($\langle \Gamma, E, T \rangle, \mu$)
5: $T^{A'} \leftarrow$ AbstractTable($\langle \Gamma, E, T \rangle, \mu$)	16: $\mathcal{H} \leftarrow$ ConstructHypothesis($T^{A'}$)
6: **while** $\neg$IsClosedConsistentComplete($T^{A'}$) **do**	17: cex $\leftarrow$ ConformanceTest($\mathcal{H}$)
7: $\Gamma \leftarrow$ MakeClosed($T^{A'}$)	18: **if** cex $\neq \epsilon$ **then**
8: $\langle \Gamma, E, T \rangle \leftarrow$ FillTable($\langle \Gamma, E, T \rangle, \Pi$)	19: $\langle \Gamma, E, T \rangle \leftarrow$ AddCex(cex, Π)
9: $T^{A'} \leftarrow$ AbstractTable($\langle \Gamma, E, T \rangle, \mu$)	20: **while** cex $\neq \epsilon$
	21: **return** $\mathcal{H}$

$\langle \Gamma, E, T, T^{A'}, \mu \rangle$ where $T^{A'}$ is a mapping $\Gamma \times E \rightarrow 2^{\Sigma_O^{A'+}}$ to the second level abstracted outputs and $\mu : \Sigma_O^A \rightarrow \Sigma_O^{A'}$ is the second level abstraction function.

Example 3 (Multi-Client Connection Observation Table). Table 1 shows an intermediate observation table in the learning procedure of the system depicted in Fig. 3. Table 1 is then abstracted with the equivalence classes defined in Example 2. The abstracted observation table is presented in Table 2.

3.4 Learning Algorithm

In the following, we introduce our learning algorithm for ONFSMs. Especially, we explain the integration of the second level abstraction in the L^*-based learning setup and how this abstraction technique generates a more generic hypothesis.

Algorithm 1 describes the procedure performed by the learner to learn an ONFSM. For this, the learner requires the abstract input alphabet Σ_I^A of the SUT, the second level abstraction mapping μ, and the teacher Π which provides access to the mapper and SUT. In Line 1 and 2 we start with the initialization of the observation table and the counterexample (cex). Remember that the classic observation table is a triplet $T = \langle \Gamma, E, T \rangle$. Γ is a prefixed-closed set of sequences, which can be written as $\Gamma = \Gamma_S \cup \Gamma_P$ where $\Gamma_S \cap \Gamma_P = \emptyset$. Γ_S contains the sequences that identify the states of the ONFSM and $\Gamma_P = \Gamma_{P_S} \cup \Gamma_{P'}$, where $\Gamma_{P_S} \subseteq \Gamma_S \cdot (\Sigma_I^A \times \Sigma_O^A)$, $\Gamma_{P'} \subset \Gamma \cdot (\Sigma_I^A \times \Sigma_O^A)$ and $\Gamma_{P_S} \cap \Gamma_{P'} = \emptyset$. We initialize T by adding the empty sequence ϵ to Γ_S and the input alphabet Σ_I^A to E.

After the initialization we fill the observation table T (Line 4) by performing output queries to the teacher Π. The mapper translates the first level abstracted inputs of Σ_I^A to concrete inputs of Σ_I and the observed concrete outputs of Σ_O to first level abstracted outputs Σ_O^A. Every time we fill the table with the query outputs we extend the observation table $T = \langle \Gamma, E, T \rangle$ to the abstract observation table $T^{A'} = \langle \Gamma, E, T, T^{A'}, \mu \rangle$ by translating observed outputs with μ as explained in Sect. 3.3. Note that the second level abstraction only changes the mapping $T^{A'}$; Γ, E and T stay unchanged.

After the abstraction in Line 5 we check in Line 6 if the abstracted observation table $T^{A'}$ is *closed*, *consistent* and *complete*. To the best of our knowledge, this part is different to other learning algorithms.

Table 3. Observation table of Example 1 after the first output queries.

$\Gamma \backslash E$	Connect
ϵ	Ack
(Connect, Ack)	Ack, Closed_All

Table 4. Abstraction of Table 3 using the mapping defined in Example 2

$\Gamma \backslash E$	Connect
ϵ	Ack
(Connect, Ack)	Ack, Closed

Closedness. First, we check if the abstracted table $T^{\mathcal{A}'}$ is *closed*. This check is similar to the closed check proposed by El-Fakih et al. [7], however, instead of checking the values in the mapping T, we check if the second level abstracted outputs in $T^{\mathcal{A}'}$ are equal. For this, we denote that two rows $\gamma, \gamma' \in \Gamma$ in the abstracted table are equal, i.e. $\gamma \cong_{\mathcal{A}'} \gamma'$, iff $\forall e \in E, T^{\mathcal{A}'}(\gamma, e) = T^{\mathcal{A}'}(\gamma', e)$. The abstract observation table $T^{\mathcal{A}'}$ is not closed if there exists a $\gamma' \in \Gamma_P$ such that no $\gamma \in \Gamma_S$ fulfills $\gamma \cong_{\mathcal{A}'} \gamma'$.

Consistency. Unlike the other learning algorithms for ONFSMs, we have to check if our abstract observation table $T^{\mathcal{A}'}$ is *consistent*. The consistency check is necessary due to queries that are added through the abstraction mechanism and due to the counterexample processing which we discuss later in this section. Our check is based on the consistency check for Mealy machines introduced by Niese [15]. We define that $T^{\mathcal{A}'}$ is consistent if for every $\gamma, \gamma' \in \Gamma$, where $\gamma \cong_{\mathcal{A}'} \gamma'$ holds, no input/output pair $(i, o) \in (\Sigma_I^{\mathcal{A}} \times \Sigma_O^{\mathcal{A}})$ exists where $\gamma \cdot (i, o) \not\cong_{\mathcal{A}'} \gamma' \cdot (i, o)$.

Completeness. The *completeness* check is different to other active learning algorithms. Here we check, if we have added all necessary sequences to construct a hypothesis. Since the final hypothesis contains the first level abstracted outputs, but is constructed based on the second level abstraction outputs, it may be necessary to add additional sequences to Γ. These sequences are required to identify the target state of all observed input/output pairs. For this, we define that two rows $\gamma, \gamma' \in \Gamma$ in the classic observation table are equal, denoted by $\gamma \cong \gamma'$, iff $\forall e \in E, T(\gamma, e) = T(\gamma', e)$. For each $\gamma \in \Gamma_S$ we select each $\gamma' \in \Gamma_P$ where $\gamma \cong_{\mathcal{A}'} \gamma'$ but $\gamma \not\cong \gamma'$ holds. We then check if Γ contains all sequences $pre(\gamma' \cdot (e, s_O^+))$ where $e \in E$ and $T(\gamma, e) \neq T(\gamma', e)$, and $s_O^+ \in T(\gamma', e)$. If no such sequence is required or all required sequences already exist, $T^{\mathcal{A}'}$ is complete.

If either the abstracted table $T^{\mathcal{A}'}$ is not *closed* or not *consistent* or not *complete*, we continue our procedure in Line 7. Here, we make $T^{\mathcal{A}'}$ closed if necessary. To make $T^{\mathcal{A}'}$ closed, we move every row $\gamma' \in \Gamma_P$ to Γ_S, where $\forall \gamma \in \Gamma_S : \gamma \not\cong_{\mathcal{A}'} \gamma'$ holds. Informally, we move every row from Γ_P to Γ_S where the set of abstracted outputs for all $e \in E$ is unique. This introduces a new state in our hypothesis. If we have found such a $\gamma' \in \Gamma_P$, we have to add all observed outputs in the mapping T from the row γ' to Γ_{P_S}. For this, we concatenate γ' with each observed input/output pair in that row, i.e. for each $i \in \Sigma_I^{\mathcal{A}}$ we add for each observed output sequence $o \in T(\gamma', i)$ the concatenation $\gamma' \cdot (i, o)$ to Γ_{P_S}. Afterwards, we fill the table T according to the updated Γ in Line 8 and in the next line we construct again $T^{\mathcal{A}'}$.

Table 5. Final observation table of the connection protocol of Example 1. The input Connect is abbreviated by Conn.

$\Gamma \backslash E$	Conn
ϵ	Ack
(Conn, Ack)	Ack, Closed_All
(Conn, Ack)(Conn, Ack)	Ack, Closed
(Conn, Ack)(Conn, Closed_All)	Ack
(Conn, Ack)(Conn, Ack)(Conn, Closed)	Ack, Closed_All

Table 6. Final abstracted observation table generated from Table 5. The input Connect is abbreviated by Conn.

$\Gamma \backslash E$	Conn
ϵ	Ack
(Conn, Ack)	Ack, Closed
(Conn, Ack)(Conn, Ack)	Ack, Closed
(Conn, Ack)(Conn, Closed_All)	Ack
(Conn, Ack)(Conn, Ack)(Conn, Closed)	Ack, Closed

Example 4 (*Closed Abstracted Observation Table*). Table 3 shows the observation table after the first output queries. We abstract the table using the mapping function μ introduced in Example 2. The result of the abstraction is shown in Table 4. According to Algorithm 1 we then check if the abstracted table is closed. Since the row (Connect, Ack) is in Γ_P and the produced outputs are not in Γ_S, Table 4 is not closed. To make the table closed, we move (Connect, Ack) to Γ_S and add the corresponding sequences of the observed outputs to Γ_P. The result including the additionally performed output queries is shown in Table 1. We then again abstract this table – shown in Table 2 – and check if the abstracted table is closed. Our closed check on Table 2 is now satisfied. Note that we do not bother that Table 1 is not closed.

After making the abstract table closed and performing the required queries to fill the table, we add in Line 10 all necessary queries to make the table complete. For this, we select for all $\gamma \in \Gamma_S$ every $\gamma' \in \Gamma_P$ where $\gamma \cong_{\mathcal{A'}} \gamma'$. If then $\gamma \not\cong \gamma'$, we select the input sequence $e \in E$ where $T(\gamma, e) \neq T(\gamma', e)$ and the output sequence where the observed outputs are different, i.e. $s_O^+ \in T(\gamma', e) \setminus T(\gamma, e)$. The sequences $pre(\gamma' \cdot (e, s_O^+))$ are added to $\Gamma_{P'}$, if the sequence is not already part of Γ. Therefore, $\Gamma_{P'}$ only contains sequences that are added to fulfill the completeness of the abstracted observation table.

Example 5 (**Complete Abstracted Observation Table**). We continue the learning procedure of Example 4 by checking if the observation table is complete. For this, we consider Table 1 and the abstracted Table 2. We see that the row (Connect, Ack) is equal to (Connect, Ack), (Connect, Ack) in the abstracted table. However, in Table 1 we see that the outputs Closed_All and Closed are different. Hence, we add the sequence (Connect, Ack), (Connect, Ack), (Connect, Closed) to the classic observation table (Table 5). After making Table 5 complete, we abstract the table (Table 6). Table 6 is now closed and complete.

If the table is *closed* and *complete*, we make in Line 13 the abstracted observation table *consistent*. For each two rows $\gamma, \gamma' \in \Gamma$ where $\gamma \cong_{\mathcal{A'}} \gamma'$ and an input/output pair $(i, o) \in (\Sigma_I^{\mathcal{A}} \times \Sigma_O^{\mathcal{A}})$ where $\gamma \cdot (i, o) \not\cong_{\mathcal{A'}} \gamma' \cdot (i, o)$ exists, we add $i \cdot e$ to E, where $e \in E$ and $T(\gamma \cdot (i, o), e) \neq T(\gamma' \cdot (i, o), e)$.

When the table is closed, complete and consistent, we construct a hypothesis from our abstract observation table in Line 16 of Algorithm 1. Since we consider two different levels of abstraction in our observation table, we have to modify the classical construction approach from El-Fakih et al. [7]. Algorithm 2 describes

---

Algorithm 2. Hypothesis construction

Input: abstract obs. table $\mathcal{T}^{\mathcal{A}'} = \langle \Gamma = \Gamma_S \cup \Gamma_P, E, T, T^{\mathcal{A}'}, \mu \rangle$, input alphabet $\Sigma_I^{\mathcal{A}}$
Output: ONFSM $\mathcal{M} = \langle \Sigma_I^{\mathcal{A}}, \Sigma_O^{\mathcal{A}}, Q, q_0, h \rangle$
1: **function** CONSTRUCTHYPOTHESIS
2:     $q_0 \leftarrow \epsilon \in \Gamma_S$
3:     $Q \leftarrow \Gamma_S$
4:     **for all** $\gamma_S \in \Gamma_S$ **do**
5:         $Q_{\gamma_S} \leftarrow \{\gamma | \gamma \in \Gamma \wedge \gamma \cong_{\mathcal{A}'} \gamma_S\}$
6:         **for all** $\gamma \in Q_{\gamma_S}$ **do**
7:             **for all** $i \in \Sigma_I^{\mathcal{A}}$ **do**
8:                 **for all** $o \in T(\gamma, i)$ **do**
9:                     $\gamma' \leftarrow \gamma \cdot (i, o)$
10:                    **if** $\gamma' \in \Gamma$ **then**
11:                        $h \leftarrow h \cup (\gamma_S, i, o, \gamma_S')$ where $\gamma_S' \in \Gamma_S \wedge \gamma_S' \cong_{\mathcal{A}'} \gamma'$
       return $\mathcal{M}$

---

the process of generating an ONFSM $\mathcal{M}$ from the abstract observation table $\mathcal{T}^{\mathcal{A}'}$. The initialization process in Line 2 and 3 of Algorithm 2 is equal to other L^*-style algorithms. For this, the empty sequence ϵ indicates the initial state q_0 of $\mathcal{M}$. In addition, the states are defined by the rows of Γ_S. However, due to the second level abstraction, not all observed outputs are represented in the row $\gamma_S \in \Gamma_S$. To consider these outputs in the hypothesis, we have to check also the observations in the mapping T. For this, we filter in Line 5 the equal rows of γ_S in Γ according to the second level abstraction and then add all transitions with the corresponding observations in the Lines 6 to 11. In Line 9 we concatenate the currently considered sequence γ with the observed input/output pair. If this sequence is part of Γ, we have to find the correct destination state of the transition. For this, we select the equal state according to the second level abstraction in Γ_S. In Line 11, we add the new transition to the transitions h.

Example 6 (Hypothesis Construction). Table 5 and Table 6 are used to construct a hypothesis of Example 1. The closed, complete and consistent Table 6 identifies the states and Table 5 contains all observed outputs. Γ_S includes two states $\{q_0, q_1\}$. From the initial state q_0 we create one transition $q_0 \xrightarrow{\text{Connect/Ack}} q_1$. In the second state we consider three different outputs, $\{\text{Ack}, \text{Closed}, \text{Closed\_All}\}$, where Closed and Closed_All belong to the equivalence class Closed. Therefore, we create three different edges $q_1 \xrightarrow{\text{Connect/Closed\_All}} q_0$, $q_1 \xrightarrow{\text{Connect/Closed}} q_1$ and $q_1 \xrightarrow{\text{Connect/Ack}} q_1$. The hypothesis is equal to the ONFSM shown in Fig. 3.

Conformance Testing. After the construction of the hypothesis (Algorithm 1, Line 16), we have to check in Line 17 whether our constructed hypothesis conforms to the SUT. Usually, in automata learning we assume that two systems are equal if the behavior of the learned hypothesis and the SUT are equal. For an ONFSM we could say that two systems are equal if all observable traces are equal. However, due to our second level abstraction, the learned model has a more generic behavior than the SUT. Therefore, the trace equivalence assumption does not hold. Instead we have to check trace inclusion, i.e., every trace produced by the SUT must also be observable in our learned hypothesis. Let $\mathcal{I}$ be our SUT and $\mathcal{H}$ the learned hypothesis. Further we define the function TRACES($\mathcal{M}$) that returns all observable traces, starting at the initial state q_0 of an ONFSM $\mathcal{M}$. The generated traces contain input and output symbols on the first level abstraction. Formally, we can define the conformance relation as follows:

$$\text{TRACES}(\mathcal{I}) \subseteq \text{TRACES}(\mathcal{H}). \tag{1}$$

This relations implies that the more generic the hypothesis the better the conformance. However, a completely generic model would not be useful, e.g. for further testing purposes. The learning of a too generic hypothesis is prevented by the mere consideration of observed outputs from the observation table. Therefore, the hypothesis only includes outputs that can be observed on the SUT.

According to the framework depicted in Fig. 1, the teacher either responds *yes* if the conformance relation in Eq. 1 is fulfilled or reports a counterexample. The counterexample is a trace that contains an output that is not included in our hypothesis $\mathcal{H}$. Note that since the model is input-enabled only outputs may lead to the violation of trace inclusion. We replace the conformance oracle by conformance testing to make the conformance check feasible. For this, a finite number of test cases is generated and then executed on the SUT. Since the test cases contain inputs and outputs on the first level abstraction, we again need a mapper that abstracts and concretizes inputs and outputs for the execution on the SUT. A test case *passes* if the trace generated by the SUT is also observable in the hypothesis, otherwise the test case *fails*. Therefore, the teacher answers with *yes*, if all traces *pass*, otherwise a failing trace is returned. In Algorithm 1 Line 17 the return of an empty sequence ϵ is equal to the answer *yes*. A practical implementation of the conformance testing approach is discussed in Sect. 4.

If no counterexample is found our algorithm terminates and returns the current hypothesis in Line 22, otherwise we add the counterexample to the observation table in Line 19. Note that every returned counterexample is cut off after the first non-conforming input/output pair.

The adding of a counterexample in Line 19 distinguishes two different types of counterexamples. The first type reveals an unobserved output in a state of the hypothesis where an output of the same equivalence class is also observable. To check if the counterexample belongs to this type, we execute all input/output pairs except the last one of the sequence on $\mathcal{H}$. This leads us to the *failing* state prior to the wrong observation. We then check if executing the remaining input generates an output of the same equivalence class. If the output is in the same equivalence class, we want to add the missing input/output transition to the state. In this case, we add any not already existing prefix of the found counterexample to Γ_P. The second type of a counterexample reveals an input/output pair, where no equivalent output is observable in the failing state. In this case, we perform the counterexample processing as proposed by El-Fakih et al. [7], since we want to introduce a new state in our hypothesis. This is done by firstly removing the longest matching prefix $\gamma \in \Gamma$ of the counterexample and secondly adding the suffixes of the remaining input sequence of the found counterexample to E. In both cases, we then jump back to Line 3 and continue to fill the observation table by asking membership queries. This procedure is repeated until no counterexample can be found.

4 Case Study

We evaluated the Message Queuing Telemetry Transport (MQTT) protocol. MQTT defines a publish/subscribe protocol, where clients can subscribe to topics and publish messages to a topic. Tappler et al. [23] already presented work on model-based testing of the MQTT protocol via active automata learning. However, in their work they only consider one or two clients interacting with the broker. Due to the proposed abstraction technique used in our learning algorithm for ONFSMs, we can deal with a multi-client setup. In this section, we first discuss technical aspects of the implementation of our learning algorithm and then present the results of the case study on five different MQTT brokers.

We weaken the *all-weather assumption* [13] for the observation of outputs, and assume like other learning algorithms for non-deterministic systems [11,16,26] that all outputs are observable after performing a query n times. Regarding the challenge that not all outputs are observable at once, we discuss three technical aspects of our implementation: (1) repeated execution of output queries, (2) stopping criterion for output queries, and (3) shrinking of the observation table.

(1) We need to repeat an output query since the abstraction done by the mapper introduces non-determinism. The mapper takes an abstract input and randomly chooses an input from a set of corresponding concrete inputs. Therefore, the observed outputs may differ. The number of repetitions $n_q \in \mathbb{N}$ depends on the SUT, e.g. for the multi-client setup on MQTT we executed each query at least as often as the number of used clients.

(2) Repeating every output query each time the table is filled leads to a vast amount of queries. In practice, performing queries on the SUT can be expensive, e.g. due to the latency of the response. Thus, we want to reduce the number of performed queries. In our implementation, we extended each cell of the observation table by a score $s \in \mathbb{R}_{\geq 0}$ that indicates how often the outputs in the cell change. The value of s is between 0.0 and 1.0, and each time we perform the output queries and no new output is observed, s increases by a value $s_i \in \mathbb{R}_{\geq 0}$. If at least one new output is observed, the score decreases by $s_d \in \mathbb{R}_{\geq 0}$. Note that s cannot increase above 1.0 and decrease below 0.0. If $s = 1.0$, we do not perform the output query again. The initial value of s and the values of s_i and s_d depend on the SUT and how often output queries are repeated in general.

(3) The size of the observation table significantly influences the runtime of the learning algorithm. Our abstraction techniques keep the size of the observation table small. However, due to the assumed non-determinism, it may happen that rows become equal after repeating output queries. For this, we remove equal rows in Γ_S and the corresponding suffixes in Γ_P. The shrinking

of the table is performed before the closedness, consistency and completeness check.

In Sect. 3.4, we explained that the equivalence oracle is replaced by conformance testing. Due to our conformance relation defined in Eq. 1, we cannot check if the outputs of all traces are equivalent, since our hypothesis is more generic than the SUT. We generate input sequences by randomly walking through the hypothesis model. The random walk selects outgoing transitions from the current state uniformly at random and append the input of the transition to the input sequence. This input sequence is then executed once on the SUT to generate an input/output sequence. We then check if the generated sequence is observable on our hypothesis. When we execute the input sequence on the SUT, we use the mapper to translate the abstracted inputs to concrete inputs. Since the number of possible concrete inputs is extremely large and executing all possible inputs would be infeasible, we limit the number of executed test cases to a finite number $n_{test} \in \mathbb{N}$. Due to the assumption of non-deterministic behavior, we may observe different sequences if we repeat the execution on the SUT. Instead of repeating each input sequence several times, we assume that the generation via random walk reflects the non-deterministic behavior sufficiently.

In this case study, we learned the ONFSMs of MQTT brokers. In the MQTT protocol, a client can connect to a broker. A connected client can subscribe to a topic and/or publish a message on a topic, which is then forwarded by the broker to the subscribed clients. The task of the MQTT broker is to handle the connection/disconnection of the clients and to forward publish-messages to subscribed clients. The five learned MQTT brokers are listed in Table 7. All of them implement the current MQTT standard version 5.0 [14]. To communicate with the different brokers, we used our own client implementation.

We used an akin learning setup for all five MQTT brokers. The goal was to learn the behavior of the MQTT broker that interacts with multiple clients. In our experiments, we used five clients. We defined the abstract input alphabet by $\Sigma_I^A = \{\mathsf{Connect}, \mathsf{Disconnect}, \mathsf{Subscribe}, \mathsf{Unsubscribe}, \mathsf{Publish}\}$. The mapper translates each abstract input to a concrete input for one of the five clients. Furthermore, the clients can subscribe to one topic and publish a message to this topic. For the second level abstraction we defined the following mapping

Table 7. Learning setup and results of our case study on MQTT brokers

Broker	ejabberd[a]	EMQ X[b]	HiveMq[c]	Mosquitto[d]	VerneMQ[e]
Version	20.3	v4.0.0	2020.2	1.6.8	1.10.0
Timeout	100	50	100	50	50
# Output Queries	18 315	18 375	15 950	13 975	14 800
# Equivalence Checks	1	1	1	1	1
Runtime (h)	11.28	5.48	9.04	3.98	4.30

[a] https://www.ejabberd.im/
[b] https://www.emqx.io/
[c] https://www.hivemq.com/
[d] https://mosquitto.org/
[e] https://vernemq.com/

μ for the equivalence classes {Closed, Closed_all, Closed_Unsuback_all} → Closed, {Unsuback, Unsuback_all} → Unsuback, and all other outputs map to an equally named singleton equivalence class. To make the approach feasible for a large number of clients, our mapper saves translations from the abstract sequences in Γ to sequences with concrete input/output values, i.e., we cache concrete input/output sequences of the sequences in Γ. For each of these saved translations, we repeat the output query times the number of clients. Using this querying technique, we assume that we do not frequently observe new outputs when we repeat the output queries. Therefore, we set the change indicator $s = 0.9$, $s_i = 0.2$ and $s_d = 0.1$. Furthermore, we assume that 2 000 input/output sequences sufficiently represent this system. Thus, we set $n_{\text{test}} = 2\,000$.

Figure 5 represents the learned ONFSM of an MQTT broker interacting with multiple clients. The symbol "+" represents a wildcard for several inputs or outputs that are not critical for the behavior system and, therefore, are skipped to keep the model clear. The three states of the MQTT model distinguish between the state where no client is connected (q_0), at least one client is connected, but no client is subscribed (q_1) and at least one client is connected and subscribed (q_2). Note that Fig. 5 represents a valid model for all setups where more than two clients interact with the MQTT broker.

Table 7 shows the learning setup and the results of our case study. The first three rows of the table define the MQTT broker, the tested version and the required timeout on responses. The timeout defines the duration how long (in milliseconds) the socket listens for incoming messages. An equal behavior of the five brokers could only be achieved by the adaption of the timeouts. Selecting a too low timeout, we may not receive all messages in time. Our proposed learning algorithm can deal with such a non-deterministic behavior. For example, when we learn the *HiveMQ* broker with a timeout of 50, we receive messages from old sessions or some messages are not delivered in time. Therefore, we set the timeout for the brokers individually. The last three rows of Table 7 represent the learning results which state the number of performed output queries and equivalence queries, and the required time to learn the MQTT broker. The timeout directly affects the runtime of the learning algorithm, which can be seen in the experiments for *ejabberd* and *HiveMQ*. The experiments were conducted with a MacBook Pro 2019 with an Intel Quad-Core i5 operating at 2.4 GHz and with 8 GB RAM. All learned models correspond to the ONFSM presented in Fig. 5.

Furthermore, we compared our algorithm with a deterministic learning algorithm. For this, we learn a deterministic model of the MQTT broker that interacts with five clients. The experiment was performed with the tool **LearnLib** [10] using the improved version of L^* proposed by Rivest and Schapire [19]. We only learned the model for the Mosquitto broker with a timeout of 50, all other brokers of Table 7 showed non-deterministic behavior during learning. The learning of the Mosquitto broker for five clients took more than two days (58.29h). The final model had 243 states and 6 075 transitions. The model size shows that even if we learn a small part of a rather simple system the complexity of the system increases significantly in a multi-client setup. To learn the deterministic

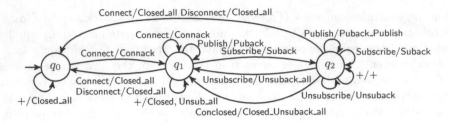

Fig. 5. The ONFSM of an MQTT broker that interacts with multiple-clients.

model, 151 900 output queries and one equivalence query were required. These results stress that our algorithm enables a faster learning-based testing technique and provides a simpler model of a large system.

5   Related Work

Our proposed learning algorithm for ONFSM is based on Angluin's L^* [4]. In the literature, the majority of learning algorithms for non-deterministic systems [6,7,11,16,25,26] also follows the same principle. Bollig et al. [6] introduced a learning algorithm for residual finite-state automata, which are a subclass of non-deterministic finite automata. Using this modeling formalism, they can represent a deterministic finite-state automaton by a more succinct non-deterministic automaton. However, they assume that the SUT behaves deterministically.

All Angluin-based algorithms for ONFSMs [7,11,16] basically follow the approach that was first proposed by El-Fakih et al. [7]. Their algorithm is based on the *all-weather assumption*, i.e. all possible outputs are observable at once. Pacharoen et al. [16] revise this assumption by assuming that all outputs are observed, after executing a query $n \in \mathbb{N}$ times. Kahlili and Tacchella [11] also considered more practical aspects and learned the non-deterministic model of TFTP server. However, as explained in Sect. 3 these algorithms might not scale well when an alphabet is abstracted by a mapper component.

Volpato and Tretmans [25,26] introduced two learning algorithms for non-deterministic input/output labelled transition systems. In their first work [25], they posed the all-weather assumption on the observation of outputs and assume an Angluin-style equivalence oracle. In their second work [26], they weakened these assumptions and proposed a conformance relation based on the **ioco**-theory [24] for an over- and under-approximation of the SUT. In contrast to our algorithm, they try to improve the observation table by increasing it, which leads to more states like in the previously mentioned algorithms for ONFSMs.

Petrenko and Avellaneda [18] proposed an algorithm for ONFSM that is not based on Angluin's MAT framework. Instead of a teacher they create a hypothesis using a SAT solver. However, the algorithm is based on the assumption that the final number of states of the ONFSM must be known in advance.

Tappler et al. [22] presented an L^*-based learning algorithm for Markov decision processes. For this, they also considered the observed frequencies of stochastic events in their models. Their algorithm rather learns the stochastic behavior instead of the non-deterministic behavior like our algorithm.

6   Conclusion

We presented an active automata learning algorithm for observable non-deterministic finite state machines. Unlike previous work on L^*-based algorithms for ONFSMs, our algorithm learns a more abstract model of the SUT by merging akin states. For this, we defined two levels of abstraction and explained how to combine them. Firstly, we showed how the mapper component proposed by Aarts et al. [2] can be used in an active learning setup for ONFSMs. Secondly, to further improve the scalability of our learning algorithm, we introduced a new abstraction scheme for the observation table based on equivalence classes for outputs. This abstraction technique made it possible to learn a more abstract model of a system that has a large input/output alphabet. We showed the applicability of our implementation by learning the ONFSMs of different MQTT brokers that interact with multiple clients.

Our proposed learning algorithm offers a more feasible technique to apply learning-based testing in a broader field of applications. For future work, it would be interesting to show a more elaborated case study, e.g. considering more features of the MQTT protocol, so that our abstract model can reveal unexpected behavior of the SUT. Currently, the abstraction refinement relies on expert knowledge, but we assume that an automatic abstraction is possible. Aarts et al. [1] proposed an automatic abstraction refinement for the abstracted input/output alphabet that ensures deterministic learning. Following a similar idea, we could refine the outputs for the first level-abstraction to ensure observable non-determinism. Regarding the second level abstraction, an equivalence measurement for states could support the definition of equivalence classes.

Acknowledgments. This work is supported by the TU Graz LEAD project "Dependable Internet of Things in Adverse Environments". We would like to thank student Jorrit Stramer for the implementation of the MQTT client.

References

1. Aarts, F., Heidarian, F., Kuppens, H., Olsen, P., Vaandrager, F.: Automata learning through counterexample guided abstraction refinement. In: Giannakopoulou, D., Méry, D. (eds.) FM 2012. LNCS, vol. 7436, pp. 10–27. Springer, Heidelberg (2012). https://doi.org/10.1007/978-3-642-32759-9_4
2. Aarts, F., Jonsson, B., Uijen, J., Vaandrager, F.: Generating models of infinite-state communication protocols using regular inference with abstraction. Formal Methods Syst. Des. **46**(1), 1–41 (2014). https://doi.org/10.1007/s10703-014-0216-x

3. Aichernig, B.K., Burghard, C., Korošec, R.: Learning-based testing of an industrial measurement device. In: Badger, J.M., Rozier, K.Y. (eds.) NFM 2019. LNCS, vol. 11460, pp. 1–18. Springer, Cham (2019). https://doi.org/10.1007/978-3-030-20652-9_1

4. Angluin, D.: Learning regular sets from queries and counterexamples. Inf. Comput. **75**(2), 87–106 (1987). https://doi.org/10.1016/0890-5401(87)90052-6

5. Berg, T., Grinchtein, O., Jonsson, B., Leucker, M., Raffelt, H., Steffen, B.: On the correspondence between conformance testing and regular inference. In: Cerioli, M. (ed.) FASE 2005. LNCS, vol. 3442, pp. 175–189. Springer, Heidelberg (2005). https://doi.org/10.1007/978-3-540-31984-9_14

6. Bollig, B., Habermehl, P., Kern, C., Leucker, M.: Angluin-style learning of NFA. In: Boutilier, C. (ed.) IJCAI 2009, Pasadena, CA, USA, 11–17 July 2009, pp. 1004–1009 (2009). http://ijcai.org/Proceedings/09/Papers/170.pdf

7. El-Fakih, K., Groz, R., Irfan, M.N., Shahbaz, M.: Learning finite state models of observable nondeterministic systems in a testing context. In: 22nd IFIP International Conference on Testing Software and Systems, Natal, Brazil, pp. 97–102 (2010). https://hal.inria.fr/hal-00953395

8. Fiterau-Brostean, P., Jonsson, B., Merget, R., de Ruiter, J., Sagonas, K., Somorovsky, J.: Analysis of DTLS implementations using protocol state fuzzing. In: 29th USENIX Security Symposium (USENIX Security 2020), pp. 2523–2540. USENIX Association (2020). https://www.usenix.org/conference/usenixsecurity20/presentation/fiterau-brostean

9. Gold, E.M.: System identification via state characterization. Automatica **8**(5), 621–636 (1972). https://doi.org/10.1016/0005-1098(72)90033-7

10. Isberner, M., Howar, F., Steffen, B.: The open-source LearnLib. In: Kroening, D., Păsăreanu, C.S. (eds.) CAV 2015. LNCS, vol. 9206, pp. 487–495. Springer, Cham (2015). https://doi.org/10.1007/978-3-319-21690-4_32

11. Khalili, A., Tacchella, A.: Learning nondeterministic Mealy machines. In: Clark, A., Kanazawa, M., Yoshinaka, R. (eds.) Proceedings of the 12th International Conference on Grammatical Inference, ICGI 2014, Kyoto, Japan, 17–19 September 2014. JMLR Workshop and Conference Proceedings, vol. 34, pp. 109–123. JMLR.org (2014). http://proceedings.mlr.press/v34/khalili14a.html

12. Margaria, T., Niese, O., Raffelt, H., Steffen, B.: Efficient test-based model generation for legacy reactive systems. In: Ninth IEEE International High-Level Design Validation and Test Workshop 2004, Sonoma Valley, CA, USA, 10–12 November 2004, pp. 95–100. IEEE Computer Society (2004). https://doi.org/10.1109/HLDVT.2004.1431246

13. Moller, F., Tofts, C.: A temporal calculus of communicating systems. In: Baeten, J.C.M., Klop, J.W. (eds.) CONCUR 1990. LNCS, vol. 458, pp. 401–415. Springer, Heidelberg (1990). https://doi.org/10.1007/BFb0039073

14. OASIS Message Queuing Telemetry Transport (MQTT) TC. Standard, Organization for the Advancement of Structured Information Standards, Burlington, MA, USA (2019). https://docs.oasis-open.org/mqtt/mqtt/v5.0/mqtt-v5.0.html

15. Niese, O.: An integrated approach to testing complex systems. Ph.D. thesis, Technical University of Dortmund, Germany (2003). https://d-nb.info/969717474/34

16. Pacharoen, W., Aoki, T., Bhattarakosol, P., Surarerks, A.: Active learning of nondeterministic finite state machines. Math. Prob. Eng. **2013**, 1–11 (2013). https://doi.org/10.1155/2013/373265

17. Peled, D.A., Vardi, M.Y., Yannakakis, M.: Black box checking. J. Autom. Lang. Comb. **7**(2), 225–246 (2002). https://doi.org/10.25596/jalc-2002-225

18. Petrenko, A., Avellaneda, F.: Learning and adaptive testing of nondeterministic state machines. In: 19th IEEE International Conference on Software Quality, Reliability and Security, QRS 2019, Sofia, Bulgaria, 22–26 July 2019, pp. 362–373. IEEE (2019). https://doi.org/10.1109/QRS.2019.00053

19. Rivest, R.L., Schapire, R.E.: Inference of finite automata using homing sequences. Inf. Comput. **103**(2), 299–347 (1993). https://doi.org/10.1006/inco.1993.1021

20. de Ruiter, J., Poll, E.: Protocol state fuzzing of TLS implementations. In: Jung, J., Holz, T. (eds.) 24th USENIX Security Symposium, USENIX Security 2015, Washington, D.C., USA, 12–14 August 2015, pp. 193–206. USENIX Association (2015). https://www.usenix.org/conference/usenixsecurity15/technical-sessions/presentation/de-ruiter

21. Shahbaz, M., Groz, R.: Inferring Mealy machines. In: Cavalcanti, A., Dams, D.R. (eds.) FM 2009. LNCS, vol. 5850, pp. 207–222. Springer, Heidelberg (2009). https://doi.org/10.1007/978-3-642-05089-3_14

22. Tappler, M., Aichernig, B.K., Bacci, G., Eichlseder, M., Larsen, K.G.: L^*-based learning of Markov decision processes. In: ter Beek, M.H., McIver, A., Oliveira, J.N. (eds.) FM 2019. LNCS, vol. 11800, pp. 651–669. Springer, Cham (2019). https://doi.org/10.1007/978-3-030-30942-8_38

23. Tappler, M., Aichernig, B.K., Bloem, R.: Model-based testing IoT communication via active automata learning. In: 2017 IEEE International Conference on Software Testing, Verification and Validation, ICST 2017, Tokyo, Japan, 13–17 March 2017, pp. 276–287. IEEE Computer Society (2017). https://doi.org/10.1109/ICST.2017.32

24. Tretmans, J.: Test generation with inputs, outputs and repetitive quiescence. Softw. Concepts Tools **17**(3), 103–120 (1996)

25. Volpato, M., Tretmans, J.: Active learning of nondeterministic systems from an IOCO perspective. In: Margaria, T., Steffen, B. (eds.) ISoLA 2014. LNCS, vol. 8802, pp. 220–235. Springer, Heidelberg (2014). https://doi.org/10.1007/978-3-662-45234-9_16

26. Volpato, M., Tretmans, J.: Approximate active learning of nondeterministic input output transition systems. ECEASST **72** (2015). https://doi.org/10.14279/tuj.eceasst.72.1008

Security Testing

APPregator: A Large-Scale Platform for Mobile Security Analysis

Luca Verderame[1] , Davide Caputo[1] , Andrea Romdhana[1,2] ,
and Alessio Merlo[1(✉)]

[1] DIBRIS, University of Genoa, Genoa, Italy
{luca.verderame,davide.caputo,andrea.romdhana,
alessio}@dibris.unige.it
[2] Security & Trust Unit, FBK-ICT, Trento, Italy

Abstract. The Google Play Store currently includes up to 2.8M apps. Nonetheless, it is rather straightforward for a user to quickly retrieve the app that matches her tastes, as Google provides a reliable search engine. However, it is likewise almost impossible to select apps according to a security footprint (e.g., all apps that enforce SSL pinning). To overcome this limitation, this paper presents APPregator, a platform which allows security analysts to i) download apps from multiple app stores, ii) perform automated security analysis (both static and dynamic), and iii) aggregate the results according to user-defined security constraints (e.g., vulnerability patterns).

The empirical assessment of APPregator on a set of 200.000 apps taken from the Google Play Store and Aptoide suggests that the current implementation grants a good level of performance and reliability. APPregator will be made freely available to the research community by the end of 2020.

Keywords: App analysis · Static and dynamic analysis · Security and privacy

1 Introduction

Risk assessment is crucial for IT systems, and it became a key issue for mobile apps, which are increasingly used every day for private or working activities. To deal with app security problems, several tools for the analysis of vulnerabilities have been proposed over the years. Despite this, such efforts did not provide a solution allowing to build a global view of the security status over a set of arbitrarily selected mobile apps. In particular, some research projects produced datasets that allow performing analysis on the security features of apps, however, these projects are focused mainly on malware. Indeed, automatic techniques are especially used to study malware and prevent its spread, but the same effort is

This work was partially funded by the Horizon 2020 project "Strategic Programs for Advanced Research and Technology in Europe" (SPARTA).

© IFIP International Federation for Information Processing 2020
Published by Springer Nature Switzerland AG 2020
V. Casola et al. (Eds.): ICTSS 2020, LNCS 12543, pp. 73–88, 2020.
https://doi.org/10.1007/978-3-030-64881-7_5

not applied to find vulnerabilities exposed in apps that could be exploited both by malicious apps or external attackers (i.e., confused deputy attacks). Albeit there exist some proposals that allow assessing the number of apps affected by a specific vulnerability, the results and the tools are kept mostly private so that only a few information is available and the tools cannot be used to replicate the analysis in the wild.

To overcome previous limitations, we designed and implemented a large scale platform for mobile security analysis called **APPregator**. The purpose of APPregator is to help researchers and developers to discover new vulnerabilities in Android apps, allowing them to aggregate and analyze a subset of Android apps that match specific security and privacy constraints as well as examining the distribution of security flaws. The proposed platform can automatically download apps from multiple stores and aggregate information about them, perform automated security analysis (both static and dynamic), and moreover, it is able to notify the results of the security analysis to apps' developers in a fully automatic way. Furthermore, our proposal allows researchers to aggregate the results according to defined security constraints and privacy.

To prove the scalability and reliability of our proposal, we collected in one month 200, 000 apps information from app stores and we performed a security analysis on 3, 500 apps. Furthermore, the 3, 500 apps were subjected to statistical analysis with the aim of examining the distribution of security flaws (i.e., insecure connections, privacy leaks, and hard-coded keys).

Structure of the Paper. The rest of the paper is organized as follows: Section 2 introduces the vulnerability assessment of mobile apps, while Sect. 3 presents the current state of the art. Section 4 defines the requirements of a large-scale platform, Section 5 presents the design of APPregator. Section 6 discusses the implementation choices for APPregator, while Sect. 7 shows the capabilities of the platform proposed. Finally, the Sect. 8 concludes the paper and points out some extensions of this work.

2   Vulnerability Assessment of Android Apps

The vulnerability assessment of Android apps is based on two main approaches: static and dynamic analysis. Static analysis techniques enable the evaluation of an app by examining the source code and the package content without executing it. Static analysis examines all possible execution paths and variable values, not just those invoked during execution. Thus, it can reveal errors and vulnerabilities that may not manifest themselves during the code execution, thereby leading to false positives.

Dynamic analysis techniques, instead, explore and evaluate the behavior of the app during its execution. Unfortunately, its effectiveness is influenced by the current limitations imposed by automated testing techniques that fail to analyze the whole app surface, leading to false negatives.

To this aim, the typical assessment workflow combines both the approaches, and it is composed of the following steps:

- *APK Reverse Engineering.* In this step, the Android Package (APK) is unpacked to retrieve manifest, resources, certificate and the app compiled code (dex files). The compiled code can be disassembled or decompiled. In the first case, the dex files are transformed using a disassembler (e.g., apktool [1]) in order to obtain a human-readable representation of the dex format called Smali [14]. In the second case, the dex files are reconverted in the original source code (or a representation of it) using tools like dex2jar [7] or jadx [11].
- *Static Analysis.* The app code is analyzed to evaluate the presence of security misconfigurations, vulnerable APIs, and security patterns. Static analysis of an app package often relies on the model representation of the app logic (e.g., through control flow graphs or call graphs [19,45]). Furthermore, static analysis techniques also evaluate non-code elements, i.e., the manifest file and all the resources files. These files are analyzed to detect misconfiguration or essential information about the app (e.g., exported activities, debug information, hard-coded keys, etc.). The most famous used tools are FlowDroid [21], TaintDroid [26] and AmanDroid [41].
- *Dynamic Analysis.* During the dynamic analysis, the app is installed and executed in a controlled environment (usually a virtual machine) in order to monitor its runtime behavior. During this phase, the behavior observed is the interaction with the file system, with the OS (i.e., all APIs invoked at runtime), and with the network by sniffing and collecting all traffic exchanged by the app during the execution. The app is stimulated using automatic tools that simulates human behavior like Droidbot [33] or Monkey [12].

3   Related Work

The typical vulnerability assessment workflow has been adopted by several frameworks and tools to either evaluate the security state of the apps (e.g., SCanDroid [28], CHEX [34], DroidChecker [23], DroidSafe [30], AppAudit [43]) or to monitor apps behavior (e.g., ProfileDroid [42], CopperDroid [39], AppIntent [46], DroidMiner [44], AsDroid [31]). However, all the above solutions focus on the security evaluation of a single app and do not provide mechanisms to i) retrieve sets of apps automatically, ii) evaluate the app's security posture in the different versions and the various application stores, and iii) prune, query and filter apps according to their security evaluation.

In the last years, both the scientific and industrial communities have proposed datasets that collect security information about apps. In [29] the authors identified that there are five datasets that collect information of more than 1 million of apps: Appannie [3], AppBrain [2], AndroZoo [32], AndroVault [38], and Andrubis [35]. While the first two are commercial data aggregation tools that use the information to study clients' competitors and improve their market position, the others have a research purpose and provide collections of apps enriched with some metadata and analyzed with several static or dynamic analysis techniques. For instance, AndroZoo collects information from: (1) the Google Play

Store, (2) the manifest file, (3) the *classes.dex* files, (4) the presence of native and encrypted code, and (5) the reports of the antivirus and vulnerabilities detection services. Unfortunately, Meng et al. [35] claim that it is complex to extract valuable information from the AndroZoo dataset and therefore they build a graph of attributes to extract these data. Androvault and Andrubis are two datasets that also perform dynamic analysis. Still, in the former, the authors were unable to execute the dynamic analysis of many apps due to time and technological constraints. The latter, instead, is discontinued and it is no longer updated from 2015. All in all, the primary purpose of those datasets is to analyze and study mobile malware, where most of them are obtained from alternative app stores or virus collections. To the best of our knowledge, there are no solutions able to aggregate apps coming from several stores (including the Google Play Store) and perform both static and dynamic analysis in order to make available to the researchers and developers community the security state of the app and its evolution.

4   Requirements for a Large-Scale Platform

In this section, we identify the requirements for a large-scale platform with the capability to perform automated security analysis (both static and dynamic) and aggregate the results according to user-defined security constraints. In detail, the aim of our proposal is to design and implement an architecture that is able to:

1. automatically collect a large set of mobile apps from several app stores;
2. perform static and dynamic analysis of those apps following the typical workflow, as described in Sect. 2;
3. store all the security-relevant information of the analysis to build a security dataset that can be queried and used to infer statistical results;
4. automatically check the release of app updates to create a security history of mobile apps releases, and
5. automatically notify the developers about security issues founded in their apps.

Apps Collection, Update and Filtering. Since the architecture needs to retrieve large sets of apps from the application stores automatically, it must crawl and download app packages from the leading Android app stores, i.e., Google Play and Aptoide [4]), being two of the most widespread Android market places. For each analyzed app, the architecture should also collect a set of app metadata, to enable fine-grained filtering of the dataset. In detail, we are interested in recording: (1) package name, (2) title, (3) icon, (4) category, (5) developer, (6) number of installs, (7) privacy policy, (8) number of ratings, (9) average ranking, (10) existence of advertising, (11) timestamp of the last update, (12) market of origin, (13) app version, (14) file hash, and (15) the analysis date.

Security Analysis. The architecture needs to perform a systematic security evaluation of the Android apps, thereby adopting the workflow described in

Sect. 2. To this aim, the platform needs to perform *Reverse Engineering, Static Analysis*, and *Dynamic Analysis*. The reverse engineering step is necessary to obtain information about the files that compose the app and the structure of the app itself (i.e., activities, services, providers, and receivers).

Regarding the static analysis, we are interested in evaluating the following information:

- the permissions (used and requested),
- the invoked APIs;
- the presence of patterns that could bring to security vulnerabilities. Such a vulnerability analysis should follow security frameworks and standards, e.g., the OWASP Mobile Applications Security Verification Standard (MASVS) [37] and the NIST Mobile Threat Catalogue [36];
- the usage of third-party libraries or frameworks;
- the obfuscation level;
- the presence of malicious code.

Regarding the dynamic analysis techniques, our platform needs to cover all of the main security measurements. Since most apps communicate over the Internet, the security assessments of network traffic and the communication protocols [20] is an essential feature. Among the possible checks, the platform needs to evaluate the absence of unencrypted communication and the presence of miss configuration, such as permissive certificate checks or the lack of security enforcement mechanisms (e.g., SSL Pinning) [27]. Furthermore, the platform should also identify the domain reputation of all the accessed URLs. Such a feature would help to detect privacy and security leaks affecting multiple apps by checking if they interact with the same unsafe endpoint.

The proposed platform also needs to detect all vulnerable third-party components since unpatched and obsolete third-party libraries are the primary source of security vulnerabilities in mobile apps, as described in [22,24,40]. The platform should also report the usage of tracking or advertising libraries to evaluate the presence of potential privacy leaks.

Furthermore, the dynamic analysis performed by the platform should also include additional information such as i) the application access to internal and external memory files, ii) the disclosure of sensitive information in the system and application logs, and iii) the use of hard-coded keys, passwords, or private token. Besides the filtering and sorting features, the system should also provide general security statistics such as the most commonly used libraries and contacted domains or the most requested files and leaks found at the same location reported for more apps.

Developers Notification. The platform needs to follow the responsible disclosure guidelines imposed by both application stores and the involved vendors. In detail, we designed our platform to be compliant with the Google's vulnerability disclosure policy [10]. In order to meet the requirements, after each security analysis, the platform automatically notifies the app's developer, waiting for 90 days for the inclusion in the dataset. The developer will be able to evaluate the security analysis and apply the required fixes to their apps within that time.

Platform Requirements. To formalize the platform requirements, we organize its features in functional requirements (FUNR), security measures (SECM), and statistical measures (STAT). The first group indicates the primary functionalities of our platform; the second one includes all the security measurements that need to be extracted by the mobile apps, while the last group collects the global metrics that can be computed by the platform. Table 1 presents the full list of requirements and their corresponding IDs.

Table 1. Platform requirements

ID	Description
FUNR1	Filter apps using the package name or a keyword in the title
FUNR2	Filter apps from a specific developer or category
FUNR3	Filter apps by the number of installations or their score
FUNR4	Filter apps that do not include a privacy policy on the Google Play Store page
FUNR5	Filter apps that requires a specific permission
FUNR6	Filter apps that use a certain category of APIs
FUNR7	Filter apps that include a specific library
FUNR8	Filter apps that use a low obfuscation level
FUNR9	Filter apps that interact with a specific internet domain
FUNR10	Filter apps that use insecure connections
FUNR11	Filter apps that access to a specific file path
FUNR12	Filter apps for which a leak is reported or an hard-coded key is found
FUNR13	Notify the app developers of security issues found in their app
SECM1	The list of components included in an app
SECM2	The list of permissions required by an app
SECM3	The list of APIs used by an app
SECM4	The list of libraries included in an app
SECM5	The request to read the Device ID
SECM6	The list of vulnerabilities reported for an app
SECM7	The obfuscation level of an app
SECM8	The probability for an application to be a malware
SECM9	The list of hosts contacted by an app with network security settings
SECM10	The list of files in the external memory used by an app
SECM11	The list of leaks found for an app
SECM12	The list of hard-coded keys reported for an app
STAT1	The most required permissions
STAT2	The most used APIs
STAT3	The most imported libraries
STAT4	The most common vulnerabilities
STAT5	The most contacted domains
STAT6	The domains most involved in a leak
STAT7	The most used files
STAT8	The files most involved in a leak

5   APPregator: A Large-Scale Platform for Mobile Security Analysis

In order to meet all requirements described in the previous section, we propose a modular architecture called APPregator. APPregator is composed of several modules, namely **Database, Crawler, Worker,** and **Server.** These modules allow to retrieve app information, to analyze its security, and to manage the obtained reports and statistics.

The **Database** stores all apps information, while the **Crawler** module identifies and collects the mobile apps. The Crawler also keeps track of the various versions of the apps. The **Worker** downloads the apps and performs the security analysis. A set of rest API is exposed by the **Server** to interact with the platform; moreover, the **Server** features a responsive GUI to extract and filter the data. Figure 1 depicts the modules of APPregator.

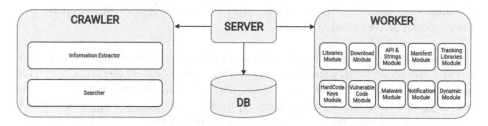

Fig. 1. APPregator architecture

Crawler. The Crawler uses the sub-module *Searcher* to collect all free apps that appear in Store categories. Once started, the *Searcher* looks for new apps in the categories TOP FREE and GROSSING. The keywords used come from the most common terms provided by the sub-module *Information Extractor. Information Extractor* relies on the Google Trends [9] service to function properly. At last, the *Searcher* starts examining TRENDING and NEW FREE categories searching for apps belonging to the same developer or similar to those already chosen during the current step. The similarities between apps are suggested by the store in use.

Worker. The Worker is structured as a micro-service, where each security measure is conducted by a specific sub-module (Fig. 1). The *Manifest* module retrieves information about app components and permissions (SECM1, SECM2). The *API & Strings* module is able to retrieve all APIs and string used by the app dividing them into categories (SECM3). The list of libraries included in the app are retrieved by two sub-modules: the *Libraries* and the *Tracking Libraries* (SECM4). The *Vulnerable Code* sub-module reports all vulnerabilities found in the app (SECM6), together with the obfuscation level of the app code (SECM7). The virus scan is performed by the *Malware* sub-module (SECM8). The *Dynamic* sub-module performs the dynamic analysis and stores the list of: (1) the host contacted by the app (SECM9),(2) the files used by the app (SECM10) and (3) the information leaked (SECM11). The Device ID access (SECM5) can be retrieved combining the information obtained from Vulnerable Code module and the Dynamic module, while the *HardCoded Keys* module detects the usage of hard-coded keys (SECM12).

The *Download* service downloads apps and checks if the latest version available in Google Play Store matches the one in Aptoide. The comparison is done through a specific API [5]. The version of an app is denoted by a name (verName) and a code (verCode). The Worker compares the SHA-2 of the downloaded APKs from the Play Store with those that have the same verName coming from unofficial markets. If the hashes are different, the Worker performs a new security analysis. If the apps have the same verName and the same verCode but a different hash, the Worker executes the malware analysis, to detect whether those apps are embedding malicious code.

Once the analysis is completed, the Worker uses the **Notification** submodule to send the analysis result to the app developer. At last, the Worker publishes the results on the platform, after the 90-day period imposed by the Google policy has expired (FUNR13).

Database. The Database stores the information collected during the analysis and provides the server with data which allows the user to execute the queries. The stored data are organized into two tables. One contains information available in app stores about apps (i.e., Play Store, Aptoide), in which each app is identified by the appId (package name). The other one contains the results of the security analysis, which has a unique verCode (version) for each app associated to the source store. The schema of the **Database** is described in Fig. 2.

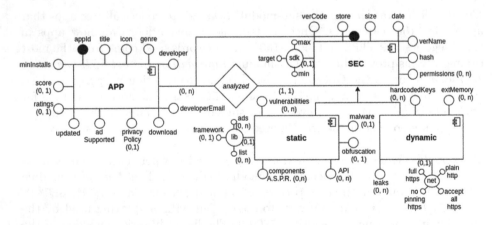

Fig. 2. Conceptual schema

Server. The Server exposes an endpoint of the REST API and a web interface that facilitates searching, sorting, and selecting the results of the application database.

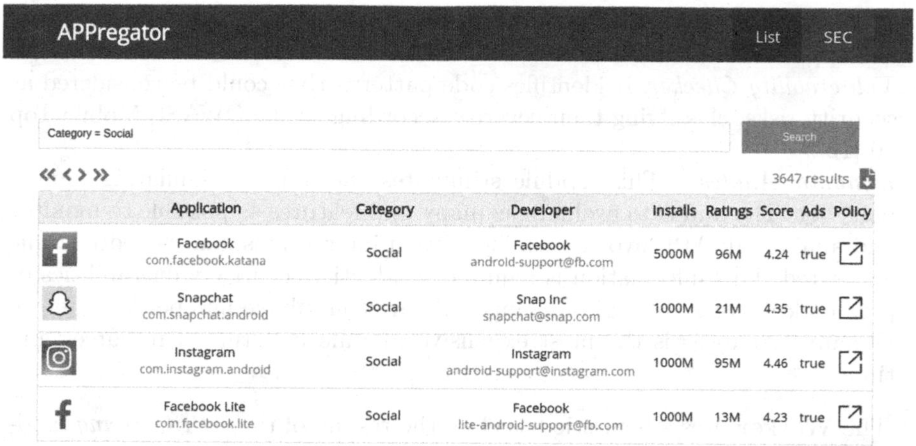

Fig. 3. Example of APPregator web interface

The **Server** also adopts operators typically implemented in the query language, such as count, limit and offset, in order to improve user experience and prevent the retrieving of large sets. If the client filters the data, an estimate of the number of query results is returned. Several navigation buttons allow to navigate through the results (Fig. 3). In addition, the server offers the possibility to download all the filtered results which could also represent the entire dataset: the server provides a stream from the database to the client to avoid storing the object in the main memory.

6   Implementation

The APPregator platform has been designed by leveraging state-of-the-art technologies and tools. The following section explains the implementation of each module.

Worker. The **Worker** consists of a set of micro-services developed in Java and Python languages. The security analysis is performed through Approver, a Saas developed by Talos [15]. Approver consists of:

- The *Decompiler*. It extracts the code and the resources from the app. The code is disassembled from *.dex* to *Smali* format. The resources (e.g., the Android manifest and the accessible strings) are stored on the disk.
- *Manifest Parser*. It analyzes the Android manifest and produces a JSON file containing permissions, activities, services, version and name of the app.
- *String and API Analysis*. This module analyzes the code searching for strings. Moreover it categorizes the Android API calls contained in the app.
- *Permission Checker*. It produces a list of permissions, taking into account both those used in the code and those declared in the manifest.

- *Library Detector*. This module searches for known third-party libraries inside the app.
- *Vulnerability Checker*. It identifies code patterns that could be considered as security risks, classifying their severity according to the OWASP Mobile Top 10 [13].
- *Dynamic Analysis*. This module stimulates the app by simulating human behavior. The aim is to evaluate as many app features as possible to monitor and analyze all API invocations, file system interactions, and network traffic generated. This information is required to identify security vulnerabilities or privacy leaks (e.g., SSL pinning misconfiguration, phone number leaks, etc.). Dynamic Analysis is the most expensive module in terms of resources and time.

The **Worker** uses a heuristic based on the results of the *API & String* module in order to perform the *Dynamic Analysis* module only when it is necessary. In detail, the Worker executes it only if the app uses at least one APIs in at least three of the following categories: INTERNET, FILE, CRYPTO, and PHONE. The Worker is composed also by another module named *HardCoded Keys*. It verifies the presence of hard-coded keys and monitors the functions categorized as CRYPTO. In details, this module compares the strings extracted from the app with the arguments passed to the caller. We decided to ignore arguments with fewer than four characters in order to reduce false positives, because they were too short to be considered as tokens. We also saved the most frequent results for creating lists of exclusion and false-positive.

Databases. The Database Management System of APPregator relies on MongoDB. The choice of a document-based solution (i.e., MongoDB) allow clients to query nested values efficiently. The database empowers multi-key index to seamlessly support the addition of new analysis modules or a new crawler. This solution prevents already existing data from being invalidated.

Crawler and Server. APPregator exploits the npm library google-play-scraper[1], and the query-to-mongo library[2] to extract app data from the Google Play Store. In this way, the users can filter the apps in the **Database** that match specific security-constraint. As a result of the libraries' choice, we used Node.JS and the framework Express for the HTTP server. We used Docker [8] in order to provide portability and fast deployment of the platform. Docker allows to stop (and eventually restart) the containers when a failure occurs or when a task is completed, thereby reducing memory usage.

7   APPregator Query Capabilities

We tested APPregator, on real-world apps extracted from the app stores between November 2019 and February 2020. The analysis has been carried out on a

---

[1] https://github.com/facundoolano/google-play-scraper.
[2] https://www.npmjs.com/package/query-to-mongo.

single machine with a quadcore 3.40 GHz processor, an SSD with 256 GB of storage, and 24 GB of RAM. Using this setup, we were able to collect in one month 200.000 apps information from the market and analyzed 3500 different app versions from the app stores. All queries described in this section were executed in a time-span between 200 ms and 800 ms. The analysis was carried out inspecting two different aspects of mobile apps: Privacy and Security.

7.1 Privacy

Using the Web Server Interface, the user can filter the apps that do not contain a field just using the search bar. For example, if the operator wants to filter apps that do not include a privacy policy on the Play Store page (FUNR4), he can execute the search !policy. If he also wants to find the subset which declared to include advertisements, he can append a semicolon with the new command ads=true, as shown in Code-Snippet 1. By using Code-Snippet 1 query on the entire dataset, APPregator reports that almost 13.000 apps do not include a privacy policy in the Play Store page on the last check, and about 7.000 of these use advertising anyway. Furthermore, we can sort them out by the number of installations by clicking on the table column name (FUNR3): four apps have at least 100 or 50 million users (Fig. 4), 35 apps have more than 10 million installations, 350 more than 1 million installations, and more than 1.500 have at least 100.000 users. Using a search bar the operator can look for apps involved in a leak (FUNR12) by using the *leaks* keyword in the search bar. By using this query on the dataset of analyzed apps, we discovered 21 apps with a potential leak, 17 of which come from the Play Store. In detail, 12 privacy leaks are saved to file, 12 exposed on the net, 19 refer to the device ID, and 5 to the user email.

```
!policy; ads=true
```

Code-Snippet 1: Query to find apps with advertising and without a privacy policy

	Application	Category	Developer	Installs	Ratings	Score	Ads	Policy
	TubeMote com.tubemote.app	Entertainment	TubeMote contact@tubemote.com	100M	419565	3.43	true	
	Chess com.jetstartgames.chess	Board	Chess Prince help.chess@mail.ru	100M	1M	4.33	true	
	Checkers com.dimcoms.checkers	Board	English Checkers help.checkers@mail.ru	50M	388279	4.32	true	
	Escaping the Prison air.com.puffballsunited.escaping...	Casual	PuffballsUnited puffballsunited@gmail.com	50M	471042	3.89	true	

Fig. 4. Top 4 most installed apps without a privacy policy on the Google Play Store

Since the *Android best practices for unique identifiers* [6] recommends developers to avoid using hardware identifiers like the device ID and use GUIDs to identify app instances uniquely, we inspected the collected dataset. Figure 5 presents the results obtained by the query in the Code-Snippet 2: 9 Google Play Store apps send the Device ID to a server.

```
leaks.net.category=device; store=play
```

Code-Snippet 2: Query to find Device ID leaks via net in the Play Store

Such an issue is particularly relevant when using advertisement libraries as a user-resettable identifier needs to be used. Despite this, the authors of *Ad IDs Behaving Badly* [25] reported to Google how ads libraries transmit over the net the device ID instead of a user-generated Advertising ID. The results obtained by APPregator confirm, one year later, the worries pointed out in the report, thereby also proving the usefulness of the website search feature (FUNR9) since some of the domains involved are the same reported in the study.

	Application	verName	verCode	Store	Hash	Size	Date
i	com.junerking.archery	3.1	20	play	1b357561a3bb...	23MB	16/2/2020, 07:40
i	com.neuralprisma	3.2.4.413	7000413	play	e0e7dec8bacb...	11MB	17/2/2020, 15:43
i	paint.by.number.pixel.art.colori...	2.12.1	1020	play	5771f49e796d...	36MB	5/3/2020, 12:07
i	com.gamebasics.osm	3.4.51.5	345105	play	0b58546fed86...	11MB	6/3/2020, 19:25
i	com.yahoo.mobile.client.android....	1.20.3	91596454	play	b2414799b92c...	30MB	8/3/2020, 07:04
i	com.hypermedia.songflip	1.1.10	1803131913	play	5d4c704f932c...	9MB	9/3/2020, 10:09
i	com.pinssible.fancykey	4.7	4146	play	431eb17ff9e8...	19MB	9/3/2020, 19:30
i	com.trulia.android	11.8.1	719	play	9b9c16c8455e...	13MB	11/3/2020, 21:03
i	com.chatous.chatous	3.9.87	379	play	216c107efb72...	46MB	11/3/2020, 21:03

Fig. 5. Play Store apps that send the Device ID to a server

7.2   Security

Further we tested some of the capabilities offered by APPregator to evaluate the security of the app.

Insecure Connections. To find the usage of insecure connections (FUNR10), the security operator can execute the query net.plain-http. By using the collected dataset, the query reports 7 results. Among the vulnerable apps, six of them come from the Play Store and have between 10 and 100 million installations. On of them apps is a web browser and reading its description in the store, we noticed that one of the features offered is the advertising block during the navigation. However, the app itself contains ads and tracking libraries, which is a behavior far from a privacy-oriented adblocker. Studying connections in a browser app is especially tricky due to the strong dependency on the user input for the URL browsing. However, also the static code analysis reports the presence of http URLs. The connection is related to the usage of the *Tencent Login* library [16], indeed APPregator also collects the reference to which part of code is involved to facilitate researchers to discover security issues.

Vulnerable Libraries. Another operation that we tested regards finding the usage of a vulnerable library just by inserting its package name (FUNR7) or searching its common name. For instance, 50 apps of the dataset include *Tencent Login*, but the version described above is used only by the web browser app. Unfortunately, APPregator does not always provide information about the library version, due to the current limitation of the library recognition technology. Indeed, library recognition is not precise due to obfuscation techniques (see, e.g., [18]) or the lack of libraries signatures. To mitigate such an issue, some additional filter operations should be performed and to help in this process, the permissions related to the methods used in the instance of the library for a specific app are saved.

Malware. The malware field is a probability obtained by adding up the number of positive responses between different antivirus services and dividing the result for the total number of scans. In our dataset, we only find 5 occurrences with malware>0 raging from 0.016 to 0.032, i.e., a minimal probability. By using the same approach of Meng et al. [35] that allows identifying repackaging of an app by checking the developer certificate w.r.t. the one in the Play Store, we identify an app between the possible malware with a different value of the certificate. This information is included in the vulnerabilities field with the flag level=Info.

Looking for the hash value of apps on Virus Total, we have retrieved an app analysis that reports an Android.PUA.DebugKey issue. This issue indicates that the app has a debug certificate: the Play Store would not have allowed the app upload, which is instead possible on Aptoide. However, the differences between the app within Play Store and within Aptoide are all related to third parties libraries: it looks like a patched version of the app with ads removed. The other 4 results are false positives.

Hard-Coded Keys. APPregator reports 8 apps that contain hard-coded keys (FUNR12): as explained in Sect. 5, we inserted a check in the code to exclude configuration parameters and manually remove the most frequent values like HmacSHA1 or HmacSHA256. The platform collects the string, the method, and the number of the parameter: the most common method is *javax.crypto.spec.SecretKeySpec*, which is used to construct a Secret key starting from the string.

This method should be used to store keys generated at run time as authentication tokens, but these strings are inserted into the code and therefore, could represent a security vulnerability depending on the specific case. Usually, the main problem is the usage of API keys for third-party services, that are saved within this method, to be used later in the code. The best practice is to perform the requests server-side, but also string obfuscation is often used.

8   Conclusion

In one month, APPregator was able to collect information from almost 200.000 apps and performed the security analysis on the 2.000 most installed apps in the Play Store, using only a single machine. It saved more than 3.500 database entries and APK files, including updates and the Aptoide app versions. The aim of this work was to build a platform able to manage large scale studies, and therefore we used technologies optimized for big data and we designed the platform with a distributed architecture. Other works (Sect. 3) collected a lot of more data, but reached one million results only after a couple of years [38] or three million in several months using seven nodes and starting from other datasets [17]. While finding information about new apps from the store becomes more difficult over time since repetitions often occur, the number of results produced in the analysis step is constant and depends on the performance of the computer (more than 100 new analyses per day in our case). After comparing the library statistics with the AppBrain [2] list of top development and advertising tools, we noticed that we obtained equivalent results also concerning the order of the elements, especially in the first positions. Consequently, the analyzed apps are relevant for this metric, and therefore also the other measures could be valid for a larger set of apps. In any case, our objective was to build an architecture able to download, analyze, aggregate a large number of apps in a totally automatic way. The produced results by our architecture show how the static analysis is useful for computing general statistics, while the dynamic tests are essentials to find security and privacy vulnerabilities.

Future Work. First, we aim to make APPregator available to the research community by the end of 2020. APPregator can be extended with new modules in order to carry out new types of analysis. Furthermore, APPregator can be extended to retrieve apps from other stores (e.g., APK Mirror, Amazon, Galaxy Store, or F-Droid) and to support iOS apps. The main limitation of our proposal is related to the results obtained during the dynamic analysis, as a full exploration of the app requires to bypass login activities with valid user's credentials. Currently, APPregator is unable to bypass this step. However, we argue that new modules, leveraging machine learning techniques to identify the fields to fill, can overcome this limitation.

References

1. Apktool. https://ibotpeaches.github.io/Apktool/. Accessed 27 May 2020
2. App brain. https://www.appbrain.com/. Accessed 27 May 2020
3. Appannie. https://www.appannie.com/. Accessed 27 May 2020
4. Aptoide. https://en.aptoide.com/. Accessed 27 May 2020

5. Aptoide api. https://co.aptoide.com/webservices/docs/7/apps/search. Accessed 27 May 2020
6. Best practices for unique identifiers. https://developer.android.com/training/articles/user-data-ids. Accessed 27 May 2020
7. Dex2jar. https://github.com/pxb1988/dex2jar. Accessed 27 May 2020
8. Docker. https://www.docker.com/. Accessed 27 May 2020
9. Google trends. https://trends.google.it/trends. Accessed 27 May 2020
10. Google's vulnerability disclosure policy. https://www.google.com/about/appsecurity/. Accessed 27 May 2020
11. Jadx. https://github.com/skylot/jadx. Accessed 27 May 2020
12. Monkey runner. https://developer.android.com/studio/test/monkeyrunner/. Accessed 27 May 2020
13. Owasp mobile top 10. https://owasp.org/www-project-mobile-top-10/. Accessed 27 May 2020
14. Smali. https://github.com/JesusFreke/smali/wiki. Accessed 27 May 2020
15. Talos sec. https://talos-sec.com/. Accessed 27 May 2020
16. Tencent. https://intl.cloud.tencent.com/. Accessed 27 May 2020
17. Allix, K., Bissyandé, T., Klein, J., Le Traon, Y.: AndroZoo: collecting millions of Android apps for the research community (2016)
18. Aonzo, S., Georgiu, G.C., Verderame, L., Merlo, A.: Obfuscapk: an open-source black-box obfuscation tool for android apps. SoftwareX **11**, 100403 (2020). https://doi.org/10.1016/j.softx.2020.100403. http://www.sciencedirect.com/science/article/pii/S2352711019302791
19. Armando, A., Costa, G., Merlo, A., Verderame, L.: Enabling byod through secure meta-market. In: WiSec 2014, New York, NY, USA. Association for Computing Machinery (2014)
20. Armando, A., Pellegrino, G., Carbone, R., Merlo, A., Balzarotti, D.: From model-checking to automated testing of security protocols: bridging the gap. In: Brucker, A.D., Julliand, J. (eds.) Tests and Proofs, pp. 3–18. Springer, Heidelberg (2012). https://doi.org/10.1007/978-3-642-30473-6_3
21. Arzt, S., et al.: Flowdroid: precise context, flow, field, object-sensitive and lifecycle-aware taint analysis for android apps. ACM SIGPLAN Notices **49**, 259–269 (2014)
22. Backes, M., Bugiel, S., Derr, E.: Reliable third-party library detection in android and its security applications (2016)
23. Chan, P.P., Hui, L.C., Yiu, S.M.: Droidchecker: analyzing android applications for capability leak. In: Proceedings of the Fifth ACM Conference on Security and Privacy in Wireless and Mobile Networks (2012)
24. Derr, E.: The impact of third-party code on android app security. In: Enigma 2018 (Enigma 2018). USENIX Association (2018)
25. Egelman, S.: Ad ids behaving badly. Technical report (2019)
26. Enck, W., et al.: Taintdroid: an information-flow tracking system for realtime privacy monitoring on smartphones. ACM Tran. Comput. Syst. (TOCS) **32**, 1 29 (2014)
27. Fahl, S., Harbach, M., Muders, T., Baumgärtner, L., Freisleben, B., Smith, M.: Why eve and mallory love android: An analysis of android SSL (in)security. In: Proceedings of the 2012 ACM Conference on Computer and Communications Security. CCS 2012, New York, NY, USA. Association for Computing Machinery (2012)
28. Fuchs, A.P., Chaudhuri, A., Foster, J.S.: Scandroid: automated security certification of android applications. Manuscript, Univ. of Maryland. https://www.cs.umd.edu/avik/projects/scandroidascaa (2009)

29. Geiger, F.X., Malavolta, I.: Datasets of android applications: a literature review (2018)
30. Gordon, M.I., Kim, D., Perkins, J.H., Gilham, L., Nguyen, N., Rinard, M.C.: Information flow analysis of android applications in droidsafe. In: NDSS (2015)
31. Huang, J., Zhang, X., Tan, L., Wang, P., Liang, B.: Asdroid: detecting stealthy behaviors in android applications by user interface and program behavior contradiction. In: Proceedings of the 36th International Conference on Software Engineering (2014)
32. Li, L., et al.: Androzoo++: collecting millions of android apps and their metadata for the research community (2017)
33. Li, Y., Yang, Z., Guo, Y., Chen, X.: Droidbot: a lightweight ui-guided test input generator for android. In: 2017 IEEE/ACM 39th International Conference on Software Engineering Companion (ICSE-C). IEEE (2017)
34. Lu, L., Li, Z., Wu, Z., Lee, W., Jiang, G.: Chex: statically vetting android apps for component hijacking vulnerabilities. In: Proceedings of the 2012 ACM Conference on Computer and Communications Security (2012)
35. Meng, G., Xue, Y., Siow, J., Su, T., Narayanan, A., Liu, Y.: Androvault: constructing knowledge graph from millions of android apps for automated computing (2017)
36. NIST: Mobile threat catalogue. https://pages.nist.gov/mobile-threat-catalogue (2018). Accessed Sept 2020
37. OWASP: OWASP mobile security testing guide (2020). https://owasp.org/www-project-mobile-security-testing-guide/. Accessed Sept 2020
38. Platzer, C., et al.: Andrubis - 1,000,000 apps later: a view on current android malware behaviors (2014)
39. Tam, K., Khan, S.J., Fattori, A., Cavallaro, L.: Copperdroid: automatic reconstruction of android malware behaviors. In: NDSS (2015)
40. Verderame, L., Caputo, D., Romdhana, A., Merlo, A.: On the (un)reliability of privacy policies in android apps. In: Proceedings of the IEEE International Joint Conference on Neural Networks (IJCNN 2020) (2020)
41. Wei, F., Roy, S., Ou, X.: Amandroid: a precise and general inter-component data flow analysis framework for security vetting of android apps. In: Proceedings of the 2014 ACM SIGSAC Conference on Computer and Communications Security (2014)
42. Wei, X., Gomez, L., Neamtiu, I., Faloutsos, M.: Profiledroid: multi-layer profiling of android applications. In: Proceedings of the 18th Annual International Conference on Mobile Computing and Networking (2012)
43. Xia, M., Gong, L., Lyu, Y., Qi, Z., Liu, X.: Effective real-time android application auditing. In: 2015 IEEE Symposium on Security and Privacy. IEEE (2015)
44. Yang, C., Xu, Z., Gu, G., Yegneswaran, V., Porras, P.: DroidMiner: automated mining and characterization of fine-grained malicious behaviors in android applications. In: Kutyłowski, M., Vaidya, J. (eds.) ESORICS 2014. LNCS, vol. 8712, pp. 163–182. Springer, Cham (2014). https://doi.org/10.1007/978-3-319-11203-9_10
45. Yang, W., Xiao, X., Andow, B., Li, S., Xie, T., Enck, W.: Appcontext: differentiating malicious and benign mobile app behaviors using context. In: 2015 IEEE/ACM 37th IEEE International Conference on Software Engineering, vol. 1. IEEE (2015)
46. Yang, Z., Yang, M., Zhang, Y., Gu, G., Ning, P., Wang, X.S.: Appintent: analyzing sensitive data transmission in android for privacy leakage detection. In: Proceedings of the 2013 ACM SIGSAC Conference on Computer & Communications Security (2013)

Vulsploit: A Module for Semi-automatic Exploitation of Vulnerabilities

Arcangelo Castiglione[1] , Francesco Palmieri[1] , Mariangela Petraglia[2],
and Raffaele Pizzolante[1(✉)]

[1] Dipartimento di Informatica, Università degli Studi di Salerno,
84084 Fisciano, Salerno, Italy
{arcastiglione,fpalmieri,rpizzolante}@unisa.it
[2] Università degli Studi di Salerno, 84084 Fisciano, Salerno, Italy
m.petraglia9@studenti.unisa.it

Abstract. Penetration testing (PT) is nowadays one of the most common and used activities to evaluate a given asset's security status. Penetration testing aims to secure networks and highlights the security issues of such networks. More precisely, PT, which is used for proactive defense and information systems protection, is a structured process, made up of various phases that typically needs to be carried out within a limited period.

In this work, we first define a modular semi-automatic approach, which allows us to collect and integrate data from various exploit repositories. These data are then used to provide the penetration tester (i.e., the *pentester*) with information on the best available tools (i.e., *exploits*) to conduct the exploitation phase effectively. Also, the proposed approach has been implemented through a proof of concept based on the *Nmap Scripting Engine (NSE)*, which integrates the features provided by the Nmap *Vulscan* vulnerability scanner, and allows, for each vulnerability detected, to find the most suitable exploits for this vulnerability. We remark that the proposed approach is not focused on the vulnerability mapping phase, which is carried out through *Vulscan*. Instead, it is focused on the automatic finding of the exploits that can be used to take advantage of the results achieved by such a phase.

Keywords: Penetration testing · Automation of security testing · Security assessment · Security monitoring · Nmap · Nmap Scripting Engine (NSE)

1 Introduction

The increasing diffusion of hardware and software technologies have significatively extended the attack surface available to malicious users since such technologies are not perfect and can be affected by bugs, vulnerabilities, and other security issues. An attack could damage an organization, impacting the economic, social, and image aspects of such an organization. Attacks are typically

© IFIP International Federation for Information Processing 2020
Published by Springer Nature Switzerland AG 2020
V. Casola et al. (Eds.): ICTSS 2020, LNCS 12543, pp. 89–103, 2020.
https://doi.org/10.1007/978-3-030-64881-7_6

carried out by finding a weakness in the systems and then exploiting it. Thus, this is the reason why this weakness is called *vulnerability*.

Nowadays, information is more vulnerable than ever. Every technological advance raises new security threat that requires new security solutions. For example, *Internet of Things (IoT)* objects offer new services and pose new security threats. The IoT paradigm application to smart communities, smart cities, and smart homes, connecting objects to the Internet, brings to light new security challenges [4,11,12,20]. These challenges make smart communities/cities/homes extremely vulnerable to several kinds of attacks [2]. Again, cloud and *mobile cloud computing (MCC)* enables mobile devices to exploit seamless cloud services via offloading, offering several advantages but increased security concerns [1,7,8]. More precisely, one of the most critical issues for the security assessment of cloud-based environments is the lack of control over the involved resources. Besides, this kind of assessment requires knowledge of the possible security tests to carry out and the hacking tools used for the analysis. To address this issue, in [7,8] the authors propose a methodology that allows them to efficiently carry out a security assessment of cloud-based applications, by automating the set-up and execution of penetration tests. This methodology is based on the knowledge of the application architecture and security-related data collected from multiple sources. However, unlike the method proposed by us, the authors' methodology focuses more on coarse-grained architectural aspects, rather than on host-based scans. Besides, security threats are increasing in mobile payment environments, and in particular, in *mobile banking applications (MBAs)* since such applications store, transmit, and access sensitive and confidential information [6]. Moreover, many everyday life activities are based on interconnected electronic devices. Most of such devices are based on *Third-Party Intellectual Property (3PIP)* cores that could not be trustworthy. Therefore, if one of these 3PIP cores is vulnerable, the security of the device could be affected [14]. Finally, the rapid growth of *Artificial Intelligence (AI)* has made this even more challenging since machine learning algorithms are now used to attack such systems. On the other hand, the current defense mechanisms protect such systems by using traditional security facilities [10]. In detail, the primary use of AI in the penetration testing field concerns using reinforcement learning (RL) techniques [10,15,16,25,29] to perform regular and systematic security testing, saving human resources. Using RL techniques, penetration testing systems can learn and reproduce average and complex penetration testing activities. We point out that the system proposed by us does not use intelligent techniques, even if, as future developments, we aim to integrate these techniques in our proposal.

Penetration testing (PT) is an activity carried out to assess the security posture of an organization by safely exposing its vulnerabilities [9]. PT also helps evaluate the efficiency of the defense methodologies, policies, and tools used by an IT organization (or IT *asset*). Penetration testing is conducted regularly to identify risks and manage them to achieve higher security standards. Nowadays, penetration testing is one of the most common and used activities to assess the health of a given IT asset in terms of security. This activity deals with detecting the vulnerabilities of a given asset in a completely legal and structured way, trying to exploit them by mimicking an attacker (i.e., a *black hat hacker*). The attacker could be driven by various malicious objectives, such as compromising or disabling the system, stealing data from it, etc. [13]. The penetration tester (*pentester*) takes care of detecting potential vulnerabilities existing in the system, trying to fix them. The main aim of PT is to provide the most appropriate solutions to fix or mitigate the consequences deriving from the exploitation of vulnerabilities found, thus increasing the security posture of the organization. Furthermore, due to the recent regulations introduced by the *General Data Protection Regulation (GDPR),* [28], and the *Cybersecurity Act* [21], penetration testing activity finds an ever-increasing application in the context of the so-called cyber-physical systems and, in particular, in cyber-physical critical infrastructures [2].

We remark that PT is a structured process, made up of various phases, typically conducted over a limited time [24]. The success of this process depends mainly on two factors: the skills of the person who conducts it, typically called *penetration tester* or *pentester* for short, and the information available to him. On the other hand, one of the main problems with this process is that the data needed to conduct it often lies in distinct and heterogeneous sources. Therefore, these data must first be collected, then integrated, and finally used appropriately. This problem assumes great importance, especially in the *vulnerability mapping* and *exploitation* phases of the penetration testing process. Through these phases, the pentester, given a vulnerability, tries to find the most appropriate tools to exploit it [26], typically called *exploits.*

However, PT is a very time- and money-consuming activity that needs specialized security skills and tools. More precisely, penetration testing is a typically human-driven procedure that requires an in-depth knowledge of the possible attack methodologies and the hacking tools available to carry out the security assessment. Therefore, automated tools to assist the pentester in his activity are increasingly needed, and often become crucial to the success of the PT activity [3].

It is essential to point out that our approach is not focused on the vulnerability mapping phase, which is carried out through *Vulscan.* However, it is focused on the automatic finding of the exploits that can be used to take advantage of the results achieved by such a phase.

1.1 Contribution

This paper defines a modular semi-automatic approach, which allows us to collect and integrate data from various exploit repositories. These data will then be used to provide the pentester with indications on the best available tools (i.e., exploits) to conduct the exploitation phase effectively. We stress that since potentially a broad set of automatic tools can support this phase, it could be challenging to choose the most suitable one. Furthermore, the architecture of the proposed approach has been implemented and integrated into a module for the *Nmap* vulnerability scanner. In detail, this architecture has been realized through an NSE (Nmap Script Engine) script [23], which integrates the features provided by the *Vulscan* vulnerability scanner. This script provides the pentester with the most suitable tools to exploit these vulnerabilities for each detected vulnerability. The experimental results obtained from the evaluation of our proposal have shown its effectiveness. As a future development, we intend to parallelize the proposed approach to improve performance in terms of detection times and choose the most appropriate exploits. Again, we intend to explore the potential of artificial intelligence to enhance penetration testing and vulnerability identification in complex network scenarios.

1.2   Organization

The paper is organized as follows. In Sect. 2, we present the proposed semi-automated approach and highlight its main characteristics and the motivations behind it. In Sect. 3, we introduce the Vulsploit module, which is a Nmap module implementing our semi-automated approach. In Sect. 4, we show and discuss the preliminary test results achieved by evaluating the Vulsploit module. Finally, in Sect. 5, we give some final considerations and draw future research directions.

2   The Proposed Semi-automated Approach

In this section, we show the reasons that led us to the introduction of our proposal. Furthermore, we describe the architecture underlying the proposed approach.

2.1   Motivations

The Penetration Testing (PT) process is quite costly and takes a considerable amount of time, ranging from days to weeks. The main phases of a typical PT process are the following: *information gathering, network scanning, target enumeration, vulnerability assessment, target exploitation, target post exploitation*, and *final reporting*. Since each phase takes time and may require procedures usually carried out manually, our goal is to automate some of these phases. This way, the whole process turns out to be faster and less prone to human error. This paper aims to automate the phases ranging from the network scanning to the exploitation as much as possible. Notice that when the target asset's vulnerabilities are detected through the vulnerability assessment phase, the next step is to understand if and how they can be exploited. More precisely, to take advantage of a detected vulnerability, we need to look for an exploit that allows us to exploit such vulnerability, typically gaining access to the vulnerable asset. Nowadays, this process is mostly done manually. Besides, we remark that the process described above should be done for all the vulnerabilities detected during the vulnerability assessment phase. Therefore, when the vulnerabilities found are few, the time taken to find all the possible exploits for such vulnerabilities is not relevant. However, when there are thousands of vulnerabilities, such a manual approach becomes impractical. In fact, by calculating with hypothetical data, we can obtain roughly the following time estimate:

- 1 min to search for the exploit of a given vulnerability;
- 1000 total vulnerabilities;
- $1 \times 1000 = 1000\,min \approx 16.6\,h$.

The semi-automated approach proposed in this paper is intended to significantly reduce the search time effort required to find suitable exploits for the found vulnerabilities. In particular, the main objective of our approach is to merge and automate, in a single phase, the following phases of a typical PT process, so that they result in the eyes of the pentester as a single phase:

1. *Network Scanning*
2. *Enumeration*
3. *Vulnerability Assessment*
4. Mid-stage of *Exploitation*, because it searches for the exploit, but does not execute it.

The idea behind our proposal is shown in Fig. 1(a) and Fig. 1(b).

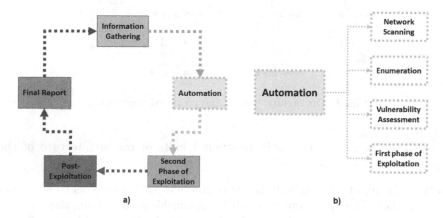

Fig. 1. (a) Phases of the PT process with the *automation*; (b) The subphases of the *automation*.

The benefits arising from the use of the proposed approach are twofold. First of all, it allows an experienced pentester to save resources in terms of time and costs, reducing the likelihood of making errors. On the other hand, our approach allows inexperienced pentesters to conduct the penetration testing process more efficiently and effectively since various stages of this process are automated [27].

2.2   Architecture

In Fig. 2, we show abstraction and generalization of our proposal. We first provide an abstract architectural view of our proposal, which abstracts the approach we have introduced from the relative implementation details. In this way, the proposed approach can be adapted according to the evolution of technologies and methodologies and based on the specific operational requirements of the context in which this approach will operate.

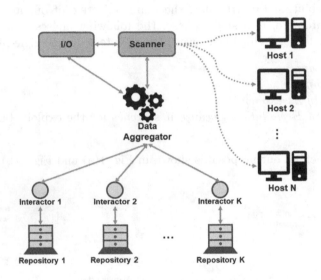

Fig. 2. The architecture of the proposed approach.

As shown in Fig. 2, the main functional units of the architecture of the proposed module are the following:

- **I/O**. The Input/Output unit is the component that allows us to send and receive data. More precisely, this unit is responsible for managing the *standard input (stdin), standard output (stdout)* and *standard error (stderr)*.
- **Host**. Hosts are the target machines (i.e., the *asset*) scanned to find vulnerabilities.
- **Scanner**. The scanner is the unit that deals with finding and analyzing vulnerabilities on the asset.
- **Data Aggregator**. The Data Aggregator is the unit that takes care of collecting, aggregating, and transferring data to the I/O unit.
- **Interactor**. This unit takes care of interacting with the Repository.
- **Repository**. The Repository is the unit that contains a list of vulnerabilities, categorized by port, service, and service version.

The information flow between the functional units is shown in Fig. 2 and can be characterized as follows:

1. The *Scanner* is started using the *I/O* unit.
2. Once started, the *Scanner* interacts with the *Hosts* and finds vulnerabilities for each of them.
3. These vulnerabilities are then sent to the *Data Aggregator*, which deals with:
   - Collecting the data achieved through the searches carried out to find vulnerabilities;
   - Aggregating them in a structured way, for example, through *JSON* structures;
   - Showing them to the user through the I/O unit.

   More precisely:

- Each *Repository* interacts with a dedicated *Interactor*, the output of each *Interactor* is then passed to a *Data Aggregator* once the processing is finished.
- The *Data Aggregator* aggregates the outputs of all the *Interactors* and then returns the output to the user.
- *Interactors* can be distributed, and their execution can be parallelized.
- The primary role of the *Interactors* is to mitigate the performance issues deriving from the massive query execution for each detected vulnerability.

3   The Vulsploit Module

This section shows the design and implementation choices that led us to create the proposed Nmap module (script), called `Vulsploit`, implementing our semi-automated approach. Vulsploit has been realized through an NSE (Nmap Script Engine) script, called "vulsploit.nse", which integrates the features offered by the *Vulscan* vulnerability scanner. This script provides the most suitable tools for the exploitation of the detected vulnerabilities.

In Fig. 3 we show an overview of the `Vulsploit` module.

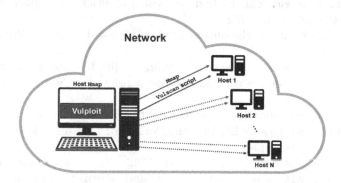

Fig. 3. An overview of the logical functioning of the proposed module.

Vulsploit automatically provides the exploits available for the vulnerabilities detected on a given asset. In detail, the general functioning of Vulsploit can be summarized as follows.

- We have a network scenario composed of $N + 1$ connected hosts.
- The component represented on the left side of Fig. 3 is the host where the Nmap scanner is running. This scanner will start the execution of Vulsploit. More precisely:
  1. Nmap scans the asset (i.e., the hosts);
  2. The Nmap Scripting Engine (NSE) executes Vulsploit.
- On the right side of Fig. 3 there is the asset (i.e., the N hosts) on which the target enumeration phase is carried out through Nmap. More precisely, Nmap
  1. using Vulscan searches for vulnerabilities of each port/service returned by Nmap;
  2. using Vulsploit searches for exploits related to the vulnerabilities found on each host.

3.1   Execution Flow

Vulsploit is composed of several logic components that interact with each other to carry out its duties. The actions performed by Vulsploit can be summarized as follows:

1. Execution of Vulscan, whose output is redirected to a file. Each line of this file roughly characterizes a vulnerability;
2. For each vulnerability present in this file, Vulsploit SEARCHES the relative exploits, making calls to local and/or remote repositories.

The following diagram outlines the detailed execution flow of vulsploit.nse.

As shown in Fig. 4, the general execution flow of Vulsploit can be summarized by the following main actions:

1. Vulsploit runs Vulscan to find the vulnerabilities on a given host, and redirects the output to a file.
2. After running Vulscan, the output file is read, row by row, by Vulsploit.
3. For each row:
   - If the row does not characterize a vulnerability but just a port number, a service, and a service version, this row is printed without performing any other action.
   - If the row corresponds to a vulnerability database:
     - If the database is Exploit-DB, Vulsploit makes a local query and returns the exploits.
     - If the database is OSVDB or MITRE CVE or any other database, Vulsploit makes a remote query and returns the exploits.
   - The exploits found by each local or remote query (or call) are eventually manipulated, returned, and then printed.

We remark that in general, for each database that requires making a remote query via API, the type of query to perform could change. In the following, we focus on the main components of the Vulsploit module.

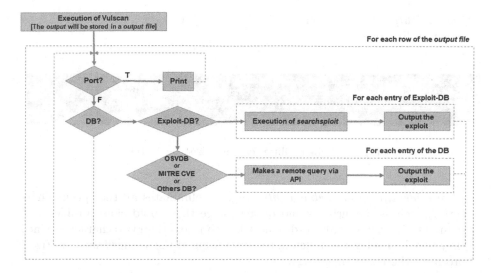

Fig. 4. `vulsploit.nse` execution flow.

3.2   Main Components

Scan and Search for Vulnerabilities. In detail, the first step performed by Vulsploit during its execution is searching for vulnerabilities. This search, whose output is redirected to a file, is performed through a script, called *Vulscan*, that provides the vulnerabilities found for a given host (or asset). An example of this step is shown in Fig. 5.

```
Starting Nmap 7.80 ( https://nmap.org ) at 2020-03-06 13:11 CET
Nmap scan report for 10.0.2.6
Host is up (0.00022s latency).
Not shown: 977 closed ports
PORT      STATE SERVICE      VERSION
21/tcp    open  ftp          vsftpd 2.3.4
| vulscan: VulDB - https://vuldb.com:
|   [43110] vsftpd up to 2.0.4 Memory Leak denial of service
|
|   MITRE CVE - https://cve.mitre.org:
|   [CVE-2011-0762] The vsf_filename_passes_filter function in ls.c in vsftpd before 2.3.3
| allows remote authenticated users to cause a denial of service (CPU consumption and process
| slot exhaustion) via crafted glob expressions in STAT commands in multiple FTP sessions, a
| different vulnerability than CVE-2010-2632.
|
```

Fig. 5. Initial output of the `Vulscan` script.

Data Parsing. As mentioned above, for each database that requires making a remote query via API, the type of query to perform could change. Therefore, before searching for the exploits through the appropriate query, depending on how this query needs to be structured, Vulsploit performs a different type of parsing of the data generated by Vulscan:

– *Vulnerability ID*: get the number in the square brackets, such as "*17491*", as shown in Fig. 6.

```
| Exploit-DB - https://www.exploit-db.com:
| [17491] VSFTPD 2.3.4 - Backdoor Command Execution
| [16270] vsftpd 2.3.2 - Denial of Service Vulnerability
|
```

Fig. 6. Vulnerabilities characterized by an ID.

– *Phrase identifying the vulnerability* (Fig. 7): eliminates all the special characters, such as parentheses and quotes, since they could cause problems in requests, and removes all words whose length is less than two characters since they may be irrelevant. In detail, the processing of the strings shown in Fig. 7 produces the following strings:

```
[13563] linux/x86 overwrite MBR on /dev/sda with `LOL!' 43 bytes
[13553] Linux - linux/x86 execve() - 51bytes
```

Fig. 7. Vulnerabilities characterized by a phrase.

- ''linux/x86 overwrite MBR/dev/sda with LOL43 bytes''
- ''Linux linux/x86 execve 51bytes''

– *CVE*, if present: The processing of the string shown in Fig. 8 produces the following string: CVE-2011-0762.

```
| MITRE CVE - https://cve.mitre.org:
| [CVE-2011-0762] The vsf_filename_passes_filter function in ls.c in vsftpd before 2.3.3
allows remote authenticated users to cause a denial of service (CPU consumption and process
slot exhaustion) via crafted glob expressions in STAT commands in multiple FTP sessions, a
different vulnerability than CVE-2010-2632.
|
```

Fig. 8. Vulnerabilities characterized by CVE.

Also, regarding the parsing of the other rows of the file which are not vulnerabilities:

– if it is a row of the type shown in Fig. 9 this line is printed;
– if instead it is a row of the type shown in Fig. 10 this line is ignored.

```
21/tcp     open  ftp              vsftpd 2.3.4
```

Fig. 9. Row of type:PORT STATE SERVICE VERSION

```
Starting Nmap 7.80 ( https://nmap.org ) at 2020-03-06 13:11 CET
Nmap scan report for 10.0.2.6
Host is up (0.00022s latency).
Not shown: 977 closed ports
```

Fig. 10. Initial script output.

Vulnerability Analysis and Exploit Research. After the parsing of each row of the file, local and/or remote queries are performed by Vulsploit to search for exploits related to detected vulnerabilities.

Data Presentation. We use the JSON format for the presentation of the data. More precisely, the result of both local and remote calls is returned in JSON format.

In detail, for remote calls, since no other manipulation of the result of such calls is performed, this result is printed. On the other hand, for local calls, the result is manipulated as follows:

1. Check if there are any working exploits, or if the response is empty or contains only the payloads of the found exploits.
2. Isolate the result if there are multiple exploits in the response. Notice that for each request, there may be multiple exploits that contain the ID between the fields, for example, in the date, in the title, etc.
3. Retrieve the exploit which matches the vulnerability (Fig. 11).

```
[17491] VSFTPD 2.3.4 - Backdoor Command Execution

    *** Exploits ***

    {"Title":"vsftpd 2.3.4 - Backdoor Command Execution
    (Metasploit)""EDB-ID":"17491""Date":"2011-07-05""Author":"Metasploit""Type":"remote""
    Platform":"unix"
    "Path":"/usr/share/exploitdb/exploits/unix/remote/17491.rb"}
```

Fig. 11. Vulnerability and related exploit (*partial output*).

3.3 Vulsploit Usage

The Vulsploit script can be executed with the following command:
nmap --script vulsploit/vulsploit.nse --script-args ''IP = 10.0.2.6'' 10.0.2.6
where:

- --script vulsploit/vulsploit.nse allows to execute the vulsploit.nse script;

- --script-args ''IP = 10.0.2.6'' pass arguments to the script, ''IP = 10.0.2.6'' is the IP address of the scanned hots;
- 10.0.2.6 is the IP address passed to Nmap for network scanning.
  - We remark that the IP passed to the script and the one passed to Nmap must be the same, otherwise the Vulsploit script analyzes one machine and Nmap another.

4   Preliminary Test Results

In this section, we show and discuss the preliminary experimental results obtained from the evaluation of Vulsploit. In particular, the purpose of the testing phase is twofold. First, we evaluate the effectiveness of Vulsploit in finding the appropriate exploits for the detected vulnerabilities. Second, we assess the performance of Vulsploit in terms of time when it deals with a large number of vulnerabilities to analyze. Before showing and discussing the experimental results obtained from the evaluation of our proposal, we first define the hardware and software environment used for the testing phase.

4.1   Hardware and Software Environment

To carry out the testing phase, we used Kali Linux, a distribution explicitly designed for security analysis. Besides, we used Metasploitable 2, a vulnerable by-design server distribution, which is based on Ubuntu (32- bit). This distribution was created by the *Rapid7 Metasploit* team. Again, Kali Linux is virtualized using VirtualBox, on the Microsoft Windows 10 operating system. Vulsploit is executed by Kali Linux on the Metasploitable 2 distribution.

In detail, we assigned the following resources to the virtual machine:

- 4 GB of RAM DDR3;
- 2 virtual cores on Intel® Core™ i5 4200M;
- 20 GB of memory, out of 237 GB of SSD available.

4.2   Execution Times and Discussions

The execution of the Vulscan script on Metasploitable2 found 23 open ports and roughly 220000 vulnerabilities.

Moreover, using the testing environment mentioned above, Vulsploit was able to process about half (i.e., 113489 vulnerabilities) of the file produced by Vulscan, containing the found vulnerabilities. The processing of such part of the file took considerable time, i.e., about 51 h, that is, 2 days and 3 hours. Although this is a large amount of time, it is nevertheless a tolerable amount. Notice that the PT activity is generally not conducted in real-time, but periodically, at dates typically not very close to each other.

However, we remark that manually searching for exploits would take a significantly longer amount of time. The following rough calculation can show the amount of time spent by the pentester using a manual approach. In detail, assuming that an exhaustive manual exploits search for each vulnerability takes about 1 minutes, that search would take 113489 minutes $\approx$ 1891.48 hours $\approx$ 78.81 days.

5 Conclusions and Future Work

The process of finding an exploit is a very time-consuming activity, even more so when the vulnerabilities detected are many, and the pentester is not very experienced or prepared. One of the most challenging tasks of this activity is searching for exploits to take advantage of the detected vulnerabilities. This activity becomes even more challenging when, for each detected vulnerability, there could be many exploits.

First of all, this paper aimed to define a general approach that allows the collection and integration of data from various exploit repositories. Any exploits collected are then used to provide the pentester with indications on which exploit to choose to conduct the *exploitation* phase of the Penetration Testing process effectively.

We highlight that our approach is not focused on the vulnerability mapping phase, which is carried out through *Vulscan*. On the other hand, our approach is focused on the automatic finding of the exploits that can be used to take advantage of the results achieved by such a phase.

A proof of concept of the proposed approach has been implemented and integrated through a Nmap script. More precisely, our proposal has been implemented through a NSE script. This script, called Vulsploit, is based on technologies such as Nmap [19], the Lua language [17,18], searchsploit, cURL, and the Shodan API [5]. The information provided by the Shodan API is important and will be increasingly important, given the ever-increasing diffusion and heterogeneity of connected devices. In detail, Vulsploit makes use of another NSE script, which is a *vulnerability scanner* provided by Nmap called Vulscan, to find the exploits available for the vulnerabilities detected by this scan.

The results obtained were quite satisfying since we could obtain the exploit information on thousands of vulnerabilities in a tolerable amount of time, obtaining a substantial saving compared to the manual approach. This time improvement is a considerable advantage, especially if we consider that penetration testing is a routine activity that is typically not conducted in real-time.

Although the results obtained are satisfactory, we could do better in future work, considering more efficient approaches. A first improvement that could be applied is to parallelize the execution of Vulsploit, in order to make calls to the various exploit repositories in parallel. Furthermore, after having parallelized the script, it could be distributed across multiple hosts, using a distributed or fully distributed paradigm. Besides, we want to improve the performance of Vulsploit through caching mechanisms. The three improvements mentioned above could increase the efficiency of our proposal, reducing execution times. Besides, some other data sources could be integrated to provide a broader set of available exploits. Moreover, current PT practice is becoming repetitive, complex, and resource-consuming despite automated tools. Therefore, since there is an ongoing interest in exploring the potential of *artificial intelligence (AI)* to enhance penetration testing and vulnerability identification of systems [22], we intend to investigate AI techniques to enhance the automation of the PT process further. In particular, we intend to investigate intelligent PT approaches using *reinforcement learning (RL)* that will allow regular and systematic testing, saving human resources [15, 16]. Using trained machine learning agents to automate this process is an important research area that still needs to be explored. Moreover, to decrease the time required by remote fetches, we want to use pre-fetching techniques to get the full remote repositories and keeping them updated.

To conclude, we remark that despite all the extensions and improvements described above to integrate and enhance our proposal, Vulsploit may still be very useful at present to those who carry out PT activities.

References

1. Al-Ahmad, A.S., Kahtan, H., Hujainah, F., Jalab, H.A.: Systematic literature review on penetration testing for mobile cloud computing applications. IEEE Access **7**, 173524–173540 (2019)
2. Ali, B., Awad, A.: Cyber and physical security vulnerability assessment for IoT-based smart homes. Sensors **18**(3), 817 (2018)
3. Almubairik, N.A., Wills, G.: Automated penetration testing based on a threat model. In: 2016 11th International Conference for Internet Technology and Secured Transactions (ICITST), pp. 413–414 (2016)
4. Ankele, R., Marksteiner, S., Nahrgang, K., Vallant, H.: Requirements and recommendations for IoT/IIoT models to automate security assurance through threat modelling, security analysis and penetration testing. In: Proceedings of the 14th International Conference on Availability, Reliability and Security. ARES 2019. Association for Computing Machinery (2019)
5. Bodenheim, R., Butts, J., Dunlap, S., Mullins, B.: Evaluation of the ability of the Shodan search engine to identify internet-facing industrial control devices. Int. J. Crit. Infrastruct. Prot. **7**(2), 114–123 (2014)
6. Bojjagani, S., Sastry, V.N.: VAPTAi: a threat model for vulnerability assessment and penetration testing of android and iOS mobile banking apps. In: 2017 IEEE 3rd International Conference on Collaboration and Internet Computing (CIC), pp. 77–86 (2017)
7. Casola, V., De Benedictis, A., Rak, M., Villano, U.: Towards automated penetration testing for cloud applications. In: 2018 IEEE 27th International Conference on Enabling Technologies: Infrastructure for Collaborative Enterprises (WETICE), pp. 24–29 (2018)
8. Casola, V., De Benedictis, A., Rak, M., Villano, U.: A methodology for automated penetration testing of cloud applications. Int. J. Grid Util. Comput. **11**(2), 267–277 (2020)
9. Ceccato, M., Scandariato, R.: Static analysis and penetration testing from the perspective of maintenance teams. In: Proceedings of the 10th ACM/IEEE International Symposium on Empirical Software Engineering and Measurement. ESEM 2016. Association for Computing Machinery (2016)
10. Chaudhary, S., O'Brien, A., Xu, S.: Automated post-breach penetration testing through reinforcement learning. In: 2020 IEEE Conference on Communications and Network Security (CNS), pp. 1–2 (2020)
11. Chen, C., Zhang, Z., Lee, S., Shieh, S.: Penetration testing in the IoT age. Computer **51**(4), 82–85 (2018)

12. Chu, G., Lisitsa, A.: Penetration testing for internet of things and its automation. In: 2018 IEEE 20th International Conference on High Performance Computing and Communications; IEEE 16th International Conference on Smart City; IEEE 4th International Conference on Data Science and Systems (HPCC/SmartCity/DSS), pp. 1479–1484 (2018)
13. Denis, M., Zena, C., Hayajneh, T.: Penetration testing: concepts, attack methods, and defense strategies. In: 2016 IEEE Long Island Systems, Applications and Technology Conference (LISAT), pp. 1–6 (2016)
14. Fischer, M., Langer, F., Mono, J., Nasenberg, C., Albartus, N.: Hardware penetration testing knocks your SoCs off. IEEE Des. Test **PP**, 1 (2020)
15. Ghanem, M.C., Chen, T.M.: Reinforcement learning for intelligent penetration testing. In: 2018 Second World Conference on Smart Trends in Systems, Security and Sustainability (WorldS4), pp. 185–192 (2018)
16. Ghanem, M.C., Chen, T.M.: Reinforcement learning for efficient network penetration testing. Information **11**(1), 6 (2019)
17. Ierusalimschy, R., De Figueiredo, L.H., Filho, W.C.: Lua - an extensible extension language. Softw. Pract. Exp. **26**(6), 635–652 (1996)
18. Ierusalimschy, R., de Figueiredo, L.H., Celes, W.: The evolution of Lua. In: Proceedings of the third ACM SIGPLAN Conference on History of Programming Languages, pp. 1–2 (2007)
19. Lyon, G.F.: Nmap Network Scanning: The Official Nmap Project Guide to Network Discovery and Security Scanning. Insecure, Sunnyvale (2009)
20. Mahmoodi, Y., Reiter, S., Viehl, A., Bringmann, O., Rosenstiel, W.: Attack surface modeling and assessment for penetration testing of IoT system designs. In: 2018 21st Euromicro Conference on Digital System Design (DSD), pp. 177–181 (2018)
21. Markopoulou, D., Papakonstantinou, V., de Hert, P.: The new EU cybersecurity framework: the NIS directive, ENISA's role and the general data protection regulation. Comput. Law Secur. Rev. **35**(6), 105336 (2019)
22. McKinnel, D.R., Dargahi, T., Dehghantanha, A., Choo, K.K.R.: A systematic literature review and meta-analysis on artificial intelligence in penetration testing and vulnerability assessment. Comput. Electr. Eng. **75**, 175–188 (2019)
23. Pale, P.C.: Mastering the Nmap Scripting Engine. Packt Publishing Ltd., Birmingham (2015)
24. Rahman, A., Williams, L.: A bird's eye view of knowledge needs related to penetration testing. In: Proceedings of the 6th Annual Symposium on Hot Topics in the Science of Security. HotSoS 2019. Association for Computing Machinery (2019)
25. Schwartz, J., Kurniawati, H.: Autonomous penetration testing using reinforcement learning. CoRR abs/1905.05965 (2019)
26. Shebli, H.M.Z.A., Beheshti, B.D.: A study on penetration testing process and tools. In: 2018 IEEE Long Island Systems, Applications and Technology Conference (LISAT), pp. 1–7 (2018)
27. Stefinko, Y., Piskozub, A., Banakh, R.: Manual and automated penetration testing. Benefits and drawbacks. Modern tendency. In: 2016 13th International Conference on Modern Problems of Radio Engineering, Telecommunications and Computer Science (TCSET), pp. 488–491 (2016)
28. Voigt, P., Von dem Bussche, A.: The EU General Data Protection Regulation (GDPR). A Practical Guide, 1st Edn. Springer, Cham (2017). https://doi.org/10.1007/978-3-319-57959-7
29. Zennaro, F.M., Erdodi, L.: Modeling penetration testing with reinforcement learning using capture-the-flag challenges and tabular Q-learning. arXiv preprint arXiv:2005.12632 (2020)

About the Robustness and Looseness of Yara Rules

Gerardo Canfora, Mimmo Carapella, Andrea Del Vecchio, Laura Nardi,
Antonio Pirozzi$^{(\boxtimes)}$, and Corrado Aaron Visaggio

Department of Engineering, University of Sannio, Benevento, Italy
{canfora,pirozzi,visaggio}@unisannio.it,
{m.carapella1,a.delvecchio2,l.nardi}@studenti.unisannio.it

Abstract. The tremendous and fast growth of malware circulating in
the wild urges the community of malware analysts to rapidly and effectively share knowledge about the arising threats. Among the other solutions, Yara is establishing as a de facto standard for describing and
exchanging Indicators of Compromise (IOCs). Unfortunately, the community of malware analysts did not agree on a set of guidelines for writing
Yara rules: a plethora of very different styles for formalizing IOCs can be
observed, indeed. Our thesis is that different styles of Yara rule writing
could affect the quality of IOCs. With this paper we provide: (i) the definition of two dimensions of Yara rules quality, namely *Robustness* and
Looseness; (ii) a taxonomy for describing the kinds of IOCs that can be
formalized with the Yara grammar, and (iii) a suite of metrics for measuring the quality of an IOC. Finally, we carried out a study on 32,311
Yara rules for examining the different existing styles and to investigate
the relationship between the writing styles and the quality of IOCs.

Keywords: Yara · Malware classification · Threat intelligence ·
Threat hunting

1 Introduction

The information necessary to recognize and classify malware is captured through
the indicators of compromise (IOCs in the remainder of the paper), which are
generally divided into three categories [9]: Network, Host-based indicators and
Email indicators. An indicator of compromise for a malware is a set of properties
regarding the structure or the behavior of a malicious software, which are able
to identify a specific malicious software. An IOC is written by an analyst who
intercepted and dissected the malware, likely in the early stages of its diffusion in
the network. Thus the analyst propagates this IOC through informative channels.
So far, many formats for writing IOCs have been proposed and used [3,6,11].
Even if none of them has yet been chosen as an official standard, without any
doubt we can state that Yara is establishing as the de facto standard in the
malware analysts' community. Yara allows analysts to define IOC in the form of

© IFIP International Federation for Information Processing 2020
Published by Springer Nature Switzerland AG 2020
V. Casola et al. (Eds.): ICTSS 2020, LNCS 12543, pp. 104–120, 2020.
https://doi.org/10.1007/978-3-030-64881-7_7

a program, namely a Yara Rule. Different papers in literature mention the quality of an IOC as a relevant issue to face; authors in [10] point two dimensions of an IOC's data quality which need to be evaluated: verifiability and believability. Tounsi and Rais [12] observe that a strong limit of IOC is to keep up to date with respect to the high variability of malware. Currently, there is not a defined process for writing a Yara Rule which could take into account these aspects of an IOC quality. Therefore analysts still rely on their own experience and ability. Such a lack of a shared discipline for writing a Yara Rule determines a high variety of styles among the authors. It may be reasonable to hypothesize that the style can have a relationship with the *quality* of the Yara Rules, as it happens in the programming languages. Measuring rule's quality would mean being able to choose the best use case in which to use them. This point is paramount for the implementation of an effective Threat Intelligence Toolchain for classification or hunting tasks and to speed up the whole malware triaging process. There is not a definition of *quality* for a Yara Rule: at the best knowledge of the authors this is the first work that attempts to investigate the aspects determining the *quality* of a Yara Rule. With *quality* of a Yara Rule we mean the ability of the Rule to be accurate in detecting the intended malware. We propose a model for defining and measuring the *quality* of a Yara Rule, namely the $\mathcal{R}$-$\mathcal{L}$ Model. In our model, we consider two aspects of the *quality* of a Yara Rule. The first aspect concerns the *robustness* of the Rule, i.e. richness and diversity of IOC types used to detect the malware. The second aspect regards the *looseness* of the Yara Rule, i.e. the ability to recognize some behaviors or features of a certain malware occurring in other malware. The concept of *looseness* is balanced by the opposite concept of *tightness*. A tight rule is not able to recognize a malware family or a malware behavior, but only an exact malware instance. Finally, we carried out a study on 32,311 Yara Rules, investigating the relationships between the indicators identified with our model and the quality of a Yara Rule. This paper provides for a triple contribution:

- a definition of *quality* of a Yara Rule, declined in the two concepts of *Robustness* and *Looseness*;
- a set of metrics for measuring the *Robustness* and *Looseness*;
- a study that correlates our measurement model with the actual *detection performances* of a Yara Rule.

The paper continues as follows: Sect. 2 discusses the novelty brought by this work with respect to the state of the art. Section 3 explains in depth the definitions of Robustness and Looseness, while Sect. 4 describes how the study was designed and carried out. Finally, results are analyzed in Sect. 5 and the main findings along with the evolution of this work are summarized in Sect. 6.

2 State of the Art

So far, not many efforts have been spent for investigating Yara Rules. However, none till now has directly addressed the problem of quality assessment of Yara Rules.

At the best of authors' knowledge, the only paper that explores the relationship between Yara Rules and malware analysis is [7], that describes a mechanism to boost the triaging performances of Yara Rules by adding references to *fuzzy hashing* of a specific sample. Scientific research in this area focused mainly on automatizing the process of rules and patterns generation and, consequently, on the automatic generation of IOCs, in order to ease and accelerate the work of malware analysts. Biondi et al. in [1] define a tool with a modular *client/server* architecture which generates new Yara Rules with dynamic and static analysis. Similarly, authors in [5] describe a IDA-Pro plug-in which can identify imported cryptography functions, used by a malware specimen, and generate a Yara hexadecimal signature for each of the captured functions.

Other researchers, instead, in order to achieve quality and resilience of detection, focused on the difference between *Observable Patterns* and *Observable Instances*, as described by [2]. Basically, the difference is that an *Observable Pattern*, also defined as Pattern Based IOC, describes a specific class of IOCs, while an *Observable Instance* is an actual instance of a class. To achieve this goal, the already cited [2] and [4] propose respectively a method and a tool to automatically produce pattern based IOCs, in order to make the detection as reliable as possible, ensuring accuracy, elasticity and interpretability. The proposed study aims to address the quality assessment in a holistic way investigating the key properties of a Yara Rule and how these properties affect the reliability of the Rule in different circumstances.

3   The $\mathcal{R}$-$\mathcal{L}$ Model

The $\mathcal{R}$-$\mathcal{L}$ model is aimed at evaluating the quality of a Yara Rule. It describes two properties of a Yara Rule: the **Robustness** ($\mathcal{R}$) and the **Looseness** ($\mathcal{L}$).

The **Robustness** of a Yara Rule is the capability of matching the intended malware, the intended malware families or the intended malicious behavior. The term "*Robustness*" refers to the desirable property of a Yara Rule to keep valid even when some IOCs of the malware change over time. This may happen in several cases; typical cases include but are not limited to: change in IP and domain of C&C, dropped files with different names, different names for mutexes, different signatures.

The **Looseness** of a Yara Rule is the capability of matching some behaviors or characteristics of the intended malware or malware families also in other malware or malware families.

This property allows a Yara Rule to identify malware variants of the intended malware, or malware families the intended malware belongs to. An inherent peculiarity of the malware evolution is the proliferation of malware variants. A malware variant is a modified version of an existing malware. It is important to recognize that a malware is a variant, because it may accelerate the triage stages, increasing the probability of an early intervention. Moreover, the reuse of (parts of) existing malware or the replication of some features in new malware is a common practice among the malware authors, as every analyst may experience, and that is often documented by the malware analysis reports. If a Yara Rule is able to identify specific behaviors, like a certain evasion technique, a boot survival mechanism, a system for realizing a lateral movement, it could help analysts profile more quickly the malware. Similarly, finding behaviors of known malware families in new malware through a Yara Rule can allow analysts to obtain a more accurate malware phylogeny, i.e. all the malware families the malware derives from. The Robustness of a Yara Rule concerns the *reliability* of its accuracy, i.e. it remains valid even when malware changes. For this reason, we could state that Robustness is a *vertical* capability of a Yara Rule. The Looseness of a Yara Rule concerns the *versatility* of its accuracy, i.e. it can be used to catch features of one malware within other instances. For this reason, we could state that Looseness is a *horizontal* capability of a Yara Rule. Yara syntax offers a malware analyst the opportunity to define many types of IOCs for classifying a malware. Of course, some of them could be *malware-redundant*, i.e. adequate for many instances, besides the malware to match. Others could be *malware-specific*, i.e. they are verified uniquely by the malware to match. In order to evaluate the Robustness, we drew up the catalogue of all the types of IOCs that can be expressed with the Yara language. For each IOC, Table 1 and Table 2 show the regular expressions which help localize the respective IOCs in the Yara Rule, respectively in the *strings* section and in the *conditions* section.

```
rule APT17_Sample_FXSST_DLL
{

    meta:
        description = "Detects Samples related to APT17 activity - file FXSST.DLL"
        author = "Florian Roth"
        reference = "https://goo.gl/ZiJyQv"
        date = "2015-05-14"
        hash = "52f1add5ad28dc30f68afda5d41b354533d8bce3"

    strings:
        $x1 = "Microsoft? Windows? Operating System" fullword wide
        $x2 = "fxsst.dll" fullword ascii
        $y1 = "DllRegisterServer" fullword ascii
        $y2 = ".cSV" fullword ascii
        $s1 = "GetLastActivePopup"
        $s2 = "Sleep"
        $s3 = "GetModuleFileName"
        $s4 = "VirtualProtect"
        $s5 = "HeapAlloc"
        $s6 = "GetProcessHeap"
        $s7 = "GetCommandLine"

    condition:
        uint16(0) == 0x5a4d and filesize < 800KB and ( 1 of ($x*)
                            or all of ($y*) ) and all of ($s*)
}
```

Fig. 1. An exemplar Yara Rule.

The $\mathcal{R}$-$\mathcal{L}$ model relies on the assumption that the Robustness and the Looseness of a Yara Rule may depend on: (i) the number of IOCs, (ii) the types of IOCs, (iii) the values of IOCs, and (iv) the conditions used in the Rule.

Given a Rule r, we can define the following metrics:

- the *amount* A_r, which counts the overall number of IOCs used in the Rule,
- the *diversity* D_r, which counts the different types of IOCs used, and
- the *distribution* N_r, which counts the density of each IOC in the rule.

Given the *diversity* of a Yara Rule D_r, the *amount* A_r is measured as:

$$A_r = \sum_{k=1}^{D_r} n_k$$

where n_k is the number of IOCs of k type. We define n_k as the *cardinality* of the k-th IOC. The *distribution* of r, N_r, is measured as:

$$N_r = \frac{D_r}{A_r}$$

It must be noticed that:

$$N_r \in]0, 1]$$

where

$$N_r = 1 \iff A_r = D_r$$

i.e. all the IOCs of the Rule belong to different types.

$$N_r \neq 0$$

$\forall r$, since it can not exist a Rule without any IOC.

The *Robustness* of r is:

$$\mathcal{R}_r = (A_r, D_r, N_r)$$

The *Looseness* of r, $\mathcal{L}_r$, is:

$$\mathcal{L}_r = (\mathcal{F}_r, \mathcal{M}_r)$$

where $\mathcal{M}_r$ is the number of malware that match r, while $\mathcal{F}_r$ is the number of malware families that match r.

As an example, let's consider the Rule r taken from a public repository[1] showed in Fig. 1. The **Robustness** parameters are computed as follows:

- $A_r = 11$
- $D_r = 2$
- $N_r = 0.18$

---

[1] https://github.com/Yara-Rules/rules/blob/master/malware/APT_APT17.yar, accessed on 12th March.

Table 1. List of the IOCs used for evaluating the Robustness of a Yara Rule.

IOC	Description	Regular Expression
Uniform Resource Locators	Captures Yara Rule's strings referring to URL.	`([A-Za-z]+://)([-\w]+(?:\.\w[-\w]+)+)(:\d+)?(/[^.!,?"<>\[\]{}\s\x7F-\xFF]*(?:[.!,?]+[^.!,?"<>\[\]{}\s\x7F-\xFF]+)*)?`
Dynamic-Link Libraries and their functions	Captures Yara Rule's strings referring to dll and their functions.	`.*\.dll\s*`
Win32 Library	Captures Yara Rule's strings referring to dll Win32 functions.	`^[A-Z]\w{2,10}([A-Z](\w){3,10}){1,6}$`
IP Addresses (IPv4)	Captures Yara Rule's strings referring to IP addresses v4.	`(?:(?:\d[01]?\d\d|2[0-4]\d|25[0-5])\.){3}(?:25[0-5]|2[0-4]\d|[01]?\d\d|\d)(?:\/\d{1,2})?`
IP Addresses (IPv6)	Captures Yara Rule's strings referring to Ip addresses v6	`((?=.*:.)(?!.*::.*::)(::)?([\dA-Fa-f]{1,4}:(:|\b)|){5}|([\dA-Fa-f]{1,4}:){6})(([\dA-Fa-f]{1,4}((?!\3)::|:\b|(?![\dA-Fa-f]))|(?!\2\3)){2}|((2[0-4]|1\d|[1-9])?\d|25[0-5])\.?\b){4})`
Domains	Captures Yara Rule's strings referring to Domain Names.	`\b((?=[a-z0-9-]{1,63}\.)(xn--)?[a-z0-9]+(-[a-z0-9]+)*\.)+[a-z^(exe)^(dll)]{2,63}(?<!exe)$(?<!dll)$(?<!png)$(?<!html)$(?<!htm)$(?<!ini)$(?<!bin)$(?<!php)$(?<!pdb)$(?<!dat)$(?<!sys)$(?<!txt)$(?<!log)$(?<!asp)$(?<!tmp)$(?<!xml)$(?<!js)$(?<!sh)$(?<!gui)$(?<!bmp)$(?<!dbg)$(?<!db)$(?<!apk)$(?<!asp)$(?<!pdf)$(?<!jpg)$(?<!dex)$(?<!qrk)$(?<!cgi)$(?<!manifest)$(?<!wc)$(?<!rtf)$(?<!gif)$(?<!lz)$(?<!nse)$(?<!plist)$(?<!sh)$(?<!ocx)$(?<!key)$(?<!gho)$\b`
Unix file Paths	Captures Yara Rule's strings referring to Unix systems file paths.	`(?:/[A-Za-z\d.][A-Za-z\d\-.]{0,61})+`
Windows file Paths	Captures Yara Rule's strings referring to Windows systems file paths.	`([A-Za-z]{1}:\\{1,2})?(\\{1,}[A-Za-z0-9]+)(\\{0,}[A-Za-z0-9]+\\{0,})+\\{0,}`
Email addresses	Captures Yara Rule's strings referring to email addresses.	`\b(\w[-.\w]*)@([-\w]+(?:\.[-\w]+)*)\.([A-Za-z]{2,4})\b`
Generic files	Captures Yara Rule's strings referring to files.	`.*\.[a-z]{3,4}\s*`
Portable Executable files	Captures Yara Rule's strings referring to pe files.	`[A-Za-z0-9_-]*\.exe\s*`
XML/HTML tags	Captures Yara Rule's strings referring to XML and Html tags, distinguishing among generic tags and open tags.	For open tag: `\<[^\>]+\>[A-Za-z\d-:]*$` For generic tag: `<[^<=~'\"\\0-9>](\s|\w)+>?(</(\s|\w)+>?)?`
Registry keys	Captures Yara Rushowed in figurele's strings referring to registry keys usage.	`((HKEY_LOCAL_MACHINE|HKLM|HKCU)\\.*)`
SQL code fragments	Captures Yara Rule's strings referring to SQL commands and code fragments.	`(?:INSERT\sINTO|SELECT|DELETE\sFROM|CREATE\s(TABLE|DATABASE)|DROP\s(TABLE|DATABASE)|FOREIGN\sKEY|GROUP\sBY|IF\sEXISTS|UNION)\s+(\s|[^;])+;*$`
Hash	Captures Yara Rule's strings referring to hash, in the form of MD5, SHA1 and SHA256.	MD5: `^(0[x|X])?[A-Fa-f0-9]{32}$` SHA1: `^(0[x\|X])?[A-Fa-f0-9]{40}$` SHA256: `^(0[x|X])?[A-Fa-f0-9]{64}$`
Universally unique Identifiers	Captures Yara Rule's strings referring to UUID (format: 8-4-4-4-12).	`[a-f0-9]{8}-[a-f0-9]{4}-[a-f0-9]{4}-[a-f0-9]{4}-[a-f0-9]{12}`
MAC Addresses	Captures Yara Rule's strings referring to MAC addresses.	`(([0-9A-F]{2}|[\%0-9a-z]{2,4})[:-]){5}([0-9A-F]{2}|[\%0-9a-z]{2,4})`
Http headers	Captures Yara Rule's strings referring to generic Http headers, including the first Http request string and the user-agent header field.	Generic: `^((\w{1}-\w{3,})|(\w{2,})|(\w[\w-]+)):\s+\w\w(\s|\w)+` Regex for first http request string and for user-agent header field: `(POST)|(GET)|(PUT)|(.?HTTP/\d\.\d)|((User-Agent:)?(Mozilla)|([A-Za-z0-9]*)/\d\.\d)`
Http payload	Captures Yara Rule's strings referring to Http payloads.	`^&?(([A-Za-z0-9\%./\[\]]{2,}=[^\s;,<>\"\\/=]*)&?)+`
Generic code fragments	Capture Yara Rule's strings refferring to code fragments.	`[^(<>&(\*\%+\\/!\?)]+\((.*)\)?`
Strings connected to keylogging	Captures Yara Rule's strings referring to keylogging.	`^\[\w[^:,(),\[\]]'.\\\"{}=_]*\]$`
Shell commands or references	Captures Yara Rule's strings related to shell commands or references to them.	`(CMD.EXE|POWERSHELL|SHELL)`
Environment Variables	Captures Yara Rule's strings referring to environment variables.	`\%[A-Za-z_]{2,}\%`
Hexadecimal Strings	No regular expression was considered to retrieve information about this field, thanks to the support of Plyara, wich is able to directly identify hexadecimal strings.	-
Regular expressions	No regular expression was considered to retieve information about this field, thanks to the support of Plyara, wich is able to directly identify strings in the form of regular expression.	-
YARA modules used	Captures references to Yara modules' used, with a special focus on pe module and its functions.	For generic module: `(\w+\.{1}\w+(\.{1}\w+)*((\([\w*.+/\\s\"=,.:?]|*))|(\s?(==)\s?[\w*.+/\\s\"=,.:?]*)))` For pe module: `(\w+\.{1}\w+(\([\w*.+/\\s\"=,()]|]\)?\s?(\.{1,}\w+)*(\([\w\\s\"=,.]*|.]*))?\s?((?!(and)|(or))\w+)?\s?((==)?\s?((\"[\w\\s\=,:/.]*\")|([\w\=,:/.]*)))?)`
Plain text strings	If a certain string did not match any of the described regular expressions, it was considered as a plain text string.	-
Base64 Strings	Captures Yara Rule's strings written in Base64 encoding scheme.	`^([A-Za-z0-9+\/]{4})*([A-Za-z0-9+\/]{2}={1,2}$\|[A-Za-z0-9+\/]{3}=$)`

D_r is 2 because \$x2 belongs to the category *Dynamic-Link libraries and their functions*, while \$x1, \$y1-2, \$s1-7 belong to the category *plain text strings*. Finally, we can conclude that:

$$\mathcal{R}_r = (11, 2, 0.18).$$

We can tell that r uses only 2 types of IOCs, with a strong density: as a matter of fact, the amount of IOCs is 11; the high value of A_r suggests that the Rule is reliable, even if the low distribution may weaken the Robustness of r, since variants of new malware could be matched with other types of IOCs. The *Looseness* measures how many correct matches a Rule has, and may be calculated with regards to a reference repository of malware. By submitting r to Hybrid Analysis (one of the two platforms used for the study discussed later), we obtain the following ***Looseness*** parameters:

- $\mathcal{M}_r = 10$
- $\mathcal{F}_r = 36$

Finally, we can conclude that:

$$\mathcal{L}_r = (10, 36)$$

The Rule r shows a good versatility, as it allows to match 10 different malware and 36 different malware families.

4   The Study Design

The goal of this study is to investigate the diversity of the styles adopted by the malware analysts for writing Yara Rules and the impact of the different styles on the quality of Yara Rules. The quality of Yara Rules will be evaluated with the $\mathcal{R}\text{-}\mathcal{L}$ model. The study is structured in three Research Questions:

- **RQ$_1$: which are the styles adopted by the authors of Yara Rules?** This RQ is aimed at profiling the main approaches used for writing Yara Rule in order to identify good and bad practices.
- **RQ$_2$: which IOCs are mostly used in versatile Rules?** This RQ is aimed at investigating which styles can be found in rules with high values of $\mathcal{M}_r$ and $\mathcal{F}_r$.
- **RQ$_3$: is Robustness correlated with the Looseness of a Yara Rule?** This RQ is aimed at understanding whether, given a Yara Rule r, A_r, N_r, and D_r are related to the $\mathcal{M}_r$ and $\mathcal{F}_r$.

Table 2. List of the Conditions used for evaluating the Robustness of a Yara Rule.

Condition	Regular Expression
and conditions	`.+?\sand\s.+?`
or conditions	`.+?\sor\s.+?`
not conditions	`.*?not\s.+?`
filesize conditions	`.+filesize.?`
all of ... conditions (e.g. all of them or $string*)	`all\sof\s(them|\(\$.*?\))`
any of ... conditions (e.g. any of them or $string*)	`any\sof\s(them|\(\$.+?(,\$.+?)*?\))`
Subset of strings conditions (e.g. 2 of them)	`\d+\sof\s(them|\(\$.+?(,\$.+?)*?\))`
Entire set of strings conditions (e.g. $string*)	`\${1}\w*\*{1}`
Offset conditions (e.g. $string1 at 200):	`.+at\s(0(x|X)[0-9a-fA-F]+|\d+|\(.+?\))`
Range conditions (e.g. $string1 in (0..filesize))	`.+in\s\((\d+|.+?)\.{2}(\d+|.+?)\)`
Position conditions (e.g. uint16(0) == ...)	`u?int(8|16|32)(be)?`
Serial number of certificates	`pe\.signatures).*serial.*==.*`
Issuer/subject conditions	`(pe\.signatures).*(issuer|subject).*(contains).*`

4.1   The Dataset

The dataset used in the study contains 32,311 Rules collected from the following sources:

- a catalogue of Yara Rules written by McAfee ATR Team[2];
- the InQuest awesome Yara collection[3];
- a catalogue of Yara Rules publicly available on github repository[4]
- the VALHALLA collection[5];
- the YOROI ZLab YARA Rules collection[6].

   Because of the many different versions of Yara used by the authors of the rules, not all the collected Rules were compliant with the process of gathering and analysis. Moreover, some Rules were affected by typos, which prevented them from being scanned. For this reason, 51 files[7] were discarded.

4.2   Data Collection

In order to evaluate how many malware and how many malware families were matched by each Rule in dataset, we submitted the Rules to two of the most

---

[2] https://github.com/advanced-threat-research/Yara-Rules, last access on 23rd march 2020.

[3] https://github.com/InQuest/awesome-yara, last access on 23rd march 2020.

[4] https://github.com/Yara-Rules/rules, last access on 23rd march 2020.

[5] https://www.nextron-systems.com/yara-rule-feed/, last access on 23rd march 2020.

[6] https://yoroi.company/research/, last access on 23rd march 2020.

[7] It must be recalled here that a file may contain more than one rule.

popular platforms for threat intelligence: Hybrid Analysis[8] (HA from here on) and VirusTotal[9] (VT from here on). In particular, Hybrid Analysis provides a list of files containing the matched instances of malware, the malware families, and the indicators that caused the match. Moreover, for each submitted Rule, we identified:

- First Sample: submission date of the least recent report returned for a certain Rule.
- Last Sample: submission date of the most recent report returned for a certain Rule.

We referred VirusTotal mainly as an oracle, in the sense that we gathered from this platform a variety of information to check the accuracy and the consistency of that collected from Hybrid Analysis.

4.3   Information Gathering Process for the Looseness

The indicators contained in a Rule were extracted through a process organized in a sequence of tasks. First, every Yara Rule of the dataset was parsed by Plyara [8] in order to transform each Rule in the form of a Dictionary data structure, i.e. a sequence of key-value pairs, where the key is the name of the Rule and the value is a string containing the body of the Rule. For each Rule, a Retrohunting task on HA was performed, in order to find and collect samples that were matched by that Rule. The submission of Yara Rules on HA and the activation of a Retrohunting task were automated by a web scraper written with Python[10] by the authors.

For each sample identified in the previous step, VT was queried through its public REST API, by submitting the hash of the malware, in order to obtain the information of interest. Then, for each sample, classification signatures from the different AVs were retrieved.

4.4   Information Gathering Process for Evaluating the Robustness

The collection process for each Rule was based exclusively on Plyara and the script described in the previous section. A set of regular expressions was defined to identify the different kinds of indicators occurring in the Rule. By using Plyara functionalities, every file of the dataset was parsed and its rules were disassembled into their basic elements, i.e. `metadata`, `strings` and `conditions`. For each Rule, Plyara returned a dictionary which contained data for type, name and value of a string. This value was compared to each regular expression in order to find a specific pattern, thus allowing the classification of each string.

---

[8] https://www.hybrid-analysis.com/, last access on 13th March 2020.
[9] https://www.virustotal.com/gui/, last access on 13th March 2020.
[10] https://www.python.org/.

5   Results

This section discusses how the study's results may help to reply to the three Research Questions.

5.1   Results for RQ$_1$: Which Are the Styles Adopted by the Authors of Yara Rules?

In order to get the picture of the styles adopted by the analysts for writing the Yara Rules, we can examine the distributions of the *amount, diversity*, and *distribution* that we have characterized through the following parameters of descriptive statistics (see Table 3): the maximum, the minimum, the mean, the median, the first and the third quartile, the mode, and the standard deviation.

The first observation is that the most Rules are very light, as the 75% of the dataset contained less than two indicators with a distribution of 1, and that this combination represents also the most common one, as the mode parameter shows; the 25% of the dataset has only one IOC. We should mention that there are some Rules that are exceptionally overloaded with IOCs, as the maximum value measured is 1361.

Table 3. The results of RQ$_1$

Amount	Diversity	Distribution	Parameter
1361	11	1	Max
0	0	0	Min
2.929	1.826	0.866	Mean
2	2	1	Median
1	1	0.8	1qt
2	2	1	3qt
2	2	1	Mode
11.24	0.89	0.25	St dev

However, the variability of the amount is not that huge ($\sigma_{amount} = 11.24$), but it is very low for the diversity ($\sigma_{diversity} = 0.89$), which confirms that malware analysts tend to use a very limited number of IOC types (one or two, as previously observed), and when the number of IOCs is greater than 2, it tends to stay small, except for very rare cases. We could distinguish between *light* Rules, i.e. the ones containing a few parameters (2 ± 1) and *overloaded* Rules, which contain many parameters (≥ 13). Two indicators mainly contribute to the maximum outliers, more precisely *domains* and *hexadecimal strings*, which means that overloaded Rules are due to an excessive number of domains and signatures. Mode, median and third quartile are zero for all the IOCs except for *hexadecimal string*, for whom the value of the three parameters is 1.

This means that the distribution of IOC types is not uniform in the dataset, while the *hexadecimal string* is the most frequent IOC. Even if the mean is a tricky parameter as it is influenced by extreme values, it can be used to confirm the previous interpretations: the *hexadecimal string* appears in almost every Rule ($\mu > 0.9$), followed by the plain text stings *text* ($0.8 < \mu < 0.9$). Except for the *Module*, which appears averagely in half of the Rules, and *Windows Path* (μ slightly greater than 0.1), all the other indicators have a frequency smaller than 0.1, thus they are used in (less than) 1 Rule out of ten. It is interesting to observe that the IOCs spanning from *HashMD5* to *IPV6 Address* are used a negligible number of times in the samples. Figure 2 shows that *domains* and *hexadecimal strings* have the highest variability, as expected by the very high values of the maximum for these indicators. Except for *Text, Module, PE File* and *Path Windows* which have a $1 < \sigma < 3$, all the other IOCs show a standard deviation much under 1, which means that their frequencies do not change a lot in the dataset.

> **RQ$_1$ Summary:** *On average a Rule contains one or two types of indicators. The distribution of IOC types is not uniform among the Rules. The most widespread IOC is the hexadecimal string, while domain is the main cause for overloaded Rules.*

5.2   Results for RQ$_2$: Which IOCs Are Mostly Used in Versatile Rules?

In order to understand which IOCs mainly contribute to the detection for a Yara Rule, we computed parameters of descriptive statistics[11] for those Rules which reported at least a true positive, i.e. a number of matches ≥ 1. 15,162 Rules out of 32,311 did not produce any match with existing malware, corresponding to the 47% of the dataset. This result may depend on several factors. First of all, many Rules are created and distributed by International Organizations such as national CERT, or by private companies that deal with Incident Response activities which provide descriptions, in the form of Yara Rules, about threats which were not necessarily been disclosed on public sandboxes. Another explanation may be that some Rules regard specific malware for platforms such as MacOSX (i.e. *OSX_MacSpy.yar*) or Android (i.e. *Android_Dendroid_RAT.yar*) that are not very popular on these public sandboxes. Finally, there are also Rules which contain signatures for specific packers (i.e. *peid.yar*) that are not widely used. It is worth observing the high values of the maximum for *domains* (almost 1,400) and for *hexadecimal strings* (1,000), while for a not negligible subset it is over 30, however. Interestingly, *domains* are not that used among successful Rules.

---

[11] These parameters are: the maximum, the minimum, the mean, the 1st and the 3rd quartile, the median, the standard deviation, and the mode.

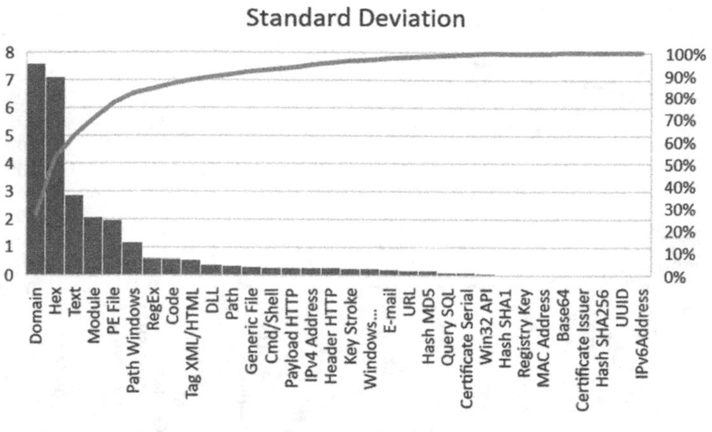

Standard Deviation

Fig. 2. The values of the standard deviation for each IOC

Figure 3 shows that *hexadecimal strings* are used more or less in all the Rules. With the only exception of *Module* and *text strings* with a $0.6 < \mu < 0.7$, all the other IOCs have values ≤ 0.2, that means they can be found, in average, in 1 successful Rule out of 5. It emerges that some IOCs are never used in Yara Rules, as well as: `Win32API`, `Hash SHA1`, `Base64`, `RegistryKey`, `HashSHA256`, `MAC Address`, `UUID`, `IPv6Address`, `Certificate Serial`, and `Certificate Issuer`.

The variability of *amount* in successful Rules remains under a threshold of 0.5 for most indicators, as Fig. 4 suggests. *Domains* and *hexadecimal strings* have the highest variability ($8 < \sigma < 11$), while a small subset has a moderate variability ($1.5 < \sigma < 2$). As shown in Fig. 2, Rules with non-zero matches are heavier, as the strong differences in variability of IOCs suggest (see Fig. 2).

The mode is 0 for all the indicators, but *hexadecimal strings* (for which it is 1). This means that the most Rules have hexadecimal strings, while all the other indicators are very sparse in the dataset. The same happens for the median and the 3rd quartile. The minimum value and the 1st quartile are overlapped on zero.

RQ$_2$ Summary: *In Rules with non-zero matches, the most widespread indicators are strings, both textual and hexadecimal, and modules. Non-zero matches Rules are heavier than zero matches rules, with a variability of amount for IOCs slightly over 3. Many indicators are never used, while domains, which have the highest number of occurrences in the entire dataset, resulted the most used IOC also in non-zero matches Yara Rules.*

Non-zero Mean

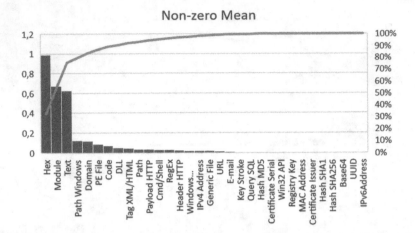

Fig. 3. The values of the Mean for each IOC of the Rules with non-zero matches

Non-zero Standard Deviation

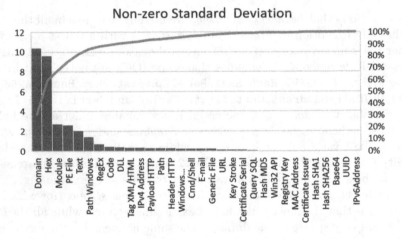

Fig. 4. The values of the Standard Deviation for each IOC of the Rules with non-zero matches

5.3   Results for RQ3: Is Robustness Correlated with the Looseness of a Yara Rule?

Data (Table 4) tell us that half of the Rules have not matches with any malware (and, thus, with malware families). But, the population of the Rules under the 3rd quartile matches with 15 malware and 22 malware families. Having a look at the maximum values, we can find a huge Looseness in some Rules, which are able to identify up to 695 malware instances, and 143 malware families.

The images of the corresponding boxplots (Fig. 5 can help to get the picture of how the values are distributed in the dataset. The most part of the Rules are extremely *tight* (half of the dataset have no matches at all), while a minority of the Rules are *loose*. In contrast, the *loose* Rules show a huge *Looseness*,

Table 4. The Parameters of the Distributions of the malware and families matched by Rules

Parameter	Number of malware	Number of families
Mean	19.82	10.13
Standard deviation	54.88	15.57
Min	0	0
1st Quartile	0	0
Median	0	0
Mode	0	0
3rd Quartile	15	22
Max	695	143

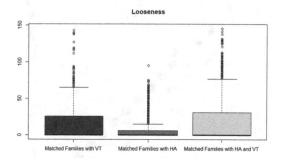

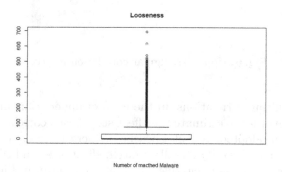

Fig. 5. The Box Plots of the number of matched families by Rule obtained on the different platforms, and of the number of matched malware by Rule.

considering the high number of outliers rising from the maximum bar in the boxplot. A similar observation can be made for the matching with the malware families, but with much smaller numbers, as expected. Let's recall here that the Looseness of a Rule is the ability of detecting a characteristic or a strain of a malware (family); a loose Yara Rule may help detect a new sample or track a new malicious campaign (threat hunting). Finally, Kendall non-parametric correlation has been computed among IOCs, conditions constraints and both Number of Malware and Number of Families. It has been decided to apply the Bonferroni method to adjust p-values in order to reduce the Type I error. The goal of the correlation analysis is to obtain statistical evidence of the correlation between the IOCs, the Robustness (*amount, diversity and distribution*) and the Looseness (*Numb of Malware, Number of Families*).

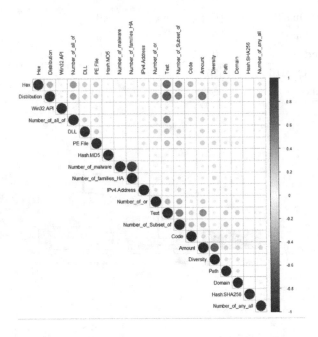

Fig. 6. Upper Triangular correlation matrix

Then, the resulting correlations, in the form of upper triangular matrix, are shown in Fig. 6. In order to estimate the effect size of each correlation, the Cohen standard has been adopted. About Looseness, there is statistical evidence for *Num of Malware* and *diversity* (small negative effect size) and *Number_of_families_HA* and *diversity* (small negative effect size) as shown in Fig. 6. Moreover, it is observed that there is not statistical evidence between Looseness and condition's constraints (*Number of OR, Number of AND, Number of Any Of, Number of All Of, Number of Subset Of*). Based on these observations, it is possible to conclude that Looseness does not depends on the amount or distribution of the IOCs but weakly depends on the diversity. This basically means that, Yara Rules with a minor diversity are better and more suitable for threat hunting activities.

RQ$_3$ Summary: *The most part of the Rules are tight. The loose Rules, which are a small portion of the examined dataset, are exceptionally powerful, as they are able to match numerous instances of malware and malware families. Unfortunately, no correlation has been observed between IOCs and Looseness and between Looseness and condition's constraints, but only a weak correlation between Looseness and the diversity.*

6   Conclusion

In this paper we propose a model, namely the $\mathcal{R}$-$\mathcal{L}$ model for defining and measuring the *quality* of Yara Rules in two dimensions: the Robustness and Looseness. The Robustness of a Yara Rule is the capability to match the intended malware even if some IOCs change over time. The Looseness of a Yara Rule is the capability of matching variants of the intended malware and regards the versatility of its accuracy. To validate the proposed model we first collected a dataset composed of 32,311 Yara Rules from different public repositories and proved them on two threat intelligence platforms: Hybrid Analysis and Virus-Total. Our results demonstrate that:

(i) Most Yara Rules have a small diversity, but a limited subset is overloaded with many IOCs;
(ii) Looseness is a very widespread property of Yara Rules;
(iii) the correlation between Robustness and Looseness is weak.

Yara is an adopted standard in the Threat Intelligence community but there are not accepted shared guidelines. These findings could be useful for integrating Yara in any process of Intelligence creation. It is possible to introduce these metrics in a recommendation tool for writing Yara signatures for specific use cases, like malware hunting, classification, detection, and sharing knowledge. A finding which can drive the writing of a Yara rule is that no correlation has been observed between Looseness and Robustness; this means that the adequacy of a rule for proactively finding new malware variant does not depend on the number or types of IoC's but probably depends on a semantic dimension of the rule.

As future work, we will also investigate more in-depth the usage of compound conditions within a Rule and how styles differ among the Rules for diverse platforms.

References

1. Biondi, F., Dechelle, F., Legay, A.: MASSE: modular automated syntactic signature extraction. In: IEEE International Symposium on Software Reliability Engineering Workshops (ISSREW), pp. 96–97. IEEE (2017)
2. Doll, C., et al.: Automated pattern inference based on repeatedly observed malware artifacts. In: Proceedings of the 14th International Conference on Availability, Reliability and Security, pp. 1–10 (2019)

3. Kampanakis, P.: Security automation and threat information-sharing options. IEEE Secur. Priv. **12**(5), 42–51 (2014)
4. Kurogome, Y., et al.: EIGER: automated IOC generation for accurate and interpretable endpoint malware detection. In: Proceedings of the 35th Annual Computer Security Applications Conference. ACSAC 2019, San Juan, Puerto Rico, pp. 687–701. Association for Computing Machinery (2019). ISBN: 9781450376280. https://doi.org/10.1145/3359789.3359808
5. Lee, H.S., Lee, H.-W.: Automatic detection of crypto-graphic algorithms in executable binary files using advanced code chain. In: 2019 International Conference on Green and Human Information Technology (ICGHIT), pp. 103–107. IEEE (2019)
6. Martin, R.A.: Making security measurable and manageable. In: MIL- COM 2008–2008 IEEE Military Communications Conference, pp. 1–9. IEEE (2008)
7. Naik, N.: Augmented YARA rules fused with fuzzy hashing in ransomware triaging. In: IEEE Symposium Series on Computational Intelligence (SSCI), pp. 625–632. IEEE (2019)
8. Plyara, 04 April 2020. https://github.com/plyara/plyara
9. Ray, J.: Understanding the threat landscape: indicators of compromise (IOCs) (2015)
10. Sillaber, C., et al.: Data quality challenges and future research directions in threat intelligence sharing practice. In: Proceedings of the 2016 ACM on Workshop on Information Sharing and Collaborative Security, pp. 65–70 (2016)
11. Steinberger, J., et al.: How to exchange security events? Overview and evaluation of formats and protocols. In: 2015 IFIP/IEEE International Symposium on Integrated Network Management (IM), pp. 261–269 (2015)
12. Tounsi, W., Rais, H.: A survey on technical threat intelligence in the age of sophisticated cyber attacks. Comput. Secur. **72**, 212–233 (2018)

Measurement-Based Analysis of a DoS Defense Module for an Open Source Web Server

Marta Catillo[✉], Antonio Pecchia, and Umberto Villano

Dipartimento di Ingegneria, Università degli Studi del Sannio, Benevento, Italy
{marta.catillo,antonio.pecchia,villano}@unisannio.it

Abstract. Denial of Service (DoS) attacks represent an ever evolving landscape, which ranges from bruteforce flooding approaches to more sophisticated low-bandwidth slow techniques. DoS has become a major threat to the availability of modern web servers because of the large number of attack tools across the Internet. In spite of the increasing number of security modules that can be usefully deployed in production servers, there is not a one-fits-all defense solution against DoS.

This paper proposes a measurement-based analysis of a well-established defense module for the Apache web server. The module is tested against both flooding and slow DoS attacks in order to quantify its capability at assuring correct service to legitimate clients. Results indicate that the module can mitigate flooding DoS attacks while causing some performance loss of the server; however, it is ineffective against slow attacks. The findings of our analysis are useful to support the deployment of proper defense mechanisms.

Keywords: Denial of Service · Web server · Defense · Availability

1 Introduction

Nowadays, web servers are broadly used for the implementation of Internet services. As a consequence, performance assurance of web servers plays a key role in satisfying the needs of a large and growing community of users. The number of **Denial of Service (DoS) attacks** against web servers has greatly increased in recent years. DoS attacks undermine the availability of a *victim* server by making access difficult, it not even impossible, to legitimate users. DoS is an important focus of interest for current research [5], because of the large number of attack tools across the Internet, frequency and disruptive effects.

Numerous surveys and research papers, such as [19] and [30], deal with DoS both from the perspective of the attack and possible defense. Several schemes [1,10,13], have been proposed to detect "traditional" **flooding DoS attacks**, i.e., attacks designed to overwhelm a targeted server by means of a massive number of HTTP requests. However, in the last years, DoS attacks evolved into

© IFIP International Federation for Information Processing 2020
Published by Springer Nature Switzerland AG 2020
V. Casola et al. (Eds.): ICTSS 2020, LNCS 12543, pp. 121–134, 2020.
https://doi.org/10.1007/978-3-030-64881-7_8

a "second generation", i.e., the so-called **slow DoS attacks** [25]. These use low-bandwidth approaches that exploit application-layer vulnerabilities and the intrinsic design of the HTTP protocol. Researchers have invested considerable effort to detect slow DoS attacks, and a wide body of literature, e.g.., [27], [6], [16], is currently on this topic.

In order to mitigate DoS attacks, practitioners can rely on a variety of security modules that are recommended for hardening "core" web server installations. Nevertheless, in spite of the increasing number of security modules that can be usefully deployed in production servers, there is not a "one-fits-all" defense solution against DoS attacks.

In this paper we propose a measurement-based analysis of a well-established **defense module** for the Apache web server called `mod_evasive`[1]. It is an Apache module intended for DoS, DDoS (*distributed* DoS) and bruteforce attacks mitigation. Our analysis is based on direct performance measurements of a victim server during a variety of DoS attacks performed in a controlled testbed. In order to emulate both flooding and slow DoS attacks, we considered three types of DoS: a classic volumetric DoS made by means of a Python script widely used in the literature, a *home-made* flood attack with a very high request rate, and a slow header DoS attack crafted with a specialized tool. Each attack is launched both against the *baseline* server, i.e., no defense module in place, and its hardened version by enabling `mod_evasive`. We collect different service metrics, such as throughput loss, number of successful requests and reply time, in case of *no* and *with defense* in order to quantify the capability of the module at assuring correct service to legitimate users.

To the best of our knowledge, we are not aware of a similar study that assesses a defense module in face of such a mixture of attack conditions and metrics. In fact, while tech blogs and references provide practical guidance for installation and functional testing the modules, there is a lack of comprehensive performance measurements to drive practitioners' choice. Our analysis provides several interesting outcomes regarding the module in hand. First, the module mitigates flooding DoS attacks; however, it may cause up to 15.74% throughput loss of the server. Second, *in none of the experiments* the defense module was able to ensure the success of all the legitimate HTTP requests, which means that a server will fail some requests anyway in spite of the defense. Finally, the module is ineffective against slow attacks. Overall, the findings of our study provide a better understanding of the capability of the module and its potential limitations in a production environment. Moreover, we recommend to accompany the module assessed in this study by means of supplemental defense mechanisms[2,3] in order to achieve comprehensive defense.

The paper is organized as follows. Section 2 discusses related work in the area of DoS and defense. Section 3 describes the experimental testbed, attack tools and service metrics. Section 4 provides a detailed analysis of the attacks and

---

[1] https://github.com/jzdziarski/mod_evasive.

[2] https://sourceforge.net/projects/mod-antiloris/.

[3] https://httpd.apache.org/docs/trunk/mod/mod_reqtimeout.html.

their impact in case of *no* and *with defense*. Section 5 concludes the work and discusses potential future directions.

2   Related Work

The escalation of DoS attacks has attracted a significant interest by the research community, which focused on specialized DoS attacks detection mechanisms. A number of countermeasures have been taken over the years to mitigate DoS attacks [29]. Some conventional approaches rely on monitoring the connection request rate [14]: for example, a client whose connection request rate is higher than a pre-established threshold is marked as an attacker. This technique is mostly ineffective for slow DoS attacks, as shown in [2]; moreover, in some cases even a legitimate requesting user could have a short-term burst of connection requests without leading to an attack [24]. Authors in [7] analyze DoS traffic from a public research dataset and measure its impact under different configurations of a victim server. Results indicate that a proper configuration of the server can strongly mitigate the impact of a DoS attack.

In recent years, with the rapid diffusion of deep learning techniques, many machine learning-based DoS detectors have spread in the literature [18], along with more classic detection techniques. In [11] the authors use three types of analyzers to detect DDoS attacks. In particular, they consider statistical analysis of HTTP flows, users' access behavior by graph modeling the paths of the web server as well as the different costs of navigating through the server, and the frequency of HTTP operations carried on the web server. The proposed model can autonomously detect bots and security scanners. However, it is ineffective against slow DoS attacks when number of involved bots is large. The work [2] presents a method that tracks the number of packets a web server receives in a given interval of time. This feature is monitored in two subsequent time intervals in order to detect normal or anomaly behavior. However, feature selection might be a long and complex activity. Monitoring the number of packets received can cause high false positive rate, because a high burst of traffic can be due to different scenarios. Authors in [9] propose a method to detect different types of attacks, such as DoS, by mining text logs in a critical industrial system.

Typically, in a production environment, misconfiguration of the web server could lead to security breaches and make DoS attacks easier for malicious users. Beside regular updating and patching the web server, it is essential to configure it for better security performance. Many popular web servers allow to enable DoS security modules with the aim to mitigate security infringements. Although the use of these modules is highly recommended, there is a lack of studies on the defense topic. Moreover, in some cases, these patches have the limitation of blocking legitimate requests from being served. As stated in [22], countermeasures against DoS/DDoS attacks can be roughly classified in three categories: *survival* techniques, *proactive* techniques and *reactive* techniques. In [23] the authors show that a web server configured with the security modules can really mitigate the attack. However, if it is launched by an increasing number of bots, there is a noticeable delay in the server response; as such, a massive attack scenario can affect the performance of the server. The work [4] provides a detailed analysis of DDoS countermeasures. It highlights the strengths of each method, and also consider some countermeasures that can be taken against each defense mechanism from the perspective of the attacker. A survey of DDoS defense mechanisms can be found in [29]. The authors provide a detailed classification of defense mechanisms driven by the moment in time when the defense should be applied: before the attack (*prevention*), during the attack (*detection*), or after the attack (*identification* and *response*). Authors in [26] present a study that highlights performance and defense mechanisms of Windows Server and Linux Server. The paper evaluates several defense mechanisms, such as *ACLs, threshold limit, reverse path forwarding* and *network load balancing*.

In the literature, many metrics have been proposed to evaluate both the impact of DoS attacks and defense strategies. However, there are no benchmarks [20] that allow to evaluate effective metrics. In [21] the authors propose the percentage of failed transactions (transactions that do not follow QoS thresholds) as a metric to measure DDoS impact. In particular, they describe a threshold-based model for traffic measurements. If a measurement exceeds the threshold, it indicates poor service quality. However, the duration of the transactions depends on the network load. Therefore, it is difficult to set the absolute duration threshold. *Server timeout* has been used as a metric in [17]. Unfortunately, the damage effects in terms of legitimate traffic drop are not indicated. Finally, in [12], Gupta et al. describe two statistical metrics namely, *Volume* and *Flow*, in order to efficiently detect DDoS attacks.

3   Testbed and Analysis Method

Our analysis is based on direct performance measurements of a victim server during DoS attacks performed in a controlled testbed. We collect a variety of service metrics to gain insight into the impact of the attacks in case of *no* and *with defense*. In the following we describe the experimental testbed, the DoS tools and the service metrics adopted.

3.1   Experimental Testbed

Experiments were conducted on a private cloud infrastructure hosted by a data-center at the University of Sannio. The experimental testbed capitalizes on our previous work [8] and consists of three Ubuntu 18.04.2 LTS nodes, described in the following using the naming shown in Fig. 1.

The **"victim" node** hosts an installation of Apache 2.4. This web server is a significant case study, given its widespread use. It can fit a wide-range of websites, ranging from personal blogs to websites that serve millions of users; moreover, it is open source and cross-platform. The Apache web server supports a variety of *modules* –including security-related capabilities– that can be enabled by adjusting the configuration of the *baseline* server installation. In our study we

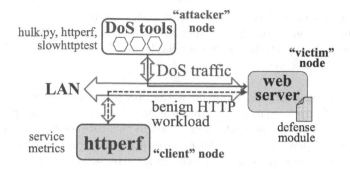

Fig. 1. Experimental testbed.

address `mod_evasive`, i.e., a consolidated **defense module** intended to protect a server from DoS, DDoS and bruteforce attacks. We carefully tuned and tested the correct functioning of `mod_evasive` according to the instructions from a well-detailed tech blog[4]. The module inspects incoming requests at the server side and blacklists malicious client IP addresses based on several thresholds and timeouts, such as *site count, page count, blocking period*. At any time, `mod_evasive` can be seamlessly enabled or disabled by acting on the configuration and re-starting the web server. We conducted an experimental campaign with different attacks both against the *baseline* server and its version hardened by means of `mod_evasive`.

As for the remaining components in Fig. 1, the **"attacker" node** generates the DoS traffic intended to disrupt server operations. To this aim, we use several state-of-the-art attack tools, which are described in Sect. 3.2. Finally, the **"client" node** hosts `httperf`[5], which is a widely-used workload generator. This tool makes it possible to set a desired level of workload by regulating different parameters, such as *total connections, connections per second* and *requests per connection* and triggers the normative HTTP requests, which aim to emulating the *benign* workload by a legitimate client. During the experiments, the web server is exercised with both DoS traffic and benign workload. We use native metrics produced by `httperf` and a set of derived metrics –detailed in Sect. 3.3– to monitor the web server and to measure the impact of the attack.

3.2   DoS Attacks and Tools

Our experiments encompass an interesting mixture of DoS attacks that exploit both flooding activities and the intrinsic design of the HTTP protocol. Attacks and their implementation in the testbed are presented in the following.

Hulk DoS. The attack aims to flood the victim server with a massive amount of HTTP requests. In particular, it continuously triggers single or multiple

---

[4] https://www.atlantic.net/vps-hosting/how-to-install-and-configure-modevasive-with-apache-on-ubuntu-18-04/.

[5] https://github.com/httperf/httperf.

requests and generates a *unique pattern* at each time by randomizing key fields of the requests. Some attack strategies are reported in [15]. We use the well-consolidated `hulk.py` Python script available at GitHub[6] to launch Hulk DoS against our victim server.

Bruteforce Flooding. We supplement the analysis with a *home-made* flooding attack performed by means of an additional installation of `httperf` at the "attacker" node. To this aim, `httperf` –used in this case for flooding purposes– is configured to open 100 concurrent connections per second and to make 1,000 HTTP requests per connections, which sum up to total 100,000 requests per second: this request rate is by far higher than the actual processing capacity of the server in our testbed. Differently from Hulk DoS, the request pattern is constant; however, the magnitude of the flooding is much higher than Hulk.

Slow Header. Differently from the above, *slow header* is not a "mere" flooding attack. Rather, it relies on an HTTP protocol design condition, which requires requests to be *completely* received by the server before they are actually processed. As such, the attack is accomplished by sending incomplete HTTP requests (i.e., without ever ending the header) that end up saturating the connections of the victim server. We use `slowhttptest`[7] to execute a *slow header* attack. The tool is configured to use a budget of 5,000 concurrent sockets, which lead to an attack duration of around 4 min in our testbed.

3.3 Collection of the Service Metrics

During the experiments we continuously probe the operational status of the server at regular intervals by alternating (i) a run of `httperf` at the "client" node and (ii) collection of the corresponding metrics. At each run, the **benign workload** implemented by means of `httperf` consists of 10 concurrent connections per second and 100 HTTP requests per connections, which sum up to a rate of 1,000 requests per second (*reqs/s*). While collecting the metrics, we set a request timeout of 10 *s* to avoid that `httperf` hangs by waiting for requests that might never succeed in case of attack. We focus on the following metrics from `httperf`:

- **reply rate** or **throughput (T)**: HTTP requests accomplished by the server within the time unit, measured in *reqs/s*;
- **mean response time (MRT)**: mean time taken to serve a request measured in milliseconds (*ms*);
- **OK requests**: number of requests served with the 200 HTTP status code by the server.

Beside the metrics above –"natively" provided by `httperf`– we compute the following derived metrics:

---

[6] https://github.com/grafov/hulk.
[7] https://github.com/shekyan/slowhttptest.

- **throughput loss (TL)**: percentage of HTTP requests that *are not* accomplished by the web server within the time unit, i.e., $TL = \frac{(1,000-T)}{1,000} \cdot 100$, where 1,000 is the request rate. TL varies in the interval $[0, 100]\%$: any point where $TL \neq 0\%$ reflect a slowdown of the server in serving the requests.
- **mean OK requests per connection**: *OK requests* divided by 10, i.e., the number of concurrent connections issued by `httperf`.

In attack-free conditions, in response to the workload of 1,000 *reqs/s*, the metrics above are equal to the following values: $T = 1,000$ *reqs/s*, $MRT = 0.4$ *ms*, OK requests $= 1,000$, $TL = 0\%$, mean OK requests per connection $= 100$. Given that in our testbed the only source of legitimate activity is the "client" node, any deviation from these "ideal" values points out the presence of a DoS activity.

4   Experimental Results

This section discusses the results obtained by running the attacks presented in Sect. 3.2 against the web server in hand. For each attack, we run two independent experiments. The former consists in performing the attack against the *baseline* server installation, i.e., no defense module in place; the latter is done by running the attack after having started the server with its defense module enabled. The two experimental scenarios are denoted by *NO defense* and *WITH defense* through the rest of the paper.

The duration of each experiment is 300 s, which is long enough to collect a sample of service metric observations for statistical purposes (e.g., 30 observations); in all the cases, the attack starts at $t = 20$ s since the beginning of the experiment. At the end of each experiment we (i) store measurement data and logs for subsequent analysis, (ii) clear the logs of the web server, such as `access` and `error` log (iii) stop the workload generator, attack scripts and the web server. In the following, the results are presented by increasing service loss levels caused to the server.

4.1   Hulk DoS

Figure 2a (□-*marked* dashed series) shows how TL varies during the progression of the Hulk attack in case of *NO defense* for our server: the attack causes sporadic spikes of the TL, whose maximum observed value is 77.06% at $t = 140$ s since the beginning of the run (x-axis). In order to gain insight into the effect of the attack, we complement TL with the *mean OK requests per connection* metric described above. It is worth noting that an increase of TL reflects the slowdown of the server at serving HTTP requests; however, it does not account for the correctness of the requests, which is summarized by the latter metric in Fig. 2b (□-*marked* dashed series) for the *NO defense* scenario. Interestingly, for several data points the metric drops from 100, i.e., the *normative* value for attack-free conditions, to a lower value, such as 57.68 –the worst case– when $t = 70$ s. Overall, when the server is not properly protected, Hulk DoS causes both the slowdown of the server and a relevant loss of correct requests at sporadic times.

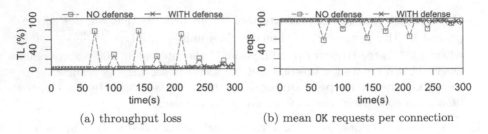

(a) throughput loss   (b) mean OK requests per connection

Fig. 2. Impact of the attack (`hulk` script).

```
—— access.log ——
[01/Aug/2020:22:44:31 +0200] "GET /index.html?ZBWRUMRX=ANINEAZY HTTP/1.1"
 200  11192 "http://engadget.search.aol.com/search?q=PPQOBOV" "Mozilla/4.0
(compatible; MSIE 8.0; Windows NT 6.1; WOW64; Trident/4.0; SLCC2;.NET CLR
2.0.50727; InfoPath.2)"
```

Fig. 3. Response to a Hulk DoS HTTP request (*NO defense*).

```
—— access.log ——
[01/Aug/2020:22:27:50 +0200] "GET /index.html?TOIHJNNI=ZXGMI HTTP/1.1"
 403  459 "http://www.google.com/?q=QILIYIIDL" "Mozilla/5.0 (X11; U;Linux
x86_64; en-US; rv:1.9.1.3) Gecko/20090913 Firefox/3.5.3"
—— error.log ——
[Sat Aug 01 22:27:50.377578 2020] [evasive20:error] [pid /*omitted*/]
[client 192.168.111.65:54508] client denied by server configuration:
/var/www/html/index.html, referer: http://www.google.com/?q=QILIYIIDL
```

Fig. 4. Response to a Hulk DoS HTTP request (*WITH defense*).

Figure 2a and Fig. 2b (×-*marked* solid series) show TL and mean OK requests per connection when the defense module is on, i.e, *WITH defense*. It can be noted that the defense module is able to mitigate significant spikes and drops observed in the previous scenario. Nevertheless, in spite of the defense, the attack can still affect the server at some extent: the maximum TL is 7.88% and the minimum mean OK requests is 93.12. This is an interesting finding, which indicates that a server may fail to handle some requests also in case of defense.

We closely looked into the logs of the web server, i.e., *access.log* and *error.log*, to motivate the difference in the service loss caused by the Hulk DoS attack in both *NO* and *WITH defense* conditions. As mentioned above, the attack *floods* the server by means of malicious HTTP requests that consist of random URL query string, user agent and referee. Figure 3 shows an example of such a request, logged by the web server in the *access.log* in case of *NO defense*. Surprisingly, the server accomplishes the malicious request with the 200 (OK) HTTP status code (enclosed in a box in Fig. 3): as a consequence, the computation overhead of serving a malicious request is the same as any other normative request. On the other hand, Fig. 4 shows how a malicious HTTP request by Hulk is tracked by the logs of the server in the *WITH defense* scenario. The most striking

Table 1. Service metrics (`hulk` script).

	Availability	Max TL	Max MRT	Percentage OK requests by MRT		
				[0, 10] ms	(10, 100] ms	(100, +∞]
NO defense	0.938	77.06%	0.9 ms	100.0%	0.0%	0.0%
WITH defense	0.988	7.88%	0.4 ms	100.0%	0.0%	0.0%

outcome is that the malicious request is now **forbidden** the access to the resource with the **403** HTTP status code (enclosed in a box in Fig. 4) and it raises a corresponding "`client denied`" notification in the *error.log*. Differently from *NO defense*, the malicious request is aborted before it triggers the normative computation; however, it still needs some handling cycles by the server in order to be flagged as forbidden. As a consequence, although *per-request* overhead is negligible, the overall contribution of a significant flooding activity can affect the server also in case of defense.

Table 1 summarizes key service metrics obtained for Hulk DoS, such as the *availability*. Through the rest of the paper, we compute the **availability** as the ratio between the number of successful HTTP requests observed during an attack-injection experiment divided by the number of successful HTTP requests that the server would accomplish in attack-free conditions over the same interval. The number of successful HTTP requests is related to an interval of 300 s (i.e., the duration of the experiment). *Availability* can be seen here as the probability that the server will successfully handle a HTTP request under attack.

As shown in Table 1, *availability* is 0.988 in case of defense and thus higher than the value measured in *NO defense*, i.e., 0.938; however, it is not exactly 1 (i.e., attack-free conditions) because –although with defense– the server fails to successfully handle some HTTP requests, as presented above. Another interesting outcome is given by the *percentage of OK requests by MRT*, shown in the rightmost columns of Table 1, where we break down the total number of successful requests reported by the workload generator based on their MRT. It can be noted that both in *NO* and *WITH defense* scenarios, 100% of OK requests are served with a MRT in [0, 10] ms. Noteworthy, 10 ms is seen as a typical maximum tolerable delay for a response of a web server in order to be usefully deployed in multilayer workflows [3]. As such, in our testbed Hulk DoS did not affect the *usability* of successful requests. Nevertheless, it is worth noting that the maximum MRT observed in case of *NO defense*, i.e., 0.9 ms, is significantly higher than *WITH defense*, i.e., 0.4 ms.

4.2   Bruteforce Flooding

The following paired runs encompass our *home-made* bruteforce flooding; again, we assess the behavior of the server in case of *NO* and *WITH defense*.

Figure 5a and Fig. 5b (□-*marked* dashed series) show how TL and mean OK requests per connection vary during the *NO defense* run. At three data points, i.e., $t = 74$, 144, and 240 s the metrics reach 100% and 0, respectively. This means

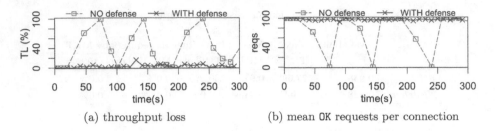

(a) throughput loss (b) mean OK requests per connection

Fig. 5. Impact of the attack (`httperf` bruteforce flooding).

Table 2. Service metrics (`httperf` bruteforce flooding).

	Availability	Max TL	Max MRT	Percentage OK requests by MRT		
				[0, 10] ms	(10, 100] ms	(100, +∞]
NO defense	0.498	100.00%	46.5 ms	86.6%	13.4%	0.0%
WITH defense	0.975	15.74%	0.6 ms	100.0%	0.0%	0.0%

that, during those runs of `httperf` at the "client" node, the web server succeeds to accomplish *none* of the requests. Overall, the attack strongly affects the normative operation of the server through all the duration of the run. For example, it can be noted that TL = 0% in almost no point of the x-axis in Fig. 5a. As for the *WITH defense* run, Fig. 5a and Fig. 5b (×-*marked* solid series) make it possible to appreciate the invaluable benefit of the defense module for both the throughput and OK requests. TL is constantly around its mean value of 3.36% over the duration of the run with a peak of 15.74% in the worst case; similarly, *mean OK requests per connection* varies around a mean of 97.20. Both the values are really close to 0% and 100, i.e., the ideal values in attack-free conditions. Again, in spite of the strong mitigation effect, there is a performance loss in the *WITH defense* scenario. Such as for Hulk DoS, this is due to the server cycles needed to forbid the massive amount of malicious requests with the 403 HTTP status code, which is more significant in this attack.

Table 2 summarizes key service metrics obtained in face of bruteforce flooding. *Availability* is 0.498 in *NO defense*: the server failed to successfully reply around half of the HTTP requests issue by the workload generator when compared to the attack-free scenario. Moreover, 13.4% out of the total successful requests are replied with a MRT in (10, 100] *ms* (i.e., *percentage of OK requests by MRT* in Table 2), which means that a substantial number of correct replies is strongly delayed because of the attack. *Availability* in case of defense is 0.975, such as shown in bottom row of Table 2. This value is lower than 0.988, which was measured for *WITH defense* in Hulk DoS. Although far from the "ideal" value of 1, it is reasonably satisfactory given the magnitude of the flooding. Noteworthy, the defense module allows all successful requests to be served with a MRT in [0, 10] ms.

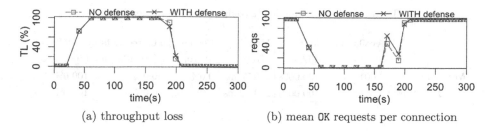

(a) throughput loss   (b) mean OK requests per connection

Fig. 6. Impact of the attack (`slowhttptest` slow header).

4.3   Slow Header

The last attack addressed in this study is *slow header*. Figure 6a and Fig. 6b (□-*marked* dashed series) show how TL and mean OK requests per connection vary during the *NO defense* run. It can be noted that the attack is able to quickly saturate the web server: TL is 99.8% starting from $t = 60$ s –thus 40 s since the beginning of the attack– up to $t = 190$ s, which means that the server fails to handle almost all benign HTTP requests of the workload generator during this timeframe. Similar considerations apply to mean OK requests per connection, whose value is 0 over the same timeframe. The server resumes it normative operations at $t = 210$ s after a short transitory. Figure 6a and Fig. 6b (×-*marked* solid series) show the metric for the *WITH defense* run: the appearance of both the time series is very close the to *NO defense* experiment.

Since the presence of the defense module reflects into *no* significant change of the service metrics at application level, we performed further analysis to support the claim that the module assessed in this study provides no mitigation for *slow header* attacks. To this objective, we leverage the outcome of `slowhttptest`, which accounts for the *socket usage*. Figure 7 compares the number of *opened* and *connected* sockets during the progression of the attack for *NO* and *WITH defense* (dashed and solid series, respectively). The 5,000 sockets mentioned in Sect. 3.2 are opened at the beginning of the attack at $t = 20$ s and progressively closed later on. Moreover, the number of connected sockets reaches a maximum of 1,400 around $t = 150$ s, which is consistent with the TL in Fig. 6b. Interestingly, mitigation actions implemented by the defense module do not affect at all the attacker's *socket usage*, which is the same in *NO* and *WITH defense*.

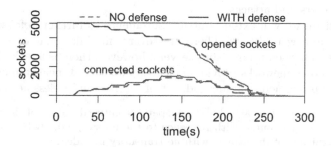

Fig. 7. Socket usage by `slowhttptest`

Table 3. Service metrics (`slowhttptest` slow header).

| | Availability | Max TL | Max MRT | Percentage OK requests by MRT | | |
				[0, 10] ms	(10, 100] ms	(100, +∞]
NO defense	0.001	100.00%	2107.8 ms	0.0%	0.0%	100.0%
WITH defense	0.001	100.00%	2132.2 ms	0.0%	0.0%	100.0%

As for the summary of the metrics[8], shown in Table 3, we note that *availability* is 0.001 in both the runs: during the attack, the server accomplished almost none of the requests of the workload generator with respect to an attack-free scenario. It is worth noting that out of the very small number of requests (e.g., 120 in the *WITH defense* run) that occasionally succeed during the attack, 100% are served with a MRT higher than 100 ms and thus unable by a potential client.

Overall, it can be reasonably claimed that the defense module assessed in this study provides no mitigation for *slow header* attacks. As such, the module should be accompanied by supplemental defense mechanisms in order to achieve comprehensive defense in production environments.

5   Conclusion

This paper proposed an initial measurement study assessing a DoS defense module for a widely-used web server. Results highlighted *pros* and *cons* of the module. Most notably, we observe that, in spite of the defense, a web server may occasionally fail to serve legitimate requests; moreover, the module in hand does not protect from *slow header* attacks.

Our study builds around the intuition that existing defense modules might not provide exhaustive coverage for all modern DoS attacks: this is pursued by instantiating the study in the context of a widely-used web server. As for any measurement study, there may be concerns regarding the validity and generalizability of results, based on the aspects listed in [28]. We rely on a mixture of experiments consisting of direct emulation of DoS attacks by means of state-of-the-art tools. More important, we support our findings with a significant range of service metrics and by direct inspection of socket usage. Overall, these mitigate internal validity threats and provide a reasonable level of confidence on the experimental results. Noteworthy, our analysis can be reasonably ported to other web servers and attacks.

In the future we will extend our measurements to further defense modules, attack types and web servers. There are several modules that can be used by practitioners to harden productions servers; however, there is a lack of comparative studies and frameworks providing clear guidance and measurements. In this respect, we will augment the method, set of metrics and assessment framework

---

[8] Differently from previous attacks, which span the entire duration of the experiment, here metrics are computed with reference to the interval [60, 160] s, which reflects the full magnitude of the attack, with no transitory included.

–currently focused on DoS attacks– based on the type of attacks and corresponding defense modules. Our work is extremely useful to tune defense mechanisms, to find a well-balanced mix between defense modules and performance overhead, and to discover attacks that are not covered yet by existing modules.

References

1. Agarwal, M., Pasumarthi, D., Biswas, S., Nandi, S.: Machine learning approach for detection of flooding DoS attacks in 802.11 networks and attacker localization. Int. J. Mach. Learn. Cybern. **7**(6), 1035–1051 (2014). https://doi.org/10.1007/s13042-014-0309-2

2. Aiello, M., Cambiaso, E., Mongelli, M., Papaleo, G.: An on-line intrusion detection approach to identify low-rate DoS attacks. In: Proceedings of the International Carnahan Conference on Security Technology, pp. 1–6. IEEE (2014)

3. Alizadeh, M., et al.: Data center TCP (DCTCP). ACM SIGCOMM Comput. Commun. Rev. **40**(4), 63–74 (2010)

4. Beitollahi, H., Deconinck, G.: Analyzing well-known countermeasures against distributed denial of service attacks. Comput. Commun. **35**(11), 1312–1332 (2012)

5. Bonguet, A., Bellaiche, M.: A survey of denial-of-service and distributed denial of service attacks and defenses in cloud computing. Future Internet **9**(3), 43 (2017)

6. Cambiaso, E., Aiello, M., Mongelli, M., Vaccari, I.: Detection and classification of slow DoS attacks targeting network servers. In: Proceedings of the International Conference on Availability, Reliability and Security, pp. 1–7. ACM (2020). Article No.: 61

7. Catillo, M., Pecchia, A., Rak, M., Villano, U.: A case study on the representativeness of public DoS network traffic data for cybersecurity research. In: Proceedings of the International Conference on Availability, Reliability and Security, pp. 1–10. ACM (2020). Article No.: 6

8. Catillo, M., Pecchia, A., Villano, U.: Towards a framework for improving experiments on DoS attacks. In: Shepperd, M., Brito e Abreu, F., Rodrigues da Silva, A., Pérez-Castillo, R. (eds.) QUATIC 2020. CCIS, vol. 1266, pp. 303–316. Springer, Cham (2020). https://doi.org/10.1007/978-3-030-58793-2_25

9. Cinque, M., Della Corte, R., Pecchia, A.: Contextual filtering and prioritization of computer application logs for security situational awareness. Future Gener. Comput. Syst. **111**, 668–680 (2020)

10. Dharini, N., Balakrishnan, R., Renold, A.P.: Distributed detection of flooding and gray hole attacks in wireless sensor network. In: Proceedings of the International Conference on Smart Technologies and Management for Computing, Communication, Controls, Energy and Materials, pp. 178–184. IEEE (2015)

11. Giralte, L.C., Conde, C., de Diego, I.M., Cabello, E.: Detecting denial of service by modelling web-server behaviour. Comput. Electr. Eng. **39**(7), 2252–2262 (2013)

12. Gupta, B.B., Misra, M., Joshi, R.: An ISP level solution to combat DDoS attacks using combined statistical based approach. Int. J. Inf. Assur. Secur. **3**, 102–110 (2012)

13. Ismail, M.N., Aborujilah, A., Musa, S., Shahzad, A.: Detecting flooding based DoS attack in cloud computing environment using covariance matrix approach. In: Proceedings of the International Conference on Ubiquitous Information Management and Communication, pp. 1–6. ACM (2013). Article No.: 36

14. Kang, B., Kim, D., Kim, M.: Real-time connection monitoring of ubiquitous networks for intrusion prediction: a sequential KNN voting approach. Int. J. Distrib. Sens. Netw. **11**(10), 1–10 (2015)
15. Kaur, H., Behal, S., Kumar, K.: Characterization and comparison of distributed denial of service attack tools. In: Proceedings of the International Conference on Green Computing and Internet of Things, pp. 1139–1145. IEEE (2015)
16. Kemp, C., Calvert, C., Khoshgoftaar, T.: Utilizing netflow data to detect slow read attacks. In: Proceedings of the International Conference on Information Reuse and Integration, pp. 108–116. IEEE (2018)
17. Ko, C., Hussain, A., Schwab, S., Thomas, R., Wilson, B.: Towards systematic IDS evaluation. In: Proceedings of the DETER Community Workshop, pp. 20–23 (2006)
18. Liu, H., Lang, B.: Machine learning and deep learning methods for intrusion detection systems: a survey. Appl. Sci. **9**(20), 4396 (2019)
19. Mahjabin, T., Xiao, Y., Sun, G., Jiang, W.: A survey of distributed denial-of-service attack, prevention, and mitigation techniques. Int. J. Distrib. Sens. Netw. **13**(12), 1–32 (2017)
20. Mirkovic, J., Arikan, E., Wei, S., Thomas, R., Fahmy, S., Reiher, P.: Benchmarks for DDOS defense evaluation. In: Proceedings of the Military Communications Conference, pp. 1–10. IEEE (2006)
21. Mirkovic, J., et al.: Towards user-centric metrics for denial-of-service measurement. In: Proceedings of the Workshop on Experimental Computer Science, pp. 1–14. ACM (2007)
22. Mirkovic, J., Reiher, P.: A taxonomy of DDoS attack and DDoS defense mechanisms. ACM SIGCOMM Comput. Commun. Rev. **34**(2), 39–53 (2004)
23. Moustis, D., Kotzanikolaou, P.: Evaluating security controls against HTTP-based DDoS attacks. In: Proceedings of the IISA, pp. 1–6. IEEE (2013)
24. Nagaratna, M., Prasad, V.K., Kumar, S.T.: Detecting and preventing IP-spoofed DDoS attacks by encrypted marking based detection and filtering (EMDAF). In: Proceedings of the International Conference on Advances in Recent Technologies in Communication and Computing, pp. 753–755. IEEE (2009)
25. Sikora, M., Gerlich, T., Malina, L.: On detection and mitigation of slow rate denial of service attacks. In: Proceedings of the International Congress on Ultra Modern Telecommunications and Control Systems and Workshops, pp. 1–5. IEEE (2019)
26. Treseangrat, K., Kolahi, S.S., Sarrafpour, B.: Analysis of UDP DDoS cyber flood attack and defense mechanisms on Windows Server 2012 and Linux Ubuntu 13. In: Proceedings of the International Conference on Computer, Information and Telecommunication Systems, pp. 1–5. IEEE (2015)
27. Tripathi, N., Hubballi, N.: Slow rate denial of service attacks against HTTP/2 and detection. Comput. Secur. **72**, 255–272 (2018)
28. Wohlin, C., Runeson, P., Höst, M., Ohlsson, M.C., Regnell, B., Wesslén, A.: Experimentation in Software Engineering: An Introduction. Kluwer Academic, Norwell (2000)
29. Zargar, S.T., Joshi, J.B.D., Tipper, D.: A survey of defense mechanisms against distributed denial of service (DDoS) flooding attacks. IEEE Commun. Surv. Tutorials **15**, 2046–2069 (2013)
30. Zhijun, W., Wenjing, L., Liang, L., Meng, Y.: Low-rate DoS attacks, detection, defense, and challenges: a survey. IEEE Access **8**, 43920–43943 (2020)

Trust Is in the Air: A New Adaptive Method to Evaluate Mobile Wireless Networks

Alexandra-Elena Mocanu (Mihaita)[1](✉), Bogdan-Costel Mocanu[1](✉),

Christian Esposito[2](✉), and Florin Pop[1,3](✉)

[1] University Politehnica of Bucharest, Bucharest, Romania
{alexandra_elena.mihaita,bogdan_costel.mocanu}@cti.pub.ro,
alexa.mihaita@gmail.com, florin.pop@cs.pub.ro
[2] University of Salerno, Fisciano, Italy
esposito@unisa.it
[3] National Institute for Research and Development in Informatics (ICI),
Bucharest, Romania
florin.pop@ici.ro

Abstract. During this new world pandemic, a lot of technical issues have come to life, forcing all industries to reinvent themselves and how the day to day operations are performed. Remote working has become not only a trend but a necessity. Starting from online lecturing to online meetings on a need to know basis, people are concerned about their privacy and security in the online environment. Thus, in this paper, we focus our attention to the concepts of trust and reputation models in Wireless Mobile Networks (WMN), Wireless Sensor Networks (WSN) more accurately, for secure routing of large data packets with respect to Quality of Service (QoS). This paper analyses the current context in wireless mobile networks, more specifically in wireless sensor networks, and proposes a novel adaptive method to evaluate it by defining a Markov based trust function and a new model to manage it.

Keywords: Trust · Reputation · Mobile wireless networks · Secure routing · Adaptive methods

1 Introduction

Nowadays, while all industries have tried to find a new way to perform daily operations remotely, the IT industry has been the one to offer the means to do. This goal has been able to be achieved through video conferences regardless of the geographical location of the parties involved. As the learning curve has adjusted, it has also brought to life multiple issues regarding user and data privacy. One of the most used conference applications, Zoom [18], has faced numerous damning issues: from scandals about sending data to third parties without user awareness,

© IFIP International Federation for Information Processing 2020
Published by Springer Nature Switzerland AG 2020
V. Casola et al. (Eds.): ICTSS 2020, LNCS 12543, pp. 135–149, 2020.
https://doi.org/10.1007/978-3-030-64881-7_9

to the *lack of end-to-end encryption*. This type of problems had gathered more visibility than before and forced the authorities to take action [2,10].

Another issue which has developed from the increased number of stay-at-home people, has been the increased usage of *video streaming apps* or *bandwidth hogs*, as the media has called them. According to their official statements, HBO Now has reported an increase of 65% of binge-watching and 70% of movie viewing, Twitch an overall increase usage of 31%. In contrast, YouTube Games has reported an increase of 15% [3]. These significant numbers have translated into increased stress on the networks and forced major vendors like Netflix or YouTube to deliver their services at lower qualities to accommodate all the users [7] until better solutions can be found.

The day-to-day applications of security have become more relevant to the end-user and, hence, have enforced the need for research in securing WSN. The impact of privacy violations has made apparent the need for an added level of security when talking about mobile wireless networks. The desired effect is that even if the encryption element of the system is broken, there is still little-to-no-damage to be done on the user part. The extra layer of security mentioned previously can be represented by that of trust and reputation, taking into account the network's requirements for low latency and without increasing the network's offload and overhead significantly.

This paper presents a brief analysis of current research trends in Mobile Wireless Sensors Networks (Sect. 2). Second, we introduce a novel method for trust management of WSN based on Markov chains (Sect. 3) and an adaptive method trust management method with respect to QoS concerns (Sect. 4). Finally, we conclude this paper and present our experimental result in (Sect. 5).

2   Analysis Is in Our Hands

The leading technologies which make the communication possible represent an integrated part of wireless sensor networks. A significant opportunity for scientific research has been brought forward towards the next generation of wireless communication systems of 6G by the last milestone of the 5G mobile communication standard worldwide release. According to the authors in reference [12], the technologies considered to be too immature for 5G networks will emerge for the upcoming 6G networks, improving the data transfer rates significantly. Therefore, researchers estimate that 6G networks will be faster than the 5G ones by up to 1000 times [14]. This next-generation communication standard will have to meet more requirements than the 5G technology, though, not necessarily, at the same time.

These requirements include a multi-band, high-spread spectrum beyond 300 GHz, allowing hundreds of Tbps links for the interconnection of trillion-level nodes with an undetectable human latency of less than 1ms. In [15], authors estimate that 6G networks will be developed in conjunction with the actual stringent network demands such as low latency, reliability, efficiency, and QoS for indoor and outdoor scenarios, taking into account the security constraints holistically. All these factors have a significant impact on WSN and their applicability.

Another critical use case of 6G networks resides in the evolution of both augmented reality (AR) and virtual reality (VR) with direct application in e-Health and Smart Cities. The authors in reference [31] confirm that line of thought by stating that the bandwidth requirements for a full human 3D hologram are about 4.32 Tbps. This bandwidth is in the realm of the 6G networks. Even though the use cases mentioned above show a wide range of applications for the 6G networks, a new set of challenges emerges.

Besides the challenges that the 6G networks bring, the authors of [20] talk about the fact that user devices have started to carry more and more sensitive information. That information varies from banking data to actual data about the health of the user or the activity the user makes and when he does it. This information can be gathered and used directly or indirectly to damage the user, thus enforcing the idea of deploying an added level of security which can guarantee the data is unaltered and secure. Trust and reputation in WSN help a user know what elements of the network are to be trusted, including itself from the other's perspective.

In paper [5], the authors describe the concept of trust and reputation in WSN as depending on a set of attributes such as "reliability, scalability, and reconfigurability". Authors in reference [27] have emphasised three main goals for a trust and reputation model in a wireless communication network as follows:

- able to provide accurate information about the worthiness of the nodes, making it clear if they can be reliable or not;
- secure enough to encourage the nodes actually to try and cooperate and earn trustworthiness;
- dissuasive of untrustworthy nodes in the network.

Having spoken about the attributes of trust and reputation models, we also have to highlight their properties. In reference [1], the authors talk about those properties being asymmetry, context-sensitivity, subjectivity and partial transitivity. Asymmetry refers to the fact that: if node A trusts node B, then it is not mandatory that node B also trusts node A. Context sensitivity refers to the fact that node A might trust node B with respect to some tasks but not necessarily with all of them. Subjectivity refers to the fact that the trust each node can compute of any other nodes in the network depends on its perspective. For example, an öptimisticïode will have an average trust value more prominent than a pessimistic one with respect to the same tasks. Partial transitivity refers to the fact that if node A trusts node B and node B trusts node C, then it is not compulsory for node A to trust node C.

As stated by authors in reference [1], one of the main problems when dealing with WMN is the high computational cost of the nodes. This problem, along with their limited resources, leads to an increased level of vulnerability to attacks. Trust and reputation models can, therefore be a viable alternative to security through encryption in WSN. Based on the way that the network includes the trust and reputation model, we can split it into different categories as follows:

- security mechanisms like intrusion detection systems or dynamic access control policies. The role of trust and reputation, in this case, is that of detecting abnormal behaviour and then adjusting the level of trust of the nodes in the network;
- service management. Their use, in this case, can boost the solutions concerning multiple problems like routing and service provider selection;
- service provider (SP) selection. Their use, in this case, gives better performances according to reference [6];
- routing. In reference [9] authors have proved that trust and reputation models can be used for secure data-forwarding even through malicious isolating devices before making routes and finding the best and trustworthy route.

According to authors in reference [28], the trust and reputation models can also be classified according to the initial value that each node is given when entering the system, as follows:

- full trust. Each node is considered to be trustworthy and based on its malicious behaviour, that level of trust decreases. When the trust value drops under a fixed value named threshold, the node becomes untrustworthy. This approach is considered to be an optimistic one;
- no trust. Each node is considered to be untrustworthy and therefore has to prove its benevolence to become trustworthy. This approach is considered to be a pessimistic one;
- neutral value. Each node in the network is given a neutral value of trust and based on its actions that trust level can increase or decrease thus determining the trustworthiness of the node. This approach is considered, as the name suggests it, to be neutral.

According to the same paper [28], there are two possibilities for computing the trust and reputation values of the nodes. The first model is based solely on first-hand information, while the second one takes into account both first-hand information, as well as the second-hand information. If in the first case, each node takes into consideration only its experience to determine if a node is trustworthy, in the second case, it will base its trust and reputation value on its experience but also on the experience of its neighbours. Two systems, OCEAN [4] and Pathrater [22], have implemented both first hand and second-hand information and have shown that this model of computing the trust and reputation value is more robust.

Another interesting classification of trust and reputation models can be made according to the way that the trust and reputation value of the node in the network is updated. According to [19], the system can update the trust and reputation value either event-driven or time-based. Updating the value of the nodes in the system according to the first type of trigger is made after a transaction with the node has been completed. Updating the trust and reputation value in a time-driven system is made periodically by using an aggregation technique.

Multiple scenarios of use-cases for WSN have been built based on each of the priory mentioned classifications and characteristics of trust and reputation models. Multiple models have been proposed and tested in WMN, each presenting their way of analysing the network, suggesting a formula for trust level estimation and results showing the advantages and disadvantages of the selected approach (Table 1).

Authors in paper [17] have shown that several models can be implemented for wireless mobile networks. These models have applicability in fields like "cloud-computing, identity management and identity federation, web services and Internet of things".

Table 1. Proposed models for implementing trust in mobile wireless networks [21].

Trust model	Description
ATRM [8]	This model of trust and reputation is carried out locally with low delays and overhead for the networks
QDV [13]	Is an ant colony inspired model for trust and reputation with good results against packet injection by malicious nodes in a network
ATSN [11]	Is a watchdog-based approach for trust and security in a network
RFSN [30]	This is a reputation-table based approach for ensuring security
CORE [24]	Measures trustworthiness in a network by its implications to common network operations
DRBTS [29]	Is a two-level structure reputational model to assist user gather the best information available
BTRM-WSN [23]	Represents another ant colony inspired trust and reputation model adapted to maintain a trace of its neighbors at all times

A novel trust model for Mobile Cloud computing [25] was developed by the Distributed Systems Laboratory from the Politehnica University of Bucharest. The authors proposed an adaptive trust management algorithm for structured overlay networks based on the honeycomb structure.

3 Trust Is in the Air

Trust model-based systems give the advantage of not using the classic approach of adding a level-upon-level of security but, instead, they enforce it from the beginning and the general level of protection of the network grows along with the system itself. Although the idea of an evolving trust is appealing, the accuracy of the computed value of the trust levels of a node in a WMN is rather difficult to ensure.

After analysing various models of trust and reputation in WMN, we want to set the premises for a new Markov based approach for trust and reputation in WMN. We consider a WMN with a number of N independent nodes whose trust values are dynamic, asymmetric, context-sensitive, subjective and partial transitive.

Almost all the trust and reputation model we have analysed have taken into consideration only the behaviour of the node and have ignored the wireless aspect of the network, therefore bypassing the importance of the link between two nodes.

We have proposed this model to help emulate the behaviour of the connection between two nodes, oversimplifying the problem into three states: the node has a stable connection and is available for tasks, is offline to the network or is in a volatile state in which it is online but not entirely open for tasks. The trust levels of the nodes in the proposed system are influenced by only one type of fault. That fault is that any given node can be offline for an undefined period. Each node fails according to a sum of exponentially distributed function with parameter α. In the system, each node can have one of three states: online and available for communication, offline and non-existing and volatile in which the node has recovered from an offline state, but it is still not available for communication. The volatile state can be assimilated to the error diagnosis state after a sudden shut down of a node.

The trust and reputation model we propose is implemented to help boost the routing of packets and to help find a reliable service provider, therefore being included in the system for service management.

The proposed model represents an optimist approach and therefore grants each node full trust when entering the system. The trust and reputation value of any node in the system, at the starting point, is 1.

The trust and reputation value of a node in the system for this proposed model is computed based solely on first-hand information. This model implies that each node computes the trust of the other nodes and the access points of the system are used for the data aggregation. The number of transitions of a node can be counted by the node itself upon unusual behaviour and also by the nodes and the access points in its surroundings by checking the node's status. Further work on the proposed model will include analysing if second-hand information adds robustness to the system, as references [4] and [22] suggest.

For this model of trust and reputation, we suggest using a hybrid approach of both event-trigger and time-based for updating the trustworthiness of a node. The event-trigger update refers to the oscillating state of the node between online and offline and between the states offline and volatile. The time-based aspect of the proposed model refers to the fact that, if a node is in the volatile state for a period of time larger than a set threshold τ, then it will be automatically placed in the online state again. Along with resetting the state of the node from volatile to online, the trust and reputation value of the node will be restored to 1, therefore allowing a node to redeem from bad behaviour. That bad behaviour in this proposed model is represented by a bad connection, either from subjective causes like battery drainage or objective one like weather events.

The time during which the node is offline is considered downtime. We assume that the downtime of a node is according to a sum of exponentially distributed function with parameter β.

Parameter β, as well as α, can have either a fixed value for the lifespan of the node or a variable one, thus generating two different scenarios (Fig. 1). We assimilate these two scenarios in real life to the power supply a node. For example, we can use the fixed-parameter to map, for instance, a node which is constantly power plug and, thus, has little-to-no variations during its lifespan. In contrast, a battery-based node may vary according to the battery usage curve.

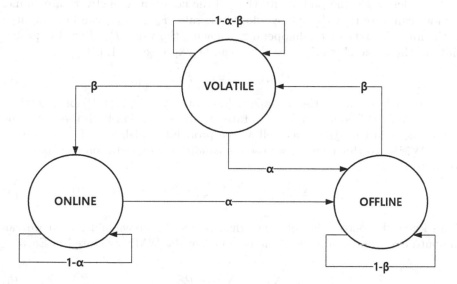

Fig. 1. Each node fails with a probability based on α parameter and recovers to an online state with a probability based on β parameter.

For research purposes, we consider that only one node recovers at a time as well as the fact that the nodes' variations between the state of online, offline and volatile are independently and that the state of one node does not influence that of those surrounding it. Therefore, for each node i from the N number of nodes existing in the network, there is a different α and β generically referred to as α_i and β_i. The premises previously stated represent an adaptation of a model presented in [16].

Given the previous premises, one of the main objectives of this paper is to discover what is the probability that a given number of nodes i, smaller than N, are online at any given time t in the WMN. To this respect, firstly, we modelled the proposed WMN as a Markovian system. We introduce

$$\gamma_i = \frac{\alpha_i}{\beta_i} \tag{1}$$

where α_i and β_i are the coefficients for the exponentially distributed functions which represent the states when a node is offline, respectively online.

Given the Eq. 1 and knowing the total number of nodes N in the network, we can state the probability that a given number i of nodes, smaller than N, are online at any given time t, from balance equations of continuous-time Markov chain as follows in Eq. 2.

$$P_i = \frac{\gamma_i}{i! \sum_{j=1}^{N} \frac{\gamma_j}{j!}} \tag{2}$$

Another goal of this paper is to estimate what is the average downtime rate (i.e. the average number of nodes that breaks down per time unit) as well as the average failure rate for our given WMN.

Considering P_N the probability that all the nodes in the network are online, then we can state that the average downtime rate ($P_{down.rate}$) can be computed as the improbability of P_N happening. Knowing the value P_N, then the probability of the whole network to be down can be expressed in Eq. 3.

$$P_{down.rate} = 1 - P_N \tag{3}$$

In order to estimate the average failure rate ($\lambda_{fail.rate}\epsilon[0;1]$) of a network with N number of nodes, we have to take into consideration both the downtime of each node in the system as well as the probability of having i nodes online in the WMN. To this respect, we use the conditional expectation calculation to compute Eq. 4.

$$\lambda_{fail.rate} = \sum_{i=1}^{N} i \times \alpha_i \times P_i \tag{4}$$

If we know the percentage of time when nodes are unavailable, then we can compute the average number of online nodes in the WMN as stated in Eq. 5.

$$N_{avg} = \sum_{i=1}^{N} i \times P_i \tag{5}$$

Trying to find the equation for the average downtime rate, a new challenge has arisen. If we can determine what the average number of online nodes is in a network, could we address the problem in reverse and find out what would be the minimum number of nodes that a WMN would have to have to ensure that at any given time there are at least N nodes online? The mathematical equation which can estimate the lowest number M of nodes which can guarantee at least N online nodes can be stated as follows $N_{avg}(M) \geq N$. The extended computation of that inequality can be observed in Eq. 6.

$$\sum_{i=1}^{M} \frac{i \times \gamma_i}{i! \sum_{j=1}^{M} \frac{\gamma_j}{j!}} \geq N. \tag{6}$$

These equations have been tested and validates by considering a network with a number of $N = 10$ independent nodes whose values of the parameters α and β can be observed in Table 2.

Table 2. Values of α and β for the test network formed by 10 nodes.

α	β
0.20	0.99
0.14	0.72
0.20	0.86
0.11	0.97
0.21	0.87
0.11	0.85
0.21	0.81
0.11	0.43
0.10	0.88
0.20	0.98

During the validation we have observed that a low rate a failure, stated by a low value of parameter *alpha*, along with a high recovery rate, translated in a high value of parameter *beta*, increase the probability of i number of nodes to be online in the network. These simulation results can be observed in Fig. 3.

In Fig. 2 we show the dependency of the probability of having a certain number of nodes online in the network according to the existing number of failed nodes. As seen, the value of the probability P is decreasing significantly with the number of offline nodes.

4   Adaptive Method Bases on Probabilities

Given the WMN described in the previous section, with N number of nodes which can switch their state between online and offline independently, we consider each of the node's initial trust to be 1 ($T_0 = 1$). That is to say that all the nodes start from the presumption of being fully reliable, with capabilities to be a part of the network (online). Each transition to offline and online again affect the reliability of the node and therefore it's trust.

We choose the variable w to express the probability that an offline node can not go online immediately, thus remaining in the volatile state. It's value can be computed as the ratio of the rate of node break-downs that can not go online immediately, over the total average rate of node break-downs as shown in Eq. 7.

$$w = \frac{\sum_{j=1}^{N-1} \alpha_j \times P_j}{\sum_{j=1}^{N} \alpha_j \times P_j}. \tag{7}$$

We can define the trust of a node i in a WMN with M nodes, an average number of N_{avg} online nodes with a probability w that after a break down they cannot become immediately online, after k number of transitions as follow in Eq. 8.

P value depending of the number of offline nodes

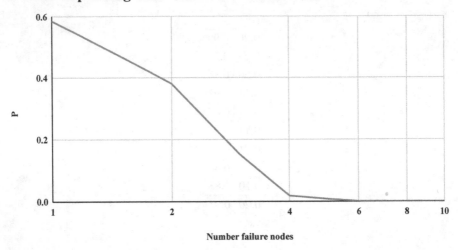

Fig. 2. Values of the probability P of having a certain number of online nodes in the network with respect to the number of failed nodes.

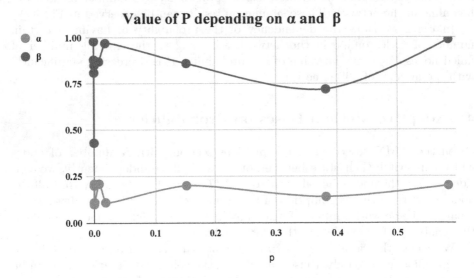

Fig. 3. Values of the probability P of having a certain number of online nodes in the network with respect to the α and β parameters.

$$T_i^k = \frac{1}{k} \times \left((1 - w) \times T_i^{k-1} + w \times \frac{N_{avg}}{M} \right) \tag{8}$$

Translating this formula for the trust and reputation level computation into pseudo-code can be observed in algorithm 1. Considering that when a node is going offline is it not voluntarily, then when it is rebooting it will have a system error to detect the abnormal behaviour.

Algorithm 1. Calculate the trust and reputation level of a node

1: M the number of nodes in the network
Require: $M \geq 0$
2: **for** $i < M$ **do**
3:    Compute for each node its γ_i and probability to be i nodes online at any given time in the network with M nodes
4:    $\gamma_i \leftarrow \frac{\alpha_i}{\beta_i}$
5:
6:    $P_i \leftarrow \frac{\gamma_i}{i! \sum_{j=1}^{M} \frac{\gamma_j}{j!}}$
7:
8: **end for**
9: $N_{avg} \leftarrow \sum_{i=1}^{M} i \times P_i$
10:
11: $w \leftarrow \frac{\sum_{j=1}^{M-1} \alpha_j \times P_j}{\sum_{j=1}^{M} \alpha_j \times P_j}$
12:
13: **for** $i < M$ **do**
14:    update the trust and reputation value for all the nodes in the network
15:    **if** node is recovering after being offline **then**
16:       **if** time recovering $> \tau$ **then**
17:          change node state to online
18:          $T_i = 1$
19:       **else**
20:          node state is considered volatile with k_i transitions
21:          $T_i^{k_i} = \frac{1}{k_i} \times \left((1-w) \times T_i^{k_i-1} + w \times \frac{N_{avg}}{M} \right)$
22:       **end if**
23:    **end if**
24:
25: **end for**

Furthermore, we evaluate the proposed trust method using the same sample values of the parameters of the network, as shown in Table 2. In Fig. 4 we show the obtained results where it can be seen that the trust value for each node decreases in the same manner as the value of the probability P of having a certain number of nodes online in the network.

If after a certain number of transitions during the volatile state, a node will remain stable, the trust and reputation model allows the possibility of redemption by reinstating its trust value to the initial one, $T_0 = 1$. Further work will determine how long does the time τ has to be to represent that a node has become stable and available properly.

One of the possible applications of this adaptive method for trust and reputation in WMN is to ensure secure routing of video streams taking into account QoS over a number of N online nodes.

Adaptive Trust

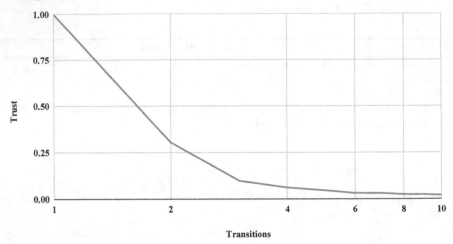

Fig. 4. Evolution of trust with respect to the number of failed nodes in the network

The authors of [26] present a novel lightweight trust decision-making framework named LEACH (Low Energy Adaptive Clustering Hierarchy) for secure video streaming. The stakeholders of this protocol are master nodes, member nodes, and base station, where sensor nodes are organised in small clusters. The base stations are power-plugged nodes, while the master nodes are chosen by taking into consideration the largest battery life of sensors. The low probability of being offline of the master nodes ensures a high level of trust, which is to be expected due to their high availability in the system.

Other applications of this adaptive trust model can be ubiquitous systems.

5   Conclusions

Taking into consideration the heterogeneous devices in a network along with the different operating systems and all-changing topology, it becomes difficult and consuming in terms of resources (time, money etc.) to implement classical security models with respect to QoS.

In this paper, we have proven that the trust and reputation based new paradigm of security may be able to solve these issues efficiently. The Markov based approach for trust and reputation in WMN proposed in this paper manages to compute trust values of the nodes that are dynamic, asymmetric, context-sensitive, subjective and partial transitive.

Each node in the system can have one of three states: online and available for communication, offline and non-existing and volatile in which the node has recovered from an offline state, but it is still not available for communication. The volatile state can be assimilated to the error diagnosis state after a sudden shut down of a node.

The trust and reputation model proposed represents an optimist approach and therefore grants each node full trust when entering the system. The trust and reputation value of any node in the system, at the starting point, is 1. Each update of the trust and reputation value is computed based solely on first-hand information. This approach has managed to avoid single point of failure but presents less accuracy, each user being limited to its history when considering if trusting other nodes. Extending the model to aggregate data from both first-handed and second-handed data represents future work.

This information is gathered using a hybrid approach of both event-trigger and time-based for updating the trustworthiness of a node. The obtained results of the proposed trust and reputation model present great potential regarding further simulations and determining the accuracy of the proposed algorithm.

Multiple challenges need to be addressed in terms of heterogeneous devices in a network. The first set of challenges addresses the hardware design, especially in the microcircuits and microprocessors manufacturing areas to deal with high propagation loss, especially in terahertz frequencies. Beyond the hardware implementation, the use of distributed user-centric architectures means a significant challenge in the distribution of data to the end-points in a secure and trustful manner. Another issue is creating an efficient and trusted system based on the next-generation 6G networks taking into consideration energy efficiency. Another challenge in these networks is the modelling and optimisation of the network topology for the scheduling of tasks.

One of the use cases involves the concept of unmanned mobility that will evolve to fully autonomous transportation systems with high efficiency, taking into consideration traffic safety and infrastructure management in a green manner.

Our statements are as follow: the trust model is defined and theoretically proved considering the probabilistic model presented in Sect. 3. The adaptive model (see Sect. 4) considers that adaptive factor, w, is changing over time, and that fact is reflected in the trust computation of a node. Further work will present the level of trust that the Markov based security approach which has been discussed in Section 3 can offer concerning similar other techniques presented in Sect. 2.

References

1. Ahmed, A.I.A., Ab Hamid, S.H., Gani, A., Khan, M.K., et al.: Trust and reputation for internet of things: fundamentals, taxonomy, and open research challenges. J. Netw. Comput. Appl. **145**, 102409 (2019)
2. Aiken, A.: Zooming in on privacy concerns: video app zoom is surging in popularity. In our rush to stay connected, we need to make security checks and not reveal more than we think. Index Censorsh. **49**(2), 24–27 (2020)
3. Alexander, J.: The entire world is streaming more than ever - and it's straining the internet: governments and ISPs are trying to manage strain (2020)
4. Bansal, S., Baker, M.: Observation-based cooperation enforcement in ad hoc networks. arXiv preprint cs/0307012 (2003)

5. Baras, J.S., Jiang, T.: Managing trust in self-organized mobile ad hoc networks. In: Proceedings of the 12th Annual Network and Distributed System Security Symposium Workshop (2005)
6. Billhardt, H., Hermoso, R., Ossowski, S., Centeno, R.: Trust-based service provider selection in open environments. In: Proceedings of the 2007 ACM symposium on Applied Computing, pp. 1375–1380 (2007)
7. Blose, T., Umar, P., Squicciarini, A., Rajtmajer, S.: Privacy in crisis: a study of self-disclosure during the coronavirus pandemic. arXiv preprint: 2004.09717 (2020)
8. Boukerche, A., Li, X.: An agent-based trust and reputation management scheme for wireless sensor networks. In: IEEE Global Telecommunications Conference, GLOBECOM 2005, vol. 3, pp. 5-pp. IEEE (2005)
9. Brenner, M.: Classifying ITIL processes; a taxonomy under tool support aspects. In: 2006 IEEE/IFIP Business Driven IT Management, pp. 19–28. IEEE (2006)
10. Chawla, A.: Coronavirus (COVID-19) - 'zoom' application boon or bane. SSRN 3606716 (2020)
11. Chen, H., Wu, H., Zhou, X., Gao, C.: Agent-based trust model in wireless sensor networks. In: Eighth ACIS International Conference on Software Engineering, Artificial Intelligence, Networking, and Parallel/distributed Computing (SNPD 2007), vol. 3, pp. 119–124. IEEE (2007)
12. David, K., Berndt, H.: 6G vision and requirements: is there any need for beyond 5G? IEEE Veh. Technol. Mag. **13**(3), 72–80 (2018)
13. Dhurandher, S.K., Misra, S., Obaidat, M.S., Gupta, N.: QDV: a quality-of-security-based distance vector routing protocol for wireless sensor networks using ant colony optimization. In: 2008 IEEE International Conference on Wireless and Mobile Computing, Networking and Communications, pp. 598–602. IEEE (2008)
14. DOCOMO, N.: White paper 5G evolution and 6G. Accessed 1 2020
15. Giordani, M., Polese, M., Mezzavilla, M., Rangan, S., Zorzi, M.: Toward 6G networks: use cases and technologies. IEEE Comm. Mag. **58**(3), 55–61 (2020)
16. Glaropoulos, I.: Queuing theory 2014-exercises (2014)
17. Gómez Mármol, F., Marín-Blázquez, J.G., Martínez Pérez, G.: LFTM, linguistic fuzzy trust mechanism for distributed networks. Concurr. Comput. Pract. Exp. **24**(17), 2007–2027 (2012)
18. Gray, L.M., Wong-Wylie, G., Rempel, G.R., Cook, K.: Expanding qualitative research interviewing strategies: zoom video communications. Qual. Rep. **25**(5), 1292–1301 (2020)
19. Guo, J., Chen, R., Tsai, J.J.: A survey of trust computation models for service management in internet of things systems. Comput. Commun. **97**, 1–14 (2017)
20. Kambourakis, G., Gomez Marmol, F., Wang, G.: Security and privacy in wireless and mobile networks (2018)
21. Mármol, F.G., Pérez, G.M.: Providing trust in wireless sensor networks using a bio-inspired technique. Telecommun. Syst. **46**(2), 163–180 (2011)
22. Marti, S., Giuli, T.J., Lai, K., Baker, M.: Mitigating routing misbehavior in mobile ad hoc networks. In: Proceedings of the 6th Annual International Conference on Mobile Computing and Networking, pp. 255–265 (2000)
23. Marzi, H., Li, M.: An enhanced bio-inspired trust and reputation model for wireless sensor network. Procedia Comput. Sci. **19**, 1159–1166 (2013)
24. Michiardi, P., Molva, R.: Core: a collaborative reputation mechanism to enforce node cooperation in mobile ad hoc networks. In: Jerman-Blažič, B., Klobučar, T. (eds.) Advanced Communications and Multimedia Security. ITIFIP, vol. 100, pp. 107–121. Springer, Boston (2002). https://doi.org/10.1007/978-0-387-35612-9_9

25. Pop, F., Dobre, C., Mocanu, B.C., Citoteanu, O.M., Xhafa, F.: Trust models for efficient communication in mobile cloud computing and their applications to e-commerce. Enterp. Inf. Syst. **10**(9), 982–1000 (2016)
26. Ramesh, S., Yaashuwanth, C.: Enhanced approach using trust based decision making for secured wireless streaming video sensor networks. Multimed. Tools Appl., 10157–10176 (2019). https://doi.org/10.1007/s11042-019-7585-5
27. Resnick, P., Zeckhauser, R.: Trust among strangers in internet transactions: empirical analysis of eBay's reputation system. Econ. Internet E-Commer. **11**(2), 23–25 (2002)
28. Sen, J.: A survey on reputation and trust-based systems for wireless communication networks. arXiv preprint arXiv:1012.2529 (2010)
29. Srinivasan, A., Teitelbaum, J., Wu, J.: DRBTS: distributed reputation-based beacon trust system. In: 2006 2nd IEEE International Symposium on Dependable, Autonomic and Secure Computing, pp. 277–283. IEEE (2006)
30. Srinivasan, A., Teitelbaum, J., Wu, J., Cardei, M., Liang, H.: Reputation-and-trust-based systems for ad hoc networks. Algorithms Protoc. Wirel. Mob. Ad Hoc Netw. **375**, 375–404 (2009)
31. Xu, X., Pan, Y., Lwin, P.P.M.Y., Liang, X.: 3D holographic display and its data transmission requirement. In: 2011 International Conference on Information Photonics and Optical Communications, pp. 1–4. IEEE (2011)

Enabling Next-Generation Cyber Ranges with Mobile Security Components

Enrico Russo⬛, Luca Verderame⬛, and Alessio Merlo$^{(\boxtimes)}$⬛

DIBRIS, University of Genoa, Genoa, Italy
{enrico.russo,luca.verderame,alessio.merlo}@unige.it

Abstract. The number of security incidents involving mobile devices has risen in the past years. This means that organizations must seriously consider such devices within their threat landscape and prepare their cybersecurity operators to prevent, identify, and manage security issues involving them. Nowadays, cyber ranges represent the most effective and versatile systems for training skills in the cybersecurity domain as they provide hands-on experiences in large, sophisticated infrastructures. Nevertheless, cyber ranges are capable of emulating components and interactions of the Information and Operational Technology domains, but they lack the support of mobile devices with the same effectiveness and realism. In this paper, we propose an enhancement of the architecture and the training environments of an existing cyber range, which properly integrates mobile security components. The effectiveness of such an integration is due to a thorough review of the mobile threat landscape and the functional components of a cyber range.

Keywords: Cyber range · Mobile security · Cybersecurity training

1 Introduction

Cyber ranges are virtualized environments that allow defining specific training in cybersecurity for a plethora of different students. A cyber range emulates an actual cybersecurity-relevant scenarios (e.g., the ICT deployment of a corporation or a small city) in which teams of several trainees compete to reach different (and conflicting) aims. A typical (and simplified) cyber range deployment involves a simulated ICT environment in which all components of the environment suffer from specific vulnerabilities, properly inserted before the competition start. On one side, a red team is aimed at discovering and exploiting such vulnerabilities, while, on the other side, a blue team aims to discover and fix the same vulnerabilities, before the red one can exploit them.

The granularity of the exercises, as well as the kind of vulnerabilities to play with, depends on the number and kind of emulated ICT infrastructures in the cyber range. A missing brick is the mobile component of the emulated ICT infrastructure. As a consequence, a lot of high impact vulnerabilities and attack

ⓒ IFIP International Federation for Information Processing 2020
Published by Springer Nature Switzerland AG 2020
V. Casola et al. (Eds.): ICTSS 2020, LNCS 12543, pp. 150–165, 2020.
https://doi.org/10.1007/978-3-030-64881-7_10

patterns cannot be tried in current cyber ranges. In fact, a vulnerable mobile node may act as a Trojan Horse to contact other connected devices, perform harmful commands or spread malicious software. Furthermore, a compromised mobile device may allow the attacker to steal, publicly reveal, or sell any personal information extracted from the device and the installed apps, including the user's information, information about contacts, or credentials.

To try bridging this gap, in this paper we discuss the importance of adding mobile components in actual cyber ranges, by illustrating a training motivating scenario (Sect. 2). Then, we point out the mobile threat landscape (Sect. 3) in order to identify the most promising family of vulnerabilities and attack patterns that can be fruitfully ported on cyber ranges. Furthermore, we detail a taxonomy and an architectural model of a generic cyber range (Sect. 4), before pointing out how such architectures can be extended and integrated with a mobile component (Sect. 5). Finally, we discuss some related work and some future steps towards the implementation of a next-generation cyber range emulating mobile components.

2   Motivating Scenario

In this section, we introduce a motivating scenario concerning a security testing against the employees and the Information Technology (IT) infrastructure of an enterprise.

2.1   A Penetration Testing Activity

A penetration test [9], also knows as a pentest, is a simulation of an attack against a given system or environment. The purpose of a pentest activity is identifying weaknesses and vulnerabilities in the target before an attacker can identify and exploit them for malicious activities.

This scenario is inspired by [25] and refers to the pentest conducted to find possible ways to steal reserved documents from a target enterprise. The initial conditions require the actors, namely the pentesters, to have no internal knowledge of the target system and negligible privileges. In detail, the pentesters have only a time-limited access to the guest network, i.e., the wireless network granting visitors access to the Internet and isolated from corporate resources. Nevertheless, the entire attack sequence led to the gain of the admin rights and the creation of a special Kerberos ticket, namely the Golden Ticket [32], which guarantees a long-term and hard-to-detect persistence. For the sake of presentation, here we only report the relevant steps that involve the mobile components.

First, the pentesters leverage their connection to execute a quick scan of the network and discover that even the employees use the guest wireless. In particular, they discover that the receptionist accesses the guest network to connect her own personal *smartphone* to the Internet.

Then, they exploit social engineering techniques [34] against the receptionist and gather the information that (*i*) she has a young daughter and (*ii*) often uses the connected smartphone to make the daughter play with some games inside.

This information allows the pentester to conduct a spear phishing [35] campaign to invite the receptionist to download and install an Android application for children. The suggested application is a real puzzle for children but modified with an injected code to grant the attackers a shell access to the mobile device.

The success of the phishing campaign provides a more stable link to the guest network through the receptionist's smartphone. This connection enables the pentesters to obtain a more in-depth knowledge of the network configuration, as depicted in Fig. 1.

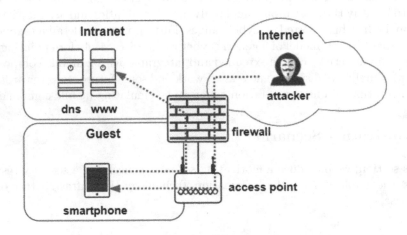

Fig. 1. The diagram of the penetration testing scenario.

Notice that the connected device can contact a name resolution server, namely *dns*, and a web server, namely *www*, hosted in a different network, probably the corporate *Intranet*. Moreover, a misconfiguration on the corporate *firewall* allows the guest hosts to access the login page of the manager application of the www server.

The pentesters use the smartphone as a gateway for attacking the www server. In particular, they obtain the admin password with a brute force attack [33], upload a web shell, and gain access to the Intranet.

A sequence of further lateral movements leads to the achievement of admin rights. We refer the interested reader to [25] for a detailed description of these steps.

3   The Mobile Threat Landscape

The involvement of vulnerable mobile devices in an attack can have severe consequences. Indeed, the attack discussed in Sect. 2 underlines the strategic importance of including mobile devices and applications in a cyber range exercise.

From a general standpoint, mobile devices share the same IT infrastructure of other connected devices. As shown in Fig. 2, the device can connect through a Wi-fi or cellular network to the Enterprise systems and consequently to the exposed Back-end Services such as Email servers, File Shares, and Enterprise App servers. Furthermore, the mobile device may host third-party apps retrieved by either Public or Enterprise App Stores.

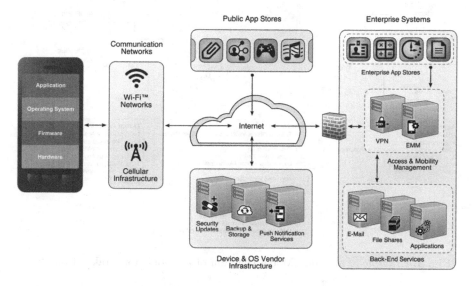

Fig. 2. Mobile ecosystem landscape.

To cope with the complexity of evaluating the security risks posed by such a mobile ecosystem, several initiatives propose frameworks and procedures for the threat modeling and the vulnerability assessment and penetration testing of mobile apps and devices. Notable examples include the Mobile Applications Security Verification Standard (MASVS) from the OWASP consortium [23] and the Mobile Threat Catalogue by NIST [19].

For instance, Fig. 3 depicts the Threat Model Diagram for a mobile app that can interact with a company workstation and its back-end services [2]. The diagram details the *Assets* controlled or accessed by the app, the possible *Threat Agents* that can interact with the ecosystem and, finally, describes a set of *Controls* that enable the mitigation of security breaches.

We can use the Threat Model Diagram to map the attack exploited in the Motivating Scenario: the attacker crafted a malicious app without specific permissions (TA04 - Malicious App (Sandboxed)) and then delivered it to the victim using a phishing message (e.g., [6]). Once installed, the app grants access to the device functionalities and the credentials of the victim (A06 - A03). After this stage, the mobile app acted as a Trojan Horse to contact other connected devices, perform harmful commands, or spread malicious software.

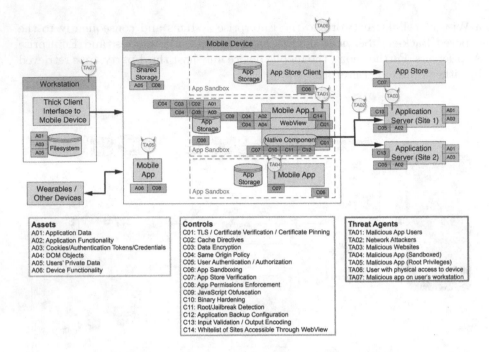

Fig. 3. Example of a Threat Model Diagram of a mobile app, taken from [2]

4 Cyber Ranges

In this section, we provide a taxonomy and an architectural model of a generic cyber range. The overall layout and its key components, core technologies, and capabilities are inspired by [12,39].

In detail, the architectural scheme of a cyber range is depicted in Fig. 4. It represents the two main levels, namely the *Management* and the *Training Environment* level, the core functionalities and related components. Two specific functionalities, i.e., the Orchestration and the Data Collection, enables interfacing between the two levels. A description of the above elements follows.

4.1 Management Level

The Management Level supports the planning and execution of the activities conducted within the cyber range. It can be accessed through a standalone *User Interface* (UI) or through an *Application Program Interface Gateway* (API GW). UI simplifies human interaction with the management functionalities. API GW provides a unified entry point for integrating external entities. This level makes also available the *Exercise Design* and the *Competency Management* functionalities.

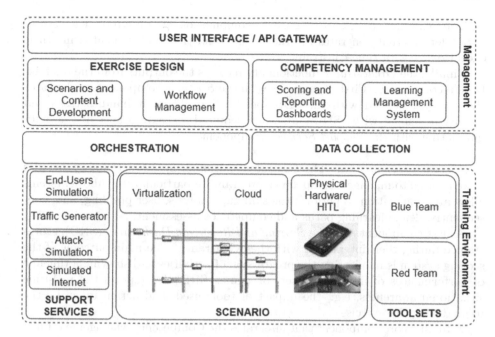

Fig. 4. The architectural scheme of a cyber range.

Exercise Design. The outcomes of the activities carried out in a cyber range are highly correlated to the quality of the training scenario. This means that the exercise designers must be able to build complex and heterogeneous infrastructures and reproduce events that characterize them, e.g., the users' activity. The Exercise Design functionality includes all the facilities to help designers to create training environments complying with the above constraints.

The definition of the infrastructure and its initial configuration is handled through the *Scenario and Content Development* (SCD) component. The primary function of SCD is allowing exercise designers to compose scenarios without having to know the underlying technologies and the complexity to configure the running environment. A common solution is to provide SCD with a domain-specific language (see, for example, [11,29]) for detailing the training environments of a cyber range. In particular, the above language, also identified as the *Scenario Definition Language* (SDL), allows the declarative specification of the scenario elements (e.g., a server, a firewall, or an IoT device), and their (mis)configurations (e.g., the installed software, the configured users, or the affected vulnerabilities).

A further component, namely the *Workflow Management* (WM), is in charge of scheduling and programming events, i.e., scenario injections, that are performed during the simulation. The WM supports the configuration of scenario injections through an extension of SDL, namely *extended SDL* (eSDL), that resembles the languages for business process modeling. Briefly, an exercise designer can use eSDL to configure (a combination of) activities, e.g., a scenario element that generates Internet traffic, and the conditions allowing their executions, e.g., a time constraint.

Finally, the *Orchestrator* functionality receives the outputs from the Exercise Design components. First, it interacts with the *Scenario* components and creates the sandbox defined with the SDL specification. Then, it handles tasks and condition defined with eSDL and, when required, execute a specified activity interacting with the *Support Services* component.

Competency Management. The *Competency Management* functionality includes systems used to manage a competence program. In particular, the above systems allow an organization to perform the skill gap analysis, user profiling, and, consequently, define learning paths and competence assessment.

A first component, i.e., the *Scoring and Reporting Dashboards* (SRD), scores trainee during their interaction with the cyber range. The main outcome of the scoring system is monitoring the progression of activities and showing a timeline of performances of individual users or teams. SRD also reports the real-time situational awareness, e.g., the impact of tools used, and action taken by the users during the exercise.

A further core component that integrates the Competency Management functionality is the *Learning Management System* (LMS). LMS is required for the administration, documentation, tracking, reporting, and delivery of learning and assessment content.

The *Data Collection* functionality extracts from the training environment most of the data used by these components, e.g., services status, generated traffic, memory dumps, logs, or other artifacts.

4.2   Training Environment

The Training Environment level represents the sandbox in which teams and individual users carry out their activities during the exercise execution. It includes the *Scenario* along with the *Support Services* and *Toolsets* functionalities.

Scenario. The Scenario functionality includes the digital infrastructure where all the activities are staged as well as all the game-specific aspects such as targets, vulnerabilities and rules of engagement. To this aim, it mainly leverages *Virtualization* and *Cloud Computing* components to host the virtual instance of all the required components.

Nevertheless, the Scenario may also require the inclusion of physical devices such as network equipment or IoT systems. The *Physical Hardware* (PH) component manages the interfacing with these hardware items.

PH also enables the *Hardware-in-the-Loop* (HITL) capability and allows real systems to interact with virtual stimuli received from the training environment.

Support Services. Actions performed by the *Support Services* functionality take place during the execution of the exercise and help to improve the realism of the training experience. Support Services interact directly with the Scenario and include the following components.

- *End-User Simulation* (EUS). It simulates the presence and behavior of benign users in the training environment. User simulation may refer to both internal users or fictitious clients accessing exposed services of the simulated environment. Examples of such user activity can include browsing the Internet, sending emails, or interacting with cloud or external services.
- *Traffic Generator* (TG). This component is capable of automatically generating both benign and malicious traffic. The function of traffic generators is crucial as the ability to identify and react to attacks by defense systems and operators lies in the precision with which traffic can be distinguished.
- *Attack Simulation* (AS). It refers to the ability to simulate attacks within and to the simulated environment. This component made available an attack library which contains a list of pre-defined attacks together with the ability to import/create custom operations. Attacks are performed interacting with the *Red Team Toolset*, and they may aim at exploiting vulnerabilities, executing lateral movements, and injecting malware or backdoors.
- *Simulated Internet*. It provides services outside the main simulated environment that are required for the realization of specific use cases. For example, this component can simulate social media (e.g., Twitter, Facebook, or LinkedIn), internet routing protocols, global services such as name resolution, remote API endpoints, or update and software repositories for various operating systems.

Toolsets. A cyber range is also equipped with state-of-the-art attack and defense tools made available to attackers (red team) and defenders (blue team) by the *Red Team* (RTB) and *Blue Team Toolsets* (BTT), respectively.

RTB consists of a collection of tools that aid in attacker operations, e.g., reconnaissance, weaponization, command-and-control, escalate privileges, lateral movements, or data exfiltration.

BTT includes services for the identification and prevention of intrusions, e.g., anti-malware or intrusion detection systems [17,18], and tools for carrying out analysis and managing security incidents, e.g., a System Information and Event Management (SIEM) software or digital forensic tools.

5 Extending Cyber Ranges with Mobile Ecosystems

As previously discussed, one of the main strengths of cyber ranges is the execution of exercises with a high degree of realism. Unfortunately, state-of-the-art cyber ranges cannot easily cope with a scenario that comprises mobile devices and apps. Indeed, current cyber ranges threat models do not include mobile ecosystems specifically, and thus the corresponding Assets, Threats, and Controls are coarse-grained and inaccurate. This implies that designers cannot create mobile-first exercises - like the one presented in Sect. 2 - and thus, red and blue teams cannot train their attack and defense skills in a mobile ecosystem.

To this aim, we define and present here an extension of the cyber range architectural model to support mobile ecosystems.

5.1 Mobile-Aware Cyber Range Architecture

The support of the mobile ecosystem requires a revision of the components of a cyber range (see Sect. 3) following the analysis of their functionalities that need to be updated or added. In Table 1, we summarize the results of the above analysis presenting the required integration tasks for revising each component.

Table 1. Integration tasks for mobile security components.

Management level (M)	
1. Exercise Design	
a. *Scenario and Content Development*	− M.a1.1: extend SDL with new components. − M.a1.2: add configuration script for new components.
b. *Workflow Management*	− M.b1.1: extend SDL+ with new actions and conditions.
2. Competency Management	
a. *Scoring and Reporting*	− M.2a: extend goals and metrics with ones related to mobile components.
b. *Learning and Management System*	− M.2b: introducing learning material and hands-on specific to mobile security.
Training environment (T)	
1. Scenario	
a. *Virtualization/Cloud*	− T.1a: extend automation tool for supporting mobile-specific connectivity.
b. *Physical Hardware*	− T.1b: support the interfacing with physical mobile devices.
2. Support services	
a. *End-Users Simulation/-Traffic Generator*	− T.2a: execute mobile-specific actions.
b. *Attack Simulation*	− T.2b: supporting the interaction with mobile-specific attack tools.
c. *Simulated Internet*	− T.2c: introducing the mobile-specific components.
3. Toolsets	
a. *Blue Team*	− T.3a: extending the weapon rack with mobile-specific tools for BTs.
a. *Red Team*	− T.3b: extending the weapon rack with mobile-specific attack tools.

Scenario and Content Development. A major set of updates concerns functionalities providing facilities for personnel involved in designing exercises, i.e., the SCD and WM components.

A first update consists of extending SDL languages to support the addition of mobile components and their configurations in the scenario specification (Task M.a1.1). For instance, cyber ranges can use easily expandable languages, e.g., *CRACK* SDL [29], to reproduce mobile elements and configurations through typed nodes. Fig. 5 depicts the CRACK SDL diagram for the receptionist's smartphone as described in the motivating scenario.

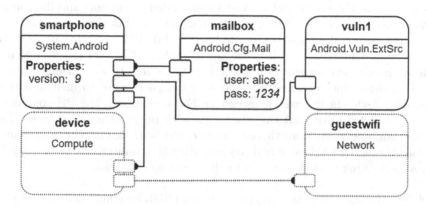

Fig. 5. An excerpt from the CRACK SDL diagram for the motivating scenario.

In detail, the *device* and *guestwifi* nodes represent components of the existing *Compute* and *Network* types, respectively. They represent the compute node, i.e., a virtual machine, connected to the guest network. The *System.Android*, *Android.Cfg.Mail*, and *Android.Vuln.ExtSrc* types are an example of an extension of the existing CRACK SDL. The *smartphone* node is the instance of the Android system running on the compute node. Its type allows the designer to specify the Android version through the *version* property. The *mailbox* node represents an Android configuration. In particular, it configures the mailbox used by the receptionist for reading emails on the smartphone. Its type allows the designer to specify the credential for accessing the mailbox through the *user* and *pass* properties. The *vuln1* node is a vulnerability that arises from a misconfiguration of the smartphone.

In addition to the support of an extended SDL language, the SCD needs to associate a corresponding configuration script to each new component (Task M.a1.2). For example, the Android.Vuln.ExtSrc type presented in Fig. 5 must be translated into a sequence of operations required on Android for allowing the installation of apps from unknown sources.

Scenario. Hence, the scenario deployment is handled by an SDL Orchestrator that (*i*) parses the specification, (*ii*) selects all the configuration scripts associated with the scenario, and (*iii*) executes the script on the related System node.

Typically, the execution phase is managed using automation IT tools, e.g., *Ansible* [27], that use Secure Shell (SSH) daemons to access each compute node and execute the scripting operations to configure the scenario. However, mobile OSes do not support by default the SSH connectivity, and thus, it is not the best method to configure them. For example, the *Android debug bridge* [3] (ADB) can run over a TCP connection and facilitates a variety of device configuration and actions.

To this aim, the Orchestrator must be extended to support specific connectivity methods (i.e., an ADB plugin) for configuring mobile devices (Task T.1a).

The operations described above apply to mobile OSes running inside a virtual machine. Unfortunately, in some cases, mobile OSes can not be executed inside a virtual environment. For instance, this is due to a licensing problem, virtual hardware incompatibility, or because designers want to include a physical mobile device in the exercise scenario. For this reason, the PH component must be extended to support the interfacing with physical mobile devices (Task T1.b). A suitable solution for this extension could be (*i*) having the management interface through a USB cable and (*ii*) providing the connectivity to the training environment using a wireless access to the scenario networks.

Workflow Management. As it happened for the SDL language, a further update consists in extending eSDL in the Workflow Management to support activities and conditions related to a mobile ecosystem (Task M.b2.1). As an example, Figure 6 depicts the eSDL diagram of the spearphishing attack described in the motivating example. The diagram represents an injection event that is programmed to possibly occurs during the running exercise.

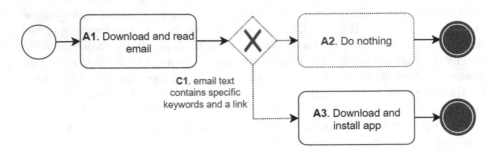

Fig. 6. A eSDL diagram for the spearphishing attack of the motivating scenario.

Differently from the traditional eSDL language, we introduced two activities, A1 and A2, to mimic the user operations on Android devices. The A1 activity download and read an email using the Android mail app. The A2 activity download and install an app from a HTML link in input and install it on Android.

Support Services. As detailed in Sect. 4, eSDL activities are executed in the running environment by the Orchestrator but through the EUS and TG components of the Support Services. Therefore, EUS and TG must be extended to execute mobile-specific actions on running devices (Task T.2a). To do so, the Support Services need to include specific software to interact and simulate the user interaction, such as the monkeyrunner tool [4] and DroidBot [16] for Android OS.

Another fact that features the mobile ecosystem is its close relationship with Internet services. As described in Sect. 3, apps installed on mobile devices are typically retrieved from stores hosted on the public Internet. Moreover, many mobile apps implement their functionalities interacting with remote API services exposed by servers from the Internet. For this reason, the SI component must be integrated with services that simulate App Stores and remote API services (Task T.2c). For instance, the SI can include a customized application market based on the F-Droid [10] open-source marketplace and a system to mock remote API services based on the Mocky [13] tool.

Toolsets. Concerning the Toolsets component, the cyber range needs to include mobile-specific tools for both the Red and Blue teams (Tasks T.3a and T.3b).

For example, as described in the motivating scenario, the red team could use an injection tool, namely Metasploit framework [26], to generate a malicious payload and pack it into a legitimate Android application as a Trojan to compromise the user device. Other red team tools can include Owasp ZAP Proxy [21], zAnti [40], and iNalyzer [7].

Notice that some of these attacking tools need to be integrated with the AS component (Task T2.b) if they are used to perform operations during automatic attacks.

On the other hand, blue teams can use vulnerability assessment tools, e.g., apktool [37], jadx [31], and Mobile Security Framework (MobSF) [1], to detect vulnerabilities and patch mobile apps [5].

Competency Management. Mobile-aware cyber ranges requires also to extend the Competency Management. In particular, trainees must practice on topics and hands-on specific to mobile security before tackling an exercise on a complex and mixed scenario. These new resources need to be added to the LMS component (Task M2.b). For example, the contents hosted by LMS could be enriched with documentation and related exercises about the security of mobile ecosystems, such as fundamentals of decompilation of mobile apps, static analysis techniques, fundamentals of app repackaging and instrumentation, how to intercept the network traffic of an app, or forensic techniques for mobile devices.

Similarly, the rating of the trainees' performances must be extended according to their activities related to the mobile environment. In detail, the SRD score must include the goals that involve mobile assets (Task M.2a). For example, a red team's goals could include taking control of a mobile device, exfiltrate data from smartphones and apps, or threaten the overall service availability shutting them down. On the other side, new blue team goals could be reporting how they hardened flaws in mobile devices' configuration or how they analyzed and patched an installed app.

6   Related Work

The increasing popularity of Cyber Ranges is pushing the research community to design and build advanced Cyber Ranges architectures. More in detail, most of the attention is devoted to the building and deployment of complex and heterogeneous training scenarios to reduce the learning curve of students. The KYPO cyber range [38] is a cyber exercise and research platform where security experts can carry out exercises and experiments in a secure and isolated environment. KYPO simulates complex scenarios through virtual environments hosting different types of infrastructural components. These scenarios can also include mobile devices running virtual machines with Android images.

ADLES [15], CyRIS [8], CRACK [29] are tools for creating cyber range scenarios and use virtualization for deploying them. Like [38] they can potentially emulate mobile devices running Android in the instantiated virtual machines.

Unlike [8,15,29,38], a proficient training on mobile security can not be limited only to the integration of Android virtual machines in the running scenario. It requires at least the support of specific configurations and vulnerabilities, the emulation of their strong relationship with the user activity through ad-hoc runtime injections, and the support of targeted tools like the preliminary proposal we discussed here.

Many other initiatives offer hands-on solutions for training security experts on mobile security. Among them, the MSTG Playground [20], the Android Security Sandbox [36], DIVA Android [24] and InsecureBankv2 [30] provide vulnerable apps to be used as the target of VAPT sessions. Other similar forms of hands-on activities are Capture the Flag (CTF) challenges like UnCrackable Mobile Apps [22], KGB Messenger [14] and Mobile CTF [28].

However, although these hands-on solutions represent an effective way to learn mobile security, they are unable to cover the comprehensive process of cybersecurity defense like Cyber Ranges and our proposal do.

7   Conclusion

This paper is an early step towards enhancing generic cyber ranges with the full integration of the mobile security ecosystem in their training environments. We briefly reviewed the mobile threat landscape along with the component and functionalities of the current state-of-the-art cyber ranges. The above analysis allowed us to detail a list of tasks and examples to simplify and carry out such an integration. This project is still on-going and we identify the following main next steps.

First, a complete implementation of the proposal on an existing and running cyber range. During this activity, we strongly require to focus our effort on extending the SDL and its orchestrator engine with the support of a rich catalog of configurations, vulnerabilities and runtime actions for mobile components.

Then, after a survey of real-world case studies involving the use of mobile components in complex IT infrastructures, we need to identify key aspects to be reproduced in training exercises. This effort should lead us to proficiently extend the current training scenarios with mobile components and make the most of the new features.

Finally, we need to validate our proposal by using an extended scenario and evaluating the training outcome after an exercise session.

Acknowledgments. This work was partially funded by the Horizon 2020 project "Strategic Programs for Advanced Research and Technology in Europe" (SPARTA) and by the Italian Ministry of Defense PNRM project "UNAVOX".

References

1. Abraham, A.: Mobile Security Framework. https://github.com/MobSF/Mobile-Security-Framework-MobSF. Accessed Sept 2020
2. Sethi, A., Bergman, N., Kozyrakis, J., Gagnon, C., Scambray, J.: The Developer's Guide to Securing Mobile Applications: Threat Modeling. https://www.synopsys.com/software-integrity/resources/ebooks/securing-mobile-applications-threat-modeling.html. Accessed Sept 2020
3. Android: Android Debug Bridge. https://developer.android.com/studio/command-line/adb (2020). Accessed Sept 2020
4. Android: monkeyrunner tool. https://developer.android.com/studio/test/monkeyrunner (2020). Accessed Sept 2020
5. Aonzo, S., Georgiu, G.C., Verderame, L., Merlo, A.: Obfuscapk: an open-source black-box obfuscation tool for android apps. SoftwareX **11**, 100403 (2020). https://doi.org/10.1016/j.softx.2020.100403. http://www.sciencedirect.com/science/article/pii/S2352711019302791
6. Aonzo, S., Merlo, A., Tavella, G., Fratantonio, Y.: Phishing attacks on modern android. In: Proceedings of the 2018 ACM SIGSAC Conference on Computer and Communications Security, CCS 2018, New York, NY, USA, pp. 1788–1801. Association for Computing Machinery (2018). https://doi.org/10.1145/3243734.3243778
7. AppSec Labs: iNalyzer. https://appsec-labs.com/inalyzer/. Accessed Sept 2020
8. Beuran, R., Pham, C., Tang, D., Chinen, K.i., Tan, Y., Shinoda, Y.: Cybersecurity education and training support system: CyRIS. IEICE Trans. Inf. Syst. **101**(3), 740–749 (2018). https://doi.org/10.1587/transinf.2017EDP7
9. Bishop, M.: About penetration testing. IEEE Secur. Priv. **5**(6), 84–87 (2007). https://doi.org/10.1109/MSP.2007.159
10. F-Droid Limited: F-Droid. https://www.f-droid.org/. Accessed Sept 2020
11. Fite, B.K.: Simulating cyber operations: a cyber security training framework (2018). https://www.sans.org/reading-room/whitepapers/bestprac/simulating-cyber-operations-cyber-security-training-framework-34510. Accessed Sept 2020
12. Gonzalez, C.P.: Cyber range the future of cyber security training. Technical report, SANS (2020)
13. Lafont, J.: Mocky.io (2020). https://github.com/julien-lafont/Mocky. Accessed Sept 2020
14. Lambert, T.: KGB Messenger. https://github.com/tlamb96/kgb_messenger. Accessed Sept 2020
15. Conte de Leon, D., Goes, C.E., Haney, M.A., Krings, A.W.: ADLES: specifying, deploying, and sharing hands-on cyber-exercises. Comput. Secur. **74**(C), 12–40 (2018). https://doi.org/10.1016/j.cose.2017.12.007

16. Li, Y., Yang, Z., Guo, Y., Chen, X.: DroidBot: a lightweight UI-guided test input generator for android. In: 2017 IEEE/ACM 39th International Conference on Software Engineering Companion (ICSE-C), pp. 23–26. IEEE (2017)
17. Migliardi, M., Merlo, A.: Modeling the energy consumption of distributed IDS: a step towards green security. In: 2011 Proceedings of the 34th International Convention MIPRO, pp. 1452–1457, May 2011
18. Migliardi, M., Merlo, A.: Improving energy efficiency in distributed intrusion detection systems. J. High Speed Netw. **19**(3), 251–264 (2013)
19. NIST: Mobile Threat Catalogue (2018). https://pages.nist.gov/mobile-threat-catalogue. Accessed Sept 2020
20. Open Web Application Security Project: MSTG Hacking Playground. https://github.com/OWASP/MSTG-Hacking-Playground. Accessed Sept 2020
21. Open Web Application Security Project: Zed Attack Proxy. https://owasp.org/www-project-zap/. Accessed Sept 2020
22. OWASP: UnCrackable Mobile Apps. https://github.com/OWASP/owasp-mstg/tree/master/Crackmes. Accessed Sept 2020
23. OWASP: OWASP Mobile Security Testing Guide (2020). https://owasp.org/www-project-mobile-security-testing-guide/. Accessed Sept 2020
24. Payatu Software Labs LLP: DIVA Android. https://github.com/payatu/diva-android. Accessed Sept 2020
25. Pierini, A., Trotta, G.: From APK to Golden Ticket, February 2017. https://www.exploit-db.com/docs/english/44032-from-apk-to-golden-ticket.pdf
26. Rapid7 LLC: Metasploit Framework (2020). https://www.metasploit.com/. Accessed Sept 2020
27. Red Hat: Ansible (2020). https://www.ansible.com/. Accessed Sept 2020
28. Rodriguez, I.: Mobile CTF. https://ivrodriguez.com/mobile-ctf/. Accessed Sept 2020
29. Russo, E., Costa, G., Armando, A.: Building next generation cyber ranges with CRACK. Comput. Secur. **95**, 101837 (2020). https://doi.org/10.1016/j.cose.2020.101837
30. Shetty, D.: InsecureBankv2. https://github.com/dineshshetty/Android-InsecureBankv2. Accessed Sept 2020
31. Skylot: jadx. https://github.com/skylot/jadx. Accessed Sept 2020
32. Soria-Machado, M., Abolins, D., Boldea, C., Socha, K.: Kerberos golden ticket protection. Mitigating Pass-the-Ticket on Active Directory, CERT-EU Security Whitepaper 7, 2016 (2014). https://cert.europa.eu/static/WhitePapers/UPDATED%20-%20CERT-EU_Security_Whitepaper_2014-007_Kerberos_Golden_Ticket_Protection_v1_4.pdf
33. The MITRE Corporation: T1110: Brute Force (2020). https://attack.mitre.org/techniques/T1110/. Accessed Sept 2020
34. The MITRE Corporation: T1268: Conduct social engineering (2020). https://attack.mitre.org/techniques/T1268/. Accessed Sept 2020
35. The MITRE Corporation: T1566.002: Phishing: Spearphishing Link (2020). https://attack.mitre.org/techniques/T1566/002/. Accessed Sept 2020
36. Toledo, R.: Android Security Sandbox. https://github.com/rafaeltoledo/android-security. Accessed Sept 2020
37. Tumbleson, C.: Apktool. https://ibotpeaches.github.io/Apktool/. Accessed Sept 2020

38. Vykopal, J., Oslejsek, R., Celeda, P., Vizvary, M., Tovarnak, D.: KYPO cyber range: design and use cases. In: Proceedings of the 12th International Conference on Software Technologies - Volume 1: ICSOFT, pp. 310–321. INSTICC, SciTePress (2017). https://doi.org/10.5220/0006428203100321
39. Yamin, M.M., Katt, B., Gkioulos, V.: Cyber ranges and security testbeds: scenarios, functions, tools and architecture. Comput. Secur. **88**, 101636 (2020). https://doi.org/10.1016/j.cose.2019.101636.   http://www.sciencedirect.com/science/article/pii/S0167404819301804
40. Zimperium: zAnti.   https://www.zimperium.com/zanti-mobile-penetration-testing. Accessed Sept 2020

Testing Methods and Applications

A Technique for Parallel GUI Testing
of Android Applications

Porfirio Tramontana(✉), Nicola Amatucci, and Anna Rita Fasolino

University of Naples "Federico II", Napoli, Italy
{ptramont,nicola.amatucci,fasolino}@unina.it

Abstract. There is a large need for effective and efficient testing processes and tools for mobile applications, due to their continuous evolution and to the sensitivity of their users to failures. Industries and researchers focus their effort to the realization of effective fully automatic testing techniques for mobile applications. Many of the proposed testing techniques lack in efficiency because their algorithms cannot be executed in parallel. In particular, Active Learning testing techniques usually relay on sequential algorithms.

In this paper we propose a Active Learning technique for the fully automatic exploration and testing of Android applications, that parallelizes and improves a general algorithm proposed in the literature. The novel parallel algorithm has been implemented in the context of a prototype tool exploiting a component-based architecture, and has been experimentally evaluated on 3 open source Android applications by varying different deployment configurations.

The measured results have shown the feasibility of the proposed technique and an average saving in testing time between 33% (deploying two testing resources) and about 80% (deploying 12 testing resources).

1 Introduction

Nowadays, the diffusion of mobile applications is continuously increasing, and these applications are often characterized by a very tight time-to-market to follow the evolution of the users needs and trends. On the other hand, this rapid development process can produce mobile applications containing a large number of faults. Crashes and other failures originated by these faults may compromise the quality of the app and can be responsible of drastic losses in terms of users that will soon uninstall an unreliable application[1]. In the last years academia and industry have shown a great interest for fully automatic testing techniques and tools as shown by the large number of proposals that can be found in literature [25, 30].

In the context of Android applications, most of these techniques can be classified in three distinct categories: Random testing techniques, Model Based testing techniques and Active Learning testing techniques [1].

---

[1] https://blog.helpshift.com/80-users-delete-mobile-apps/.

© IFIP International Federation for Information Processing 2020
Published by Springer Nature Switzerland AG 2020
V. Casola et al. (Eds.): ICTSS 2020, LNCS 12543, pp. 169–185, 2020.
https://doi.org/10.1007/978-3-030-64881-7_11

Random Testing Techniques are fully automatic testing techniques that choose user or system events at random and execute them on the application under test without taking into account the previously executed events. For example, the Monkey tool[2] is a command line executable testing tool included in the standard Android Development Toolkit (ADT) that is able to generate sequences of events on the interface of an Android application in a totally automatic manner. Other random techniques have been proposed in [13,17,20,26]. Random testing techniques can be applied without any previous knowledge of the application under test and can be easily parallelized by executing different independent testing sessions on different testing resources. Although these techniques have demonstrated their effectiveness in many contexts, a well known limitation is due to the possible redundancy of the executed test cases, that causes a remarkable inefficiency. For this reason, such techniques often require long running times before achieving significant effectiveness values [1,9]. In addition, the trend of the discovery of unexplored application behaviors tends to drastically decrease with the increase of the running time, so it is difficult to choose a termination criterion that ensures an optimal trade-off between effectiveness and efficiency [3,26].

More efficient solutions to these testing problems are represented by Model Based and Active Learning testing techniques. Model Based techniques are able to generate and execute test cases from structural and/or behavioral models of the application. Examples of models used for the automatic generation and execution of test cases are Finite State Machines [19,22,23,29], Sequence Diagrams [5], Activity Diagrams [11,15], GUI Trees [3,27,28] and Labeled State Transition Machines [24]. A limitation of these techniques is represented by the difficulty to design or reverse engineer an accurate model describing the structure and the behavior of the application under test.

A specialization of Model Based techniques is represented by Active Learning testing techniques [8]. These techniques (also called Model Learning techniques) do not need any existing model of the application under test but they are able to dynamically build models during an automatic exploration process. The exploration itself is driven by the dynamically built model. Amalfitano et al. [1] have studied the similarities between different Active Learning approaches presented in literature in the context of GUI testing of Android applications. They have found that all the approaches consist of iterative algorithms in which, at each iteration, an user or a system event that is executable on the current GUI of the application under test is scheduled and executed, and the resulting GUI is used to refine the model. Active Learning techniques usually terminate their execution when all the relevant events executable on the GUIs of the application under test have been executed at least once. Many Active Learning techniques and tools supporting GUI testing of Android applications have been proposed in the last years both by academy and industry [25], including for example Android Ripper [4], A^3E [6], SwiftHand [8], Dynodroid [17] and Sapienz [20]. Google has released and made available to developers an Active Learning testing tool in the

---

[2] http://developer.android.com/tools/help/monkey.html.

form of a cloud service called Android Robo Test[3], that represents a simple but not very effective tool.

Active Learning techniques are generally difficult to be parallelized since they are based on iterative algorithms where the selection of the next event to be tested is based on the analysis of the reconstructed model of the application, that is refined at each iteration. The need for a centralized storing and management of this model introduces a constraint for the parallelization of the testing activities.

This paper presents an evolution of an instance of the Unified Online Testing algorithm presented in [1]. This evolution allows the parallel execution of some portions of the algorithm, with a consequent saving in terms of testing time with respect to its sequential version. This technique has been implemented by a prototype tool extending the Android Ripper tool [2,4]. We carried out a preliminary experimentation of the tool by executing it on 3 different Android applications by varying the number of testing machines and the number of virtual devices instances for each machine, in order to assess the savings in testing time with respect to the non-parallel configuration.

The paper is organized as follows: in Sect. 2 the most relevant parallel Active Learning testing techniques found in the scientific literature are presented while in Sect. 3 our proposed algorithm is presented. The characteristics of the prototype tool implementing the algorithm are reported in Sect. 4. The results of some experiments carried out on 3 open source Android applications are presented in Sect. 5, together with a discussion of the obtained results and of the directions for the future improvements of the technique and of the tool. Finally, conclusions and future works are reported in Sect. 6.

2   Related Work

As highlighted in [25], only few automatic techniques and tools supporting GUI testing of Android applications have been designed having parallel execution in mind.

Neamtiu et al. [14] in 2011 presented a first technique based on the parallel execution of the Monkey tool to generate random or deterministic event sequences, while Mahmood et al. [18] in 2014 proposed EvoDroid, a tool that exploits parallel execution in the context of a cloud platform to increase the efficiency of the Search-based technique they implemented. Similarly Mao et al. [20] exploited parallel execution of test cases to reduce the execution time of their multi-objective search based testing strategy implemented by the tool Sapienz.

As regards Parallel Active Learning testing techniques, the first relevant contribution in the literature is the one provided by Meng et al. [21], that presented ATT, a master-slave testing framework supporting the parallel and distributed execution of test cases on Android applications. With ATT it is possible to distinguish an AgentManager component that acts as master and interacts with the slave nodes, called Agents. Each Agent is in charge of interacting with one

---

[3] https://firebase.g.oogle.com/docs/test-lab/robo-ux-test.

Android Virtual or Real Device: it receives information about the GUI and interacts with the target app through a service running on the target device. ATT has
been applied to different testing processes involving the re-execution of test cases
generated by the Capture and Replay tool RERAN [10], the random testing tool
called Monkey+ and the hybrid approach called UGA [16].

Wen et al. [28] proposed in 2015 a framework called PATS aiming at the
reduction of the execution time of an Active Learning testing process by using a
master-slave model. The dynamic exploration algorithm performed by the testing
process is carried out by a set of slave nodes that analyze a GUI, dynamically
elicit event sequences to be fired and actually fire events on the application
under test. These events are managed by a coordinator that guides the process
dispatching new GUIs to the slave nodes; this component is also in charge for
avoiding redundancies within the model.

More recently, Cao et al. [7] have presented ParaAim, a tool for the systematic
exploration of Android apps designed for parallel execution. It explores the GUI
states of an app using the exploration technique presented in [12]. When a newly
encountered Activity of the app is discovered for the first time, it starts a new
task considering this state as a starting point. The proposed approach is based
on the master-slave pattern where the master owns a queue of tasks that are
scheduled on independent slave nodes; each slave node restores the GUI state by
replying the event sequence leading to it, then it continues the exploration from
there. Moreover, to speed up the exploration, there are a prioritization algorithm
and an event sequence minimization heuristic to reduce the costs related to replay
the event sequences. The experiments reported in [7] show how the exploration
speed increases almost linearly as the number of devices increases. ParaAim,
similarly to our approach, adopts a master-slave architecture and distributes
tasks on the slave nodes but it also introduces a prioritization strategy and
performs an event sequence minimization task. A weakness of ParaAim with
respect to our tool is related to the granularity of the analysis: ParaAim is
guided by Activity coverage, whereas our tool is driven by the more fine grained
coverage of executable events [1].

3   A Parallel Algorithm for the Automatic Exploration of Android Applications

In this section the parallel Active Learning algorithm that we have designed
for the automatic exploration and testing of Android applications will be presented. This algorithm has been derived from a sequential Active Learning
Testing algorithm that implements an iterative exploration of an application
under test (AUT). The pseudo-code of this sequential algorithm is shown in
Algorithm 1. This algorithm has been obtained as an instance of the more general Unified Online Testing Algorithm presented in [1].

The algorithm begins by executing the *initializeAppModel* operation that
starts the AUT and initializes the model *appModel* with the description of the
first GUI of the AUT. The GUI description includes a subset of its widgets

---

Algorithm 1. Sequential Active Learning Testing algorithm

1:   $appModel \leftarrow initializeAppModel()$;
2:   $stopCondition \leftarrow evaluateStopCondition()$;
3:   **while** $(!stopCondition)$ **do**
4:      $fireableEvents[] \leftarrow extractEvents(appModel)$
5:      $eventsSequence \leftarrow scheduleEvents(fireableEvents[])$;
6:      $CurrentGUIDescription \leftarrow runEvents(eventsSequence)$;
7:      $appModel \leftarrow refineAppModel(CurrentGUIDescription)$;
8:      $stopCondition \leftarrow evaluateStopCondition()$;
9:   **end while**

---

and the values of a subset of its attributes (e.g. buttons and text fields and attributes such as id and event handlers). At each iteration, the algorithm analyzes the description of the current GUI interface in the *appModel* and evaluates if there are new events that can be fired on it. The set of considered events is limited to the ones for which an explicit event handler has been implemented in the AUT code. The *extractEvents* operation pushes this set of executable events (and the corresponding sequences of events preceding each of them) on the *fireableEvents* queue. Successively, the *scheduleEvents* operation pops an executable events sequence from the *fireableEvents* queue and executes it on the AUT (*runEvents* method). The *refineAppModel* adds the description of the GUI obtained after the execution of the sequence of events to the *appModel*. The algorithm continues until there are no more events to be scheduled, i.e. until the *fireableEvents* queue is empty.

In order to design a parallel version of this algorithm, some observations have to be taken into account. Most of the operations performed by this algorithm involve the analysis or the update of the *appModel*: (1) the *initializeAppModel* operation inserts into the *appModel* the description of the starting GUI of the AUT; (2) the *extractEvents* method extracts from the model the set of events that can be executed on the current GUI of the AUT; (3) the *refineAppModel* operation updates the *appModel* with the description of the last explored GUI. All these operations cannot be parallelized since they need the exclusive access to the *appModel* data structure.

The *scheduleEvents* and the *runEvents* methods, instead, can be concurrently executed. In particular, a Degree of Parallelism P can be achieved for these operations if P testing resources (i.e. virtual or real devices) are available. In this case, the semantic of the *scheduleEvents* method is modified in order to select a set of P sequences of events. The *runEvents* method can be transformed in the *runParallelEvents* one, that sends each of the P scheduled sequences of events to one of the P available resources. The Algorithm 1 is consequently transformed in the Parallel Active Learning testing algorithm (Algorithm 2).

In details, the *scheduleParallelEvents* method returns a set of P sequences of events *eventsSequence[]* that is passed to the *runParallelEvents* method. This method distributes the P sequences of events to the P different testing resources. The *refineAppModel* operation sequentially updates the *appModel* taking into

Algorithm 2. Parallel Active Learning Testing Algorithm

1: $appModel \leftarrow initializeAppModel()$;
2: $stopCondition \leftarrow evaluateStopCondition()$;
3: **while** ($!stopCondition$) **do**
4:     $fireableEvents[] \leftarrow extractEvents(appModel)$
5:     $eventsSequence[] \leftarrow scheduleParallelEvents(P, fireableEvents[])$;
6:     $CurrentGUIDescription[] \leftarrow runParallelEvents(P, eventsSequence[])$;
7:     $appModel \leftarrow refineAppModel(CurrentGUIDescription[])$;
8:     $stopCondition \leftarrow evaluateStopCondition()$;
9: **end while**

account all the P GUI instances received from the testing resources. Of course, if there are less than P items in the *fireableEvents* queue, only a subset of the resources will be used in that iteration of the algorithm.

4   Architecture and Implementation of the Tool

The Algorithm 2 presented in the previous section has been implemented in a prototype called *Parallel Android Ripper*, that is based on the Android Ripper[4] tool presented in [1]. The system is built according to a component based architecture and can be distributed on different machines. The architecture includes the following two types of components:

- The *Coordinator* component that is responsible of the execution of the Algorithm 2 and that has exclusive access to the *appModel* data structure; it coordinates the execution of the whole process.
- The *Test Case Executor* components that receive from the *Coordinator* sequences of events to be executed and inject them into the Android Virtual or Real Device they manage.

The abstract architecture of the Parallel Android Ripper can be deployed in different ways by changing the number of involved machines, the number of *Test Case Executor* components deployed on each of these machines and the type of testing resources (i.e. Android Virtual or Real Devices).

For example, Fig. 1 shows a possible deployment scenario where the *Coordinator* component is deployed on a physical machine storing the *appModel*, too, and there are three machines each one hosting two instances of the *Test Case Executor* component. Each *Test Case Executor* instance is connected to an Android Virtual Device (AVD) deployed on the same machine, and is able to install the AUT and run a test case corresponding to the scheduled sequence of events. The Degree of Parallelism P of this deployment scenario is equal to 6 since there are 6 different *Test Case Executor* components that can run in parallel.

---

[4] https://github.com/reverse-unina/AndroidRipper.

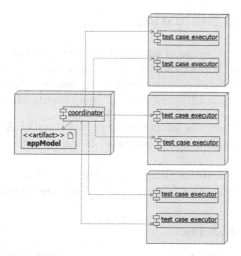

Fig. 1. Deployment of the Parallel Android Ripper with 4 distinct machines and 6 *Test Case Executor* components

A prototype of the Parallel Android Ripper tool has been implemented in order to evaluate its feasibility and to assess its performance in the context of the experiments presented in the following section.

The *Coordinator* component has been deployed on an Application Server and includes a Web Application and a REST Web Service. The Web Application allows the user (1) to upload the apk of the AUT, (2) to select the set of testing machines hosting the instances of the *Test Case Executor* components and the number of *Test Case Executor* components instantiated on each machine, (3) to start and control the execution of the whole process. The REST Web Service is directly invoked by the Web Application and is responsible for the execution of the Active Learning algorithm and for the communication with the *Test Case Executor* components. The *Coordinator* component returns as outputs the reconstructed GUI Tree Model of the AUT, the code coverage achieved by the exploration and the log files reporting the encountered failures and exceptions.

Each *Test Case Executor* component exposes an RMI interface featuring the methods needed to drive the execution of a sequence of events on an AVD and to return a description of the current GUI of the AUT. In detail, each *Test Case Executor* component generates a testing package including a JUnit test case featuring the scheduled sequence of events and the *AUT*, then it installs and starts the test case on an AVD via the Android Debug Bridge (ADB) tool. The description of the GUI obtained after the execution of this sequence of events is returned to the *Coordinator* component at the end of the execution of the test case.

5   Experimental Evaluation

This Section reports the results of an experimental evaluation of the performance
of the Parallel Android Ripper tool involving three open source Android applications and different deployment scenarios having different Degrees of Parallelism
P. In particular, the main objectives of the experiments are the following:

- to evaluate if and how the effectiveness of the Parallel Android Ripper tool
  (measured in terms of the code coverage) is influenced by the degree of parallelism P;
- to evaluate how much testing time can be saved by deploying multiple testing
  machines and multiple *Test Case Executor* instances on each testing machine.

5.1   Variables and Metrics

The independent variable of the experiment presented in this section is represented by the deployment configuration of the tool. Different deployments have
been considered by varying the following two parameters:

n_m that is the total number of different physical machines hosting the *Test
Case Executor* components;
n_e that is the number of *Test Case Executor* components deployed for each
of the n_m machines.

As a consequence, the degree of parallelism P can be defined as the product
between the number of physical machines and the number of *Test Case Executor*
components deployed for each machine:

$$P = n_m * n_e$$

We have considered 6 different deployment configurations having 1, 2 or 6
physical machines and 1 or 2 instances of the *Test Case Executor* per machine,
with resulting degrees of parallelism P between 1 and 12. The following 6 configurations have been considered:

- $C_{1,1}$: ($n_m = 1$, $n_e = 1$, $P = 1$)
- $C_{1,2}$: ($n_m = 1$, $n_e = 2$, $P = 2$)
- $C_{2,1}$: ($n_m = 2$, $n_e = 1$, $P = 2$)
- $C_{2,2}$: ($n_m = 2$, $n_e = 2$, $P = 4$)
- $C_{6,1}$: ($n_m = 6$, $n_e = 1$, $P = 6$)
- $C_{6,2}$: ($n_m = 6$, $n_e = 2$, $P = 12$)

The first configuration $C_{1,1}$ implements a sequential version of the algorithm,
with a single *Coordinator*, a single *Test Case Executor* and a single AVD. This
configuration has been considered as a benchmark for the evaluation of the
savings in testing time obtained by varying the degree of parallelism P between
2 and 12.

The dependent variables measured for each execution of the testing tool are the testing time tt needed to complete the process and the code coverage percentage cc. We have considered the code coverage instead of the number of observed failures or crashes because it provides a more detailed view of the coverage of the application behaviors.

In order to evaluate the saving of testing time due to the selection of different deployment configurations having different degrees of parallelism P, we have introduced a metric called Speed Improvement factor S. The Speed Improvement among two configurations C_i and C_j is defined by the following expression:

$$S(C_i, C_j) = \frac{tt(C_j) - tt(C_i)}{tt(C_j)} = 1 - \frac{tt(C_i)}{tt(C_j)} \tag{1}$$

For example, if we want to measure the Speed Improvement of the configuration $C_i = C_{2,1}$ with respect to the reference configuration $C_j = C_{1,1}$, and the testing time using $C_{1,1}$ is $tt(C_{1,1}) = 34$ minutes, while the testing time using $C_{2,1}$ is only $tt(C_{2,1}) = 23$ minutes, then the Speed Improvement factor is $1 - (23 \div 34) = 0.32$. In other words, 32% of the testing time can be saved by deploying two testing machines each one hosting a single *Test Case Executor* component, instead than using a single machine.

5.2   Experimental Objects

The objects of the experiments are 3 small-sized open source Android applications that have been selected from the Google Play market and for which the source code is online available. Table 1 provides some pieces of information about the selected applications including a short description, the number of classes, the number of Activity classes, the number of methods, the number of event handlers methods and the number of LOCs. These applications have been already considered as case studies in the experiments carried out in [1].

Table 1. Characteristics of the AUTs involved in the experiments

ID	Application	Version	Description	# Classes	# Activ.	# Methods	# Event handlers	# LOCs
AUT1	TicTacToe	1.0	Simple game	13	1	47	16	493
AUT2	TippyTipper	1.2	Tip calculator app	42	6	225	70	999
AUT3	Tomdroid	0.7.1	Note-taking app	133	10	707	117	3860

5.3   Experimental Setup and Procedure

The tool has been deployed according to the architecture presented in Sect. 4 based on a single *Coordinator* component and a set of *Test Case Executor* components deployed on a set of different testing machines and driving AVDs running on the same machines.

More in details, the *Coordinator* component has been deployed on a PC running the Windows 7 Operating System, featuring an Intel I5 3.0 GHz processor and 8 GB of RAM; each *Test Case Executor* component has been deployed on PCs having the same characteristics. Each *Test Case Executor* manages the execution of the test cases on a different Android Virtual Device (AVD) running on the same machine; the AVD is configured to emulate an Android device having 2 GB of RAM, a 512 MB SD Card, and running the Android Nougat (7.0) operating system. All the machines are deployed in the context of the same network infrastructure, featuring a static network configuration.

Each AUT has been tested for each of the six configurations $C_{1,1}$, $C_{1,2}$, $C_{2,1}$, $C_{2,2}$, $C_{6,1}$, $C_{6,1}$. For each run the testing time needed to complete the execution of the testing process and the achieved code coverage percentage have been measured. The code coverage has been measured exploiting the Emma code coverage tool[5] included in the standard distribution of the Android development kit. The Speed Improvement factor has been evaluated for each possible pair of different configurations. No specific preconditions have been set for each of the 3 AUTs; moreover, each AUT has been re-installed after the execution of each test case. A delay of two seconds has been added before each execution of two consecutive events.

5.4 Results

Table 2 reports the testing time tt (in minutes) measured for each of the 3 AUTs and for each of the 6 considered configurations. In addition, the last column reports the corresponding code coverage cc, measured in percentage. In the last row, the Degree of Parallelism P of each configuration is reported, too.

Table 2. Measured Results for each Configuration and each AUT

	tt (minutes)						
	$C_{1,1}$	$C_{1,2}$	$C_{2,1}$	$C_{2,2}$	$C_{6,1}$	$C_{6,2}$	cc %
AUT1	34	23	19	14	12	7	78%
AUT2	85	62	59	44	26	19	75%
AUT3	164	113	107	74	50	32	36%
P	1	2	2	4	6	12	

The data reported in Table 2 show that the code coverage percentage does not depend on the deployment configuration, thus the introduction of the parallelism in the sequential algorithm does not produce any variation in its effectiveness. By observing the data from left to right, it is clear that the testing time is strongly affected by the degree of parallelism P and it decreases as P increases.

---

[5] http://emma.sourceforge.net/.

More in detail, we have evaluated the Speed Improvement that can be obtained (1) by increasing the number of machines and (2) by increasing the number of *Test Case Executor* components. Table 3 reports the values of the Speed Improvement factor (measured in percentage) evaluated by comparing deployment configurations having different numbers of machines and the same number of *Test Case Executor* components per machine.

Table 3. Values of the Speed Improvement factor evaluated among configurations having the same number of *Test Case Executor* components per machine

	$S(C_{2,1}, C_{1,1})$	$S(C_{2,2}, C_{1,2})$	$S(C_{6,1}, C_{1,1})$	$S(C_{6,2}, C_{1,2})$
AUT1	42%	38%	63%	69%
AUT2	31%	29%	69%	69%
AUT3	35%	35%	70%	72%
Average	36%	34%	66%	70%

By analyzing the second and the third column of Table 3 we can observe that if the number of machines is doubled (from 1 to 2), there is a speed improvement between 29% and 42% for the three considered AUTs (35% in average). Analogously, the last two columns show that if the number of machines is increased of 6 times (from 1 to 6), the speed improvement varies between 63% and 72% (68% in average).

Table 4 reports the values of the Speed Improvement factor (measured in percentage) evaluated by comparing deployment configurations having the same number of machines and, respectively, 1 or 2 *Test Case Executor* components per machine. The table shows that doubling the number of *Test Case Executor*

Table 4. Values of the Speed Improvement factor measured between configurations having the same number of machines and different numbers of *Test Case Executor* components per machine

	$S_i(C_{1,2}, C_{1,1})$	$S_i(C_{2,2}, C_{2,1})$	$S_i(C_{6,2}, C_{6,1})$
AUT1	32%	27%	43%
AUT2	27%	26%	26%
AUT3	31%	31%	36%
Average	30%	28%	35%

components per machine, the speed of the testing process is increased in average only of 31% against the average of 36% of improvement obtained by doubling the number of testing machines. So, doubling the testing machines is preferable to doubling the testing resources deployed on the same machines.

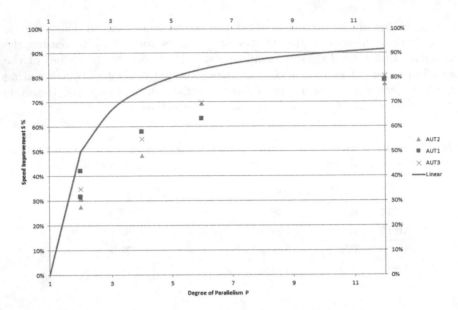

Fig. 2. Trend of the Speed Improvement with respect to the configuration $C_{1,1}$ for different configurations having different degrees of parallelism P

Figure 2 shows that the increase in Speed Improvement is always less than linear with respect to the corresponding increase of the degree of parallelism P. In detail, the continuous line in the figure represents the ideal trend of the Speed Improvement evaluated with respect to the configuration $C_{1,1}$ and the points represent the measured values of S with respect to the $C_{1,1}$ configuration. Figure 2 shows that all the points are below the line, in particular the ones corresponding to configurations having two instances of the *Test Case Executor* for machine.

These data can be compared with the ones reported in [28] according to which the PATS tool provides in average a Speed Improvement S of 27% on a configuration having two different test executors deployed on two different machines instead that only one, whereas our tool has provided in average a Speed Improvement of 35% with two *Test Case Executor* components deployed on two different machines and of 31% when deployed on the same machine. The ParaAim tool [7] obtains slightly better results in time saving when deploying two or four devices, with a corresponding increase in testing effectiveness, too. However, the testing effectiveness obtained by ParaAim is measured in terms of Activity coverage and is quite small since it does not exceed 15% on average. Although these data are related to different sets of applications (3 AUTs for our tool, 4 AUTs for PATS, 20 AUTs for ParaAim) and different coverage metrics, it appears that the performance of our tool are encouraging.

In conclusion, this experimental evaluation has shown that the introduction of a parallel algorithm does not influence the effectiveness of the testing tool in terms of achieved code coverage, whereas it provides a reduction of the testing time with respect to the sequential algorithm. More in detail, a larger speed improvement can be obtained by increasing the number of testing machines, whereas an increase of the number of the *Test Case Executor* components deployed on the same testing machine provides minor improvements.

5.5   Discussions and Possible Improvements

In this section a discussion of the results obtained by the analysis of the experimental results will be presented, with the aim of proposing ideas for further improvements of the efficiency of the proposed algorithm and of its prototype implementation.

Four limiting factors affecting the performance of the proposed tool have been recognized: (1) the presence in the algorithm of methods that are not parallelized at all; (2) the losses in efficiency occurring when the number of testing resources grows, (3) the delay due to the waiting for the termination of the different scheduled event sequences, (4) the concurrency between different *Test Case Executor* components deployed on the same machine. In the following, we will discuss each of these factors and will indicate some proposals to reduce their influence on the performance of the tool.

Parallelization of the Algorithm. The unique operation of the Algorithm 2 that has been parallelized is the *RunParallelEvents* operation. We have primarily focused our attention on the parallelization of this operation since it is usually the most costly one in terms of testing time.

Other methods of the algorithm could be partially parallelized. For example, by adopting the *Breadth First* scheduling strategy, the *extractEvents* operation extracts from the *appModel* some events executable on the last explored GUIs and pushes them on the bottom of the *fireableEvents* queue, while the *scheduleParallelEvents* operation selects the first P events on top of the same queue. When the queue contains more than P events, the two operations can be executed concurrently. The restart time needed to uninstall and reinstall the AUT can be reduced by performing these operations in parallel just after the returning of the GUI description to the coordinator.

Reduction of the Speed Improvement for Growing Degrees of Parallelism. The experiments have shown that an increase of the degree of parallelism P progressively reduces the testing time needed to execute the proposed algorithm. Anyway, it is possible to observe that, when the degree of parallelism P grows, there are iterations of the algorithm for which there are less than P fireable events, so that not all the testing resources can be used in parallel. In order to have an idea of this phenomenon, we measured the number of iterations of the Algorithm 2 executed on *AUT1* for different values of P. Table 5 shows the number of iterations needed to complete the testing algorithm and, in the last row, the minimum number of iterations needed if all the testing resources are

Table 5. Number of iterations of Algorithm 2 executed on *AUT1* for different values of the Degree of Parallelism *P*

	P				
	1	2	4	6	12
Measured number of iterations	69	37	20	14	9
Minimum number of iterations	69	35	18	12	6

used at each iteration (i.e. the ratio between the total number of executed events and the the degree of parallelism).

We can observe that the difference between the minimum number of iterations and the measured number of iterations tends to increase. In particular, with 12 testing resources, 9 iterations are needed instead than only 6.

Delay Due to the Waiting of the Termination of the Scheduled Event Sequences. The *runParallelEvents* concurrently starts the execution of at most *P* test cases on the *P* available testing resources, and terminates when all the test cases have been terminated and all the descriptions of the obtained GUIs have been returned. The waiting for the termination of all the test cases may represent a waste of time, in particular if the different test cases need different times to be executed. The *Breadth First* scheduling strategy selects for the execution sequences of events having similar length, so the delays due to the different lengths of the sequences of events are small. The Algorithm 2 should be improved by partially refining the *appModel* every time a single GUI description is returned by a *Test Case Executor*, in order to execute the *refineAppModel* operation in concurrence with the *runParallelEvents* operation.

Delay Due to Concurrency Between Different Test Case Executor Components Deployed on the Same Machine. The deployment of more than one *Test Case Executor* and of more than one AVD on the same machine may cause a reduction of the performance of the tool due to the concurrency between these instances in the access to the resources of the machine. In particular, we have experienced in our experimental configurations that the concurrency of three or more AVDs on the same machines involved in our experiments brings to drastic reductions of the performance of the testing tool that makes these configurations very inefficient. This phenomenon worsen with the most recent Android versions, that needs many more memory resources than the first ones. Technologies such as containers could reduce the weight of this phenomenon.

Efficiency improvements may be obtained by adopting different architectural and technological solutions, too. First of all, the use of real Android devices instead of AVDs may provide an improvement in speed due to the better performance of some devices with respect to the corresponding virtual versions. In particular, by using real devices, it is possible to deploy many *Test Case Executor* components on the same machine having a limited concurrency between them since most of the time spent in the *RunParallelEvents* operation is devoted to the execution of the events on the devices. In this case, the *Test Case Executor* components may also be deployed on the same machine hosting the *Coordinator* component with a consequent saving in terms of number of physical machines.

6   Conclusions and Future Work

This paper proposes a fully automated parallel GUI testing solution for Android applications based on Active Learning techniques. The techniques previously proposed in the literature have been mainly developed having in mind the optimization of their effectiveness, whereas a lesser attention has been paid to their efficiency. The parallel Active Learning algorithm supporting the exploration of the GUIs of Android applications has been obtained by instantiating the Unified Online Testing algorithm proposed in [1] and by modifying it to allow the concurrent execution of some of its operations. The algorithm has been implemented in a prototype tool, whose feasibility and performance have been evaluated against 3 open source Android applications and 6 different deployment configurations. The experimental evaluation has shown that the proposed tool provides a significant reduction of the testing time both with respect to its sequential implementation and with respect to the average reduction of testing time obtained by the PATS tool [28]; moreover, when compared to the ParaAim [7] tool, our tool appears to be more effective. The experiments have shown how the algorithm efficiency depends mainly on the number of deployed machines, whereas an increase in the number of *Test Executor* components per machine does not cause strong improvements in efficiency. This may have happened because the AVDs involved in our experiments shared the same resources on a single machine running concurrently, so we think that this problem can be mitigated by using more machines to host AVDs or exploit real Android devices.

Future work will address the optimization of the algorithm and of the tool and the execution of larger experiments aiming at the evaluation of their scalability. In particular, the migration of the proposed tool from a component based architecture to a service based architecture and its deployment within public cloud infrastructures will be studied and realized.

References

1. Amalfitano, D., Amatucci, N., Memon, A., Tramontana, P., Fasolino, A.: A general framework for comparing automatic testing techniques of android mobile apps. J. Syst. Softw. **125**, 322–343 (2017)
2. Amalfitano, D., Fasolino, A., Tramontana, P., De Carmine, S., Imparato, G.: A toolset for gui testing of android applications. In: IEEE International Conference on Software Maintenance, ICSM, pp. 650–653 (2012)
3. Amalfitano, D., Fasolino, A., Tramontana, P., Ta, B., Memon, A.: Mobiguitar: automated model-based testing of mobile apps. IEEE Softw. **32**(5), 53–59 (2015)

4. Amalfitano, D., Fasolino, A.R., Carmine, S.D., Memon, A., Tramontana, P.: Using GUI ripping for automated testing of android applications. In: ASE 2012: Proceedings of the 27th IEEE International Conference on Automated Software Engineering. IEEE Computer Society, Washington, DC, USA (2012)
5. Anbunathan, R., Basu, A.: Data driven architecture based automated test generation for android mobile. In: 2015 IEEE International Conference on Computational Intelligence and Computing Research, ICCIC 2015 (2016)
6. Azim, T., Neamtiu, I.: Targeted and depth-first exploration for systematic testing of android apps. SIGPLAN Not. **48**(10), 641–660 (2013)
7. Cao, C., Deng, J., Yu, P., Duan, Z., Ma, X.: Paraaim: testing android applications parallel at activity granularity. In: 2019 IEEE 43rd Annual Computer Software and Applications Conference (COMPSAC), vol. 1, pp. 81–90 (2019)
8. Choi, W., Necula, G., Sen, K.: Guided GUI testing of android apps with minimal restart and approximate learning. In: Proceedings of the 2013 ACM SIGPLAN International Conference on Object Oriented Programming Systems Languages & Applications, pp. 623–640. ACM (2013)
9. Choudhary, S.R., Gorla, A., Orso, A.: Automated test input generation for android: are we there yet? (E). In: 2015 30th IEEE/ACM International Conference on Automated Software Engineering (ASE), pp. 429–440, November 2015
10. Gomez, L., Neamtiu, I., Azim, T., Millstein, T.: Reran: timing- and touch-sensitive record and replay for android. In: Proceedings of the 2013 International Conference on Software Engineering, ICSE 2013, pp. 72–81. IEEE Press, Piscataway, NJ, USA (2013)
11. Griebe, T., Hesenius, M., Gruhn, V.: Towards automated UI-tests for sensor-based mobile applications. Commun. Comput. Inf. Sci. **532**, 3–17 (2015)
12. Gu, T., et al.: AimDroid: activity-insulated multi-level automated testing for android applications. In: 2017 IEEE International Conference on Software Maintenance and Evolution (ICSME), pp. 103–114 (2017)
13. Hao, S., Liu, B., Nath, S., Halfond, W.G., Govindan, R.: Puma: programmable UI-automation for large-scale dynamic analysis of mobile apps. In: Proceedings of the 12th Annual International Conference on Mobile Systems, Applications, and Services, MobiSys 2014, pp. 204–217. ACM, New York (2014)
14. Hu, C., Neamtiu, I.: Automating gui testing for android applications. In: Proceedings of the 6th International Workshop on Automation of Software Test, pp. 77–83 (2011)
15. Li, A., Qin, Z., Chen, M., Liu, J.: Adautomation: an activity diagram based automated GUI testing framework for smartphone applications. In: Proceedings - 8th International Conference on Software Security and Reliability, SERE 2014, pp. 68–77 (2014)
16. Li, X., Jiang, Y., Liu, Y., Xu, C., Ma, X., Lu, J.: User guided automation for testing mobile apps. In: Software Engineering Conference (APSEC), 2014 21st Asia-Pacific, vol. 1, pp. 27–34, December 2014
17. Machiry, A., Tahiliani, R., Naik, M.: Dynodroid: An input generation system for android apps. In: Proceedings of the 2013 9th Joint Meeting on Foundations of Software Engineering, ESEC/FSE 2013, pp. 224–234. ACM, New York (2013)
18. Mahmood, R., Mirzaei, N., Malek, S.: Evodroid: segmented evolutionary testing of android apps. In: Proceedings of the 22nd ACM SIGSOFT International Symposium on Foundations of Software Engineering, FSE 2014, pp. 599–609. ACM, New York (2014)

19. Majeed, S., Ryu, M.: Model-based replay testing for event-driven software. In: Proceedings of the ACM Symposium on Applied Computing, 04–08-April-2016, pp. 1527–1533 (2016)
20. Mao, K., Harman, M., Jia, Y.: Sapienz: multi-objective automated testing for android applications. In: Proceedings of the 25th International Symposium on Software Testing and Analysis, ISSTA 2016, pp. 94–105. ACM, New York (2016)
21. Meng, Z., Jiang, Y., Xu, C.: Facilitating reusable and scalable automated testing and analysis for android apps. In: Proceedings of the 7th Asia-Pacific Symposium on Internetware, Internetware 2015, pp. 166–175. ACM, New York (2015)
22. Nguyen, C., Marchetto, A., Tonella, P.: Combining model-based and combinatorial testing for effective test case generation. In: 2012 International Symposium on Software Testing and Analysis, ISSTA 2012 - Proceedings, pp. 100–110 (2012)
23. Su, T.: FSMdroid: Guided GUI testing of android apps. In: Proceedings of the 38th International Conference on Software Engineering Companion, ICSE 2016, pp. 689–691. ACM, New York (2016)
24. Takala, T., Katara, M., Harty, J.: Experiences of system-level model-based GUI testing of an android application. In: Proceedings of the 2011 Fourth IEEE International Conference on Software Testing, Verification and Validation, ICST 2011, pp. 377–386. IEEE Computer Society, Washington, DC (2011)
25. Tramontana, P., Amalfitano, D., Amatucci, N., Fasolino, A.R.: Automated functional testing of mobile applications: a systematic mapping study. Softw. Qual. J. 27(1), 149–201 (2018). https://doi.org/10.1007/s11219-018-9418-6
26. Tramontana, P., Amalfitano, D., Amatucci, N., Memon, A., Fasolino, A.R.: Developing and evaluating objective termination criteria for random testing. ACM Trans. Softw. Eng. Methodol. 28(3) (2019)
27. Wang, P., Liang, B., You, W., Li, J., Shi, W.: Automatic android GUI traversal with high coverage. In: Proceedings of the 2014 Fourth International Conference on Communication Systems and Network Technologies, CSNT 2014, pp. 1161–1166. IEEE Computer Society, Washington, DC (2014)
28. Wen, H., Lin, C., Hsieh, T., Yang, C.: Pats: a parallel GUI testing framework for android applications. In: 39th IEEE Annual Computer Software and Applications Conference, COMPSAC 2015, Taichung, Taiwan, 1–5 July 2015, vol. 2, pp. 210–215 (2015)
29. Zaeem, R.N., Prasad, M.R., Khurshid, S.: Automated generation of oracles for testing user-interaction features of mobile apps. In: Proceedings of the 2014 IEEE International Conference on Software Testing, Verification, and Validation, ICST 2014, pp. 183–192. IEEE Computer Society, Washington, DC (2014)
30. Zein, S., Salleh, N., Grundy, J.: A systematic mapping study of mobile application testing techniques. J. Syst. Soft. 117, 334–356 (2016)

Trigger Alarm: A Smart NFC Sniffer for High-Precision Measurements

Martin Erb[1(✉)], Christian Steger[1], Martin Troyer[1],
and Josef Preishuber-Pflügl[2]

[1] Institute of Technical Informatics, Graz University of Technology, Graz, Austria
{martin.erb,steger,martin.troyer}@trugraz.at
[2] CISC Semiconductor GmbH, Lakeside B07, 9020 Klagenfurt, Austria
j.preishuber-pfluegl@cisc.at
https://www.cisc.at

Abstract. In this paper, we present a new design and proof of concept of a smart Near Field Communication (NFC) sniffer, including special trigger features for high-precision measurements during NFC interoperability testing. Even though interoperability testing is not mandatory for successful NFC-device certification, the fast increasing amount of electronic consumer devices providing NFC functionality strongly increases the need for interoperability testing. Nowadays, used automated interoperability test systems require time-consuming and expensive manual debug sessions in case of a communication error, to compensate missing test data for analyzing the failure root cause. To highly decrease costs and time required to perform these manual measurements, we developed a proof of concept of a sniffer tool providing intelligent trigger functionalities. It supports the test engineer during manual debug session and can be integrated into a fully automated interoperability test and analysis system. Hence, we drive the development of automated interoperability test systems and want to encourage standardization bodies to include interoperability testing to the certification procedure.

Keywords: Near Field Communication · Software Defined Radio · Measurement system · Test platform · Interoperability

Near Field Communication has experienced a steep marked ramp up in recent years. The rapidly increasing amount of mobile phones pushed to the global market led to the increasing integration of NFC technology in consumer electronic devices. NFC provides a convenient, easy, and secure possibility to transfer wireless data between two electronic devices [6,12]. Integrating NFC, which has been

This work is part of the ANITAS project in cooperation with CISC Semiconductor, NXP Semiconductors, and the Institute of Technical Informatics at the Graz University of Technology. This project is partly founded by the Kärntner Wirtschaftsförderungsfonds and the Steirischen Wirtschaftsförderungsgesellschaft mbH under the FFG (Austrian Research Promotion Agency) grant number 864323.

© IFIP International Federation for Information Processing 2020
Published by Springer Nature Switzerland AG 2020
V. Casola et al. (Eds.): ICTSS 2020, LNCS 12543, pp. 186–200, 2020.
https://doi.org/10.1007/978-3-030-64881-7_12

evolved from the Radio Frequency Identification (RFID) technology, to smartphones enables the possibility to replace identity documents for access control or debit cards for payment [17]. Furthermore, NFC allows initiating device connectivity such as Bluetooth or WLAN, thus allowing the user to easily exchange security-sensitive data between their devices [3,7,9,18,25].

To keep the NFC technology on the course of further success and to enlarge the influence to the market, the user acceptance needs to be increased. To achieve this and to encourage more people to use NFC-enabled devices for a wide range of different applications in their daily life, interoperability needs to be guaranteed. The ultimate goal is to achieve full interoperability among all devices from various manufactures. To reach this goal, the NFC Forum follows the approach of harmonizing the different standards and ensuring interoperability by extensive conformance testing [10,23,24].

However, interoperability testing cannot entirely be replaced by conformance testing because during the certification process one communication party is always simulated. Additionally, the setup for conformance testing has to be entirely defined to make the test procedure reproducible [13]. This leads to the drawback that conformance testing cannot represent all real-world scenarios and misses to include many user requirements [14,15]. The problem of missing user requirements is shown in various current systems where certified products have interoperability lacks [1].

In contrast to other wireless technologies where interoperability issues may occur due to interference [21], such as Bluetooth or WiFi or test systems where the physical layer is excluded from testing [26], NFC interoperability test systems have to analyze the whole data transfer across all communication layers. CISC Semiconductor, a leading supplier of RFID measurement and test solutions, developed an automated interoperability test system to gain significant speedup for testing [2]. In the case of a communication error, however, manual debugging with different additional measurement and analysis equipment is required. We analyzed projects over the last years from our research partners (CISC Semiconductor and NXP Semiconductors) and found out that setting up the measurement devices and performing additional communications to detect the error root cause consumes a massive amount of the overall test time.

Lack of All-In-One Solution. As defined by the NFC test standard [13], the sample rate of the measurement device to properly analyze communication parameters must be at least 500MS/s. Existing test platforms such as presented by the works [5,11,16] have implemented protocol decoder and further analysis tasks based on the baseband signal. They use the baseband signal because the required bandwidth is only 847 KHz (the subcarrier generated by the Proximity Inductive Coupling Card (PICC)) plus the data rate such as 106 KHz used for payment applications. Therefore, a digital sample data rate of about 6 MS/s is sufficient to decode the protocol. Such measurement devices are essential and very useful for interoperability error debugging; however, not all communication relevant parameters can be analyzed. Therefore, an additional oscilloscope is still required, with which a test engineer can capture parts of the communication with a sufficiently high sample rate. To capture exactly the appropriate part of the communication mostly requires multiple tries to set up the oscilloscope.

The time to set up the measurement system correctly, perform the measurements again, and analyze the results prolongs the debug time and makes interoperability testing very expensive.

Oscilloscope for Specific Parameters. The trigger functionalities of an oscilloscope are sufficient to analyze simple parameters like the field strength or modulation index. For such measurements, no specific parts of an NFC communication are required, which means that one configuration of the measurement is sufficient, and only one communication needs to be performed per measurement point. In work [19] they present an automated test system with various measurement devices to analyze interoperability problems. In this case, the oscilloscope is used to measure the high frequency (HF)-field strength. Nevertheless, the system can analyze only the HF-field strength automatically. Otherwise, manual interaction from a test engineer would be required to reconfigure the oscilloscope, which would again increase the test and measurement time.

Lack of Intelligent Trigger Features. During conformance testing, one communication partner is always simulated, meaning the test controller is generating either a Proximity Coupling Device (PCD) command or a PICC response. Therefore, it is straightforward to control a high precision analog measurement device with a high sampling rate, such as an oscilloscope, to capture exactly the communication parts required to check if the Device Under Test (DUT) fulfills the requirements defined by the standards. This is not true for interoperability testing where both communication partners have finalized products and have to be handled as black-box. Additionally, interoperability testing mostly requires to analyze a specific command or response within the whole communication. However, it is time-consuming to configure the oscilloscope each time to capture exactly the required command or response using a sample rate of at least 500 MS/s. The high sample rate prevents the user from capturing the whole communication. Furthermore, the time between the start of the communication and the occurrence of a certain command may differ between multiple test runs due to re-transmissions. To the best of our knowledge no analog measurement system including such features to trigger an external high-precision oscilloscope exists.

Our Contribution. In this paper, we present a smart sniffer tool providing intelligent trigger functionality for NFC interoperability testing based on software-defined radio (SDR) platform. The sniffer tool presented does not close the gap of an all-in-one solution but implements intelligent trigger features for easy communication capturing using an external oscilloscope. Precise and easy triggering at the position before an error happens or where additional investigations should be made is essential to reduce the time for a manual debug session significantly. Therefore, we implemented three options for the communication types described in ISO-14443, which apply rising edges on different general-purpose input outputs (GPIO): (i) HF-field on, (ii) every command typeA or typeB, and (iii) selected command typeA or typeB. In Sect. 3, we present how the different trigger functionalities can be used to achieve significant speedup during testing. In this paper, we make the following contributions:

- We design three different trigger functionalities not yet used for interoperability testing to reduce the manual debug session duration (Sect. 1).
- We implement the designed features based on an SDR platform, the LimeSDR (Sect. 2).
- We experimentally show the functionalities and the performance of the three different trigger features (Sect. 3).

After describing related work in Sect. 4 we conclude our paper in Sect. 5, along with a discussion on future work.

1 Trigger Design

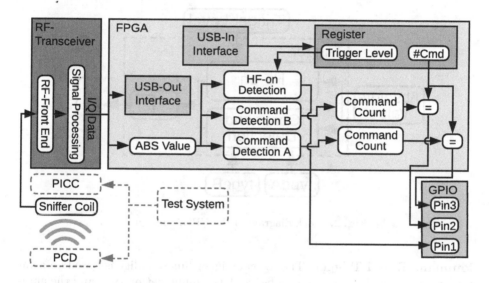

Fig. 1. Block diagram of the FPGA implementation

As a basis for our Field Programmable Gate Array (FPGA) design, we used the work [5] of the researcher from the University of Technology Graz. In their work, they implemented a simple HF-field on trigger using the RedPitay platform [28]. Our design is not restricted to any hardware platform. However, the input to the trigger block is the absolute value of the baseband of the captured communication. Nevertheless, it makes sense to include the trigger functionality to a similar measurement device as the RedPitaya. Figure 2 shows a simplified version of the design of the trigger functionality. The green blocks show the input values enabling the possibility to configure the behavior of the trigger. The HF-on block and the Command Detection block show the two main components of the trigger. We split up the FPGA and the RF-transceiver because different FPGA hardware platforms may not include an RF-transceiver but, for sure multiple connection possibilities for an RF daughterboard.

HF-on Trigger. The HF-on trigger is the simplest version of a trigger and could also be realized using an oscilloscope. The HF-on trigger outputs a single rising edge on a GPIO pin when the absolute value exceeds the trigger level the first time after the user armed the trigger. The trigger level is configurable by the user. Implementing this simple trigger feature enables the possibility to synchronize the time between the captured I/Q data by the measurement device and the signal captured by the oscilloscope. This can be useful for further signal analysis tasks. Additionally, this trigger is internally connected to the streaming block. Meaning, the host PC starts receiving I/Q data from the measurement device when the HF-on trigger fires. This is useful during testing because, in most cases, a test engineer is not interested in the signal before a communication start.

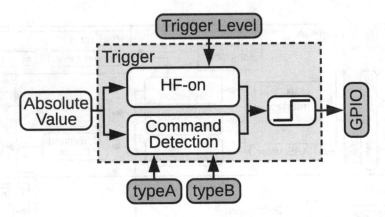

Fig. 2. Block diagram of the FPGA design

Command Based Trigger. The second trigger functionality is based on command recognition. The user can configure the communication type and the number of the command when the trigger should fire. For simplicity, only the number of the command can be defined because triggering on a specific command name would require a complete protocol decoder implemented on the FPGA. The command detection block is responsible for finding all commands, either typeA or typeB, within the absolute value of the baseband signal and counting them. The trigger fires whenever the number of found commands of one single communication type is equal to the configured value by the user. If the user does not define any number of commands to trigger on, typeA and typeB trigger fire on every detected command.

The command base trigger feature is handy and time saving for a test engineer when it comes to capturing a specific command within a communication. If an interoperability issue should be analyzing the error mostly happens in the same position within the protocol, but not at the same time after the communication start. Therefore, a standard oscilloscope trigger would not be sufficient to always trigger at the correct point in time. The functionality where every command triggers a rising edge significantly simplifies error cases where either the PCD waits for a response of the PICC or the PICC does not understand the command. In these cases, the oscilloscope shows the last command sent by the PCD and can easily be analyzed by a test engineer.

2   Implementation

2.1   Hardware

Before thinking of implementation details, we used the design described in Sect. 1 to find a suitable hardware platform to implement our smart sniffer. As mentioned above, the absolute value of the baseband signal is required as input for the trigger function. NFC technology uses a 13.56 MHz carrier frequency and a sub-carrier with a frequency of 848 KHz. For our implementation, we are focusing on the payment application, which supports a data rate of 106 kBit/s, but the hardware should support higher data rates too. During our research, we tried to focus on only a few important hardware requirements: (i) Radio Frequency (RF)-front end capabilities such as center frequency, bandwidth, and sample rate, (ii) FPGA specification, (iii) configurable GPIOs, and (iv) connection interface to the host PC. Because we are using only the baseband of the signal, we decided to use a sample rate of about 10 MS/s for the I/Q data transmitted to the host PC. Therefore, the data throughput of the connection interface between measurement hardware and host PC is not critical, and a lot of different hardware platforms are available. After our evaluation phase, we decided to use the LimeSDR from Lime Microsystems [20] in the USB configuration. The advantage of this hardware platform is the powerful RF-transceiver chip, which includes already highly configurable analog and digital signal processing units. These units enable the possibilities to shift the signal to the baseband and to apply the required filters to have clean I/Q data ready even before sent to the FPGA. Using such a powerful RF-transceiver chip saves many hardware resources on the FPGA for other tasks. The FPGA provides enough computational power and memory resources to implement the trigger features described in Sect. 1. The LimesSDR provides a USB 3.0 interface to connect the host PC. The data throughput of this interface is far enough to transfer the I/Q data shifted to the baseband.

2.2   Software

Figure 1 shows the high-level block diagram of our FPGA implementation. The sniffer coil is connected to the RF-front end and placed between PICC and PCD. The signal processing units of the RF-transceiver convert the captured communication to the digital domain and shift the signal to the baseband. Furthermore, the RF-transceiver applies the corresponding filters and sends the I/Q data to the FPGA. Further, the FPGA sends the captured baseband I/Q data to the USB-Out interface and computes the absolute value of the signal. As shown in

Fig. 1, the calculated absolute value is than used as input for the three different main functional blocks of the FPGA implementation: (i) HF-on detection, (ii) command detection typeA and typeB, and (iii) command count.

The HF-on detection block compares the received absolute value with the trigger level defined by the user using the configuration register. The first time the absolute value exceeds the threshold, the HF-on trigger fires a rising edge on GPIO Pin1. Additionally, this trigger signal is used to start the I/Q data streaming to the USB-Out interface, more precisely to the host PC. This feature gives a lot of flexibility during testing. It reduces the data to be transferred because the unwanted signal before a communication start is not sent to the host PC. Furthermore, this trigger allows a precise synchronization between captured I/Q data on the host PC and the recorded data on an external oscilloscope.

The command detection blocks for typeA and typeB use a min-max method with fixed thresholds based on the modulation values defined in the standard to detect rising edges within the received signal. Using the peak-to-peak values and the frequency of the rising edges, the detector blocks check if the absolute value belongs to a request sent by the PCD or not. If one of the detection blocks identifies a command, it increases the command count by one. The command count block counts the number of commands for a single type, which has been decoded after the acquisition has been started. The count of recognized commands is further compared with the number defined by the user in the configuration register. If the number counted by the command count block is equal as configured by the user, GPIO Pin2 is set to high for typeB and GPIO Pin3 for typeA, respectively. If the user configures the number of commands with zero, a short peak is applied to the corresponding GPIO pin whenever a command is detected. For our use case, which is the payment application, the data rate is always 106 kBit/s. Therefore, the communication between PCD and PICC takes place via Amplitude Shift Keying (ASK) 10% amplitude modulation of the RF operating field for communication typeB and around 100% for typeA. This is not true for data rates higher than 424 kBit/s for which the thresholds for the min-max method need to be adapted.

As depicted in Fig. 1 the different trigger features are implemented in parallel. This means that the HF-on trigger can be used simultaneously to the different command detection features. Therefore, a test engineer can configure the oscilloscope in a way that triggers first on the HF-on trigger to show the start of the communication and later trigger again if a certain amount of commands were detected. This increases the flexibility of performing manual measurements using an oscilloscope and reduces the amount of required additional communications because multiple events can be observed at once.

3   Evaluation

We used the design described in Sect. 1 to implement the functionality as presented in Sect. 2 and performed an evaluation shown in this section. We used one PCD and two PICCs to show the trigger functionalities for communication typeA and typeB. The three NFC-enabled devices implement the payment application according to the EMVCo standard. Therefore, they are communicating at 106 kBit/s. As shown in Fig. 3, we placed the sniffer coil, which is connected to the LimeSDR and the oscilloscope, between PCD and PICC. The LimeSDR was connected to the host PC, which was responsible for configuring the device, controlling the measurement procedure as well as starting the communication on the PCD. Furthermore, we connected the three different GPIO pins of the LimeSDR to the remaining analog input channels of the oscilloscope. The trigger of the oscilloscope was configured in single-shot mode using one of the analog inputs as a trigger source. The sample rate of the oscilloscope was set to 2 GS/s.

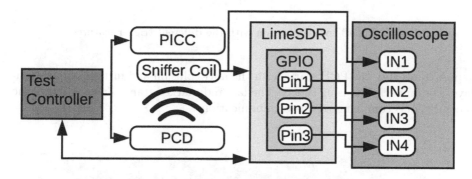

Fig. 3. Evaluation setup

Figure 4 shows the beginning of an NFC communication between PCD and PICC using communication typeB. One can see the four captured signals by the oscilloscope: (i) *HF* signal capture by the sniffer coil, (ii) *typeA* trigger signal for typeA commands, (iii) *typeB* trigger signal for typeB commands, (iv) and *HF-on* trigger signal when the HF-field exceeds the configured threshold. The fifth signal (*SDR*) shown in Fig. 4 is the absolute value captured and processed by the LimeSDR. The LimeSDR was configured to trigger on HF-on and on the second typeA and typeB command. The five red marked frames show three zoom regions, explained more detailed later, and the shape of the commands for the different communication types.

The default activation procedure for payment transactions starts with the HF-field activation by the PCD shown in the first red marked frame *Zoom 1*. Afterward, the PCD tries to activate the card using a typeA command, as shown in the second red-marked frame *TypeA cmd 1*. The activation was not successful because we used a typeB only PICC, and therefore, no typeA response can be found. Further on, the PCD tries to activate the card using a typeB command, as shown in the third red marked frame *TypeB cmd 1*. This time one response after the command can be found. The default procedure of the PCD is to check again if a typeA card is present. Therefore, a second typeA command is sent thus marked with a red frame *Zoom 2*. Since the PICC did not respond to the second

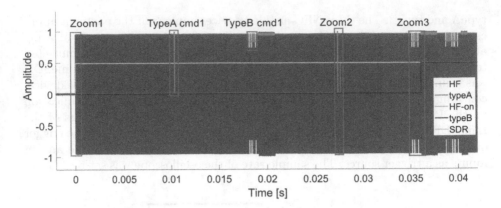

Fig. 4. TypeB communication with the different trigger features

typeA command, the PCD starts with the anti-collision and further application-layer communication using typeB. The last red marked frame *Zoom 3* shows the second typeB command of this communication.

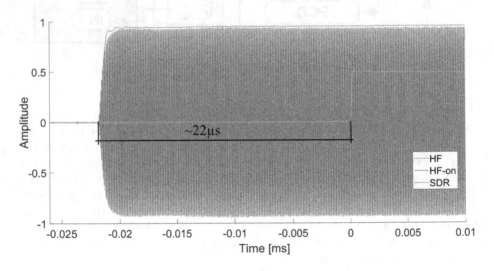

Fig. 5. TypeB communication showing Zoom 1

Figure 5 shows a close-up of the HF-on trigger functionality more precisely the *Zoom 1* frame in Fig. 4. On the time axis, one can observe that the oscilloscope triggered on the rising edge of the HF-on signals generated by the LimeSDR because time equals zero. The time delay between actual HF-field on captured by the oscilloscope and the rising edge of the signal generated by the LimeSDR of about 22 µs is introduced by the processing time of the implemented detection algorithm and the time required to control the GPIO pin. Nevertheless, this time delay is constant and thus can be used to synchronize the captured signal from the oscilloscope and the LimeSDR. All the different figures show the SDR signal synchronized to the HF signal using this time delay. As explained in Sect. 2, the streaming of the I/Q data to the host PC is started at the same time when the HF-on trigger fires. Figure 5, however, shows that the SDR signal (depicted in green) starts about 22 μs earlier. This feature was set as an additional requirement not to lose any important information and was realized using ring buffers for data streaming to the host PC.

Figure 6 shows an enlarged view of the LimeSDR command trigger for typeA. One can see that the rising edge of the command recognition appears after around 220 μs. The reason, therefore, is, on the one hand, the implemented command detection algorithm, which analyzes the whole command and waits until the command is finished to reduce the probability of wrong command detection. On the other hand, the ring buffer, which has to be bigger than for the HF-on trigger, and the overall processing time of the LimeSDR, is larger. The constant time shift between command end and the rising edge of the trigger can be ignored because conventional oscilloscopes have a changeable pre-trigger time. This measurement shows that a user can trigger very precisely on a predefined command even if the between communication start and the specified command changes.

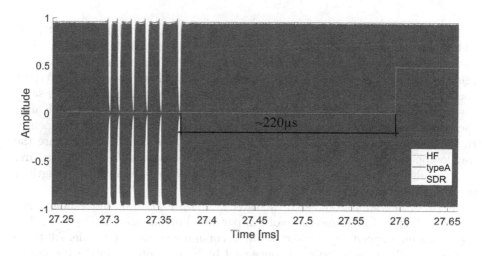

Fig. 6. TypeB communication showing Zoom 2

The last red marked frame in Fig. 4 shows the second typeB command, specifically the command the LimeSDR triggers on. Figure 7 displays a close-up of the mentioned frame. One can see that the rising edge of the trigger signal from the LimeSDR is again 220 μs after the end of the command. This has, of course, the same reasons as explained in the previous paragraph. However, we tried to keep the time delay for both command triggers as similar as possible to ensure that the test engineer can use the same oscilloscope settings independent of the communication type.

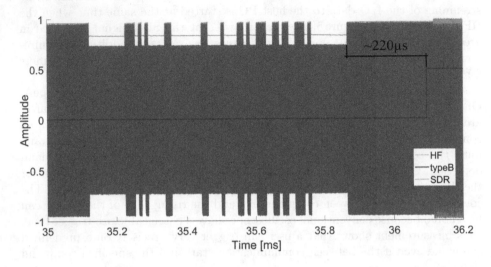

Fig. 7. TypeB communication showing Zoom 3

Figure 8 shows the last missing trigger functionality, applying a short peak to the appropriated GPIO for every command within the whole communication. For clarity reason, the HF-on trigger is not shown in this figure, but it can be used in parallel for this configuration case as well. This figure shows a typeA communication to prove further that the trigger functionalities work the same way for typeA communications. Observing Fig. 8, one can see a short peak after each command of typeA and typeB captured by two different input channels of the oscilloscope. This shows that the test engineer can decide to configure the oscilloscope to trigger either on typeB or typeA commands. Using this feature, it is possible to quickly capture the last command independent of the length of the communication.

Figure 4 in combination with the three close-up Figs. 5, 6, and 7 shows that the three trigger functionalities work in parallel. Furthermore, it is proven that triggering on a specific command within a communication is possible. All these features enable the possibility of convenient high-precision communication snippet capturing using an external oscilloscope and, therefore, reduce the time for manual debug sessions.

4   Related Work

In the field of NFC testing, a lot of research already exists. Research dealing with measurement methods of various communication parameters, design, and implementation of test systems focusing on different NFC applications, and design of

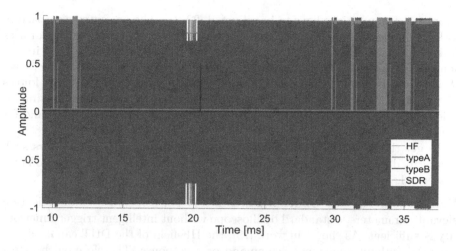

Fig. 8. TypeA communication trigger on all commands

measurement devices to be as accurate as possible. Furthermore, the development of automated conformance and interoperability test systems is ongoing.

Baseband Measurement Systems. For interoperability testing, first of all, it is essential to analyze the whole communication in general. However, for some specific communication relevant parameters, the baseband signal is not sufficient. The required information is lost during the mixing and filtering process. In the works [5,11,16], different hardware, and measurement methodologies are used to analyze the communication between two NFC-enabled devices regarding interoperability issues. These works have one thing in common: the complete signal analysis and error evaluation are based on the baseband signal. This can be very useful to find protocol errors or to analyze which communication partner led to the communication fault. Furthermore, it is helpful to find the position of the error within the communication quickly. However, it is not suitable to analyze specific parameters that require an exact representation of the HF-carrier signal of the PCD.

To find all possible interoperability issues a high-precision oscilloscope is essential. Therefore, the designed trigger functionality presented in this paper could be used to improve the already existing functionality presented in [5,11,16] as long as the used hardware provides configurable GPIOs and enough computation power.

Special Setup. In contrast to conformance testing, where a well-defined measurement setup is required, this is not true for interoperability testing. The standard ISO/IEC 10373-6 [13] defines this specific setup, and it is taken over by the NFC-Forum in their analog parameter comparison and alignment [24]. Since interoperability testing is performed as black-box testing with finished products, the specific setup and most of the given specifications of the various standards cannot be applied anymore. Furthermore, the algorithms for many parameter computations have to be adjusted [22,27]. The presented approach in work [4] implements some of the specific parameter computation but again uses the specific setup. Furthermore, the transmitter is included in the FPGA implementation, which simulates one communication partner. This makes it very easy to capture only a snipped of the communication because the FPGA well knows the point in time when a command is sent. However, simulating one communication partner and not using two complete NFC-enabled devices is not valid for interoperability testing.

To get the specific snippet of a communication to analyze parameters such as described in [8,22,27] a measurement system with smart trigger functionality is essential.

High Resolution but Limited Parameter. For some NFC communication relevant parameters, a standard oscilloscope without intelligent trigger functionality is sufficient. As shown in work [19], the HF-field of the DUT can easily be measured without analyzing a command or a response. Therefore, such a test system is suitable and can be used to find some interoperability issues if they are related to the HF-field strength.

5   Conclusion and Future Work

In this paper, we present an NFC interoperability sniffer tool providing smart trigger functionalities to reduce test time during manual debug sessions. Furthermore, we provide a solution to capture NFC communication frames with very high sample rates. Before elaborating on the design of the sniffer tool we point to the importance of interoperability testing and the need for an additional device supporting the test engineer to analyze the signal of interest. In Sect. 2 we present the used hardware and explain implementation details. We evaluated the proof of concept and show how the different trigger features work. Furthermore, we show how the sniffer tool including the smart trigger functionalities connected with an external oscilloscope can be used to capture the communication snippet of interest for further interoperability analysis. The parallel implementation of the different features additionally increases the usability of the whole system also for other measurement purposes. Using the proposed smart NFC sniffer for high-precision measurements significantly reduces the time required to set up an oscilloscope and to capture the correct communication snippet. Our goal is to improve interoperability testing for NFC-enabled devices to on the one hand increase the user acceptance and user experience. On the other hand, interoperability testing should be included in the product development life cycle and into the certification process.

This system can be improved by implementing a real-time protocol decoder on the FPGA to support triggering on a specific command and not on a command number. Furthermore, we would like to support more different data rates and applications. Within the ANITAS project [29] we will integrate this system to the automated NFC interoperability test system at CISC Semiconductor. This will significantly reduce the time required during manual debug sessions.

References

1. Boada, L.: Near field communication devices: having interoperability issues, February 2016. https://blog.applus.com/nfc-devices-having-interoperability-issues/
2. CISC Semiconductor: CISC semiconductor interoperability website, November 2018. https://www.cisc.at/services/nfc-interoperability-tests/. Accessed: 06 May 2020
3. Coskun, V., Ozdenizci, B., Ok, K.: The survey on near field communication. Sensors **15**(6), 13348–13405 (2015). https://doi.org/10.3390/s150613348
4. Couraud, B., Vauche, R., Deleruyelle, T., Kussener, E.: A very high bit rate test platform for ISO 14443 and interoperability tests. In: 2015 IEEE 16th International Conference on Communication Technology (ICCT), pp. 353–356, October 2015. https://doi.org/10.1109/ICCT.2015.7399857
5. Erb, M., Steger, C., Preishuber-Pfluegl, J., Troyer, M.: A novel automated NFC interoperability test and debug system. In: Smart SysTech 2019, European Conference on Smart Objects, Systems and Technologies, pp. 1–8, June 2019
6. Finkenzeller, K.: RFID Handbook: Fundamentals and Applications in Contactless Smart Cards, Radio Frequency Identification and Near-Field Communication. Wiley, New York (2010)
7. Fischer, J.: NFC in cell phones: the new paradigm for an interactive world [Near-Field Communications]. IEEE Commun. Mag. **47**(6), 22–28 (2009). https://doi.org/10.1109/mcom.2009.5116794
8. Gebhart, M., Wienand, M., Bruckbauer, J., Birnstingl, S.: Automatic analysis of 13.56 mhz reader command modulation pulses. In: Eurasip RFID Workshop (2008)
9. Global Industry Analysts Inc.: Consumer Preference for Contacless Payment & Automated Ticketing Supported by Speed & Convenience Benefits Drives Demand for NFC Enabled Phones, October 2018. https://www.strategyr.com/blog/blog-post.asp?bcode=MCP-7852
10. GSMA, NFC Forum, S.J.: Joint position paper on interoperability of NFC mobile devices, March 2013
11. Hawrylak, P.J., Ogirala, A., Cain, J.T., Mickle, M.H.: Automated test system for ISO 18000-7 - active RFID. In: 2008 IEEE International Conference on RFID. IEEE, April 2008. https://doi.org/10.1109/rfid.2008.4519355
12. Heinrich, C.: RFID and Beyond - Growing your Business Through Real World Awareness. Wiley, New York (2005)
13. ISO/IEC: ISO 10373-6 Identification cards: Test methods (2016)
14. Kang, S.: Relating interoperability testing with conformance testing. In: IEEE GLOBECOM 1998 (Cat. NO. 98CH36250), vol. 6, pp. 3768–3773, November 1998. https://doi.org/10.1109/GLOCOM.1998.776013
15. Kindrick, J.D., Sauter, J.A., Matthews, R.S.: Improving conformance and interoperability testing. StandardView **4**(1), 61–68 (1996)
16. Kun, G., Yigang, H., Zhouguo, H., Bin, L., Kai, S., Yanqing, Z.: Design and development of a open frame RFID system unite test platform. In: Proceedings. The 2009 International Symposium on Information Processing (ISIP 2009), p. 205. Academy Publisher (2009)
17. Lacmanović, I., Radulović, B., Lacmanović, D.: Contactless payment systems based on RFID technology. In: The 33rd International Convention MIPRO, pp. 1114–1119, May 2010
18. Langer, J., Roland, M.: Anwendungen der NFC-technologie. Anwendungen und Technik von Near Field Communication (NFC), pp. 205–241. Springer, Heidelberg (2010). https://doi.org/10.1007/978-3-642-05497-6_9

19. Langer, J., Saminger, C., Grunberger, S.: A comprehensive concept and system for measurement and testing Near Field Communication devices. In: IEEE EUROCON 2009. IEEE, May 2009. https://doi.org/10.1109/eurcon.2009.5167930
20. Lime Microsystems: Lime Microsystems Website (2019). https://myriadrf.org/. Accessed06 May 2020
21. Marinčić, A., Kerner, A., Šmunić, D.: Interoperability of IoT wireless technologies in ambient assisted living environments. In: 2016 Wireless Telecommunications Symposium (WTS), pp. 1–6, April 2016. https://doi.org/10.1109/WTS.2016.7482046
22. Muehlmann, U., Gebhart, M.: Automated analysis of ISO/IEC14443a interrogator command pulse shapes. In: SoftCOM 2009–17th International Conference on Software, Telecommunications Computer Networks, pp. 75–79, September 2009
23. NFC Forum: The Keys to Truly Interoperable Communications, October 2007. http://nfc-forum.org/wp-content/uploads/2013/12/NFC-Forum-Marketing-White-Paper.pdf
24. NFC Forum: ISO/IEC 14443 Analog Parameter Comparison and Alignment, January 2017
25. Shobha, N.S.S., Aruna, K.S.P., Bhagyashree, M.D.P., Sarita, K.S.J.: NFC and NFC payments: a review. In: 2016 International Conference on ICT in Business Industry Government (ICTBIG), pp. 1–7, November 2016. https://doi.org/10.1109/ICTBIG.2016.7892683
26. Song, E.Y., Lee, K.B.: An interoperability test system for IEEE 1451.5–802.11 standard. In: 2010 IEEE Sensors Applications Symposium (SAS), pp. 183–188, February 2010. https://doi.org/10.1109/SAS.2010.5439406
27. Stark, M., Gebhart, M.: How to guarantee phase-synchronicity in active load modulation for NFC and proximity. In: 2013 5th International Workshop on Near Field Communication (NFC). IEEE, February 2013. https://doi.org/10.1109/nfc.2013.6482449
28. StemLabs: RedPitaya Website, November 2018. https://www.redpitaya.com. Accessed 16 March 2020
29. Österreichische Forschungsförderungsgesellschaft: Project homepage, June 2019. https://projekte.ffg.at/projekt/2893228. Accessed 05 May 2020

Methods for Live Testing of Cloud Services

Oussama Jebbar[1(✉)], Ferhat Khendek[1], and Maria Toeroe[2]

[1] Gina Cody School of Engineering and Computer Science, Concordia University,
Montreal, Canada
ojebbar@encs.concordia.ca, ferhat.khendek@concordia.ca
[2] Ericsson Canada Inc., Montreal, Canada
maria.toeroe@ericsson.com

Abstract. Service providers use cloud to reduce the cost of their services and speed up their time to market. There is a huge gap between the environment where the services are developed and first tested, and the environment where they operate. Live testing is defined as testing a service in its production environment without causing any intolerable disruption to its usage. It is considered as one of the solutions to overcome the impact of the difference between the development environment and the production environment on the reliability of the test results. Test interferences are a major challenge for live testing as they may lead to the system mishandling the production traffic. Existing solutions to alleviate the risk of interferences have limited applicability. In this paper we propose a set of test methods, applicable in different situations, for live testing to improve the reliability of test results without causing any intolerable disturbance to the cloud services. To reduce the complexity of these test methods we define the concept of boundary environments and a set of coverage criteria to aim at during live testing.

Keywords: Live testing · Cloud · Test method · Boundary environment · Runtime configuration state

1 Introduction

Cloud is a commonly adopted paradigm due to the flexibility of resource provisioning and the improved resource utilization it enables. Whether it is dedicated (private cloud) or shared (public cloud), a cloud is considered a complex system due to its scale and the configurations involved in its setup and management. This raises the question of how the differences between the test environment (lab, staging, dev.) and the cloud as production environment may impact software engineering activities such as software testing. Indeed, testing in the test environment is not enough anymore. In [2] for instance, Google reports a 43 min outage of the compute engine service due to a bad configuration. Although the configuration was tested pre-deployment, unexpected errors manifested once it was deployed in production. [7] presents a similar yet more elaborated issue encountered by Microsoft Azure as a configuration and code change errors that were not detected prior to the deployment and which lead to an almost 3 h outage of several services. These errors

© IFIP International Federation for Information Processing 2020
Published by Springer Nature Switzerland AG 2020
V. Casola et al. (Eds.): ICTSS 2020, LNCS 12543, pp. 201–216, 2020.
https://doi.org/10.1007/978-3-030-64881-7_13

manifested as a result of the new code and configuration being exposed to a specific traffic pattern not known/considered pre-deployment. To reveal such scenarios, services hosted in clouds need to be re-tested in their production environments as (1) the multiple configurations involved in a cloud system lead to differences between the configurations used in the test environment and the ones deployed in production [3]; and, (2) clouds may be subject to unexpected scenarios (requests or traffic patterns) that may not have been covered by testing activities.

Live testing, as we define it [24], is testing a service in its production environment without causing an intolerable disruption to its usage. Live testing becomes more challenging as the tolerable disruption constraints become more stringent as in the case of carrier grade services. Interferences between test traffic and production traffic are among the main challenges of live testing as they result in violations of one or more of the functional or non-functional requirements of the cloud service. Test interferences may be due to internal characteristics of the services being tested (statefulness, nature of interactions, etc.), or the shared resources among services hosted in the same environment. Test interferences can manifest at the level of the services being tested or at the level of other services that share resources with them. A concrete example of such cases can be found in [4] where Google describes how testing an experimental feature for Java and Go applications in the Google App Engine caused instances of Java, Go, and Python applications to malfunction for almost 20 min.

The countermeasures taken to alleviate the risk associated with test interferences are known as test isolations. Some test methods provide isolation by using only components that can be tested live, i.e. they incorporate specialized modules called Built-In Test modules (BITs) that provide isolation [12]. Other test methods rely on other mechanisms such as cloning (used in canary releases and gradual rollout [6] test methods), snapshot and restore, resource negotiation, or scheduling tests when interferences are less likely to happen [13]. Canary releases and gradual rollouts are two test methods that are commonly used for testing a system in production. They rely on the use of production traffic to test new versions of existing features. In addition to the limitation of not being able to address new features, the reliability of the test results they provide needs to be improved. [1] reports an incident in which a canary tested configuration turned out to be erroneous after being propagated to the rest of the system. The failure, according to [1], was due to the fact that the feature was canary tested in network locations where some of its scenarios were not executed. These un-covered scenarios have been executed in other network locations after the change was propagated system wide. Had the new feature been tested in all possible network locations, this problem could have been avoided. Similarly, [5] reports on an issue caused by a bug in a feature that was not detected using gradual rollout. Although we cannot confidently claim that this could have been avoided if the feature was tested in other locations under different conditions, we cannot rule it out as a possibility either.

In this paper, we propose a set of test methods, applicable under different conditions, for live testing. These methods offer more flexibility compared to the existing ones and help alleviate the risk of potential test interferences. Testing of cloud services can be very complex and resource/time consuming. Therefore, we define the concept of boundary environment and different coverage criteria to reduce the cost of proper testing of cloud services and avoid situations such as in [1] and [5].

The rest of this paper is organized as follows. In Sect. 2 we provide the background knowledge. We present the test methods we propose in Sect. 3. We introduce the boundary environment concept and its related coverage criteria in Sect. 4 and discuss how they can be integrated with our test methods as well as with other methods. Before we conclude in Sect. 6, we review the related work in Sect. 5.

2 Background and Definitions

Cloud service providers accommodate tenants with a varying range of requirements. To reduce the cost of their services, cloud service providers realize their systems using configurable software which can be configured differently to satisfy different requirements. Configurations can be of different types, *tenant configuration, application configuration,* or *deployment configuration.* Tenant requirements are realized using services. A *service* consists of one service instance or multiple service instances chained together to compose the service. A *service instance* is the workload which is assigned to a *single configured instance.* Service providers create service instances using configurations of all the aforementioned types. These configurations play various roles in tuning the behavior of the configurable software. *Tenant configurations* for instance are used to parametrize the service instances composing the service of a specific tenant. *Application configurations* are used to expose/refine features of the configurable software which may be required to be parameterized differently for different tenants. When instantiated, a configured instance yields a set of *components* which are providing the actual service instance. The number of such components, their locations, their interactions with components of other configured instances, the policies that govern the number of such components, etc. are aspects set using *deployment configurations.*

A *configured instance* may be deployed on several physical or virtual nodes, i.e. its *components* may be running on any of the nodes on which it is deployed. Such design is usually used for capacity and/or fault tolerance purposes. Therefore, at any moment of the system's lifespan, components of configured instances may be running on same nodes, on different nodes, bounded to the same or different components of another configured instance, etc. The locations of those components, their numbers per configured instance, and their binding information is called a *runtime configuration state.* The set of

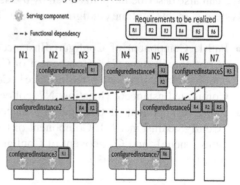

Fig. 1. Example of systems under consideration.

runtime configuration states in which a system can be depends on the system's configuration. This is also called the viability zone for self-adaptive systems [22]. When the system is in a given runtime configuration state, each component is located on a specific node, in a specific network, sharing that node with a set of components from other configured instances. The location information (node and network) and collocation information define the *environment* under which the component is actually serving. Therefore, a runtime configuration state is identified by the set of environments under which the components of the configured instances are serving when the system is in that runtime configuration state. Furthermore, we can also identify runtime configuration states by the environments under which the service instances that compose each service are provided. For each service, such a combination of environments is called the *path* through which the service is provided. Note that for services that are composed of a single service instance the concept of path coincides with the concept of environment as there are no combinations of environments to consider at this level. As a result, the concept of path, as we define it, is not to be confused with path in white box testing which may refer to control flow path or data flow path. To evaluate the compliance of the services with the requirements, cloud service providers use test cases as needed. These test cases may involve one or more configured instances depending on the realization of the requirements the test case covers.

Figure 1 depicts an example of a system we are interested in and addressing in this paper. Some requirements such as R3 are realized using services composed of a single service instance (assigned to ConfiguredInstance4). Other requirements such as R2 are realized through services that are compositions of more than one service instance (service instances assigned to ConfiguredInstance2, ConfiguredInstance4, and ConfiguredInstance6). The figure also captures a runtime configuration state where ConfiguredInstance2, ConfiguredInstance3, and ConfiguredInstance7 have two components running, while the rest of the configured instances have only one. These numbers of components can change as a result of configured instances scaling in or out. We can identify and describe the environment under which the component of ConfiguredInstance4, for instance, is serving as {location: N4, collocation: comps of {ConfiguredInstance7}}. We can also describe the paths taken by the service realizing R2, for instance, when the system is in this runtime configuration state. These paths are as follows:

- Path1: Component of ConfiguredInstance4: {location: N4, collocation: comps of {ConfiguredInstance7}}, Component of ConfiguredInstance2: {location: N2, collocation: comps of {ConfiguredInstance1, ConfiguredInstance3}}, and Component of ConfiguredInstance6: {location: N7, collocation: none}.
- Path2: Component of ConfiguredInstance4: {location: N4, collocation: comps of {ConfiguredInstance7}}, Component of ConfiguredInstance2: {location: N3, collocation: none}, and Component of ConfiguredInstance6: {location: N7, collocation: none}.

3   Test Methods

This section describes the various live testing methods we propose to avoid the interferences between the test traffic and the production traffic of different conditions, i.e. configured instances with different characteristics.

3.1 Goals and Assumptions

We aim for solutions that are capable of covering all runtime configuration states. Therefore, the coverage of runtime configuration states must be incorporated in our test methods. Furthermore, our solution should be independent of the configured instances under test (not assuming any capabilities of the configured instances under test); and, independent of the test cases being executed and the features being tested (like testing only features for which we only have production traffic). To meet these goals, we assume that the environment in which the configured instances run has the capability: (1) to snapshot the components of the configured instances composing the system. The snapshot image that is taken should be enough to clone these components. The environment has also the capability to clone a component from a snapshot; and, (2) to relocate service assignment from one component to another. These assumptions are aligned with the cloud paradigm. Due to containerization, snapshotting and cloning, for instance, can be done independent of the technologies used to realize the configured instances. Tools such as CRIU enable the snapshotting and cloning of processes running in various container technologies such as Docker [8] and LXC [9]. Furthermore, production like setups containerize even infrastructure services (kubelet and kubeproxy for Kubernetes [10], nova and neutron for openstack [11], for instance) which makes this assumption applicable also to infrastructure services. Service relocation is a feature also supported by cloud orchestrators. Such feature is usually needed to meet QoS requirements such as availability and service continuity. However, not all orchestrators may support service continuity.

3.2 Illustrative Example

Figure 2 shows a setup we will use to explain some concepts used in our test methods. It is composed of two configured instances which share three out of five nodes. The two configured instances share nodes N1, N2, N3, while nodes N4 and N5 can only be used by ConfiguredInstance1. At the time of the testing, ConfiguredInstance1 and ConfiguredInstance2 have two components each.

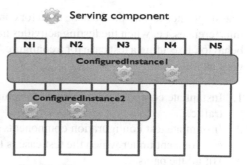

Fig. 2. Setup for the illustrative example.

To cover all runtime configuration states of the system, one should reproduce these states during testing. Therefore, during testing a component can be either a serving component, a component under test, or a test configuration component. A *serving component* is a component that handles production traffic. A *component under test* is a component that receives the test traffic. A *test configuration component* is a component, which is not under test, which receives a duplicated production traffic, but does not handle it. Such components are used to recreate the runtime configuration state corresponding to the component being tested. The set of paths that need to be covered for testing a service composed of a single service instance provided by ConfiguredInstance2 includes but is not limited to:

- Path1: {location: N1, collocation: comps of {ConfiguredInstance1}}. If we start from the runtime configuration state illustrated in Fig. 2, this will imply instantiating a test configuration component for ConfiguredInstance1 on N1, while having the component of ConfiguredInstance2 on N1 as the component under test.
- Path2: {location: N2, collocation: comps of {ConfiguredInstance1}}. If we start from the runtime configuration state illustrated in Fig. 2, this will imply instantiating a test configuration component for ConfiguredInstance1 on N2, while having the component of ConfiguredInstance2 on N2 as the component under test.
- Path3: {location: N3, collocation: comps of {ConfiguredInstance1}}. If we start from the runtime configuration state illustrated in Fig. 2, this will imply instantiating a component of ConfiguredInstance2 on N3 as the component under test while ConfiguredInstance1 already has its component on N3 handling production traffic, so it is a serving component.

In the rest of this section we will describe various test methods that can be used to test configured instances in production while avoiding the risk of interferences. Note that these test methods are applicable at configured instance level and not at path level. That is, to test a service which is a composition of two or more service instances that are provided by different configured instances, we can use different test methods for the different configured instances on the path providing the service. Furthermore, we need to test the service for all the paths through which it can be provided.

3.3 Single Step

The single step test method can be used for configured instances with no potential risk of interferences, i.e. when the testing activities have no impact on the configured instances behavior. Executing a test case for a configured instance using the single step test method goes as follows:

1. Instantiate components under test to setup the paths that will be taken by the test traffic.
2. Instantiate test configuration components as needed to complete the creation of the environment under which the test case is to be executed.
3. Hit all the paths.

Figure 3 illustrates the iteration for using the single step method to test a service composed of one service instance which is provided by ConfiguredInstance1. From the configuration of ConfiguredInstance1 one can deduce that the service can be provided through one of the eight paths (that means also eight environments as we are in the case of a service composed of a single service instance). As shown in Fig. 3, one can exercise five paths at a time using this test method. The figure shows five out of the eight paths tested. Since there is no potential risk of interferences, components of ConfiguredInstance1 are allowed to handle test traffic and production traffic at the same time. Therefore, test components are instantiated on an as-needed basis. Starting from the runtime configuration state in Fig. 3(a), in (b), for instance, for ConfiguredInstance1 we had to instantiate test components on nodes N1, N2, and N5, but for N3 and N4 we use the components which already handle production traffic, i.e. these components play two roles: serving component and component under test (marked as serving component under test). Similarly, the instantiation of test configuration components is not necessary as existing serving components help to create the environments under which one wants to test. However, in the absence of such components, one needs to instantiate test configuration components as it is the case for ConfigurationInstance2 on node N3 in Fig. 3(b). Figure 3(c) shows the runtime configuration state after completing the single step test method. It is the same as in Fig. 3(a).

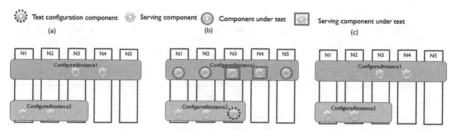

Fig. 3. Testing iteration for the single step test method applied to ConfiguredInstance1.

3.4 Rolling Paths

The rolling paths test method can be used in situations where testing may impact the configured instance to be tested (therefore, serving components under test cannot be used), and the total cost of isolation mechanisms such as snapshot-and-clone and service-relocation is not too high in terms of causing intolerable disruption to the service. The rolling paths test method applied to a single configured instance as follows:

1. Instantiate a component under test to create the path that will be taken by the test case.
2. Instantiate test configuration components as needed to setup the environments under which the test component should undergo testing.
3. Execute the test case on the created path.
4. Snapshot a serving component and replace the already tested component under test with a serving component cloned from the snapshot. Relocate the service to the new serving component.
5. Replace the snapshotted serving component with a component under test to create a new path to be tested.
6. Repeat from the second step until all the paths are exercised by the test case.

Figure 4 illustrates a few iterations of the rolling paths in the case of a service composed of a single service instance provided by ConfiguredInstance2. There are six paths to be exercised by the test case. Because of the potential risk of interferences, test traffic has to be isolated from production traffic. As a result, unless there are enough resources, one cannot test multiple paths at the same time. A single path is created at each iteration by instantiating the necessary components under test and test configuration components as shown in Fig. 4(b), (c) and (d). After executing the test case in each iteration the service is relocated, and a next path is created for it to be exercised by the test case until all paths have been exercised. Figure 4(e) shows that the runtime configuration state after the testing differs from the one in which the testing activity has started, i.e. Figure 4(a).

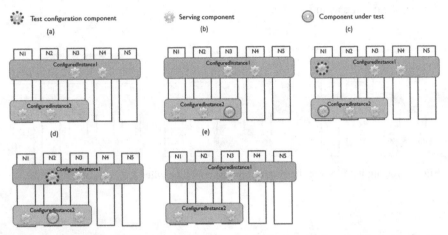

Fig. 4. Testing iterations for the rolling paths test method applied to ConfiguredInstance2.

3.5 Small Flip

The small flip test method can be used to test configured instances when there is a risk of potential interferences; and, for which the number of currently required components is less than the number of unused nodes that can be used by this configured instance. For instance, the small flip can be used for a configured instance which can have components on six nodes and that, at the time of testing, requires only two components. Assuming we are testing a configured instance that, at the time of testing, requires k components out of the maximum n, where k <= n/2, the small flip test goes as follows:

1. Instantiate k components under test for the configured instance being tested on k available nodes.
2. Instantiate the test configuration components to create the test environments under which the k components under test are to be tested.
3. Test all the paths which can be exercised and which involve the k instantiated components under test until all the paths have been covered
4. Take snapshots of the k serving components, and replace the k components under test with k serving components cloned from the snapshots. Relocate the production traffic to the k new serving components.
5. Run the test cases for components on the rest of the nodes using the single step test method.

Figure 5 shows the iterations of the small flip test method in the case of a service composed of a single service instance that is provided using ConfiguredInstance1. The small flip is used to test configured instances that present a potential risk of interferences, however, the resources available allow for exercising at least k paths in each iteration. In the first iteration shown in Fig. 5(b) two paths are exercised. The small flip results in one service relocation shown in Fig. 5(c) when used for only one configured instance involved in providing the service being tested. It shows the application of the single step test method to the remaining nodes. Figure 5(d) shows the runtime configuration state after completion of the test. Note that the test of a service composed of more than one service instance and, therefore more than one configured instance (of the configured instances providing these service instances) is being tested using the small flip, may result in more than one service relocation for some configured instances.

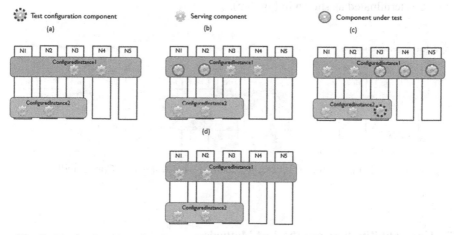

Fig. 5. Testing iterations for the small flip test method applied to ConfiguredInstance1.

3.6 Big Flip

The big flip is the test method which induces the least service disruption and takes the shortest time. However, among the test method discussed here it has the highest resource consumption. The big flip test method of a configured instance goes as follows:

1. Create a new configured instance, the test configured instance, that has the same configuration as the configured instance to be tested. The components of the test configured instance are the components under test, while the components of the configured instance to be tested remain as serving components during testing activities.
2. Create test configuration components required to test each path and run the test case.
3. After completing the tests, take a snapshot of the original configured instance to be tested, replace the test configured instance with an instance cloned from the snapshot, relocate the production traffic to the test configured instance (which will make it the

configured instance with the new serving components); and remove the original configured instance from the system.

Figure 6 shows how the big flip test method is used to test a service composed of one service instance provided using ConfiguredInstance2. As shown in Fig. 6(b), a new instance of ConfiguredInstance2 (ConfiguredInstance2') is instantiated on nodes that can host its environment. Such nodes are identified by taking into consideration information from the system configuration such as, software installed on each node, anti-affinity rules, etc. The new instance is then used to perform the tests under different paths (which are environments in this case as the service is composed of only one service instance). After the tests for all paths pass, the tested configured instance is replaced by one cloned from the original configured instance, which becomes the one with the serving components (service relocation from the original instance to the new one), and the original configured instance is terminated as shown in Fig. 6(c).

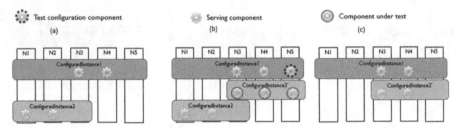

Fig. 6. Testing iterations for the big flip test method when applied to ConfiguredInstance2.

3.7 Compatibility Between the Test Methods

The test methods described in this section apply to a single configured instance, however, a test case often involves more than one configured instance. It is possible to combine our proposed test methods throughout the path traversed by the test case keeping in mind: (1) The big flip method can be combined with any test methods; (2) the single step can only be used if throughout the paths being tested only the single step or the big flip are used; and, (3) The rolling paths and the small flip methods can be used together, and even combined with the big flip method.

4   Boundary Environments and Coverage Criteria

A cloud service needs to be tested against all possible runtime configuration states of the system providing it. For cloud services we redefine the notion of *"test case passed"* to *"a test case passed only when it passed in all possible applicable runtime configuration states"*. Testing a service against all its applicable runtime configuration states is neces-sary, however it is very costly. Let us consider a service composed of only one service instance protected by a configured instance where the components can be on any one of ten dedicated nodes (not shared with any other configured instance). For a normal functional test case, one will have to run this test case ten times to test this service against all its applicable runtime configuration states (once per node). In the case of a stress test case, and if we assume the maximum size of the configured instance is four components, the test case will need to be executed 210 times (C_{10}^4 times, without considering the scaling steps). These numbers increase with the number of service instances. Thus, covering all the runtime configuration states may be impossible for complex and large systems such as cloud systems.

4.1 Boundary Environments

To tackle the aforementioned problem we propose testing against a representative set of runtime configuration states. A runtime configuration state is described via the environments in which each service instance is provided; as a result, identifying the representative set of runtime configuration states consists of identifying the environments that describe the runtime configuration states in this set. Because any environment has two elements, i.e. location and collocation, such environments can be derived in two mutually non-exclusive ways:

- Collocation-wise: for a given set of locations on which a configured instance is deployed, one can identify the environments with the largest collocations per location which we call *boundary environments*. In other words, the collocation set of an environment that has that same location is a subset of the collocation set of the boundary environment. Two environments are said to have the same boundary environment if they have the same maximum collocation and equivalent locations, i.e. same network, and hosts of identical specifications.
- Location-wise: for a given set of collocations of components of a given configured instance and a maximum number of N components, one can identify various assignments of N collocations to N locations as allowed by the configuration. Such assignments are what we call *mixtures of environments*. Such assignments may or may not allow the reuse of collocations as the configuration allows. Two mixtures are said to have equivalent assignments if their assignments involve the same set of collocations in equivalent locations with the same numbers of occurrences of each collocation per location class.

By identifying the boundary environments in a system one can group the nodes of the system into groups that have the same boundary environment. Similarly, by identifying mixtures of environments one can group them into mixtures which involve the same set of collocations with the same number of occurrences of each collocation per location class. Our main idea is to use such groupings (location-wise and collocation-wise) to group runtime configuration states into equivalence classes taking into consideration the environments they involve. In other words, test runs should cover runtime configuration states that involve: (1) boundary environments, and (2) mixtures that were derived from collocations of boundary environments and that involve as many boundary environments as possible. The rationale behind this method is based on the following assumptions:

- Boundary environments present the worst case of resource sharing under which one can put the component under test; therefore, if a property holds under the boundary environment it will hold under all its sub-environments.
- Boundary environments allow for grouping nodes into equivalence classes. As a result, one node that replicates the boundary environment is considered representative of all the equivalent nodes that can host that boundary environment. This assumption enables us to reduce the number of paths, and as a result the number of runs the test case should go through.

4.2 Coverage Criteria

Using the boundary environments, one can define the set of paths that should be exercised by the test case. Such set depends also on the nature of the test case itself. A functional test case will only need to target boundary environments of the configured instances. However, for stress test, for instance, one needs to use mixtures of boundary environments as well as check how the service behaves when these are chained with various mixtures of the other configured instances involved in the test case. Figure 7 shows an example in which a service composed of two service instances that are provided (and protected) by two configured instances (ConfiguredInstance1 and ConfiguredInstance2) undergoing a stress test. Figure 7(a) shows that ConfiguredInstance1 can have up to three components and ConfiguredInstance2 can have up to two components. If we assume all nodes are identical and are in the same network, ConfiguredIntsnace1 components may serve under environments with any of four collocations (for instance, collocation: comps of { }). Same applies to ConfiguredInstance2. Furthermore, ConfigureInstance1 has three different collocations for the boundary environments, namely one shared with only ConfiguredInstance2 (for example on N1), one shared with only ConfiguredInstance3 (for example on N4), and one shared with both (on N3). Similarly, ConfiguredInstance2 has two collocations for the boundary environments, one shared with only ConfiguredInstance1 and one shared with both ConfiguredInstance1 and ConfiguredInstance3. Figure 7(b) to (g) capture some mixtures under which the service has to be tested (as it may be provided under these mixtures).

One can use various coverage criteria of the boundary environments as well as their mixtures in order to define the paths a test case has to exercise. Among these coverage criteria we believe the following are the most relevant. They are ordered in the descending order of their respective error detection power:

- *All boundary environments mixtures (resp. boundary environments) paths*: in this coverage one identifies first all possible mixtures of boundary environments (resp. boundary environments), then tests on all the paths that chain the mixtures (resp. boundary environments) of the configured instances being tested.
- *Pairwise boundary environments mixtures (resp. boundary environments)*: in this coverage one identifies all possible mixtures of boundary environments (resp. boundary environments), then generates a set of paths such as each pair of identified mixtures (resp. boundary environments) is in at least one path. To do so, one can generate a covering array of strength two for the identified mixtures (resp. boundary environments) considering each configured instance as a factor and each mixture (resp.

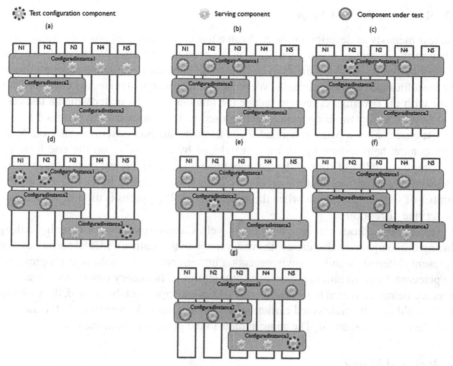

Fig. 7. Some mixtures and their combinations against which a service instance provided by ConfiguredInstance1 and ConfiguredInstance2 should be tested.

boundary environments) of a configured instance as a level of the factor representing that configured instance.

- *All boundary environments mixtures (resp. boundary environments)*: in this coverage one aims at testing a set of paths in which each mixture of boundary environments (resp. boundary environments) is used at least once.

Based on the assumptions we made, one can use any of these criteria to reduce the number of runs of a test case while maintaining an acceptable level of error detection power. To run a functional test case against the service composed of the service instances provided by the configured instances in Fig. 7, one needs twenty runs for that test case to cover all runtime configuration states (without varying the location, taking into consideration the location one will end up with ninety six runs), as compared to six runs using all boundary environments paths and pairwise boundary environments coverage criteria, or three runs for all boundary environments criterion. Similar reduction in the number of runs can be achieved for test cases that may involve environments mixtures such as stress tests.

4.3 Revisiting the Test Methods

The test methods as described in Sect. 3 run a test case against all possible paths while reducing the impact of testing activities on the production traffic. We have shown that this can be time consuming and may induce some intolerable service disruption due to service relocation for some methods. We proposed the concept of boundary environments along with the coverage criteria to reduce the number of paths under which a test case is to be run. Using these concepts the proposed test methods can be revisited to run the test cases only on paths generated given an environments-coverage criterion. Such enhancement help reduce the disruption induced by live testing on the one hand by reducing the number of runs of the test case regardless of which test method is used for isolation, which reduces the time needed for testing. On the other hand, by reducing the number of service relocations when the small flip or rolling paths is used which reduces the service disruption.

Other test methods can be enhanced as well. Canary releases can be enhanced by placing the components that expose the new version of the feature under test on nodes that represent different boundary environments. Furthermore, as the rollout is progressing, the placement should aim to cover relevant mixtures of boundary environments as new users are being redirected to the new version. Had such approach been used, the problem in [1] could have been detected earlier before retiring the older version and the damage could have been contained. The same applies to the gradual rollout method.

5 Related Work

The author in [13] proposed a set of test methods to alleviate the risk associated with interferences. The main focus was to assess the runtime testability of the SUT provided a set of test methods that can provide isolation, and propose methods for test case selection that can balance between reducing the cost of runtime testability and the cost of runtime diagnosis. The authors in [12, 14] propose alleviating the risk of interferences using BITs to test a system in production. [15] proposes the use of the methods in [12–14] to avoid interferences. Moreover, [15] extended the TTCN Test System Reference Architecture [23] to orchestrate test case execution in production. Although this solution allows for the automation of test case execution and test configuration deployment, it remains limited to the use of TTCN as a language for test case specification in specific environments, namely OSGi managed JAVA systems. Canary releases [6], gradual rollouts [6] and dark launches [17] leverage the use of production traffic for testing purposes. In canary releases a new version of an existing feature is released to a subset of customers for a period of time, the new version will be released to all the customers only if it does not show any problem during the test period. Unlike canary releases, in gradual rollouts the percentage of customers using the new version increases in small steps, 5% for instance, until the new version takes over provided no problems are revealed while it is being tested. Dark launches consist of deploying the new version without releasing it to any customers. The production traffic is duplicated, and the behavior of the new version is compared to the behavior of the old version. If no problems are detected during the test period, the new version will be made visible to the users. As they rely on duplicating the production traffic, canary release, gradual roll outs, and dark launches have limited applicability as they can only be used to test new versions of existing features, i.e. they are not applicable for new features for which there is no production traffic to duplicate. Same applies for methods such as Simplex [16] which is used for dependable live upgrade and testing of real time embedded systems. Blue-Green deployment technique [18] is used to enable zero downtime live upgrade and testing. It consists of maintaining two identical production environments, Blue and Green. One of them is used to handle the production traffic while the second remains idle. When it is time for an upgrade, the idle environment will be upgraded and tested. If the new setup passes all the tests the production traffic will be redirected to the idle environment and the active environment will become idle. The drawback of this approach is that it comes at a high cost resource wise as it poses the challenge of maintaining two environments in synch, which is not acceptable for large scale systems.

In addition to testing, software upgrade is yet another management activity performed on live systems. The main challenge of live upgrade is the potential impact on the system's availability. Our test methods follow similar patterns as some state-of-the-art live upgrade methods. The rolling paths that we propose is similar to the rolling upgrade method [19] as this latter consists on rolling on batches of nodes (of a given size) and upgrade them iteratively in order to upgrade the system while maintaining service availability. Methods proposed to deal with software incompatibility include the split mode upgrade [20] and the delayed switch upgrade [21]. They consist of upgrading half of the nodes providing the service, redirecting the traffic to the upgraded nodes, then upgrade the rest of the nodes; which makes the principles used in the small flip method similar to the principles on which these methods are based. Blue/Green deployment [18] is also nothing more than an upgrade method, the parallel universe, used for testing activities. The gradual rollouts can also be considered as a rolling upgrade in which the tests are performed as the upgrade progresses.

6 Conclusion

Testing cloud services in the production environment has implications that cannot be addressed while testing in the development environment. On one hand, the complexity and the heterogeneity of the system should be taken into consideration in order to obtain reliable test results. On the other hand, one has to alleviate the risk of test interferences. In this paper we proposed a set of test methods, applicable in different situations, that will enable live testing of cloud services. We discussed how covering all the runtime configuration states of the system is costly and infeasible in real life systems. We proposed the concept of boundary environments and a set of coverage criteria that can reduce the cost of testing cloud services when combined with our proposed test methods as well as existing ones. As future work, we plan to validate with real case studies the methods and concepts introduced in this paper.

Acknowledgement. This work has been partially supported by Natural Sciences and Engineering Research Council of Canada (NSERC) and Ericsson.

References

1. https://status.cloud.google.com/incident/compute/16012. Accessed 18 June 2020
2. https://status.cloud.google.com/incident/compute/15046. Accessed 18 June 2020
3. https://status.cloud.google.com/incident/appengine/19001. Accessed 18 June 2020
4. https://status.cloud.google.com/incident/appengine/16002. Accessed 18 June 2020
5. https://status.cloud.google.com/incident/cloud-networking/18012. Accessed 18 June 2020
6. Feitelson, D.G., Frachtenberg, E., Beck, K.L.: Development and deployment at Facebook. In: IEEE Internet Computing (2013)
7. 20th November 2019 incident. https://status.azure.com/en-us/status/history/. Accessed 18 June 2020
8. Docker. https://www.docker.com. Accessed 18 June 2020
9. Linux containers. https://www.linuxcontainers.org. Accessed 18 June 2020
10. Kubernetes. https://www.kubernetes.io. Accessed 18 June 2020
11. Openstack. https://www.openstack.org. Accessed 18 June 2020
12. Brenner, D., Atkinson, C., Malaka, R., Merdes, M., Paech, B., Suliman, D.: Reducing verification effort in component-based software engineering through built-in testing. Inf. Syst. Front. **9**(2–3), 151–162 (2007)
13. Sanchez, A.G.: Cost Optimizations in Runtime Testing and Diagnosis. Ph.D. Thesis. Delft University of Technology, September (2011)
14. Suliman, D., et al.: The MORABIT Approach to Runtime Component Testing. In the proceedings of the 30th Annual International Computer Software and Applications Conference COMPSAC 2006 (2006)
15. Lahami, M., Krichen, M., Jmaiel, M.: Safe and efficient runtime testing framework applied in dynamic and distributed systems. Sci. Comput. Program. **122**, 1–28 (2016)
16. Lee, K., Sha, L.: A dependable online testing and upgrade architecture for real-time embedded systems. In: The proceedings of the 11th IEEE International Conference on Embedded and Real-Time Computing Systems and Applications RTCSA 2005 (2005)
17. Tang, C., et al.: Holistic configuration management at Facebook. In: The proceedings of the 25th Symposium on Operating Systems Principles SOSP 2015 (2015)
18. Blue-green. https://docs.cloudfoundry.org/devguide/deploy-apps/blue-green.html. Accessed 18 June 2020
19. Roush, E.T.: Cluster rolling upgrade using multiple version support. In: The Proceedings of IEEE International Conference on Cluster Computing ICCC 2001 (2001)
20. Das, T., Roush, E.T., Nandana, P.: Quantum leap cluster upgrade. In: The Proceedings of the 2nd Bangalore Annual Compute Conference COMPUTE 2009 (2009)
21. Ouyang, X., Ding, B., Wang, H.: Delayed switch: cloud service upgrade with low availability and capacity loss. In: The proceedings of the 5th International Conference on Software Engineering and Service Science ICSESS 2014 (2014)
22. de Lemos, R., et al.: Software engineering for self-adaptive systems: a second research roadmap. In: de Lemos, R., Giese, H., Müller, H.A., Shaw, M. (eds.) Software Engineering for Self-Adaptive Systems II. LNCS, vol. 7475, pp. 1–32. Springer, Heidelberg (2013). https://doi.org/10.1007/978-3-642-35813-5_1
23. ETSI ES 201 873-5 v4.8.1. Methods for Testing and Specification (MTS): The Testing and Test Control Notation version 3; Part 5: TTCN-3 Runtime Interface (TRI)
24. Jebbar, O., Khendek, F., Toeroe, M.: Architecture for the automation of live testing of cloud systems. In: The Proceedings of the 20th IEEE International Conference on Software Quality, Reliability, and Security IEEE QRS (2020)

Testing Methods and Automation

Automated Transition Coverage
in Behavioural Conformance Testing

Lina Marsso, Radu Mateescu, and Wendelin Serwe[✉]

Univ. Grenoble Alpes, Inria, CNRS, Grenoble INP*, LIG, 38000 Grenoble, France
wendelin.serwe@inria.fr

Abstract. In the setting of ioco-based conformance testing with test purposes, we propose an automatic approach to generate a test plan (set of test purposes) with its associated test suite (set of test cases) covering all transitions of the IOLTS model of the system. The approach can also be applied to improve an existing test plan, by both, completing the coverage and eliminating redundancies. Implementing our approach on top of the CADP toolbox, we report on experiments with several examples of concurrent systems and discuss possible variants and heuristics to fine-tune the overall performance of the approach, as well as the quality of the computed test plan.

1 Introduction

MBT (Model-Based Testing) [39,41] encompasses the range of methods that exploit a model of the SUT (System Under Test) to automate testing. MBT enables to keep tests in close correspondence with the SUT's requirements and reduces the cost of the test activity, at the price of developing a model of the SUT. Conformance testing is a form of black-box MBT seeking to establish that an SUT behaves according to a model, which serves as an oracle. We make the common hypothesis that the behaviour of both, the model and the SUT, can be represented as an IOLTS (Input-Output Labelled Transition System) [22], which is a convenient semantic representation for high-level formal languages.

A popular conformance relation for IOLTSs is *ioco* [38], which served as basis for various testing approaches, such as on-line testing, as implemented in the JTorX tool [1], or on-the-fly test case generation guided by test purposes, as implemented in the TGV [22] and TESTOR [27] tools. The former approach has the advantage of being fully automatic (the tester executes the SUT and the model in a co-simulation manner), whereas the latter approach using test purposes allows the tester to build a *test plan*, i.e., set of test purposes at a similar abstraction level as the system requirements. In an approach based on *ioco* and test purposes, the test plan must be transformed into a *test suite*, i.e., a set of concrete, deterministic test cases to be executed on an SUT. Each test

---

* Institute of Engineering, Univ. Grenoble Alpes.

© IFIP International Federation for Information Processing 2020
Published by Springer Nature Switzerland AG 2020
V. Casola et al. (Eds.): ICTSS 2020, LNCS 12543, pp. 219–235, 2020.
https://doi.org/10.1007/978-3-030-64881-7_14

purpose directs the test case extraction and enables to handle large models by ignoring those parts of the model irrelevant to the considered test purpose. In both approaches, the tester is confronted with the questions of when to stop the testing process (either by terminating the co-simulation, or by devising no more test purposes), and how thoroughly the SUT has been tested. These well-known questions in the testing domain are classically addressed using *coverage criteria* [42] measuring the degree to which the internal structure of an SUT was exercised during the testing process.

Suitable coverage criteria for LTSs (and thus IOLTSs) were proposed in [37], which quantify in an increasingly stronger way how much of the LTS structure is explored during the testing process: (a) *all labels* (covering each label of the LTS, given that a same label may occur on several transitions in the LTS); (b) *all states* (covering each state of the LTS); (c) *all transitions* (covering each transition in the LTS); (d) *all proper paths* (covering each finite sequence of the LTS without repeated states); (e) *all paths* (covering each sequence of the LTS). Since criteria (d) and (e) are too costly in practice, and sometimes impossible to achieve with a finite testing process, such as criterion (e) on an LTS containing cycles, we focus on criterion (c), referred to as *transition coverage* in the sequel.

In this paper, we propose an approach to automatically generate a set of test purposes with their corresponding CTGs (Complete Test Graphs), each of which contains all necessary information to drive a (conformant) SUT towards the corresponding test purpose (if possible). This approach is iterative: in each iteration, a new test purpose is derived from a counterexample illustrating a not yet covered transition of the model. It is also possible to start from an existing, non-trivial (i.e., not empty) test plan, completing it to cover all transitions, as well as detecting redundant test purposes that do not increase the coverage. Because a CTG is not necessarily controllable (e.g., there might be a non-deterministic choice between inputs to be sent to the SUT), we further automatically extract from each CTG a deterministic test suite covering all transitions of the CTG. The union of all such generated test suites thus ensures transition coverage of the IOLTS model. We implemented the approach on top of TESTOR[1] and the CADP toolbox[2] [13], and we experimented it on several distributed systems.

The remainder of the paper is organised as follows. Section 2 recalls the essential notions of the underlying theory. Section 3 describes the main algorithms and illustrates them on a running example. Section 4 presents an experimental evaluation of our approach, declined along several variants. Section 5 compares our approach to related work. Finally, Sect. 6 gives some concluding remarks.

2   Background

Conformance testing establishes that the behaviour of an SUT corresponds to the behaviour of a model (M) modulo a conformance relation. Behaviours are represented as IOLTSs (Input-Output Labelled Transition Systems) [22].

---

[1] http://convecs.inria.fr/software/testor.

[2] http://cadp.inria.fr.

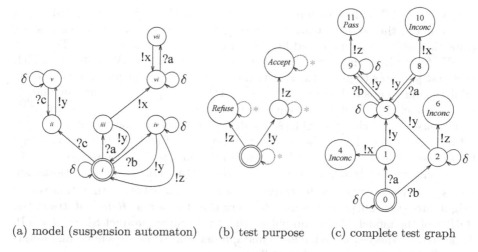

(a) model (suspension automaton)   (b) test purpose   (c) complete test graph

Fig. 1. Model, test purpose, and corresponding complete test graph [22]

An IOLTS (S, A, T, s_0) comprises a set of states S, a set of labels (or actions) A, a transition relation $T \subseteq S \times A \times S$, and an initial state $s_0 \in S$. The label set is partitioned in $A = A_I \cup A_O \cup \{\tau\}$, where A_I, A_O are the input and output labels, and τ is the internal (invisible) label. For value-passing systems, labels are of the form $G\ v_1 \ldots v_n$, where G is the name of a gate (communication link) and $v_1, \ldots, v_n$ are data values; for dataless systems, labels are simply gate names. A transition $(s_1, a, s_2) \in T$ (also noted $s_1 \xrightarrow{a} s_2$) indicates a move labelled by a between states s_1 and s_2. Input (resp. output) labels are noted $?a$ (resp. $!a$). We assume the following *testing hypothesis*: an SUT can be modelled in the same way as the formal model, i.e., in our case as an IOLTS. Input (resp. output) labels of the SUT are controllable (resp. observable) by the environment (tester).

The tester observes the execution traces of the SUT and also detects *quiescent* states, i.e., deadlocks (states without successors), outputlocks (states without outgoing output labels), or livelocks (states on τ-cycles). The quiescence present in an IOLTS $M = (S^M, A^M, T^M, s_0^M)$ is modelled by a *suspension automaton* $\Delta(M)$, an IOLTS obtained from M by adding δ-loops on the quiescent states, where δ is a special output label. In the sequel, we use the same running example as [22], whose suspension automaton $\Delta(M)$ is shown in Fig. 1(a).

An SUT conforms to the model M modulo the *ioco* relation [38] if after executing each trace of $\Delta(M)$, the suspension automaton $\Delta(\text{SUT})$ exhibits only those outputs and quiescences that are allowed by M. Since two sequences with the same observable labels (and quiescence) cannot be distinguished, the suspension automaton $\Delta(M)$ must be determinised before generating tests (this is the case for $\Delta(M)$ in Fig. 1(a), which is deterministic and minimised). A noteworthy feature of *ioco* is that an SUT with *fewer* (output) transitions than the model may be considered conformant: if the model contains a choice between several outputs, an SUT is free to implement only one of them. For such an SUT, no test suite can thus achieve transition coverage of the model, because the missing transition will never be covered by executing the test cases on the SUT.

We follow here the test generation technique of the TGV tool [22], which uses *test purposes* to guide the selection of test cases. A test purpose is a deterministic and complete IOLTS $TP = (S^{TP}, A^{TP}, T^{TP}, s_0^{TP})$, with the same labels as the model $A^{TP} = A^M$, and equipped with two sets of trap states $Accept^{TP}$ and $Refuse^{TP}$, which are used to select desired behaviours and to cut the exploration of M, respectively. The test purpose shown in Fig. 1(b) specifies a desired behaviour consisting of a label !y followed by !z and leading to an *Accept* state (the occurrence of !z before a !y is forbidden by a *Refuse* state). A transition $s \xrightarrow{*} s'$ matches every outgoing transition of s with a label other than those of its neighbours. Test purposes are used to mark the *Accept* and *Refuse* states in the IOLTS of the model M, by computing the synchronous product $SP = M \times TP$. To keep only the visible behaviours and quiescence, SP is suspended and determinised, leading to $SP_{vis} = det(\Delta(SP))$.

A *test case* is an IOLTS $TC = (S^{TC}, A^{TC}, T^{TC}, s_0^{TC})$ equipped with three sets of trap states $Pass \cup Fail \cup Inconc \subseteq S^{TC}$ denoting verdicts. The labels of TC are partitioned into A_I^{TC} and A_O^{TC} subsets. A test case TC must be *controllable*, meaning that in every state, no choice is allowed between two inputs or an input and an output (i.e., the test must either inject a single input to the SUT, or accept all the outputs of the SUT). Intuitively, a TC denotes a set of traces containing visible labels and quiescence that should be executable by the SUT to assess its conformance with the model M and a test purpose TP. From every state of the TC, a verdict must be reachable: *Pass* indicates that TP has been fulfilled, *Fail* indicates that SUT does not conform to M, and *Inconc* (inconclusive) indicates that correct behaviour has been observed but TP cannot be fulfilled. Frequently, the *Fail* state is omitted: from any state of the TC, observing an unexpected output of the SUT leads to *Fail*.

In general, several test cases can be produced from a given model and test purpose. The union of these test cases forms the CTG (Complete Test Graph) [22], which is an IOLTS similar to a TC, but possibly not controllable. Formally, a CTG is the subgraph of SP_{vis} induced by the states L2A (Lead to Accept) from which an *Accept* state is reachable, decorated with *Pass* and *Inconc* verdicts. Figure 1(c) shows the CTG corresponding to M and TP, which is not controllable (e.g., in state s_5 two inputs ?a and ?b are possible).[3] *Pass* verdicts correspond to *Accept* states (e.g., s_{11}). *Inconc* verdicts correspond either to *Refuse* states (e.g., s_6) or to states from which no *Accept* state is reachable (e.g., s_4 or s_{10}). *Fail* verdicts, not displayed on the figure, are produced for states in which the SUT can exhibit an output label or a quiescence not specified in the CTG (e.g., for label !z or quiescence in state s_1). Note that some loops of M can be unrolled in the CTG: for instance, the transitions $(s_{iii}, !y, s_i)$ and $(s_{iv}, !y, s_i)$ going back to the initial state of M correspond in the CTG to the transitions $(s_1, !y, s_5)$ and $(s_2, !y, s_5)$, respectively.

---

[3] To avoid confusion, we follow in this paper the convention of [27] and consider that the inputs and outputs of a CTG or TC are the same as those of the model.

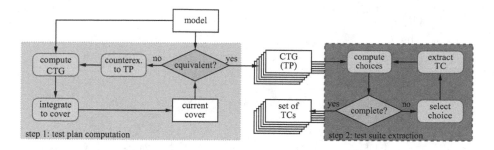

Fig. 2. Overview of the proposed approach

Our coverage approach relies on CTG generation and on several automata manipulation features provided by the tools of CADP [13], documented on the CADP web page. CTGs are generated using TESTOR [27], a new conformance test case generator that is also able to produce controllable TCs on the fly. The minimal deterministic automata of the CTGs and of the model M are obtained by applying weak trace reduction using the REDUCTOR tool, followed by strong bisimulation minimisation using the BCG_MIN tool. The coverage of M by a CTG is estimated by computing the semi-composition [24] between M and the CTG using the PROJECTOR tool, which produces a subgraph of M subsuming the regular language denoted by the CTG. Finally, M is compared with a CTG modulo strong bisimulation using the BISIMULATOR equivalence checker, which produces counterexamples (distinguishing sequences) used to generate new TPs during the coverage process. The whole coverage approach was automated using SVL [11] scripts.

3   Computation of a Test Suite Covering All Transitions

The starting point of our approach is a *finite* IOLTS model M. To ensure meaningful measurements about coverage, we first compute the (minimised) suspension automaton $\Delta(M)$. This preliminary step determinises M, removes all internal transitions and unreachable states, and marks quiescent states (with δ-loops). For readability, in the remainder of this section we use "model", rather than "suspension automaton" or "$\Delta(M)$".

Our approach, shown in Fig. 2, consists of two steps: first, we cover the model with a set of CTGs, for each of which we then extract all contained TCs. Exploiting the fact that the extraction of a CTG is completely determined by the model and the corresponding TP, our approach not only yields a test suite, but also a test plan as a set of TPs.

3.1   Covering the Model with Complete Test Graphs

We measure coverage by checking strong bisimilarity of the model with the combination of the (so far) generated CTGs; in the sequel, we refer to the latter

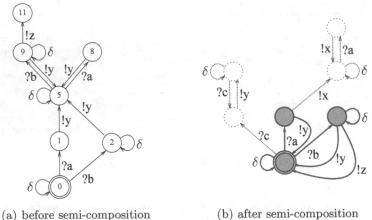

(a) before semi-composition   (b) after semi-composition

Fig. 3. Cover corresponding to the CTG (combined with the empty initial cover)

as *cover*. This naturally leads to an iterative approach in the style of CEGAR (Counter-Example Guided Abstraction Refinement) [8]: as long as the current cover is not equivalent to the model, use the counterexample generated by the equivalence checker as a new TP.

Starting with the trivial, empty cover (i.e., an empty deadlocking IOLTS, containing one single state and no transitions), our approach relies on two operations, briefly described below, that are executed at each iteration: the computation of the cover obtained by adding a new CTG and the transformation of a counterexample into a TP. At the end of this section, we present two optimisations to speed up the approach by starting with a different initial cover.

Adding a CTG to the Cover. Computing the new cover obtained by adding a CTG involves three steps. In a first step, we remove all verdict transitions from the CTG. This can be achieved by simply hiding the verdict transitions. A variant of this first step removes also all transitions leading to an inconclusive verdict, considering that such transitions do not contribute to the coverage[4], balancing thus a lower with a more significant coverage. This variant has been implemented by a simple traversal of the CTG.

In a second step, we combine the CTG with hidden verdicts (as obtained by the previous step) with the cover computed so far by the overall loop. We construct the union of both IOLTSs, considering all but their initial states as different, and minimise the resulting IOLTS for weak trace equivalence [6]. Because both the cover and the CTG are included in the model, the resulting IOLTS is also included in the model modulo trace equivalence, but it might not be a subgraph of the model (in the sense of a graph homomorphism), as illustrated by Fig. 3(a). For instance, in the model in Fig. 1(a), the output !y leads from state

---

[4] When repeatedly executing a TC until a *Pass* or *Fail* verdict is reached, there is no guarantee that a transition leading to an *Inconc* verdict has been executed.

s_{iii} back to the initial state s_i, whereas in Fig. 3(a) the corresponding transition leads from state s_1 to s_5 (which is different from the initial state s_0).

In a third step, to ensure that the resulting cover for the next iteration is a subgraph of the model, we compute the semi-composition [12,15,16,24] of the model and the IOLTS obtained after the two previous steps—by [12, Proposition 3], the result of a semi-composition is a subgraph of the left operand. Also, the resulting cover contains all visible traces of the CTG (by definition of semi-composition and because by construction all traces of a CTG are included in the model). Notice that this third step reverts any unrolling of loops induced by the synchronous product of the model with the TP. Figure 3(b) shows the cover computed using these three steps to integrate the CTG shown in Fig. 1(c) with the empty initial cover.

Transforming a Counterexample into a TP. Because the model and the cover are both deterministic, a counterexample witnessing their non-bisimilarity is necessarily a (distinguishing) sequence leading to a transition missing in the cover. Also, using a breadth-first search algorithm in the equivalence checker yields a counterexample of minimal length; this is interesting to obtain a TP as simple as possible, and to avoid reexploring parts of the model already covered.

This sequence is then transformed into a TP by simply declaring its final state as an *Accept* state. A slightly more involved transformation adds to all non-accepting states a "*"-labelled transition to a *Refuse* state, enforcing that all TCs aim to execute the precise counterexample sequence. This yields a larger TP, but in general also a smaller associated CTG, containing fewer TCs. Another variant of TP generation, suitable for value-passing systems, applies *data abstraction* by replacing the data values with wildcards in the labels of the counterexample, generalising it for a larger coverage.

The iterative approach generates a series of TPs increasing in length. This series of TPs might contain some redundancy, if TP_i is the prefix of TP_j (with $i < j$) generated later in the process. Fortunately, TP_i can be safely ignored in this case, because all transitions covered by its corresponding CTG_i are also covered by CTG_j corresponding to TP_j. Because checking for each new TP whether one of the previous TPs is a prefix has a cost quadratic in the number of TPs, it is preferable, after all TPs have been generated, to scan them only once in reverse order, and to discard those the corresponding CTG of which do not increase the coverage, as this has a cost linear in the number of TPs.

Optimisations Starting with a Non-trivial Cover. Because our approach generates TPs of increasing length, it might be advantageous to start with a non-empty cover. We consider two orthogonal possibilities for initialising the cover.

A first idea is to start with the construction of a set of TPs covering all labels of the model. To this end, one can iteratively choose a label not yet covered, construct a simple TP aiming to reach this label, and integrate the corresponding CTG into the cover as described before. Instead of considering all labels, one can also apply this idea only to all *output* (respectively, *input*) labels. By construction, this fully automatic technique generates no redundant TPs.

Another idea is to initialise the cover using a set of TPs provided by the user. Indeed, the designer of a model knows in general a set of properties the model should satisfy. More often than not, these properties have already been formalised and verified on the model—this is often the main reason for developing the model. In general, these properties can be transformed into a *test plan*, in our case, a set of TPs. Using these TPs for the first iterations has the advantage of pinpointing untested parts of the model and giving a feedback of the test plan quality in terms of coverage. In particular, if in iteration $i + 1$, the new cover is strongly bisimilar to the cover computed in iteration i, the i-th CTG (and by transitivity, the i-th TP) can be considered redundant. Although this redundancy information might depend on the order the test plan is processed, this feedback is still valuable to streamline the test plan.

When combining these ideas, inserting the cover for all labels *after* taking into account the user-provided TPs (if any) and *before* the iterative completion of the cover is the most reasonable scheme, because it increases the likelihood of starting the generic loop with an already large cover.

3.2   Extracting All Test Cases Contained in a Complete Test Graph

A CTG contains all information to drive a (conformant) SUT towards the *Accept* states of the corresponding TP. In general however, a CTG is not controllable; extracting a TC from a CTG consists in choosing a solution for all controllability conflicts. Such a TC contains thus all information to drive a (conformant) SUT towards an *Accept* state of the TP for a particular sequence of inputs provided to the SUT. Hence, a single TC is not sufficient, because other possible input sequences are discarded.

To generate a test suite covering a CTG, we propose to ensure that for each controllability conflict, all possibilities to solve this conflict are taken into account by at least one TC of the test suite.

Because solving controllability conflicts as in [22, Sect. 4.5] is tailored to the efficient extraction of a single TC, it also guarantees that the extracted TC is a subgraph of the CTG. This is achieved by enforcing the constraint that for each state of the CTG, a single solution to the controllability conflict is adopted. However, due to this additional constraint, a part of the CTG might not be taken into account when extracting TCs, potentially leaving some parts (transitions and even states) of the model outside the scope of the test suite.

For instance, for the running example, the approach of [22] allows extracting two TCs, namely those shown in Fig. 4(a) and (b). However, these two TCs ignore the state s_8 of the CTG (see Fig. 1(c)), because the controllability conflict in state s_5 (a choice between the inputs ?a and ?b) is allowed to be solved only in a single way, and solving it by always choosing the input ?a (leading to state s_8 in Fig. 1(c)) would make the *Pass* verdict unreachable, if respecting the constraint that a TC has to be a subgraph of the CTG.

To extract a test suite taking into account all the information contained in a CTG, it might thus be necessary to unroll loops, duplicating some states. This can be automated by an iterative approach keeping track of the solutions to the

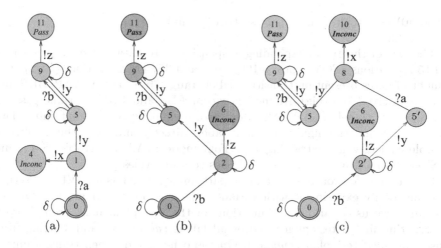

Fig. 4. Three test cases for the CTG in Fig. 1(c)

controllability conflicts of a CTG. While there is a not yet considered solution, i.e., a transition $s_1 \overset{a}{\rightarrow} s_2$ of the CTG not yet included in any TC, (1) apply the TC extraction algorithm [27] starting from the target state s_2 and (2) prefix the obtained TC by a sequence to s_1 followed by the transition $s_1 \overset{a}{\rightarrow} s_2$, duplicating the states of the CTG—states s_2' and s_5' in Fig. 4(c)—and completing the TC by appropriately handling outputs not present in the prefixed sequence, by applying the TC extraction algorithm—this adds the transition $s_2' \overset{!z}{\rightarrow} s_6$ to the *Inconc* verdict in Fig. 4(c). A more detailed discussion of this technique and possible heuristics is unfortunately out of the space limitations for the present paper.

4   Experimental Evaluation

We evaluated our approach using the following 16 models of communication protocols and distributed systems[5]: ABP (demo 1) and ABP-data (demo 2) are dataless and data-aware variants of the Alternating Bit Protocol with controllable failures of the communication links; AAP and AAP-big (demo 33) are configurations of an asynchronous agreement protocol [2,33] with 1 and 10 rounds; BRP-basic, BRP, and BRP-big (demo 16) are variants of the Bounded Retransmission Protocol [28] with controllable message-loss, larger messages, and more retries; CAR-LNT is a purely asynchronous variant of a simple autonomous car [26]; CCP (demo 28) is a multi-processor cache-coherency protocol; CFS (demo 25) is a Cluster File System [31]; CIM (demo 34) is a computer-integrated manufacturing architecture [29]; DES and DES-basic (demo 38) are variants of the Data Encryption Standard [36] with visible subkeys [27, Sect. 3.4] and less iterations; TLS (demo 6) is the Transport Layer Security 2.3 handshake protocol [5]; SMS

---

[5] The CADP demo examples are available on https://cadp.inria.fr/demos.

(demo 40) is a stock management system [7]; and TOY is the running example given in [22].

The size of the 16 corresponding suspension automata ranges from 7 states and 15 transitions (TOY) upto 71 196 states and 377 448 transitions (CFS). The number of gates present on transition labels ranges from three (AAP, BRP and CCP) to twelve (AAP-big). All models except ABP and TOY are value-passing, with up to 90 labels (CAR-LNT) and 30 input labels (CFS) containing data values. Note that the number of input labels directly influences the number of possible choices when extracting TCs. Four models (AAP, AAP-big, SMS, and TLS) contain a deadlock, and several ones contain cycles.

Because our approach is for a large part implemented as an SVL [11] script, we could easily experiment with variants, along two orthogonal axes. On the one hand, we used various initialisations of the test plan: none (*completion*), constructing first a test plan to cover all labels (*all-labels*), and starting from a user-provided test plan (*manual*). On the other hand, when transforming a counterexample into a TP, we discarded (or kept) the data values, applying data abstraction (or not).

For evaluating the efficiency of our coverage approach, we compared the different settings based on the following metrics: (i) number of TCs and CTGs generated; (ii) total number of transitions of the test suite; (iii) the total runtime and peak memory usage; (iv) number of redundant TPs; and (v) number of transitions leading to an *Inconc* state. The number of transitions of the test suite and the number of transitions leading to an *Inconc* influence the cost of actually using the test suite, because the transitions of each TC might be executed during testing, and each *Inconc* verdict requires another execution (hopefully conclusive) of the TC.

4.1 Experiments with Automatically Building a Test Plan

Table 1 summarises the results of our experiments with fully automatic settings, i.e., without user-provided test plans. Columns entitled "trans" report the total number of transitions of all TPs, CTGs, and TCs. Columns entitled "red." report the number of redundant TPs (and thus CTGs). Columns entitled "inconc." report the total number of transitions leading to *Inconc* states in all TCs. Missing lines correspond to experiments taking more than 62 h. In the case the extraction of a test suite did not finish in 62 h, the execution time corresponds to the computation of a test plan. These results were obtained using the petitprince cluster of the Grid'5000 testbed. None of the experiments required more than 65 MB of RAM.

Comparing the rows "completion—extraction" and "all-labels—completion—extraction", we observe that starting with the construction of a test plan covering all labels speeds up the approach and yields an overall smaller test plan and test suite. The speedup (of up to six times) is partially due to fewer redundant CTGs.

Comparing abstract and concrete TPs, we observe that for dataless examples (ABP and TOY), there is as expected no difference between abstract and

Table 1. Fully automatic test plan computation and test suite extraction

setting	Example	concrete TPs								abstract TPs							
		TP		CTG			TC		time	TP		CTG			TC		time
		trans	nb	trans	redun.	nb	trans	inconc.	(s)	trans	nb	trans	redun.	nb	trans	inconc.	(s)
completion — extraction	AAP	1,186	111	1,530	255	111	1,682	610	4,324	114	9	1,029	14	105	4,085	1,285	1,031
	AAP-big	66,148	1,848	127,431	7,860	1,848	1,306,679	88,711	108,947	4,756	119	104,660	435	1,819	876,200	373,044	18,246
	ABP	336	31	595	15	31	395	117	524	336	31	595	15	31	395	117	524
	ABP-data	144	22	142	6	22	162	10	363	40	6	110	2	26	282	18	281
	BRP-basic	136	16	168	12	16	179	33	323	58	6	156	4	21	357	76	230
	BRP	3,122	156	3,133	280	156	3,389	1,089	4,934	1,844	88	3,471	141	170	5,209	1,824	5,539
	BRP-big	203,186	5,122	201,791	12,643	5,122	108,700	3,777	252,529	39,976	936	206,034	2,201	5,289	172,710	134,386	73,326
	CAR-LNT	427,526	3,412	426,730	11,440	3,412	410,908	80,596	186,523	119,526	926	163,736	4,370	3,091	542,277	87,309	77,981
	CCP	22,258	1,249	19,250	1,145	1,249	21,660	4,223	30,802	622	29	11,543	88	1,590	50,856	13,291	11,876
	CIM	23,398	757	15,904	1,970	757	17,148	1,004	4,825	804	21	11,345	93	784	32,591	1,829	6,987
	DES	12,502	243	9,491	263	243	9,953	2,139	6,376	11,014	215	8,750	263	215	8,793	1,879	5,968
	DES-basic	2,364	142	2,292	89	142	2,534	422	3,182	1,884	108	2,071	89	108	2,045	352	2,705
	SMS	936	37	852	64	37	852	186	1,187	908	35	844	55	35	844	179	1,065
	TLS	1,004	61	5,471	518	61	5,471	4,908	6,115	332	19	3,679	40	65	6,123	5,411	1,034
	TOY	32	4	30	7	4	30	3	117	32	4	30	7	4	30	3	117
all-labels — completion — extraction	AAP	970	83	1,596	151	109	2,814	1,212	3,024	104	9	1,131	8	105	4,565	1,122	949
	AAP-big	34,792	848	81,973	2,302	1,427	2,578,585	345,603	37,175	4,196	100	104,693	169	1,861	545,830	452,238	15,557
	ABP	228	21	552	5	34	509	60	373	228	21	552	5	34	509	60	373
	ABP-data	2	1	36	0	6	77	0	56	2	1	36	0	6	77	0	56
	BRP-basic	2	1	52	1	7	190	0	62	54	6	155	3	21	354	72	217
	BRP	2	1	520	1	67	5,457	0	420	1,838	88	3,496	133	172	5,257	1,824	3,280
	BRP-big	2	1	19,722	1	1,673	135,429	0	11,412	39,970	936	206,203	2,177	5,340	322,324	134,506	72,635
	CAR-LNT	10	5	55,113	0	5,045	40,878,934	713,797	31,521	4	2	28,742	0	2,838	27,859,872	364,392	19,361
	CCP	2,828	155	5,734	78	1,144	134,524	522	9,747	562	25	11,423	66	1,688	57,403	13,024	12,181
	CFS	2,520	66	382,943	51		> 36,000 TCs		1,869	2	1	379,471	1		> 36,000 TCs		38
	CIM	734	19	3,235	55	485	93,555	18	4,249	116	4	4,236	3	562	48,897	94	4,128
	DES	2	1	516	0	155	30,674	0	1,033	2	1	516	1	146	32,468	0	981
	DES-basic	2	1	246	0	73	941	0	532	2	1	246	1	71	4,370	0	524
	SMS	2	1	132	0	25	2,599	75	177	2	1	132	0	25	2,599	75	170
	TLS	4	2	1,067	10	61	1,977	1,580	480	4	2	1,067	0	61	1,860	440	404
	TOY	28	4	32	3	4	33	2	76	28	4	32	3	4	33	2	76

concrete TPs. For most examples, generating abstract TPs improves the overall quality of the test plan. For all examples except the variants of BRP, we observe less TPs and a smaller total number of transitions in the test plan. An explanation is that a CTG generated for a concrete TP is in general controllable, yielding a test plan as large as the test suite. Using abstract TPs also builds the test plan faster, mostly because fewer redundant CTGs are generated. According to our experiments, the benefits of this data abstraction are particularly visible when not starting with an initial test plan covering all labels.

However, for BRP examples, abstract TPs are worse than concrete ones, because the same gate is used at the beginning of the protocol with some particular data values and at the end of the protocol with completely different values. As discarding data values annihilates this control-related distinction, the resulting abstraction is too coarse and degrades the performance. Splitting these labels of BRP using two different gates removes the ambiguity and leads to similar performance improvements as for the other examples.

As a summary for fully automatic settings, we found that, in general, starting with a test plan covering all labels and using abstract TPs (highlighted block in Table 1) is the best option. In particular, this setting produces a smaller test plan, because the abstract TPs generate fewer redundancies. However, a smaller test plan does not always yield a smaller test suite, because a more generic TP yields more TCs, in particular without an initial test plan covering all labels (see for instance CCP and CIM). These larger test suites might also contain more transitions to *Inconc* states.

4.2   Experiments with Completing a User-Provided Test Plan

We also applied our approach to complement an existing test plan for the selected models. The TPs making up the test plan either existed as such in the case study (ABP, CAR-LNT, DES, DES-basic, TLS, and TOY), or were created by transforming temporal logic properties verified in the case study. The latter step is not trivial for safety properties, which formalise bad things that (should) never happen: using such a property directly as a TP would yield a trivial CTG always resulting in an *Inconc* verdict. Thus, the property has to be transformed into a TP expressing the expected correct behaviour.

Our results when starting from a user-provided test plan are summarised in Table 2, which adds three columns to those of Table 1: the "user" column gives the number of user-provided TPs; the "ign." column gives the number of user-provided TPs that are flagged as redundant later-on; and the "gen." column gives the number of non-redundant automatically generated TPs. The "nb" column gives the number of CTGs corresponding to all non-redundant TPs (both user-provided and automatically generated). Since most user-provided TPs contain concrete, semantically meaningful data values, we did not apply data abstraction on the provided test plan. However, we applied data abstraction for all TPs automatically generated, because (for all examples but TLS) we observed that completion with abstract TPs resulted in a smaller test plan (measured in the number of TPs and their total number of transitions). We omitted CFS from Table 2, because the generation of a test plan timed out after 62 h.

Except for CCP, SMS, TLS, and TOY, the CTGs generated starting from the provided test plan cover all the labels of the model. The running example TOY comes with only one TP to illustrate test case extraction. CCP is an academic example, for which we crafted a single, rather abstract TP. For SMS and TLS, the provided test plan even covers almost all transitions. We can note many redundancies in some provided test plans (ABP, ABP-data, all variants of BRP, CIM, SMS, and TLS), which could indicate that the properties focus on a specific part of the model. Interestingly, for CFS, extending a user-provided test plan timed out, contrary to starting with a test plan covering all labels. It is worth noting that the user-provided test plan covers all labels, but only 348,327 of the 377,448 transitions in the suspension automaton for CFS—the iterative extension yields more than 8,716 TPs.

Some of the provided TPs target a particular behaviour, sometimes in a very precise manner. Therefore, the corresponding test suite contains already a large number of transitions to an *Inconc*, and this number only increases by completing the test plan. An exception is CAR-LNT, where the two provided TPs specify the two only ways to reach the final state.

Table 2. Test suite generation starting from a user-provided test plan

Example	user-provided — all-labels — completion — extraction										
	TP				CTG			TC			time
	user	ign.	gen.	sum	nb	sum	redun.	nb	sum	inconc.	(s)
AAP	2	1	8	103	9	1,131	4	107	4,583	1,122	777
AAP-big	2	0	99	4,198	101	104,975	166	1,887	546,095	452,238	15,716
ABP	3	2	0	3	1	524	2	53	2,696	0	356
ABP-data	6	4	0	15	2	92	4	40	546	0	193
BRP-basic	3	1	0	5	1	76	2	18	573	0	134
BRP	4	3	0	5	1	575	3	105	5,578	0	666
BRP-big	4	3	0	5	1	19,930	3	2,602	154,197	120	17,429
CAR-LNT	2	0	0	4	2	28,742	0	2,838	27,859,872	364,392	17,138
CCP	1	0	24	563	25	11,423	64	1,688	57,403	13,024	10,741
CIM	6	5	0	29	1	4,392	5	794	200,562	0	5,559
DES	1	0	0	6	1	1,845	0	485	354,766	0	3,209
DES-basic	1	0	0	6	1	854	0	259	32,254	0	1,663
SMS	2	1	1	4	2	263	1	50	5,174	200	356
TLS	3	3	18	302	18	3,915	23	63	6,096	5,359	824
TOY	1	1	4	28	4	32	3	4	33	2	76

5   Related Work

Although various coverage criteria have been proposed [30] and intensively studied [40] for software testing, only a few approaches target behavioural coverage of LTSs. In the following, we focus on the most closely related approaches.

The diagnostic generation features of model checkers have been used to generate test suites. For EFSMs (Extended Finite-State Machines), model checking a coverage criterion (specified as a temporal logic formula in a CTL fragment) produces as witnesses finite sequences. Two kinds of structural coverage criteria [21], based on control and data flow, are well-suited for deterministic, sequential EFSMs. Our TPs have a similar abstraction level as the CTL formulas in [21], but with the advantage of producing CTGs encompassing sets of test cases rather than individual witness sequences.

Conformance testing for concurrent systems has been studied from several perspectives, with various notions of behavioural coverage. In [10], a concurrent system is modelled as an IOPN (Input/Output Petri Net), whose semantics is its unfolding into an IOLES (Input/Output Labelled Event Structure), equipped with *co-ioco*, a generalisation of the *ioco* conformance relation to concurrent systems. TCs are generated from finite IOLESs for two coverage criteria: all paths of length n and unfolding all cycles k times, respectively. In our approach, we opted for a counterexample-driven behavioural coverage, that can be further refined towards partially covering paths of length n (by abstracting some of the concrete labels in the counterexample TPs).

Generalising a classical FSM test generation method to the IOLTS setting, *ioco*-based complete test suites can be generated from deterministic IOLTSs [9]. Completeness is achieved by generating test suites for mutant IOLTSs (aka fault domains) modelling potential faults in the SUT, so that an SUT with the faults will be detected. The considered coverage criteria ensure that each state and transition of the SUT corresponds to some state or transition of the model. Most of the classical FSM-based testing approaches [25] aim at detecting faults in the SUT, whereas conformance testing for concurrent systems aims at establishing that an SUT fulfils the requirements expressed by the formal model [17]. Therefore, we focused primarily on behavioural coverage instead of fault coverage. Experiments have shown that conformance testing has at least the same fault detection capabilities as manual testing of an SUT, and significantly better error detection capabilities in the system requirements [32].

TestComposer [23] (combining the TVEDA tool [18] with TGV [22]) and Autolink [35] were two industrial tools for the automatic test generation for SDL specifications. Similar to our approach, both first generate a test plan (a set of TPs), from which in a second step a set of test cases is extracted [34]. TestComposer relies for this second step on TGV. A notable difference to our approach is that both TestComposer and Autolink aim at structural coverage of the SDL specification, whereas we focus on (all transition) coverage of the underlying semantic model. Consequently, the techniques to construct TPs of TestComposer and Autolink differ from ours: besides manual exploration, both tools rely on specialised simulation and state space exploration algorithms, whereas we use a generic equivalence checker. Also, to the best of our knowledge, none of these tools aim at systematic generation of *all* test cases for a given TP.

Another approach for coverage-driven conformance testing was proposed in the AGEDIS project [19], by combining the test generation features of TGV and the usage of *test directives*. A test directive may specify constraints on data and also data-driven coverage criteria (e.g., cover all transitions whose source and target states satisfy specific data constraints) as in the GOTCHA tool [3]. Similarly, Uppaal-Cover uses observer automata used to express coverage criteria of test cases generated from FSM specifications [4,20]. Observer automata may specify structural criteria, dataflow criteria, and semantic coverage, but are deterministic, i.e., only a unique response and target state of the controller can be anticipated for a given state and input. Our TESTOR tool enables to describe data-handling TPs directly in the high-level language LNT [14] using multiway rendezvous. In this way, one can specify a data-driven coverage criterion by using a data-handling TP, generating the corresponding CTG, and applying the second step of our approach to extract all TCs contained in the CTG.

6   Conclusion

We proposed an automatic approach to generate a conformance test suite covering all transitions of an IOLTS M, which models the behaviour of a concurrent system. The approach proceeds in two steps. In a first step, we generate a test plan, i.e., a set of test purposes whose corresponding CTGs (complete test graphs) cover all transitions of M. This step can start either from scratch, or from a set of test purposes provided by the user. In the latter case, the approach completes the test plan to cover all transitions of M, and can also spot redundancies in the user-provided test purposes. In a second step, we produce a test suite from the test plan by extracting, from each CTG, a set of test cases covering all transitions of the CTG. We implemented this approach on top of the CADP toolbox and the TESTOR tool, and experimented it on 16 case studies. We studied possible variants and heuristics to fine-tune both the overall performance of the extraction and the quality of the resulting test plan or test suite.

Concerning future improvements, it is possible to speed up the approach by extracting test cases from different CTGs in parallel. To obtain a smaller test plan, one could also study more sophisticated heuristics when checking whether a CTG improves the overall cover, for instance by considering different, more informed orders of handling the CTGs. Finally, the built-in data abstraction (discarding the data values on the labels of counterexample sequences) could be generalised, for instance by allowing the user to specify a set of labels that should always be kept concrete.

Acknowledgments. This work was partly supported by project ArchitectECA2030 that has been accepted for funding within the Electronic Components and Systems for European Leadership Joint Undertaking in collaboration with the European Union's H2020 Framework Programme (H2020/2014-2020) and National Authorities, under grant agreement No. 877539. Experiments presented in this paper were carried out using the Grid'5000 testbed, supported by a scientific interest group hosted by Inria and including CNRS, RENATER and several Universities, as well as other organizations (see https://www.grid5000.fr). We are also grateful to Frédéric Lang for inspiring discussions.

References

1. Belinfante, A.: JTorX: a tool for on-line model-driven test derivation and execution. In: Esparza, J., Majumdar, R. (eds.) TACAS 2010. LNCS, vol. 6015, pp. 266–270. Springer, Heidelberg (2010). https://doi.org/10.1007/978-3-642-12002-2_21
2. Ben-Or, M.: Another advantage of free choice: completely asynchronous agreement protocols. In: Proceedings of PODC (1983)
3. Benjamin, M., Geist, D., Hartman, A., Mas, G., Smeets, R., Wolfsthal, Y.: A study in coverage-driven test generation. In: Proceedings of the DAC 1999, pp. 970–975 (1999)
4. Blom, J., Hessel, A., Jonsson, B., Pettersson, P.: Specifying and generating test cases using observer automata. In: Grabowski, J., Nielsen, B. (eds.) FATES 2004. LNCS, vol. 3395, pp. 125–139. Springer, Heidelberg (2005). https://doi.org/10.1007/978-3-540-31848-4_9
5. Bozic, J., Marsso, L., Mateescu, R., Wotawa., F.: A formal TLS handshake model in LNT. In: Proceedings of MARS 2018. EPTCS (2018)

6. Brookes, S.D., Hoare, C.A.R., Roscoe, A.W.: A theory of communicating sequential processes. J. ACM **31**(3), 560–599 (1984)
7. Chirichiello, A., Salaün, G.: Encoding abstract descriptions into executable web services: towards a formal development. In: Proceedings of the WI 2005, pp. 457–463 (2005)
8. Clarke, E., Grumberg, O., Jha, S., Lu, Y., Veith, H.: Counterexample-guided abstraction refinement. In: Emerson, E.A., Sistla, A.P. (eds.) CAV 2000. LNCS, vol. 1855, pp. 154–169. Springer, Heidelberg (2000). https://doi.org/10.1007/10722167_15
9. da Silva Simão, A., Petrenko, A.: Generating complete and finite test suite for ioco: is it possible? In: Proceedings of the MBT 2014, pp. 56–70 (2014)
10. de León, H.P., Haar, S., Longuet, D.: Model-based testing for concurrent systems: unfolding-based test selection. STTT **18**(3), 305–318 (2016)
11. Garavel, H., Lang, F.: SVL: a scripting language for compositional verification. In: Proceedings of the FORTE 2001, pp. 377–392 (2001)
12. Garavel, H., Lang, F., Mateescu, R.: Compositional verification of asynchronous concurrent systems using CADP. Acta Informatica **52**(4), 337–392 (2015)
13. Garavel, H., Lang, F., Mateescu, R., Serwe, W.: CADP 2011: a toolbox for the construction and analysis of distributed processes. STTT **15**(2), 89–107 (2013)
14. Garavel, H., Lang, F., Serwe, W.: From LOTOS to LNT. In: Katoen, J.-P., Langerak, R., Rensink, A. (eds.) ModelEd, TestEd, TrustEd. LNCS, vol. 10500, pp. 3–26. Springer, Cham (2017). https://doi.org/10.1007/978-3-319-68270-9_1
15. Graf, S., Steffen, B.: Compositional minimization of finite state systems. In: Clarke, E.M., Kurshan, R.P. (eds.) CAV 1990. LNCS, vol. 531, pp. 186–196. Springer, Heidelberg (1991). https://doi.org/10.1007/BFb0023732
16. Graf, S., Steffen, B., Lüttgen, G.: Compositional minimization of finite state systems using interface specifications. Formal Aspects Comput. **8**(5), 607–616 (1996)
17. Groz, R., Charles, O., Renévot, J.: Relating conformance test coverage to formal specifications. Formal Description Techniques IX. IAICT, pp. 195–210. Springer, Boston, MA (1996). https://doi.org/10.1007/978-0-387-35079-0_12
18. Groz, R., Risser, N.: Eight years of experience in test generation from FDTs using TVEDA. In: Mizuno, T., Shiratori, N., Higashino, T., Togashi, A. (eds.) Formal Description Techniques and Protocol Specification, Testing and Verification. ITI-FIP, pp. 465–480. Springer, Boston, MA (1997). https://doi.org/10.1007/978-0-387-35271-8_29
19. Hartman, A., Nagin, K.: The AGEDIS tools for model based testing. In: Proceedings of the ISSTA 2004, pp. 129–132 (2004)
20. Hessel, A., Pettersson, P.: Model-based testing of a WAP gateway: an industrial case-study. In: Brim, L., Haverkort, B., Leucker, M., van de Pol, J. (eds.) FMICS 2006. LNCS, vol. 4346, pp. 116–131. Springer, Heidelberg (2007). https://doi.org/10.1007/978-3-540-70952-7_8
21. Hong, H.S., Lee, I., Sokolsky, O., Ural, H.: A temporal logic based theory of test coverage and generation. In: Katoen, J.-P., Stevens, P. (eds.) TACAS 2002. LNCS, vol. 2280, pp. 327–341. Springer, Heidelberg (2002). https://doi.org/10.1007/3-540-46002-0_23
22. Jard, C., Jéron, T.: TGV: theory, principles and algorithms – a tool for the automatic synthesis of conformance test cases for non-deterministic reactive systems. STTT **7**(4), 297–315 (2005)
23. Kerbrat, A., Jéron, T., Groz, R.: Automated test generation from SDL specifications. In: Proceedings of the SDL 1999, pp. 135–152 (1999)

24. Krimm, J.-P., Mounier, L.: Compositional state space generation from Lotos programs. In: Brinksma, E. (ed.) TACAS 1997. LNCS, vol. 1217, pp. 239–258. Springer, Heidelberg (1997). https://doi.org/10.1007/BFb0035392
25. Lee, D., Yannakakis, M.: Optimization problems from feature testing of communication protocols. In: Proceedings of the ICNP, pp. 66–75 (1996)
26. Marsso, L., Mateescu, R., Parissis, I., Serwe, W.: Asynchronous testing of synchronous components in GALS systems. In: Ahrendt, W., Tapia Tarifa, S.L. (eds.) IFM 2019. LNCS, vol. 11918, pp. 360–378. Springer, Cham (2019). https://doi.org/10.1007/978-3-030-34968-4_20
27. Marsso, L., Mateescu, R., Serwe, W.: TESTOR: a modular tool for on-the-fly conformance test case generation. In: Beyer, D., Huisman, M. (eds.) TACAS 2018. LNCS, vol. 10806, pp. 211–228. Springer, Cham (2018). https://doi.org/10.1007/978-3-319-89963-3_13
28. Mateescu, R.: Formal description and analysis of a bounded retransmission protocol. In: Proceedings of the COST 247, pp. 98–113, University of Maribor (1996)
29. Mauw, S.: Process algebra as a tool for the specification and verification of CIM-architectures. Camb. Tracts Theor. Comput. Sci. **17**, 53–80 (1990)
30. Myers, G.J.: The Art of Software Testing, 2nd edn. Wiley, Hoboken (2004)
31. Pecheur, C.: Advanced modelling and verification techniques applied to a cluster file system. In: Proceedings of the ASE 1999 (1999)
32. Pretschner, A.: One Evaluation of Model-based Testing and its Automation. In: Proceedings of the ICSE 2005, pp. 392–401 (2005)
33. Rabin, M.O.: Randomized byzantine generals. In: Proceedings of the IEEE Symposium on Foundations of Computer Science, pp. 403–409 (1983)
34. Schmitt, M., Ebner, M., Grabowski, J.: Test generation with autolink and testcomposer. In: Proceedings of the SAM 2000, SDL Forum 2000 (2000)
35. Schmitt, M., Grabowski, J., Hogrefe, D., Koch, B.: Autolink–a tool for the automatic and semi-automatic test generation. Formale Beschreibungstechniken für verteilte Systeme, GMD-Studien **315**, 333–341 (1997)
36. Serwe, W.: Formal specification and verification of fully asynchronous implementations of the data encryption standard. In: Proceedings of the MARS, EPTCS 196 (2015)
37. Taylor, R.N., Levine, D.L., Kelly, C.D.: Structural testing of concurrent programs. IEEE TSE **18**(3), 206–215 (1992)
38. Tretmans, J.: Conformance testing with labelled transition systems: implementation relations and test generation. Comput. Netw. ISDN Syst. **29**(1), 49–79 (1996)
39. Utting, M., Pretschner, A., Legeard, B.: A taxonomy of model-based testing approaches. Softw. Test. Verif. Reliab. **22**(5), 297–312 (2012)
40. Yang, Q., Li, J.J., Weiss, D.M.: A survey of coverage-based testing tools. Comput. J. **52**(5), 589–597 (2009)
41. Zander, J., Schieferdecker, I., Mosterman, P.J., (eds.): Model-based testing for embedded systems. In: Computational Analysis, Synthesis, and Design Dynamic Systems (2011)
42. Zhu, H., Hall, P.A.V., May, J.H.R.: Software unit test coverage and adequacy. ACM Comput. Surv. **29**(4), 366–427 (1997)

An Executable Mechanised Formalisation
of an Adaptive State Counting Algorithm

Robert Sachtleben[✉]

Department of Mathematics and Computer Science,
University of Bremen, Bremen, Germany
`rob_sac@uni-bremen.de`

Abstract. This paper demonstrates the applicability of state-of-the-art proof assistant tools to establish completeness properties of a test strategy and the correctness of its associated test generation algorithms, as well as to generate trustworthy executable code for these algorithms. To this end, a variation of an established test strategy is considered, which generates adaptive test cases based on a reference model represented as a possibly nondeterministic finite state machine (FSM). These test cases are sufficient to check whether the reduction conformance relation holds between the reference model and an implementation whose behaviour can also be represented by an FSM. Both the mechanical verification of this test strategy and the generation of a provably correct implementation are performed using the well-known Isabelle/HOL proof assistant.

Keywords: Complete test methods · Finite state machines · Isabelle/HOL · Mechanised proofs · Proof assistants · Reduction

1 Introduction

Objectives. In this paper, we present a mechanised proof for a variation of the complete test strategy originally published by Petrenko and Yevtushenko in [21] and provide a formalisation of selected algorithms described by the same authors in [19] to calculate concrete test suites. We generate executable code from this formalisation to provide a trustworthy implementation of the test strategy.

The formalised strategy facilitates verifying the reduction conformance relation between two finite state machines (FSMs), of which the first serves as a reference model representing a specified behaviour, whereas the second represents the true behaviour of the system under test (SUT). Both FSMs may be nondeterministic but are assumed to be completely specified and observable. Additionally assuming an upper bound on the number of states contained in the (unknown) FSM representing the behaviour of SUT, the strategy generates finite test suites guaranteeing complete fault coverage using a state counting method. These test suites are adaptive and thus the number of tests applied to the SUT

© IFIP International Federation for Information Processing 2020
Published by Springer Nature Switzerland AG 2020
V. Casola et al. (Eds.): ICTSS 2020, LNCS 12543, pp. 236–254, 2020.
https://doi.org/10.1007/978-3-030-64881-7_15

during testing depends on its observed behaviour. In many situations, the generated test suites are therefore significantly smaller than those generated using the well-known "brute force" strategy based on product FSMs[1], which requires $O(|\Sigma_I|^{mn})$ test cases[2] for the same effect.

Motivation. We advocate an approach to systematic testing that includes formal proofs of fault coverage capabilities of test strategies, so that no doubt with respect to their test strength remains. This process entails making explicit any underlying hypotheses, such as the specification of fault domains. Since complete test strategies are of considerable importance for the verification of safety-critical systems, the correctness of fault coverage claims for a given strategy is crucial from the perspective of system certification. Thus, we further advocate the use of proof assistants to check the proofs, as we believe that due to the large number of different test strategies and the often intricate nature of their corresponding proofs it cannot be expected that each proof is manually checked by many members of the testing community. Our previous work [22] supports this view, as it uncovered an ambiguity in the textual description of a test strategy, which could lead to incomplete implementations. In [22] we also voiced our hope that mechanised proofs could be used as artefacts presented to certification authorities as a means of showing that an applied test strategy provides the fault detection capabilities claimed for it. We now additionally believe that the use of provably correct code generated from formalisations could reduce the effort required to provide convincing arguments for tool qualification of tools employing such code.

Provably correct implementations of the test strategy formalised in this paper can be employed as trustworthy components in a large variety of testing applications. These include the generation of test suites for testing whether an SUT behaves only in ways allowed in a specification that can be represented as a (possibly nondeterministic) completely specified FSM, where nondeterminism indicates that the SUT may omit some reactions. Such specifications include communication protocols that contain optional behaviour. Additionally, many interesting conformance relations can be reduced to testing for this reduction conformance relation between completely specified FSMs, including quasi-equivalence and quasi-reduction for incomplete specification FSMs (see [10]) and reduction for reactive I/O transition systems (see [12]). This in turn allows for trustworthy implementations to be employed in the process of testing, for example, embedded systems against specifications given in SysML (see [11]).

Main Contributions. To our best knowledge, this is the first time that a mechanised proof for the complete reduction test strategy elaborated in [21] is presented. Moreover, trustworthy executable code is generated from a mechanically verified formalisation of an algorithm that realises the strategy, incorporating

---

[1] This strategy has been described, for example, in the lecture notes [17, Sect. 4.5].

[2] $|\Sigma_I|$ is the size of the input alphabet, n the number of states in the reference model, and m an upper bound for the number of states in the SUT model.

selected algorithms from [19]. This provably correct implementation is used as the trustworthy core of a set of testing tools.

Related Work. The first complete state counting approach to reduction testing has been published in [20], specialising on the case of deterministic implementations being tested against nondeterministic reference models for language inclusion. Later, adaptive state counting has been proposed as an optimisation in [19]. The restriction to deterministic implementations has then been dropped in later works considering a more general formulation of the problem, admitting both nondeterministic reference models and implementations. This has been studied in [9,21], the latter being the article the present paper is based on.

To our best knowledge, applying proof assistants to testing has first been advocated in [4]. Using Isabelle/HOL at its core, an integrated testing framework has been developed by the same authors and described in [5]. This framework allows for elaboration of test strategies (called *test theorems* in [5]), fault coverage proof, test case and test data generation in the same tool. Several cases of mechanised proofs establishing the completeness of testing theories are elaborated by the authors, not including the strategy analysed in the present paper.

Our approach to model-based testing (MBT) contrasts to that advocated in [5] in that we favour the use of specialised tools for strategy elaboration (Isabelle/HOL), modelling (FSM and SysML modelling tools), and test case and test data generation (RT-Tester [16] with SMT solver [18]). We base this preference on the possibility of performing SMT solving internally, without explicit interactions with the users, which requires less specialised expertise than the interactive handling of proof assistants. In this we agree with [1].

In [22] we presented a mechanised proof for the strategy described in [9], but in contrast to the present paper, this effort did not yet focus on providing a formalisation from which provably correct executable code could be generated.

Finally, tool qualification for model-based testing tools is discussed for example in [3], where the replaying of test executions against the specification model is introduced as a measure to uncover potential faults in the untrusted test case generation. Our approach obviates the need for many such measures by employing trustworthy code to generate test suites.

Reference to Online Resources. The Isabelle/HOL session containing all the formalisations and proofs elaborated in this paper and a set of command line tools which employ the executable code generated from this session to generate test suites and apply them to SUTs, together with corresponding documentation and a short evaluation of the tools applied to a set of randomly generated FSMs, are publicly available on https://bitbucket.org/RobertSachtleben/an-executable-formalisation-of-an-adaptive-state-counting.

Overview. Section 2 provides a short overview of the test strategy presented in [21]. Next, Sect. 3 describes our formalisation of this strategy in Isabelle and outlines the strategy of our mechanical completeness proof. Thereafter, Sect. 4 describes the generation of a trustworthy implementation, its integration into a set of test tools, and experiments performed using this implementation. Finally, we provide conclusions in Sect. 5.

2 Overview of the Formalised Test Strategy

The test strategy described in [21] and formalised mechanically in this paper is employed to check whether an SUT, whose behaviour is assumed to correspond to some unknown finite state machine M', conforms to a specification, given as a finite state machine M, with respect to the reduction conformance relation. We first introduce the constructions used within this strategy as detailed in [21].

Finite State Machines. A *finite state machine* $M = (Q, q_0, \Sigma_I, \Sigma_O, h)$ is 5-tuple consisting of a finite set Q of states, an *initial state* $q_0 \in Q$, finite sets Σ_I and Σ_O constituting the input and output alphabet, respectively, and a transition relation $h \subseteq Q \times \Sigma_I \times \Sigma_O \times Q$ where $(q_1, x, y, q_2) \in h$ if and only if there exists in M a transition from q_1 to q_2 for input x that produces output y. We define the size of M, denoted $|M|$, by the number $|Q|$ of states it contains. Finally, the *language* $\mathcal{L}(M, q)$ denotes the set of all sequences $\bar{x}/\bar{y} \in (\Sigma_I \times \Sigma_O)^*$ of input-output (IO) pairs such that M can react to $\bar{x}$ applied to q with outputs $\bar{y}$. The language of M itself, denoted $\mathcal{L}(M)$, is the language of its initial state. We write $\bar{x}\bar{x}'/\bar{y}\bar{y}'$ for the concatenation of IO-sequences $\bar{x}/\bar{y}$ and $\bar{x}'/\bar{y}'$.

Primarily based on its transition relation, further properties of an FSM M can be distinguished: M is *deterministic* if for any state q in M and input x at most one transition exists. M is *observable* if for each contained state q, input x and output y there is at most one state q' that is reached from q through a transition with input/output x/y, i.e. there is at most one state q' in Q such that $(q, x, y, q') \in h$. That is, the target state reached from some state with some input can be uniquely determined using the observed output. This property also extends to IO-sequences, as the state reached by an IO-sequence $\bar{x}/\bar{y} \in \mathcal{L}(M, q)$ applied to state q is again uniquely determined. Next, M is *completely specified* if a transition exists from each contained state q for each contained input x. That is, any input $x \in \Sigma_I$ applied to a state $q \in Q$ must produce some output. Furthermore, M is *acyclic* if $\mathcal{L}(M)$ is finite, and a state q is a *deadlock state* if no transition from q exists. Also, M is *single-input* if for each state q all transitions from q share the same input component. Finally, an FSM $M' = (Q', q_0, \Sigma'_I, \Sigma'_O, h')$ is a *submachine* of M if $Q' \subseteq Q$ and $h' \subseteq h$ hold.

In the remainder of this paper we assume every FSM to be both observable and completely specified, which is no restriction, as there exist techniques to complete any FSM (see [9]) and to transform it into a language-equivalent observable minimised machine [14]. We do not, however, require any FSM to be deterministic. We furthermore assume that FSM M', representing the behaviour of the SUT, uses the same inputs as the specification M and satisfies $|M'| \leq m$.

The *product machine* (intersection) of FSMs $M_1 = (S, s_0, \Sigma_I, \Sigma_O, h_1)$ and $M_2 = (T, t_0, \Sigma_I, \Sigma_O, h_2)$ is an FSM $PM = (S \times T, (s_0, t_0), \Sigma_I, \Sigma_O, h)$, which generates the language intersection $\mathcal{L}(PM) = \mathcal{L}(M_1) \cap \mathcal{L}(M_2)$ by the following construction of h: $((s, t), x, y, (s', t')) \in h \Longleftrightarrow (s, x, y, s') \in h_1 \wedge (t, x, y, t') \in h_2$.

Finally, a state q_1 of an FSM M_1 is a *reduction* of some state q_2 of an FSM M_2 if and only if $\mathcal{L}(M_1, q_1) \subseteq \mathcal{L}(M_2, q_2)$ holds, and M_1 is a reduction of M_2 if and only if the initial state of M_1 is a reduction of the initial state of M_2.

State Preambles and Definitely Reachable States. A *state preamble P* of $M = (Q, q_0, \Sigma_I, \Sigma_O, h)$ for some $q \in Q$ is an acyclic single-input submachine of M with q being its single deadlock state such that for every state $q' \neq q$ in P all transitions of M from q' with the single input defined for q' in P are also contained in P. That is, a state preamble P of M for q can be seen as a strategy for reaching q in every completely specified submachine of M and thus, for any sequence $\bar{x}/\bar{y} \in \mathcal{L}(P) \cap \mathcal{L}(M')$ that reaches q in P, the state reached by $\bar{x}/\bar{y}$ in the SUT representation M' must be a reduction of q for M' to be a reduction of M. A state q of M is called *definitely reachable* if and only some state preamble of M for q exists. We say that a state of M' is *reached* by a preamble P if it is reached by some $\bar{x}/\bar{y}$ that reaches q in P. We call such $\bar{x}/\bar{y}$ *preamble sequences*.

Note here that the initial state q_0 of M is definitely reachable by the preamble $P_0 = (\{q_0\}, q_0, \Sigma_I, \Sigma_O, \emptyset)$. This implies that if a set PS of pairs (q, P) of states of M and corresponding preambles contains (q_0, P_0) and also $\mathcal{L}(M') \not\subseteq \mathcal{L}(M)$ holds, then a minimal length IO-sequence $\bar{x}_f/\bar{y}_f$ and additionally a sequence $\bar{x}_p/\bar{y}_p$ that reaches a deadlock state in a preamble in PS must exist such that $\bar{x}_p\bar{x}_f/\bar{y}_p\bar{y}_f \in \mathcal{L}(M') \backslash \mathcal{L}(M)$ holds, since $\mathcal{L}(P_0)$ contains only the empty sequence ϵ. In the following, we will refer to sequences such as $\bar{x}_f/\bar{y}_f$ in short as *minimal sequences to a failure extending* $\bar{x}_p/\bar{y}_p$ if the set PS is obvious from the context.

In the test strategy, for each definitely reachable state q of M a preamble P for q is used to identify states in the SUT representation that must conform to q, which include all states in M' reached by sequences that reach q in P.

State Separators. A *state separator S* of M for states q_1 and q_2 is an acyclic single-input FSM with two reachable deadlock states d_1 and d_2 such that (1) for any $\bar{x}/\bar{y} \in \mathcal{L}(S)$ it holds that if $\bar{x}/\bar{y}$ reaches d_1 then $\bar{x}/\bar{y} \in \mathcal{L}(M, q_1) \backslash \mathcal{L}(M, q_2)$ holds whereas if $\bar{x}/\bar{y}$ reaches d_2 then $\bar{x}/\bar{y} \in \mathcal{L}(M, q_2) \backslash \mathcal{L}(M, q_1)$ holds, and (2) for any sequence $\bar{x}/\bar{y} \in \mathcal{L}(S)$ reaching some non-deadlock state q in S with a single defined input x, S contains a transition from q with output y for each output y produced by any of the states reached in M by via $\bar{x}/\bar{y}$ from q_1 or q_2 to x. That is, S provides a strategy of reliably distinguishing q_1 and q_2 in all complete submachines of M. States q_1 and q_2 of M a called *r-distinguishable* if and only if a state separator of M for them exists. In the following, test separators S for states q_1 and q_2 are used to check whether certain states in M' behave like only one of q_1 or q_2, or neither of them.

Adaptively Testing of the Reduction Conformance Relation. The SUT conforms to the specification FSM M with respect to the reduction conformance relation if and only if the FSM M', which is assumed to represent the behaviour of the SUT, is a reduction of M. That is, the SUT conforms to M if and only if every behaviour of it is also admissible in M. As the languages of completely specified FSMs with nonempty input alphabets are infinite, it is not possible to check this property by simply enumerating $\mathcal{L}(M)$ and $\mathcal{L}(M')$ and therefore test suites must be applicable in a finite amount of time. In the case of nondeterministic FSMs this furthermore requires some fairness assumption that all reactions to some input can be observed within a finite number of applications of this input. In this paper, we employ the *complete testing assumption* (see [9]) and thus assume that there exists some upper bound k on the number of applications required to observe all reactions to a given sequence of inputs.

Furthermore, an SUT might exhibit only a proper subset of the behaviours of M, which enables the use of adaptivity in testing by controlling the application of inputs based on the observed behaviour of the SUT. An *adaptive test case* (ATC) A for FSM M is an acyclic single-input FSM that is output-complete for M (for every non-deadlock state there exists a transition for every output of M) and which may contain a designated deadlock state *fail*. FSM M' in state q' *passes* A if and only if there exists no sequence in $\mathcal{L}(A) \cap \mathcal{L}(M', q')$ that reaches *fail* in A. Applying A to M' thus reduces to calculating $\mathcal{L}(A) \cap \mathcal{L}(M', q')$ and checking the states reached in A, which is feasible as $\mathcal{L}(A)$ is finite.

For example, a state separator S of M for q_1 and q_1 can be transformed into an ATC I_{q_1} that checks whether the state it is applied to behaves like q_1 and not like q_2 by replacing d_2 with *fail* and adding to every non-deadlock state q a transition to *fail* for every output of M that is not produced by q in S.

Finally, adaptive test cases can be *concatenated* at their deadlock states. Given ATCs A_1 and A_2 and a deadlock state $d \neq fail$ of A_1, $A_1@_dA_2$ denotes the ATC created by replacing d in A_1 with the initial state of A_2 and inserting all transitions and other states of A_2 into A_1. For simplicity we assume here that the state sets of ATCs are pairwise disjoint, ensuring that the @ operator is associative and well-behaved when concatenating multiple ATCs.

2.1 Overview of the Formalised Adaptive State Counting Algorithm

The adaptive state counting algorithm re-verified in this paper creates a test suite for M and an assumed upper bound m on the number of states in M' as a set of adaptive test cases. This is performed by first calculating a preamble for each definitely reachable state of M and a state separator for every pair of r-distinguishable states in M, followed by a process of extending sequences from the definitely reachable states until they are too long to be proper prefixes of any minimal sequence to a failure, resulting in so-called *traversal sets*. The termination criterion for this extension is based on the number of r-distinguishable states of M encountered during the application of a sequence, which can constitute a lower bound on the number of states in any non-conforming FSM M'. Finally, a test suite is constructed by concatenating preambles, extended sequences and state separators in accordance with this termination criterion.

Traversal Sets. Let RD denote the set of all maximal sets of pairwise r-distinguishable states of Q. Given a set $R \in RD$ let R_{dr} denote the subset of R containing only definitely reachable states. Note that every state of M is contained in some such R and that R_{dr} may be empty.

For every definitely reachable state q of M the set $N^m(q)$ of *m-traversal sequences* is then constructed starting from the empty sequence by extending input sequences until they satisfy the following rule: An input sequence $\bar{x}$ is not extended further if for all $\bar{x}/\bar{y} \in \mathcal{L}(M, q)$ there exists some $R \in RD$ such that $\bar{x}/\bar{y}$ applied to q visits states from R at least $(m - |R_{dr}| + 1)$ times, where a state is *visited* if it is reached by any nonempty prefix of $\bar{x}/\bar{y}$ applied to q.

From $N^m(q)$ the *traversal set* $T^m(q)$ is constructed as the set containing for every $\bar{x} \in N^m(q)$ all $\bar{x}/\bar{y} \in \mathcal{L}(M, q)$ such there exists some $R \in RD$ whose states are visited exactly $(m - |R_{dr}| + 1)$ times along $\bar{x}/\bar{y}$ applied to q, while this does not hold for any proper prefix of $\bar{x}/\bar{y}$. We call R a *terminating* set of $\bar{x}/\bar{y}$.

Finally, from each $\bar{x} \in N^m(q)$ an acyclic observable FSM $M_{q,\bar{x}}$ with language $\mathcal{L}(M_{q,\bar{x}}) = \{\bar{x}'/\bar{y}' \in T^m(q) \mid \bar{x}'$ is a prefix of $\bar{x}\}$ is created such that any two sequences in $M_{q,\bar{x}}$ reach the same state in $M_{q,\bar{x}}$ only if they reach the same state if applied to q in M. This FSM can then be further simplified as described in [21]. The adaptive test case $TC(q, \bar{x})$ denotes the output completion of $M_{q,\bar{x}}$.

Test Suite Generation. Given a preamble P_q for every definitely reachable state q of M and for each state q in M a set ID_q containing for each q' in M that is r-distinguishable from q an adaptive test case I_q of a state separator S of M for q and q', a test suite TS is created from an empty set as follows: For each definitely reachable state q of M, each $\bar{x} \in N^m(q)$, each $TC(q, \bar{x})$ and each set $\{\bar{x}_1/\bar{y}_1, \ldots, \bar{x}_k/\bar{y}_k\}$ of all sequences of length $|\bar{x}|$ in $\mathcal{L}(TC(q, \bar{x}))$ that do not reach *fail*, a set of adaptive test cases T of the following form is added to TS, where q_i denotes the state reached by applying $\bar{x}_i/\bar{y}_i$ to q, t_i denotes the deadlock state reached by applying $\bar{x}_i/\bar{y}_i$ to the initial state of $TC(q, \bar{x})$, $TC(P_q)$ is the adaptive test case created from the output completion of P_q, and each $I_{q_i} \in ID_{q_i}$ is only concatenated onto one ATC for each $\bar{x}_i/\bar{y}_i$:

$$T := TC(P_q)@_q TC(q, \bar{x})@_{t_1} I_{q_1}@_{t_2} I_{q_2} \ldots @_{t_k} I_{q_k}$$

Applying test suite TS to an SUT thus essentially consists of applying the traversal sets after the preambles and applying after each such sequence a set of ATCs created from state separators that r-distinguish the state reached by the sequence from all states it is r-distinguishable from.

For the formalisation and implementation described in the following sections we have chosen a different representation of the test suite and its test cases, but the underlying strategy remains unchanged. We furthermore integrate the optimisation already described by Petrenko and Yevtushenko in [19] that it is not always necessary to distinguish the target of some $\bar{x}/\bar{y} \in T^m(q)$ from all states it is r-distinguishable from, as it is sufficient to r-distinguish the target from other states in some $R \in RD$ only if R is used in the termination criterion of some sequence of which $\bar{x}/\bar{y}$ is a prefix (see the use of $Id(s', R_\beta)$ in [19, Algorithm 2]).

3   The Mechanised Proof

Isabelle/HOL. Isabelle is a generic proof assistant featuring an extensive implementation of higher-order logic (Isabelle/HOL). We chosen this logic as the base for our formalisation, as it is highly expressive and already contains many useful definitions and theorems. For an introduction to Isabelle see Nipkow et al. [15]. The Isabelle core libraries are further extended by the *Archive of Formal Proofs* (see www.isa-afp.org). The Isar (*Intelligible Semi-Automated Reasoning*) proof language offered in Isabelle distributions allows for proofs to be written in a human-readable style [23]. Our previous paper [22] contains an exemplary Isar proof on FSM properties. Isabelle is also able to automatically generate executable code from many formalisations written in it, which we use in Sect. 4 to generate a trustworthy implementation of the formalised test strategy. The correctness of this translation process is proven in [8], which also describes how the code generator can serve to facilitate program and data refinement.

Data Structures. In our Isabelle/HOL formalisation we define FSMs as records (type `fsm-impl`) which we then restrict to well-formed FSMs (type `fsm`), where an FSM $M = (Q, q_0, \Sigma_I, \Sigma_O, h)$ is well-formed if its component sets are finite and additionally $q_0 \in Q$ and $h \subseteq Q \times \Sigma_I \times \Sigma_O \times Q$ hold.

record (*'state, 'input, 'output*) *fsm-impl* =
  initial :: *'state*
  states :: *'state set*
  inputs :: *'input set*
  outputs :: *'output set*
  transitions :: (*'state* × *'input* × *'output* × *'state*) *set*

typedef (*'state, 'input, 'output*) *fsm* =
  { *M* :: (*'state, 'input, 'output*) *fsm-impl* . *well-formed-fsm M*}

This follows the classical definition of FSMs more closely than the definition in our previous work [22] and also avoids cluttering proofs with well-formedness assumptions on the employed FSMs. Consider, for example, the following very natural definition of completely specified FSMs in our Isabelle formalisation[3]:

completely-specified M = ($\forall$ $q \in$ *states M*.$\forall$ $x \in$ *inputs M*.$\exists$ q' y.$(q,x,y,q') \in$ *transitions M*)

We represent state preambles and separators simply as FSMs, but we represent test suites as values of a new datatype such that a test suite $TS = (PS, tps, rds, seps)$ consists of (1) a set PS of pairs (q, P_q) for each definitely reachable state q, (2) a map tps from each definitely reachable state to the traversal sequences starting from it, (3) a map rds assigning to each pair $(q, \bar{x}/\bar{y})$, consisting of a definitely reachable state and a traversal sequence starting from it, all states that the target of $\bar{x}/\bar{y}$ needs to be r-distinguished from, and (4) a map

---

[3] Function application in Isabelle is performed in a functional programming style without braces. For example, f(x,y,z) is written in Isabelle as `f x y z`.

seps assigning to each pair of r-distinguishable states (q_1, q_2) at least one state separator S with corresponding deadlock states d_1 and d_2.

This representation also requires a new formulation of the pass relation. We say that M' passes test suite $TS = (PS, tps, rds, seps)$ for M, denoted `passes_test_suite` M TS M' in the Isabelle formalisation, if (1) M' passes $TC(P_q)$ for every $(q, P_q) \in PS$, (2) for every $(q, P_q) \in PS$ and $\bar{x}/\bar{y} \in tps(q)$, every reaction of M' in a state reached by P_q to any prefix of $\bar{x}$ is also prefix of some sequence in $tps(q)$, and (3) for every $(q, P_q) \in PS$, $\bar{x}/\bar{y} \in tps(q)$, $q' \in rds(q, \bar{x}/\bar{y})$ and $(S, d_1, d_2) \in seps(q, q')$, M' in a state reached by P_q followed by $\bar{x}/\bar{y}$ passes the adaptive test case I_q created from S. Note that this different representation and formulation does not affect the result of applying a test suite TS against the SUT: M' passes TS represented as a set of ATCs if and only if `passes_test_suite` M TS M' holds.

3.1   Proof Strategy

The first main goal of our formalisation is to prove that the formalised strategy is complete. That is, an SUT should pass a generated test suite if and only if it is a reduction of its specification. We split this proof into two parts by first formulating a sufficient condition such that any test suite satisfying it is complete, and then proving that the test suites generated by the formalised strategy do satisfy the condition. We will refer to this condition as the *completeness predicate* and describe it and its formulation in Isabelle in Subsect. 3.2.

An overview of the steps performed in the overall proof is given in Fig. 1: Let TS be a test suite generated by the formalised strategy. By construction (outlined in Subsect. 2.1, implemented in Sect. 4), TS satisfies the completeness predicate and is also finite. All further proofs then only rely on these properties and the assumptions on the structure of M' (observable, completely specified, same inputs as M, $|M'| \leq m$). M' can fail a test suite satisfying the completeness predicate only if a behaviour of M' is observed that is not admissible in M, and hence TS is *sound*: if M' is a reduction of M, then it passes TS. The main effort in establishing completeness thereafter lies in proving TS to be *exhaustive*: if M' is not a reduction of M, then M' must not pass TS. This is realised via a proof by contradiction detailed in Subsect. 3.2. Finally, completeness follows from soundness and exhaustiveness and still holds if test suites are reduced to finite prefix-free sets of IO-sequences (see Sect. 4).

The formalisation in Isabelle is split into several *theory files* covering separate aspects of the proof: First, files `FSM_Impl.thy`, `FSM.thy` and `Product_FSM.thy` provide basic definitions and properties for finite state machines. Next, the files `State_Preamble.thy`, `State_Separator.thy` and `Traversal_Set.thy` respectively introduce the three main components of the test suite and algorithms for their computation. These are then combined within `Test_Suite.thy`, which defines the completeness property and shows that each satisfying test suite is complete. Finally, an algorithm for calculating complete test suites is provided in `Test_Suite_Calculation.thy` and refined in further theory files. Overall, the formalisation effort comprises 18 theory files containing a total of 621 lemmata,

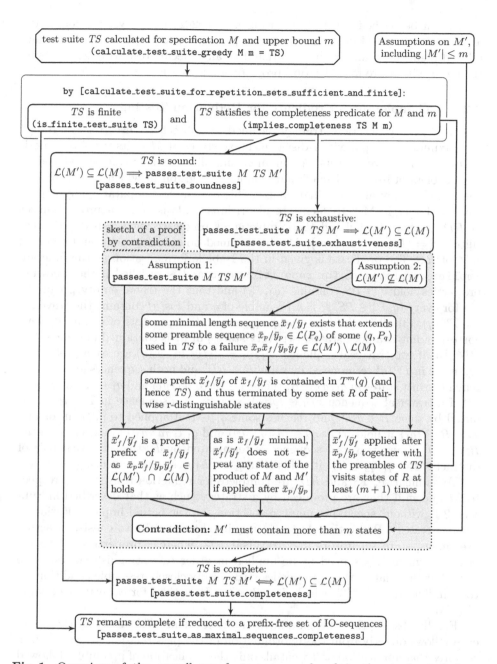

Fig. 1. Overview of the overall proof strategy employed in the mechanised formalisation, with a focus on the proof of exhaustiveness of generated test suites. Names in square brackets indicate lemmata in the Isabelle formalisation. Predicate `implies_completeness` is a shortened version of the completeness predicate described in Sect. 3.2 for a greedy strategy of calculating RD'.

which can be verified within 201 s using Isabelle2020 on a Ryzen 5 3600 CPU and Ubuntu 18.04. Most of these lemmata prove general properties on FSMs and related algorithms and are not restricted to any specific test strategy, allowing their reuse in future formalisation projects employing FSMs.

3.2   A Completeness Predicate for Reduction Testing

The test suite generation strategy outlined in Subsect. 2.1 uses the set RD of all maximal sets of pairwise r-distinguishable states of M in its termination criterion for the traversal sets. As enumerating all those sets can be reduced to the problem of listing all maximum cliques of a graph in which two states are connected if they are r-distinguishable, this can prove computationally expensive for larger FSMs. To facilitate algorithms that use only a proper subset of RD, we have formulated the completeness predicate with respect to a test suite $TS = (PS, tps, rds, seps)$, M, the assumed bound $m \geq |M'|$, and a subset RD' of RD. The predicate is given in the Isabelle formalisation as the function implies_completeness_for_repetition_sets and is satisfied if the following properties hold: (1) PS contains (q_0, P_0) and thus the trivial empty preamble, (2) for every $(q, P) \in PS$, P is a preamble of q and $tps(q)$ contains the traversal set $T^m(q)$, (3) all $(S, d_1, d_2) \in tps(q_1, q_2)$ are state separators of q_1 and q_2 with corresponding deadlock states, (4) every state q of M is contained in some set in RD', (5) if two traversal sequences $\bar{x}_1/\bar{y}_1 \neq \bar{x}_2/\bar{y}_2$ in $tps(q)$ are each prefix of a sequence in $T^m(q)$ terminated by some $R \in RD'$ and both sequences applied to q reach distinct states in $q_1, q_2 \in R$, then $q_2 \in rds(q, \bar{x}_1/\bar{y}_1)$ and $q_1 \in rds(q, \bar{x}_2/\bar{y}_2)$, (6) if a traversal sequence $\bar{x}/\bar{y} \in tps(q)$ is prefix of a sequence in $T^m(q)$ terminated by some $R \in RD'$ and reaches some $q_1 \in R$ if applied to q, then for any $q_2 \in R_{dr}\backslash\{q_1\}$ it holds that $q_2 \in rds(q, \bar{x}/\bar{y})$ and $q_1 \in rds(q_2, \epsilon)$, and (7) for each $R \in RD'$, if any traversal sequence is terminated by R, then for each pair of distinct states $q_1, q_2 \in R_{dr}$ it holds that $q_2 \in rds(q_1, \epsilon)$ and $q_1 \in rds(q_2, \epsilon)$.

To summarise, TS and RD' are complete for reduction testing with respect to M and m if they are produced by a strategy such as that described in Subsect. 2.1, without specifying many restrictions on the actual implementation of such a strategy. Properties (1) to (4) require the test suite to consist of actual preambles, state separators and traversal sets, whereas properties (5) to (7) describe where ATCs need to be applied in order to distinguish states. Note here that these latter three properties structurally closely resemble conditions 1. to 3. in Theorem 1 of [6], which describes the H-method for equivalence testing of FSMs.

Finally observe that the soundness of any test suite TS satisfying the predicate follows directly from the reformulation of the pass relation, as satisfaction requires that application of TS entails only the application of preambles followed by corresponding traversal sets followed by corresponding state separators, and thus only of IO-sequences in $\mathcal{L}(M)$, for which no reduction of M may fail.

Completeness of Test Suites Satisfying the Completeness Predicate. Let test suite TS and subset RD' of RD satisfy the completeness predicate with respect to M and an assumed upper bound $m \geq |M'|$. Then the exhaustiveness of TS follows from a classical state counting argument by establishing a lower bound greater than m on the number of states contained in any M' that is not a reduction of M but that passes TS, see for example [9, 22]. We have used this approach in a proof by contradiction: if we assume that M' passes TS while also $\mathcal{L}(M') \not\subseteq \mathcal{L}(M)$ holds, then some minimal sequence to a failure $\bar{x}_f / \bar{y}_f$ extending some preamble sequence $\bar{x}_p / \bar{y}_p$ of some (q, P_q) in the preambles of TS must exist, which is not applied in TS. Hence, some proper prefix $\bar{x}'_f / \bar{y}'_f$ of $\bar{x}_f / \bar{y}_f$ must be contained in $T^m(q)$ and terminated by some $R \in RD'$. Now $\bar{x}_p \bar{x}'_f / \bar{y}_p \bar{y}'_f$ cannot repeat any state of the product of M and M', as this would allow for a sequence to a failure shorter than $\bar{x}_f / \bar{y}_f$. Furthermore, by construction of the traversal sequences, $\bar{x}'_f / \bar{y}'_f$ applied after $\bar{x}_p / \bar{y}_p$ together with the preambles in TS must visit states of R at least $(m+1)$ times in M. These last two properties, in conjunction with M' passing all applied state separators of conditions (5) to (7) of the completeness predicate, require M' to contain at least $(m+1)$ distinct states, which provides a contradiction to the assumed upper bound $|M'| \leq m$. Completeness of TS follows from exhaustiveness and the previously established soundness. That is, M' passes TS if and only if M' is a reduction of M.

4   A Trustworthy Implementation

Complete Algorithms. The calculation of a test suite satisfying the completeness predicate can be separated into five major steps: (1) the calculation of definitely reachable states of M and corresponding preambles, (2) the calculation of r-distinguishable state pairs in M and corresponding state separators, (3) the calculation of a subset RD' of RD, (4) the calculation of traversal sets from each definitely reachable state, also storing the corresponding terminating $R \subset RD'$, and (5) the combination of these results into a test suite by calculating for each definitely reachable state and each traversal sequence from this state the states it must be r-distinguished from. Figure 2 depicts these steps and their corresponding functions in the Isabelle formalisation within the box for function `generate_test_suite_greedy`. This function implements the test strategy described above using a simple greedy algorithm to calculate a set RD'.

Step (1) of the above calculation is realised in the formalisation using function `calculate_state_preamble_from_input_choices` to construct a state preamble for a given state q if it exists, based directly on Algorithm 1 of [19]. It creates a preamble by starting from q and analysing *backward reachability*, iteratively adding not yet backwardly reached nodes q' and inputs x such that all transitions from q' for x in M reach nodes added in previous iterations, including q. If this process adds the initial state of M, then the selected states and corresponding inputs induce a valid preamble for q. State separators are calculated in a similar way to establish step (2), starting from the deadlock states of a partial separator, again as described in [19]. Based on these results, we have formalised two possible implementations for step (3): first by naively enumerating all elements of RD and second by a greedy algorithm that calculates for each state q a set $R_q \in RD$ by starting from $R_q := \{q\}$ and iteratively adding states that are r-distinguishable from all states currently in R_q until R_q is maximal. Next, we realise step (4) by performing a straightforward enumeration of paths from each definitely reachable state until the corresponding traversal sequence can be terminated by some $R \in RD'$. Finally, the implementation of step (5) follows above description.

Test Suites as Sets of IO-Sequences. To facilitate easier integration with other tools and storage of calculated test suites, we additionally provide algorithms to reduce test suites to finite prefix-free sets of IO-sequences, which might be stored by data structures as simple as lists. The previously introduced Function `generate_test_suite_greedy` performs this transformation as a final step by extracting from the calculated test suite all IO-sequences $\bar{x}_p\bar{x}_t\bar{x}_r/\bar{y}_p\bar{y}_t\bar{y}_r$ such that $\bar{x}_p/\bar{y}_p$ is a sequence reaching q in some preamble P_q, (q, P_q) is contained in TS, $\bar{x}_t/\bar{y}_t$ is a traversal sequence in $T^m(q)$ and $\bar{x}_r/\bar{y}_r$ is a sequence in some state separator applied thereafter that does not reach *fail*. The resulting finite set of IO-sequences is then simplified by removing all sequences that are proper prefixes of other contained sequences.

Let TS be the calculated test suite represented as defined in Sect. 3. Then, by construction and depicted as the last step of Fig. 1, the reduction of TS to a finite set (or list) TS_L of IO-sequences satisfies the following property:

$$\mathcal{L}(M') \subseteq \mathcal{L}(M) \Leftrightarrow \texttt{passes\_test\_suite } M \; TS \; M'$$
$$\Leftrightarrow \forall \bar{x}x\bar{x}'/\bar{y}y\bar{y}' \in TS_L : \forall \bar{x}x/\bar{y}y' \in \mathcal{L}(M') : \exists \bar{x}x\bar{x}''/\bar{y}y'\bar{y}'' \in TS_L$$

That is, an SUT representation M' passes TS if and only if for any $\bar{x}x/\bar{y}y$ that is prefix of any sequence in TS_L the SUT reacts to x applied after $\bar{x}/\bar{y}$ only with outputs y' such that $\bar{x}x/\bar{y}y'$ is also prefix of some sequence in TS_L. Note here that M is not referenced in the bottom right side of the bi-implications. Test suite TS_L can thus be applied to an SUT in practice by *applying* to the latter each contained IO-sequence (*test case*) at least k times (to satisfy the complete testing assumption). A test case $x_1 \ldots x_n/y_1 \ldots y_n$ is *applied* by iteratively applying each x_i (beginning at x_1) and observing the corresponding response y'_i of the SUT, continuing only if $y_i = y'_i$. The SUT *passes* the application of $x_1 \ldots x_n/y_1 \ldots y_n$ if and only if the observed SUT response $x_1 \ldots x_j/y'_1 \ldots y'_j$ is prefix of some sequence in TS_L. Finally, by the above property TS_L must be a subset of $\mathcal{L}(M)$ and hence the SUT passes a test case if and only if the observed response of the SUT to the test case is be admissible in M, as $\mathcal{L}(M)$ is prefix closed.

Refinement and Extensibility. Isabelle provides a powerful refinement mechanism to generate more efficient code from definitions, which we have employed in theory file `Test_Suite_Calculation_Refined.thy` to refine both data structures and algorithms. First, we have used the Containers framework [13] to represent sets using data structures such as red-black-trees wherever possible, which improves on Isabelles default set implementation as lists. Furthermore, we provide several *code equations* that allow the code generator to replace function definitions by (provably equivalent) definitions that are more efficient, for example by extracting common subexpressions to avoid repeated evaluation of identical expressions. These refinements have allowed us to use simple definitions that are easy to use within the proofs, while still being able to use more efficient definitions in code generation. They are also extensible as it is possible to add further code equations and overwrite existing ones.

New variations or optimisations of the test strategy described in this paper can furthermore easily be proven complete by establishing that they satisfy the completeness predicate, as we have decoupled implementation details from the proof of completeness via this criterion. To prove complete, for example, an alternative test strategy resulting from replacing the currently used algorithm for calculating state separators by one of the algorithms presented in [7], it is sufficient to prove in Isabelle that this new algorithm generates valid state separators and to provide for the new test strategy a lemma analogous to lemma `calculate_test_suite_for_repetition_sets_sufficient_and_finite`, which proves satisfaction of the completeness predicate.

Generated Test Tools. In theory file `Test_Generator_Export_Code.thy` we generate Haskell code for function `generate_test_suite_greedy`, which we then use to implement a comprehensive test tool set able to test an SUT given as a function in C against a specification FSM. This tool set is available at the provided online resources (see Sect. 1) and consists of two parts: a test suite generator which uses the code generated from Isabelle to generate a test suite for a given specification FSM, and a test harness which applies each test case in a given test suite against an SUT, using the above definition of applying test cases, to calculate a verdict on whether the SUT conforms to the specification. This verdict is **PASS** if and only if all test cases pass. Figure 2 depicts the workflow.

The two tools each contain fewer than 200 lines of code in addition to the generated code and serve only as interfaces between the specification FSM, test suites and the SUT. They can thus be verified manually with little effort. Together with the trustworthiness of the provably correct generated code (see [8]) facilitating the test suite generator, this has important implications on tool qualification efforts of test tools that employ the above tools: First, the fault detection capabilities of each generated test suite are established by mechanised proofs within our formalisation, providing evidence that it is complete for the fault domain of SUTs whose behaviour can be represented by an FSM M' that is completely specified, observable, contains at most m states, and has the same nonempty set of inputs as M. Verification of these proofs themselves reduces to verifying the used definitions, as any proof is verified automatically by the small trustworthy inference kernel of Isabelle, even when using sophisticated proof methods (see [2]). Furthermore, as generated test suites are a proper subsets of $\mathcal{L}(M)$, no test case application following the previously described procedure can introduce undetected SUT failures by reporting some test case as passed even though the observed response of the SUT to it is not admissible in the specification. Thus, by verification of the test case application mechanism in the test harness, the first of two hazards introduced by model-based test tools as identified in [3] can be mitigated. Mitigation of the second hazard identified there, undetected coverage failures due to test executions failing to meet test case specific pre-conditions, can for our fault domain be reduced to verifying

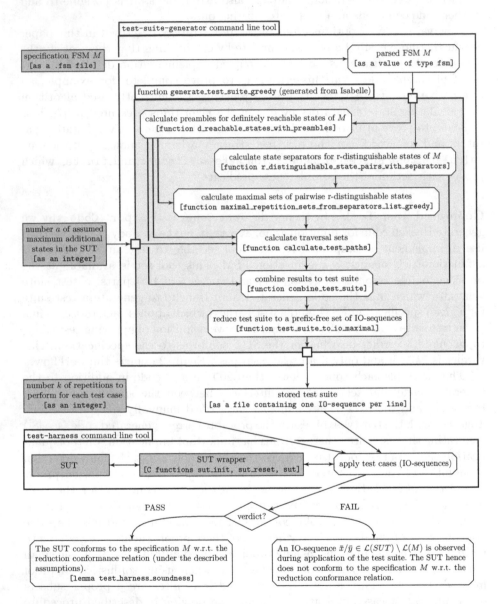

Fig. 2. Overview of the workflow of using the test suite generator and test harness command line tools to test an SUT. Dark grey shadings indicate inputs and SUT integration provided by the user, while light grey shadings indicate the trustworthy code generated from the Isabelle formalisation.

that the test harness resets the SUT to an initial state before applying each test case, as this is the only pre-condition we require. Since the integration of the SUT into the test harness is highly dependent on the SUT, we have not included the test harness in the Isabelle formalisation, but we believe that the very small provided implementation can easily be verified for a given SUT. Such a verification of the test harness tool and the integration of the generated code into the test suite generator tool then obviates measures such as replay of observed behaviours against the specification (see [3]) arising from untrusted test case generators.

Statistical Experiments. We have applied the generated implementation on a synthetic data set containing randomly generated FSMs of varying size and extend of nondeterminism, where we define the *degree of nondeterminism* of an observable FSM $M = (Q, q_0, \Sigma_I, \Sigma_O, h)$, denoted $d_{nondet}(M)$, as the ratio between the number of transitions such that other transition with the same source and input exist, and the overall number $|h|$ of transitions in M:

$$d_{nondet}(M) = |\{(q, x, y, q') \in h \mid \exists y', q'' : (q, x, y', q'') \in h \land y \neq y'\}|/|h|$$

The synthetic data set contains for each configuration (s, d) with $4 \leq s \leq 20$ and $d \in \{0.1, 0.2, 0.3, 0.4\}$ a collection of 1000 randomly generated FSMs M with 6 inputs and 4 outputs such that $|M| = s$ and M has been generated for a target value of $d_{nondet}(M) = d$ using the *fsmlib-cpp* library[4], an open source project containing many fundamental algorithms for processing FSMs. We have restricted the range of values for d to comparatively small values, as we believe that specifications of safety-critical systems often exhibit nondeterminism only to a very limited extend.

Figure 3 shows the average size (number of test cases) of test suites calculated for this data set, using an upper bound $m = |M|$, and the average time required for each calculation as measured on a Ryzen 5 3600 CPU calculating test suites for 8 FSMs in parallel. These results indicate that, for a fixed input alphabet, the average size of generated test suites correlates with the extend of nondeterminism in the specification. This follows in particular from the definition of traversal sets, since a higher degree of nondeterminism indicates, on average, a higher number of outgoing transitions for each state and thus an increase in the number of distinct IO sequences originating at each state. Note also that the calculated test suites are significantly smaller than those created using the "brute force" strategy of enumerating all input sequences of length $|M| \cdot m$, resulting in test suites of size at least $|\Sigma_I|^{m \cdot |M|}$. We conjecture that the execution time of the generated implementation can be drastically reduced by further refinement and the employment of more sophisticated algorithms in particular for the calculation of state separators.

---

[4] Publicly available for download at https://github.com/agbs-uni-bremen/fsmlib-cpp. Random FSMs for a given degree of nondeterminism have been constructed using method `createRandomFsm` of class `Fsm`.

The data set, instructions on how to employ the generated implementation to calculate test suites, and detailed results for each FSM contained in the data set are available as part of the online resources referenced in Sect. 1.

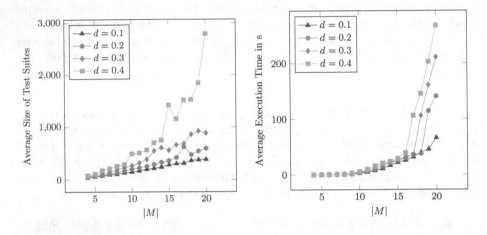

Fig. 3. Average size (left) and calculation time in s (right) of test suites for randomly generated, completely specified, observable and minimised specification FSMs M for $m = |M|$, depending on $|M|$ and target value d for $d_{nondet}(M)$.

5   Conclusions and Future Work

We have provided the first comprehensive mechanised proof of the test strategy elaborated by Petrenko and Yevtushenko in [21] and established the correctness of an implementation of this strategy. As a second main contribution, we have used the mechanised formalisation to generate from it trustworthy executable code and embedded it into a set of test tools that facilitate the calculation and application of test suites. Further investigations are required to quantitatively compare this generated implementation against hand-crafted implementations of the formalised test strategy. The theories and proofs of the formalisation, as well as the implementation of the test strategy itself, have been developed using the Isabelle/HOL tool, indicating the suitability of the latter to perform such undertakings with acceptable effort.

We advocate the use of mechanised proofs of the completeness of test strategies and the use of provably correct automatically generated implementations, because such strategies and guarantees of their fault detection capabilities are of considerable value in model-based testing of safety-critical systems, where undiscovered flaws in test strategies or their implementations might lead to insufficient actual test strength and therefore to the possibility of fatal errors in the system under test being left undiscovered. The use of provably correct automatically generated implementations can furthermore mitigate hazards introduced by model-based test tools and obviate measures against untrusted test case generators, simplifying tool qualification efforts of test tools that employ such implementations.

Acknowledgements. I would like to thank my doctoral thesis supervisor Jan Peleska for several helpful discussions.

References

1. Bjørner, N.: Z3 and SMT in industrial R&D. In: Havelund, K., Peleska, J., Roscoe, B., de Vink, E. (eds.) FM 2018. LNCS, vol. 10951, pp. 675–678. Springer, Cham (2018). https://doi.org/10.1007/978-3-319-95582-7_44
2. Blanchette, J.C., Bulwahn, L., Nipkow, T.: Automatic proof and disproof in Isabelle/HOL. In: Tinelli, C., Sofronie-Stokkermans, V. (eds.) FroCoS 2011. LNCS (LNAI), vol. 6989, pp. 12–27. Springer, Heidelberg (2011). https://doi.org/10.1007/978-3-642-24364-6_2
3. Brauer, J., Peleska, J., Schulze, U.: Efficient and trustworthy tool qualification for model-based testing tools. In: Nielsen, B., Weise, C. (eds.) ICTSS 2012. LNCS, vol. 7641, pp. 8–23. Springer, Heidelberg (2012). https://doi.org/10.1007/978-3-642-34691-0_3
4. Brucker, A.D., Wolff, B.: Interactive testing with HOL-TestGen. In: Grieskamp, W., Weise, C. (eds.) FATES 2005. LNCS, vol. 3997, pp. 87–102. Springer, Heidelberg (2006). https://doi.org/10.1007/11759744_7
5. Brucker, A.D., Wolff, B.: On theorem prover-based testing. Formal Asp. Comput. **25**(5), 683–721 (2013). https://doi.org/10.1007/s00165-012-0222-y
6. Dorofeeva, R., El-Fakih, K., Yevtushenko, N.: An improved conformance testing method. In: Wang, F. (ed.) FORTE 2005. LNCS, vol. 3731, pp. 204–218. Springer, Heidelberg (2005). https://doi.org/10.1007/11562436_16
7. El-Fakih, K., Yevtushenko, N., Saleh, A.: Incremental and heuristic approaches for deriving adaptive distinguishing test cases for non-deterministic finite-state machines. Comput. J. **62**(5), 757–768 (2019). https://doi.org/10.1093/comjnl/bxy086
8. Haftmann, F., Nipkow, T.: Code generation via higher-order rewrite systems. In: Blume, M., Kobayashi, N., Vidal, G. (eds.) FLOPS 2010. LNCS, vol. 6009, pp. 103–117. Springer, Heidelberg (2010). https://doi.org/10.1007/978-3-642-12251-4_9
9. Hierons, R.M.: Testing from a nondeterministic finite state machine using adaptive state counting. IEEE Trans. Compt. **53**(10), 1330–1342 (2004). https://doi.org/10.1109/TC.2004.85. http://doi.ieeecomputersociety.org/10.1109/TC.2004.85
10. Hierons, R.M.: FSM quasi-equivalence testing via reduction and observing absences. Sci. Comput. Program. **177**, 1–18 (2019). https://doi.org/10.1016/j.scico.2019.03.004
11. Huang, W., Peleska, J.: Complete model-based equivalence class testing. Softw. Tools Technol. Trans. **18**(3), 265–283 (2016). https://doi.org/10.1007/s10009-014-0356-8
12. Huang, W., Peleska, J.: Complete model-based equivalence class testing for non-deterministic systems. Formal Asp. Comput. **29**(2), 335–364 (2017). https://doi.org/10.1007/s00165-016-0402-2

13. Lochbihler, A.: Light-weight containers for Isabelle: efficient, extensible, nestable. In: Blazy, S., Paulin-Mohring, C., Pichardie, D. (eds.) ITP 2013. LNCS, vol. 7998, pp. 116–132. Springer, Heidelberg (2013). https://doi.org/10.1007/978-3-642-39634-2_11

14. Luo, G., von Bochmann, G., Petrenko, A.: Test selection based on communicating nondeterministic finite-state machines using a generalized Wp-method. IEEE Trans. Softw. Eng. **20**(2), 149–162 (1994). https://doi.org/10.1109/32.265636. http://doi.ieeecomputersociety.org/10.1109/32.265636

15. Nipkow, T., Wenzel, M., Paulson, L.C. (eds.): Isabelle/HOL: A Proof Assistant for Higher-Order Logic. LNCS, vol. 2283. Springer, Heidelberg (2002). https://doi.org/10.1007/3-540-45949-9

16. Peleska, J., Brauer, J., Huang, W.: Model-based testing for avionic systems proven benefits and further challenges. In: Margaria, T., Steffen, B. (eds.) ISoLA 2018. LNCS, vol. 11247, pp. 82–103. Springer, Cham (2018). https://doi.org/10.1007/978-3-030-03427-6_11

17. Peleska, J., Huang, W.l.: Test Automation - Foundations and Applications of Model-Based Testing. Lecture Notes. University of Bremen (January 2019). http://www.informatik.uni-bremen.de/agbs/jp/papers/test-automation-huang-peleska.pdf

18. Peleska, J., Vorobev, E., Lapschies, F.: Automated test case generation with SMT-solving and abstract interpretation. In: Bobaru, M., Havelund, K., Holzmann, G.J., Joshi, R. (eds.) NFM 2011. LNCS, vol. 6617, pp. 298–312. Springer, Heidelberg (2011). https://doi.org/10.1007/978-3-642-20398-5_22

19. Petrenko, A., Yevtushenko, N.: Adaptive testing of deterministic implementations specified by nondeterministic FSMs. In: Wolff, B., Zaïdi, F. (eds.) ICTSS 2011. LNCS, vol. 7019, pp. 162–178. Springer, Heidelberg (2011). https://doi.org/10.1007/978-3-642-24580-0_12

20. Petrenko, A., Yevtushenko, N., von Bochmann, G.: Testing deterministic implementations from nondeterministic FSM specifications. In: Baumgarten, B., Burkhardt, H.-J., Giessler, A. (eds.) Testing of Communicating Systems. ITIFIP, pp. 125–140. Springer, Boston, MA (1996). https://doi.org/10.1007/978-0-387-35062-2_10

21. Petrenko, A., Yevtushenko, N.: Adaptive testing of nondeterministic systems with FSM. In: 15th International IEEE Symposium on High-Assurance Systems Engineering, HASE 2014, Miami Beach, FL, USA, 9–11 January 2014, pp. 224–228. IEEE Computer Society (2014). https://doi.org/10.1109/HASE.2014.39

22. Sachtleben, R., Hierons, R.M., Huang, W., Peleska, J.: A mechanised proof of an adaptive state counting algorithm. In: Gaston, C., Kosmatov, N., Le Gall, P. (eds.) ICTSS 2019. LNCS, vol. 11812, pp. 176–193. Springer, Cham (2019). https://doi.org/10.1007/978-3-030-31280-0_11

23. Wenzel, M.: Isabelle/Isar — a versatile environment for human readable formal proof documents. Ph.D. thesis, Technical University Munich, Germany (2002). http://tumb1.biblio.tu-muenchen.de/publ/diss/in/2002/wenzel.pdf

Automatic Fairness Testing of Machine Learning Models

Arnab Sharma$^{(\boxtimes)}$ and Heike Wehrheim$^{(\boxtimes)}$

Paderborn University, Paderborn, Germany
{arnab.sharma,wehrheim}@uni-paderborn.de

Abstract. In recent years, there has been an increased application of machine learning (ML) to decision making systems. This has prompted an urgent need for validating requirements on ML models. *Fairness* is one such requirement to be ensured in numerous application domains. It specifies a software as "learned" by an ML algorithm to not be biased in the sense of discriminating against some attributes (like gender or age), giving different decisions upon flipping the values of these attributes.

In this work, we apply *verification-based testing* (VBT) to the fairness checking of ML models. Verification-based testing employs verification technology to generate test cases potentially violating the property under interest. For fairness testing, we additionally provide a specification language for the formalization of different fairness requirements. From the ML model under test and fairness specification VBT automatically generates test inputs specific to the specified fairness requirement. The empirical evaluation on several benchmark ML models shows verification-based testing to perform better than existing fairness testing techniques with respect to effectiveness.

Keywords: Fairness · Machine learning testing · SMT solving

1 Introduction

Machine Learning (ML) is gradually being used in software systems and replacing humans in decision making. The application area of such software systems now ranges from social and economical domains to even law [12]. Therefore, the quality assurance of these systems is of utmost importance. In the past few years, a significant amount of research works have been performed for checking various sorts of requirements arising in different application domains (e.g., robustness [10], security [4], balancedness [18]).

One such requirement which often needs to be ensured by the "learned" software system is *fairness*. Although there exists multiple definitions of fairness in the literature [21], the basic idea of the property is always the same. Fairness requires that changing the values of only the *protected* attributes should not change the *prediction* of an ML classifier. For example, a loan granting software

© IFIP International Federation for Information Processing 2020
Published by Springer Nature Switzerland AG 2020
V. Casola et al. (Eds.): ICTSS 2020, LNCS 12543, pp. 255–271, 2020.
https://doi.org/10.1007/978-3-030-64881-7_16

which decides whether a person gets a loan, is discriminating against "gender", if it gives a different decision (i.e., prediction) for male and female applicants when all other values of features besides "gender" are equal. Here, gender is considered to be the *protected* attribute.

Most often the use of biased training data results in such unfair predictors. However, even if the training data does not contain any unfairness, the generated ML model can still be biased. Hence, today there exists a number of specialized algorithms aiming at the generation of fair ML models (e.g. [3,22]). Galhotra et al. [8] have nevertheless shown that even the use of these fair algorithms cannot guarantee fair predictive models. They have proposed a random testing technique called THEMIS which works by generating a number of test cases testifying if and how much unfairness exists in the ML model. They have furthermore proposed *individual discrimination* as the definition of fairness, as their work suggests that the existing fairness definitions can hide unfairness in an ML model. Later, Udeshi et al. have proposed AEQUITAS [20] which generates a higher number of test cases in comparison to THEMIS in checking *individual discrimination*. More recently, Aggarwal et al. [1] have proposed a technique combining dynamic symbolic execution and local explanation which outperforms the previous two techniques in checking fairness.

Although these approaches perform quite well in detecting unfairness of a given ML model, they mostly focus on testifying one specific type of fairness. Hence, these approaches cannot be directly used to check a model for any fairness definition. As there exists several such fairness definitions depending on the application domain, a unified approach to test an ML model for a given fairness property is required.

In an earlier work, we have introduced a novel black-box testing approach [17] to test the monotonicity of a given ML model. This approach works by systematically exploring the input space of the given model by firstly inferring a white-box model *approximating* the black-box model under test (MUT), and computing the counter examples to monotonicity on the white-box model via an established verification technique. The computed counter examples on the white-box model are then checked with the black-box model. The confirmed ones are stored as test cases violating the property and further varied to generate more test cases. If unconfirmed, they serve as input to an improvement of the approximation quality of the white-box model. Here, we extend this approach to test the fairness of a given machine learning model. Our idea is to develop a property-based testing mechanism for fairness checking where the specific fairness requirement can be specified using an `assume-assert` construct. Test cases are then automatically generated attempting to violate the specified fairness property. The underlying mechanism remains the same as before and comprises four key steps: (1) White-box model inference, (2) fairness computation, (3) variation and (4) white-box model improvement.

We have implemented our approach and have experimentally evaluated it by applying it on standard benchmark ML models. Our experimental results suggest that our *verification-based testing* technique performs better than existing fairness testing techniques ([20] and [1]) for most of the test cases. Summarizing, this paper makes the following contributions:

- We provide a specification language for formulating fairness requirements on ML Models.
- We employ our verification-based-testing technique to test fairness of ML models.
- We systematically evaluate our approach on several standard benchmarks and compare our results with existing fairness testing approaches.

The paper is structured as follows. In the next section, we define fairness of machine learning models. In Sect. 3 we describe our specification language and verification-based testing. Section 4 presents the results of our experimental evaluation. We discuss related work in Sect. 5 and conclude in Sect. 6.

2   Fairness

We begin with the basic terminologies in machine learning and then give definitions of fairness.

Our interest is in testing models obtained by *supervised* machine learning. Such algorithms typically have two steps. Initially, in the *learning* phase, the algorithm is presented with a set of data instances called *training data*. The ML algorithm then generates a function (the *predictive model*), generalising from the *training data* by using some statistical techniques. The generated *predictive model* (short, model) is used in the second (prediction) phase to predict classes for unknown data instances.

Formally, the generated model (M) can be defined as a function

$$M : X_1 \times \ldots \times X_n \to Y,$$

where X_i is the value set of *feature i* (or attribute or characteristics i), $1 \le i \le n$, and Y is the set of *classes*. We define $\vec{\mathbf{X}} = X_1 \times \ldots \times X_n$. The training data consists of elements from $\vec{\mathbf{X}} \times Y$, i.e., data instances with known associated classes. During the prediction, the generated predictive model assigns a class $y \in Y$ to a data instance $(x_1, \ldots, x_n) \in \vec{\mathbf{X}}$.

In the literature, a large number of fairness definitions for ML models can be found (see [21] for a survey). They basically all build on the same concept of fairness: an ML model (or algorithm in general) is unfair if it is discriminating some individuals (i.e., data instances) on the basis of values of some of their features. This discrimination is however formally captured in completely different ways: while some works (e.g. [5,7]) employ statistical measures (probability distributions on certain outcomes of M), others employ similarity-based measures (e.g. [1,8]). Our objective here is to develop an approach for testing *black-box* models, i.e., what our approach can observe about a model are just the outputs (predictions) for certain inputs (data instances). We thus focus on similarity-based measures.

Fairness definitions first of all fix so-called protected or *sensitive* attributes which are supposed to not lead to discrimination. As an example, consider Fig. 1 which gives a decision tree for loan granting based on attributes "gender",

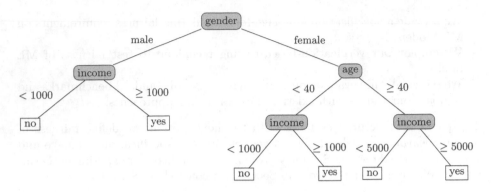

Fig. 1. A decision tree for predicting who gets a loan

"income" and "age". A fairness requirement on loan granting software might for instance state that the software should not discriminate against "gender", hence "gender" would be the sensitive attribute.

Definition 1. *A predictive model M is fair with respect to a sensitive feature i if for any two data instances $x = (x_1, \ldots, x_n), x' = (x'_1, \ldots, x'_n) \in \vec{\mathbf{X}}$, we have $(x_i \neq x'_i) \wedge (\forall j, j \neq i.x_j = x'_j)$ implies $M(x) = M(x')$.*

This fairness definition is termed *individual discrimination* and was introduced by Galhotra et al. [8]. According to this definition, all the feature values except for the protected one should have the same value. The idea is to find out whether changing only the protected feature value leads to the change of the prediction. Our decision tree model in Fig. 1 is not fair w.r.t. Definition 1 and sensitive feature "gender". Take for instance the following pair of data instances

$$\text{income} = 1000, \text{age} = 40, \text{gender} = \text{female}$$
$$\text{income} = 1000, \text{age} = 40, \text{gender} = \text{male}$$

For the first instance, the result of the prediction is 'no', while for the second data instance it will be 'yes'.

We next define *group discrimination* which extends Definition 1 to a set of protected features.

Definition 2. *A predictive model M is said to be fair with respect to a set of sensitive features $F = \{i_1, i_2, \ldots, i_m\} \subseteq \{1, \ldots, n\}$ if for any two data instances $x = (x_1, \ldots, x_n), x' = (x'_1, \ldots, x'_n) \in \vec{\mathbf{X}}$ we have $(\forall j \in F : x_j \neq x'_j \wedge \forall j \notin F : x_j = x'_j)$ implies $M(x) = M(x')$.*

In case of the tree model depicted in Fig. 1, it is evident that the decision tree is discriminating those female candidates who have age more than 40. The applicants with age less than 40 are treated equally regardless of their gender. But those who are above 40 should have a higher income than the rest.

Another similarity-based measure is *fairness through unawareness*. This requires that the protected attributes have no influence on the classification at all. Next, we directly define the group version.

Definition 3. *A predictive model M is said to be* fair *with respect to a set of sensitive features $F = \{i_1, i_2, \ldots, i_m\} \subseteq \{1, \ldots, n\}$ if for any two data instances $x = (x_1, \ldots, x_n), x' = (x'_1, \ldots, x'_n) \in \vec{\mathbf{X}}$ we have $\forall j \notin F : x_j = x'_j$ implies $M(x) = M(x')$.*

Whenever two data instances coincide on all features values except possibly for the protected attributes, they should get the same prediction.

Finally, there is also a similarity-based measure called *fairness through awareness*. This relaxes the strict equality of (some) feature values required by the definitions so far to *similar* values. The similarity is therein captured by some distance metric $d : \vec{\mathbf{X}} \times \vec{\mathbf{X}} \to [0, 1]$ on data instances[1].

Definition 4. *Let $d : \vec{\mathbf{X}} \times \vec{\mathbf{X}} \to [0, 1]$ be a distance metric on data instances and ε a threshold. A predictive model M is said to be* fair *with respect to a set of sensitive features $F = \{i_1, i_2, \ldots, i_m\} \subseteq \{1, \ldots, n\}$ if for any two data instances $x = (x_1, \ldots, x_n), x' = (x'_1, \ldots, x'_n) \in \vec{\mathbf{X}}$ we have $d(x, x') \leq \varepsilon$ implies $M(x) = M(x')$.*

For our loan-granting example, we could for instance define the distance metric as

$$d(x, x') = \begin{cases} 1 & \text{if } x_{gender} = x'_{gender} \\ \frac{|x_{age} - x'_{age}|}{100} & \text{else} \end{cases}$$

and let $\varepsilon = 0.1$. This would require that all pairs of data instances with different gender and difference in age of less than or equal 10 get the same prediction.

Next, we describe an approach for testing arbitrary given ML models with respect to some given fairness definition.

3   Testing Approach

In this section, we describe the language for specifying fairness and also briefly discuss our *verification-based-testing* (VBT) approach which we employ for testing fairness. Note that fairness testing is an instance of metamorphic testing [16] in that we cannot check violation of the tested property on a single test input, but just on *pairs* of test inputs.

3.1   Fairness Specification

Usually, approaches for fairness testing employ a fixed fairness definition and allows users to specify the set of protected features only. Our testing approach in addition allows the software engineer to state the fairness requirement itself. Our language is inspired by *property-based testing* approaches [6]. The user can specify

---

[1] Note that the definition given here differs from that of [21] as we again do not consider probability distributions of outcomes here.

```
# Train the ML algorithm with Loan data containing 3 features: income, age, gender
df = pd.read_csv('LoanData.csv')
data = df.values
x_train = data[:, :-1]
y_class = data[:, -1]
model = LogisticRegression() # Using Logistic regression  classifier  to  train
model = model.fit(x_train, y_class)
# Setting the parameters of fairCheck
fc = fairCheck(no_of_instance = 2, XML_file = 'input.xml', model = model,
instance_list = (x,y))
# Assumptions: index '0' is income, '1' is age and '2' is gender
for i in range(0, 3):
  if (i == 2):
    assume('x[i] != y[i]', i)
  else :
    assume('x[i] = y[i]', i)
# Assertion
Assert ('model.predict(x) = model.predict(y)')
```

Fig. 2. Python code snippet corresponding to Definition 1

assumptions on the inputs, in our case pairs of data instances, and *assertions*
on the outcome (the prediction). The testing technique then tries to generate
inputs satisfying the assumptions and violating the assertions.

For the specification of assumptions, the user needs to know the attributes of
data instances. These are fixed in a schema definition given in an XML configuration file (attributes and their types). Such schema files are often used to describe
the format of training data in machine learning. In the assumptions, attributes
of a data instance x can be accessed like arrays, i.e., x[0] is the value of the
first feature of instance x and so on. Assumptions are then arbitrary boolean
expressions over the attributes of two data instances, called x and y (instead of
x and x'). The model itself can be referred to by the result of training a specific
classifier on a given training data set. All parts of the fairness specification are
written in Python.

As an example, consider the loan-granting setting of the previous section.
The assumptions and assertion for individual discrimination (Definition 1) can
be found in Fig. 2. First, we train a classifier as to get the model (M). Before
specifying the property, some input parameters need to be fixed for our approach
to work. For example, the no_of_instance defines number of data instances
required to specify the property which is in this case 2 and the instance_list
contains the instance variables (in this case is x and y). Also, the XML schema
file and ML model to be checked need to be specified. There are several other
optional parameters with default values.

For example, the default value of parameter no_of_cex is set to 'single',
indicating the generation of a single counter example if the assertion is violated.
If the user assigns 'multi' to this parameter, then multiple counter examples

```
for i in range(0, 3):
  if (i == 2):
    assume('x[i] != y[i ]',  i)
  else :
    assume('0.01*(abs(x[i] − y[i ]))  <= 0.1', i)
# Assertion
Assert ('model.predict(x) = model.predict(y)')
```

Fig. 3. Python code snippet corresponding to Definition 3

would be generated. After fixing the input parameters, we state assumptions and assertion. The testing approach will subsequently generate test inputs which fulfill the assumptions and violate the assertion (if possible).

Similarly, Fig. 3 shows the code snippet for checking fairness with respect to Definition 3. Here we have elided the part on parameter setting, training etc. The only difference to the previous example is the specification of the distance function. The **assume** statement describes the distance metric we have defined earlier. The absolute value operator ($|..|$) is specified by **abs**. The expression to describe distance metric *dist* (i.e. the expression of **assume**) can be of the following form.

$$dist := d_{x,y} \bowtie \epsilon, \quad d_{x,y} := k \oplus (x[i] \oplus y[i]) \mid k \oplus (|x[i] \oplus y[i]|)$$

where $\oplus \in \{+, -, *, /\}$, $\bowtie \in \{=, \leq, \geq, >, <, \neq\}$ and $\epsilon, k \in \mathbb{R}$. Currently, our approach can deal with arbitrary distance metrics, which can be defined by using standard arithmetic operators. Although, the distance metric containing multiplication or division operations might lead to undecidability of the satisfiability question. Hence, using those operators might cause a significant slow down of our approach.

3.2   Verification-Based Testing

For generating test inputs, we employ verification-based testing which we have introduced for testing monotonicity of ML models in [17]. The basic idea is to approximate the black-box model under test (MUT) by a white-box model, essentially a decision tree. The intention therein is to be able to apply verification techniques for property checking once we have a white-box model. Decision trees are a good candidate for such a white-box model since they are easily convertible into logical formulae so that we can use an SMT solver to verify properties on the tree.

The idea of using a white-box approximator for a given black-box model is not new and studied in the areas of *interpretable* AI and testing of non-ML software. In AI, Guidotti et al. [9] uses an explainable white-box model to explain an unknown black-box model. In the testing domain, Papadopoulos and Walkinshaw [14] use the inference of a predictive model from test sets to further

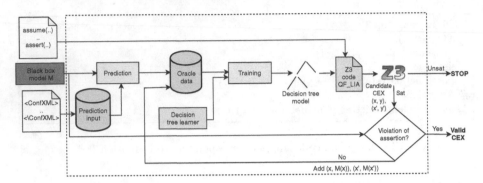

Fig. 4. Basic workflow of verification-based testing

extend this set. We use the inference of a black-box model to a white-box model to compute counter examples to specified properties.

Figure 4 depicts the basic workflow of our approach. The inputs to our approach are the predictive model M (MUT), the schema describing the set of features F and their types (e.g. `int`, `float`) used in the training of the model as an XML configuration file and an `assume-assert` fairness specification.

Our approach consists of four steps. Below, we describe the steps of our technique and explain the workflow in detail.

1. White-box model inference. First, we train a decision tree with a set of data instances called *oracle data*. We generate this oracle data (i.e., training data for the tree) by using the predictions of the MUT for some randomly chosen input instances (referred to as 'Prediction input' in Fig. 4). A decision tree learner is trained on the oracle data which results in a decision tree model approximating the given unknown black-box model.

2. Test generation. Once we have generated the decision tree, the next step is to verify the given fairness property and thereby generate test inputs. For this, we use the state of the art SMT solver Z3 [13]. First, we translate the decision tree into a logical formula describing how the classes are predicted for inputs x and x'. Figure 5 shows the Z3 code for the decision tree in Fig. 1. The data instance x (i.e. test input) is described by the features `gender1`, `age1` and `income1` whereas, test input x' is described by `gender2`, `age2` and `income2`.

The Z3 code of the tree is then complemented with code for the fairness specification. The assumptions of the fairness requirement become `assert` statements in Z3, the assertion becomes an `assert` statement in its *negated* form. The resulting formula is then checked for satisfiability, i.e., we check whether the decision tree allows for a prediction satisfying the assumptions in the fairness constraint, but not the assertion. If the formula is satisfiable, the SMT solver returns a satisfying assignment which is a counter example to this fairness constraint (however, not necessarily for the black-box model, so far just for the decision tree).

For example, consider the Python code for checking individual discrimination (Definition 1) described in Fig. 2. The `assume` statements in Python code are

```
; Declaring components of x and x' and their classes
(declare-fun gender1 () Int)   (declare-fun income1 () Real)
(declare-fun gender2 () Int)   (declare-fun income2 () Real)
(declare-fun age1() Int) (declare-fun age2() Int)
(declare-fun class1 () Int) (declare-fun class2 () Int)
; Specifying prediction of decision tree (no=0, yes=1)
(assert (=> (and (= gender1 0) (< income1 1000)) (= class1 0)))
(assert (=> (and (= gender1 0) (>= income1 1000)) (= class1 1)))
(assert (=> (and (= gender1 1) (< age1 40) (< income1 1000)) (= class1 0)))
(assert (=> (and (= gender1 1) (< age1 40) (>= income1 1000)) (= class1 1)))
(assert (=> (and (= gender1 1) (>= age1 40) (< income1 5000)) (= class1 0)))
(assert (=> (and (= gender1 1) (>= age1 40) (>= income1 5000)) (= class1 1)))
(assert (=> (and (= gender2 0) (< income2 1000)) (= class2 0)))
(assert (=> (and (= gender2 0) (>= income2 1000)) (= class2 1)))
(assert (=> (and (= gender2 1) (< age2 40) (< income2 1000)) (= class2 0)))
(assert (=> (and (= gender2 1) (< age2 40) (>= income2 1000)) (= class2 1)))
(assert (=> (and (= gender2 1) (>= age2 40) (< income2 5000)) (= class2 0)))
(assert (=> (and (= gender2 1) (>= age2 40) (>= income2 5000)) (= class2 1)))
; Unfairness constraint
(assert (and (not(= gender1 gender2)) (= income1 income2) (= age1 age2)))
(assert (not (= class1 class2 )))
; Satisfiable ?
(check-sat)
; Logical model extraction
(get-model)
```

Fig. 5. Z3 code of the decision tree with individual discrimination constraint

translated to `(assert(and(not(= gender1 gender2))(= income1 income2) (= age1 age2)))` as Z3 code in Fig. 5. The `assert` condition is then added as `(assert (not (= class1 class2)))` to Z3. The assertion specified is basically negated in the logical formula in an attempt to generate a counter example violating the specified property. The last two lines of the code ask Z3 to check for satisfiability of all assertions and – if yes (Sat) – to return a logical model. The logical model gives an evaluation for the variables such that all assertions are fulfilled. For our example, it can be found in Fig. 6.

The counter example returned by the SMT solver is a pair of data instances and their respective classes $((x, y), (x', y'))$. The corresponding classes are essentially the prediction given by the approximating decision tree. As the tree is only an approximation, the counter example produced might not be valid for the MUT. Hence, we consider it as a *candidate* counter example (candidate CEX in Fig. 4). In the next step we check whether this is a valid counter example by using the prediction of the MUT. If yes, we add the counter example as a test input to the test suite. If not, $(x, M(x))$ and $(x', M(x'))$ are added to the oracle data in order to increase precision of the approximation in later steps by re-training the decision tree.

```
sat (model
(define-fun income1 () Real 1000.0)
(define-fun age1 () Int 40)
(define-fun gender1 () Int 0)
(define-fun class1 () Int 1)
(define-fun income2 () Real 1000.0)
(define-fun age2 () Int 40)
(define-fun gender2 () Real 1)
(define-fun class2 () Int 0))
```

Fig. 6. Logical model for the query of Fig. 5

When Z3 cannot find a counter example, hence giving 'Unsat' as output, the approximated decision tree is fair w.r.t. the given fairness constraint. Still, it might be the case that the MUT itself is not fair. Then our approach was unable to generate test inputs. In all our experiments this has however not occurred so far.

3. White-box model improvement. Once we have collected a larger set of test pairs (candidate counter examples, see below on how to get multiple counter examples), we examine the validity of those for the MUT M. If any of the candidate counter examples turns out to be also a valid one for the MUT, we have found a test case violating the specified fairness property. If we cannot find such a case, then the decision tree's prediction obviously differs from the MUT for this input. These cases will then be added to the oracle data to re-train the decision tree and thereby improve the approximation. With this new tree, test generation will be started once more.

4. Variation. The basic workflow depicted in Fig. 4 is enhanced by one more step. As discussed in the previous step, if a counter example found by Z3 on computing fairness of the decision tree is invalid, the approximating tree needs to be made more precise. This can be easily achieved by adding the counter example to the oracle data and train the decision tree algorithm again. But training is a costly operation and hence it would be more efficient to train the tree only after gathering a sufficient number of invalid counter examples. To this end, we apply two strategies to produce several different logical models (i.e., counter examples) for the same logical query by using Z3 repetitively, namely *branch pruning* and *data instance pruning*. Basically, branch pruning inserts additional constraints into the logical formulae which tell the SMT solver not to generate counter examples following the same branches of the tree while data instance pruning tells Z3 to generate different data instances.

The detailed algorithms of our pruning techniques can be found in our earlier work [17]. We use these two pruning techniques to generate multiple counter examples. In the previous works of fairness testing, the effectiveness of a technique is measured in terms of the number of valid test cases generated, i.e., test cases violating the fairness constraint. Hence, we run test generation until we reach a specified limit or no further test cases can be found.

4   Evaluation

We have implemented our technique in Python. The implementation of our approach is available online at https://github.com/arnabsharma91/fairCheck. While evaluating our approach we have focused on the following two research questions.

RQ1. How does verification based testing compare to existing fairness testing approaches?

RQ2. Which pruning strategy performs better in computing unfairness?

We have carried out the following experiments to evaluate the research questions.

RQ1. We intend to compare how our approach performs in detecting unfairness compared to existing fairness testing techniques. Note however that there does not exist a fairness checking mechanism so far which can validate a black-box model with respect to a user given fairness specification. Hence, we compare our approach only to fairness testing techniques with fixed fairness definitions. For this, we have chosen AEQUITAS [20] and Symbolic Generation (SG) algorithm [1] which have both been designed to test a given black-box model for individual discrimination. We do not consider THEMIS [8] for our comparison as it has already been shown to be less effective than the other two approaches as stated by Zhang et al. [24]. The aforementioned techniques use the number of valid unfair cases generated within a specified limit of total generated test cases as their evaluation metric. The comparison between the three techniques is thus performed on this basis. We employ both data instance and branch pruning strategies for this experiment.

RQ2. For test generation, we have implemented branch and data instance pruning strategies to achieve better coverage of the decision tree. We intend to find out which strategy is better in finding unfair test cases. We use a different evaluation metric for this comparison. Instead of counting the test cases generated we compute detection rate when each of the strategies is applied individually. We have also used a similar approach in our earlier work [17] to compare our pruning strategies. The detection rate is defined as $\frac{\#\text{Valid test cases}}{\#\text{Total test cases}}$, i.e., we measure how many of the generated test cases (candidate counter examples) are really test cases violating the fairness definition.

4.1   Setup

We have performed the evaluation on two data sets, namely Adult and German credit data from the UCI machine learning repository[2]. The Adult dataset contains 13 features and 32561 data instances, the German credit dataset has 21 features and 1000 data instances. We have chosen four classification algorithms for our experiments: Naive Bayes (NB), Random Forests (RF), Logistic

---

[2] https://archive.ics.uci.edu/ml.

Table 1. Comparison of number of test cases generated for Adult dataset

Classifier	Prot. feature	VBT	SG	AEQUITAS
Logistic Regression	Gender	**133**	37	80
Logistic Regression	Race	**66**	58	25
Random Forest	Gender	**456**	90	29
Random Forest	Race	**358**	338	129
Naive Bayes	Gender	**75**	18	6
Naive Bayes	Race	**43**	40	30
Decision tree	Gender	**684**	94	156
Decision tree	Race	**739**	320	134

Regression and Decision tree. All these have been taken from `scikit-learn`. The choice of these algorithms and datasets is driven by the fact that they all have been used in the previous works of fairness testing. These ML algorithms are also frequently being used in decision making systems.

We have evaluated the accuracy score while generating predictive models and used the score to adjust the hyperparameters of the learning algorithms. We have taken AEQUITAS from the GitHub repository[3]. It was hardcoded for working with Adult dataset only. We have modified its code to make it work for any dataset. We have obtained the implementation of SG from [24]. For AEQUITAS and SG we have chosen the setting which gives the best performance. We have created oracle data in the verification-based testing approach by using a combination of random data instances and training data instances.

Finally, because all three approaches involve some sort of randomness, every experiment was carried out ten times. The results give the average of test cases generated out of these ten turns. The experiments were run on a machine with 2 cores Intel(R) Core(TM) i5-7300U CPU 2.60 GHz and 16 GB memory using Python version 3.6.

4.2   Results

Next, we report on the findings of our experimental evaluation.

RQ1. Tables 1 and 2 show the results of the experiments for RQ1. They give the number of test cases generated by each of the technique while using the four ML models obtained by training on Adult and German credit dataset, respectively. It can be inferred from the results shown that in most of the cases our technique can generate a larger number of test cases in comparison to SG and AEQUITAS.

RQ2. Figure 7 represents our results for the two pruning strategies for Adult and Credit datasets. Here, we compute individual discrimination with respect to the feature 'Gender'. It is evident from the results that data instance (short,

---

[3] https://github.com/sakshiudeshi/Aequitas.

Table 2. Comparison of number of test cases generated for German credit dataset

Classifier	Prot. feature	VBT	SG	AEQUITAS
Logistic Regression	Gender	**182**	60	38
Logistic Regression	Age	127	**164**	3
Random Forest	Gender	173	**211**	200
Random Forest	Age	**130**	118	4
Naive Bayes	Gender	**16**	3	0
Naive Bayes	Age	**27**	20	0
Decision tree	Gender	**453**	135	259
Decision tree	Age	**444**	155	3

instance) pruning performs better than branch pruning in computing individual discrimination.

We have also performed experiments to evaluate the efficiency of our approach. We have observed that for all the test cases we consider here, the maximum run time of our approach is 929.76 s. On average, our approach needs 450 s to generate test cases.

4.3 Limitations and Threats to Validity

Since we employ an SMT solver for computing fairness, verification-based testing is restricted to feature values and operations allowed by the solver. The datasets we consider in this work containing integer and real values. For categorical feature values, an encoding needs to be performed. But this is frequently done by ML algorithms in data preprocessing step.

A threat to the internal validity is the high degree of randomness involved in the techniques. First, the classifiers considered here use randomized algorithms for generating models. Thus, in principle we might get varying number of test cases to unfairness when training *with the same classifier on exactly the same data set*. To ensure a *fair* comparison, all three approaches were always started with the same model as input (training of MUTs is external to testing). All three approaches randomly generate data instances (AEQUITAS and SG for test data and VBT for oracle data). In addition to that, VBT and SG use a decision tree training algorithm which itself involves randomness. To mitigate these threats, all experiments were performed 10 times and the results give the average over these 10 runs.

5   Related Work

We divide our discussion of related works in three parts. First, we discuss some works of fairness testing of predictive models, then mention some recent techniques for machine learning testing, and third discuss approaches using model inference in testing.

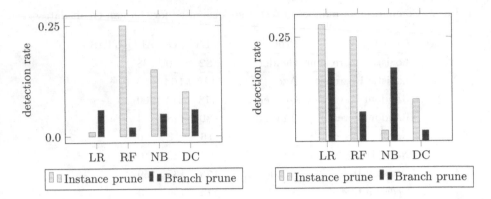

Fig. 7. Performance of data instance and branch pruning in computing individual discrimination for Adult (left) and Credit dataset (right)

Fairness Testing. There exists a number of works discussing testing fairness of ML models. Galhotra et al. first propose [8] black-box testing of predictive model for fairness. They introduce individual discrimination as a definition of fairness and give a confidence driven random testing technique to check it. They also experimentally show why the existing fairness definitions are not enough to detect discrimination in the ML model. However, their approach is less effective as they solely rely on random test case generation.

Later, Udeshi et al. propose AEQUITAS [20] for individual discrimination detection. It first randomly searches for discriminatory input test cases. Once such test cases have been found, it tries to generate more test cases by perturbing the initial ones. They propose an automated technique to use the generated test cases for retraining the given model and then obtaining a fair one.

Our approach is closest to the work of Aggarwal et al. [1]. They generate a path of a decision tree from the black-box model under test by using a tool called LIME. This tool generates a small decision tree for *local* explanations of the predictions given by the model. After generating such a *partial* decision tree, they use dynamic symbolic execution to generate multiple test cases violating *individual discrimination*. In contrast, we approximate the entire black-box model by a decision tree. We then compute the test inputs on this tree. Also, we cater for checking the predictive model with respect to several fairness definitions instead of just individual discrimination.

In a more recent work, Zhang et al. [24] propose a fairness testing technique for Deep Neural Networks (DNN). They focus on individual discrimination by generating test cases through adversarial sampling. Like AEQUITAS, they also operate in two phases. Although their approach outperforms existing fairness testing approaches, they perform a white-box testing technique, hence are limited to DNNs.

Validating Models. There exists a number of recent works which aim at validating properties of predictive models. One such important property of an ML model is *robustness*. In [10], Huang et al. first propose this as a safety property and give a verification technique showing that a Deep Neural Network (DNN) guarantees postconditions to hold on its outputs when the inputs satisfy a given precondition. Pei et al. [15] later propose the first white-box testing technique based on differential testing approach to test DNNs for *robustness*. Sun et al. [19] propose a concolic testing approach to test DNNs.

In a very recent work, Lee et al. [11] propose a white-box testing technique for DNNs to generate test cases for checking *robustness*. They use an online algorithm to select the relevant neurons during the testing process and thus do not rely on a fixed strategy of selecting neurons for coverage. The experimental results show the effectiveness of their approach across diverse DNN models.

Recently, Sharma et al. [18] have proposed a property called *balancedness* on the learning algorithm. They perform specific transformations on the training data and check whether the learning algorithm generates a different predictive model after applying such transformations. Instead of checking the predictive model, this work focuses on testing the learning algorithm. A survey of different important properties arising in Machine Learning and their validation techniques can be found in [23].

Testing via Model Inference. The inference of a decision tree describing the behaviour of software has already been pursued by Papadopoulos and Walkinshaw [14] as well as Briand et al. [2].

The former work is related to ours as it also translates the decision tree to logical formula in Z3. However, they do not use the tree to compute counter examples to the property to be tested. Instead, they use Z3 to generate test inputs covering different branches of the tree. Our approach on the other hand use the white-box model to generate targeted test inputs by using an established verification technique. Briand et al. use the decision tree in a semi-automated approach to the re-engineering of test suites. This approach requires the manual inspection of the decision tree by testers.

6 Conclusion

In this work, we have proposed a novel approach to test ML model for a user given fairness property. Our technique approximates the black-box model by a white-box model and then applies SMT solving techniques to compute fairness. It allows the user to specify the required fairness constraint herself, and with this goes beyond current fairness testing with hardcoded requirements.

We have evaluated the effectiveness of our approach by applying it to several ML models and found our approach to perform better than the existing fairness testing approaches in testifying a particular type of fairness in a large number of cases.

As future work, we plan to apply this scheme to validate other important properties of ML models. Our white-box model easily allows for checking other properties, like for instance robustness, just by applying a different check on the generated SMT code. Also, we would like to improve our framework by incorporating additional techniques to check statistical measures of fairness.

References

1. Aggarwal, A., Lohia, P., Nagar, S., Dey, K., Saha, D.: Black box fairness testing of machine learning models. In: Proceedings of the ACM Joint Meeting on European Software Engineering Conference and Symposium on the Foundations of Software Engineering, ESEC/SIGSOFT FSE, pp. 625–635 (2019). https://doi.org/10.1145/3338906.3338937
2. Briand, L.C., Labiche, Y., Bawar, Z., Spido, N.T.: Using machine learning to refine category-partition test specifications and test suites. Inf. Softw. Technol. **51**(11), 1551–1564 (2009). https://doi.org/10.1016/j.infsof.2009.06.006
3. Calders, T., Kamiran, F., Pechenizkiy, M.: Building classifiers with independency constraints. In: ICDM Workshops 2009, IEEE International Conference on Data Mining Workshops, Miami, Florida, USA, 6 December 2009, pp. 13–18 (2009). https://doi.org/10.1109/ICDMW.2009.83
4. Carlini, N., Wagner, D.A.: Towards evaluating the robustness of neural networks. In: 2017 IEEE Symposium on Security and Privacy, SP, pp. 39–57 (2017). https://doi.org/10.1109/SP.2017.49
5. Chouldechova, A.: Fair prediction with disparate impact: a study of bias in recidivism prediction instruments. Big Data **5**(2), 153–163 (2017). https://doi.org/10.1089/big.2016.0047
6. Claessen, K., Hughes, J.: QuickCheck: a lightweight tool for random testing of Haskell programs. In: ICFP 2000, pp. 268–279 (2000). https://doi.org/10.1145/351240.351266
7. Dwork, C., Hardt, M., Pitassi, T., Reingold, O., Zemel, R.S.: Fairness through awareness. In: Goldwasser, S. (ed.) Innovations in Theoretical Computer Science 2012, Cambridge, MA, USA, 8–10 January 2012, pp. 214–226. ACM (2012). https://doi.org/10.1145/2090236.2090255
8. Galhotra, S., Brun, Y., Meliou, A.: Fairness testing: testing software for discrimination. In: Proceedings of the 2017 11th Joint Meeting on Foundations of Software Engineering, pp. 498–510. ACM (2017)
9. Guidotti, R., Monreale, A., Ruggieri, S., Turini, F., Giannotti, F., Pedreschi, D.: A survey of methods for explaining black box models. ACM Comput. Surv. **51**(5), 93:1–93:42 (2019). https://doi.org/10.1145/3236009
10. Huang, X., Kwiatkowska, M., Wang, S., Wu, M.: Safety verification of deep neural networks. In: Majumdar, R., Kunčak, V. (eds.) CAV 2017. LNCS, vol. 10426, pp. 3–29. Springer, Cham (2017). https://doi.org/10.1007/978-3-319-63387-9_1
11. Lee, S., Cha, S., Lee, D., Oh, H.: Effective white-box testing of deep neural networks with adaptive neuron-selection strategy. In: ISSTA 2020: 29th ACM SIGSOFT International Symposium on Software Testing and Analysis, Virtual Event, USA, 18–22 July 2020, pp. 165–176. ACM (2020). https://doi.org/10.1145/3395363.3397346
12. Liptak, A.: Sent to prison by a software program's secret algorithms. https://nyti.ms/2qoe8FC. Accessed 01 May 2017
13. de Moura, L., Bjørner, N.: Z3: an efficient SMT solver. In: Ramakrishnan, C.R., Rehof, J. (eds.) TACAS 2008. LNCS, vol. 4963, pp. 337–340. Springer, Heidelberg (2008). https://doi.org/10.1007/978-3-540-78800-3_24

14. Papadopoulos, P., Walkinshaw, N.: Black-box test generation from inferred models. In: RAISE, pp. 19–24 (2015). https://doi.org/10.1109/RAISE.2015.11
15. Pei, K., Cao, Y., Yang, J., Jana, S.: DeepXplore: automated whitebox testing of deep learning systems. In: Proceedings of the 26th Symposium on Operating Systems Principles, pp. 1–18 (2017). https://doi.org/10.1145/3132747.3132785
16. Segura, S., Fraser, G., Sánchez, A.B., Cortés, A.R.: A survey on metamorphic testing. IEEE Trans. Softw. Eng. **42**(9), 805–824 (2016). https://doi.org/10.1109/TSE.2016.2532875
17. Sharma, A., Wehrheim, H.: Higher income, larger loan? Monotonicity testing of machine learning models. In: ISSTA 2020: 29th ACM SIGSOFT International Symposium on Software Testing and Analysis, Virtual Event, USA, pp. 200–210. ACM (2020). https://doi.org/10.1145/3395363.3397352
18. Sharma, A., Wehrheim, H.: Testing machine learning algorithms for balanced data usage. In: 12th IEEE Conference on Software Testing, Validation and Verification, ICST, pp. 125–135 (2019). https://doi.org/10.1109/ICST.2019.00022
19. Sun, Y., Wu, M., Ruan, W., Huang, X., Kwiatkowska, M., Kroening, D.: Concolic testing for deep neural networks. In: Proceedings of the 33rd ACM/IEEE International Conference on Automated Software Engineering, ASE, pp. 109–119 (2018). https://doi.org/10.1145/3238147.3238172
20. Udeshi, S., Arora, P., Chattopadhyay, S.: Automated directed fairness testing. In: Huchard, M., Kästner, C., Fraser, G. (eds.) Proceedings of the 33rd ACM/IEEE International Conference on Automated Software Engineering, ASE 2018, Montpellier, France, 3–7 September 2018, pp. 98–108. ACM (2018). https://doi.org/10.1145/3238147.3238165
21. Verma, S., Rubin, J.: Fairness definitions explained. In: International Workshop on Software Fairness, FairWare@ICSE, pp. 1–7 (2018). https://doi.org/10.1145/3194770.3194776
22. Zafar, M.B., Valera, I., Gomez Rodriguez, M., Gummadi, K.P.: Fairness constraints: mechanisms for fair classification. arXiv preprint arXiv:1507.05259 (2017)
23. Zhang, J.M., Harman, M., Ma, L., Liu, Y.: Machine learning testing: survey, landscapes and horizons. IEEE Trans. Softw. Eng. 1 (2020)
24. Zhang, P., et al.: White-box fairness testing through adversarial sampling. In: ICSE 2020: 42nd ACM SIGSOFT International Conference on Software Engineering, Virtual Event, South Korea. ACM (2020)

Inspecting Code Churns to Prioritize Test Cases

Francesco Altiero[ID], Anna Corazza[ID], Sergio Di Martino[(✉)][ID],
Adriano Peron[ID], and Luigi Libero Lucio Starace[ID]

University of Naples Federico II, Naples, Italy
{francesco.altiero,anna.corazza,sergio.dimartino,adriano.peron2,
luigiliberolucio.starace}@unina.it

Abstract. Within the context of software evolution, due to time-to-market pressure, it is not uncommon that a company has not enough time and/or resources to re-execute the whole test suite on the new software version, to check for non-regression. To face this issue, many Regression Test Prioritization techniques have been proposed, aimed at ranking test cases in a way that tests more likely to expose faults have higher priority. Some of these techniques exploit code churn metrics, i.e. some quantification of code changes between two subsequent versions of a software artifact, which have been proven to be effective indicators of defect-prone components. In this paper, we first present three new Regression Test Prioritization strategies, based on a novel code churn metric, that we empirically assessed on an open source software system. Results highlighted that the proposal is promising, but that it might be further improved by a more detailed analysis on the nature of the changes introduced between two subsequent code versions. To this aim, in this paper we also sketch a more refined approach we are currently investigating, that quantifies changes in a code base at a finer grained level. Intuitively, we seek to prioritize tests that stress more fault-prone changes (e.g., structural changes in the control flow), w.r.t. those that are less likely to introduce errors (e.g., the renaming of a variable). To do so, we propose the exploitation of the Abstract Syntax Tree (AST) representation of source code, and to quantify differences between ASTs by means of specifically designed Tree Kernel functions, a type of similarity measure for tree-based data structures, which have shown to be very effective in other domains, thanks to their customizability.

Keywords: Regression testing · Test prioritization · Code churn.

1 Introduction

Within the software maintenance, changes in the source code can introduce bugs and faults in the software, not only in the new features but also in already validated functionalities. In literature, this phenomenon is called *Software Regression. Regression Testing* is a set of activities aimed at providing confidence that

© IFIP International Federation for Information Processing 2020
Published by Springer Nature Switzerland AG 2020
V. Casola et al. (Eds.): ICTSS 2020, LNCS 12543, pp. 272–285, 2020.
https://doi.org/10.1007/978-3-030-64881-7_17

(I) the changed parts of the software behave as intended, and (II) the unchanged parts have not been adversely affected by modifications [1,13]. Although extensively used in industry, regression testing is challenging from both a process management and a resource management perspective, being extremely time consuming. This is especially true with novel software development methodologies, such as *Continuous Integration/Continuous Delivery*, where the rate of generation of new releases is very high [10]. As a consequence, many research efforts have been dedicated to propose different approaches for regression testing, with the general goal to reduce the amount of required testing efforts, while at the same time keeping a high confidence on the quality of the software, as reported in a recent survey on these techniques [19]. In the literature, the key strategies to reduce regression testing costs are:

1. Regression test selection - selecting subset of existing test cases to run on the modified software (e.g., [14,24]);
2. Regression test suite minimization - reducing the test suite size to a minimal subset, to maintain the same level of coverage as the original test suite;
3. Regression test suite prioritization - finding an ideal order of test cases according to some criteria, such that test cases with higher priority are executed earlier than ones with lower priority [18].

In this paper, we focus on the third scenario, by proposing three test suite prioritization strategies, able to meaningfully combine traditional code coverage metrics with the concept of *code churn*, a metric used in software engineering to measure the amount of code changes taking place within a software unit over the time [23]. We investigate the use of code churns for testing, since many studies have found that parts of software with higher churn exhibit also higher defect density (e.g.: [23,32]), but, to the best of our knowledge, this metric has never been significantly exploited to prioritize regression tests. We then evaluated the effectiveness of the proposed test prioritization strategies against a widely adopted strategy as a baseline, i.e. the total coverage prioritization, on an open source software system, showing promising results.

Moreover, we also sketch a novel approach which analyses the nature of the code churn, that we believe could further improve the performance of the proposed strategies. In detail, in presence of code modifications, we aim at giving higher priority to tests that stress the more changes being potentially more fault-prone (e.g., structural changes in the control flow), w.r.t. those that are less likely to introduce errors (e.g., the renaming of a variable). To do so, we propose the exploitation of the Abstract Syntax Tree (AST) representation of source code, and to quantify differences between ASTs by means of specifically designed *Tree Kernel* functions, a type of similarity measure for tree-based data structures, which turned out to be very effective in other ICT/software engineering domains (e.g. [3]), thanks to their customizability.

The paper is organized as follows. In Sect. 2 we present an overview of the state-of-the-art in test prioritization, whereas in Sect. 3 we formalize the proposed prioritization strategies. In Sect. 4, we report on the empirical study we conducted to assess the effectiveness of the proposed strategies, and discuss the results of this experiment. In Sect. 5, we sketch the new churn quantification approach we are currently investigating. At last, in Sect. 6, we draw our conclusions.

2 Related Works

With recent software development processes, like Continuous Deployment, the software codebase is updated very often, and these changes should be readily deployed to the customers. In this scenario, regression testing is a critical issue, as the re-execution of the whole test suite, for each new revision, may be too costly/time consuming. A common solution to this problem involves the use of *regression test prioritization* approaches [15,28], which aim at permuting the test suite of a software system, with the goal to give higher priority to tests with higher chance to find faults. In this scenario, in presence of time constraints, a project manager can choose to re-execute only the n most relevant test cases. A lot of research efforts have been spent in this direction (e.g., see survey [35]). Research efforts have been also devoted to defining metrics to quantify and compare the rates of fault detection of test suites [7,8]. Another class of related papers deals with prioritization techniques that are driven by requirements with higher priority, or operate in the presence of time constraints [20,33]. The application of Genetic Algorithms to determine the most effective test order has also been leveraged in different research studies, as in [16,31].

Coverage-based test case prioritization techniques are among the most widely studied approaches for regression test prioritization, as stated in [19]. These techniques aim to rank test cases according to the amount of coverage on source code they provide, considering either block coverage, decision (branch) coverage or statement coverage. A comparison of search algorithms for coverage-based regression test prioritization has been performed in [21]. A case study of several coverage-based regression test prioritization techniques on a real-world complex industrial system which includes real regression faults has been presented in [5].

Two main strategies are employed in coverage-based regression test prioritization, namely the *total* strategy and *additional* strategy [11]. *Total* strategy ranks test cases according to how much they contribute to increment the overall coverage, while *additional* strategy considers the increment of coverage supplied by a test case only on source code which was not covered by the execution of any prior test case. [12] presented a NP-hard *optimal* strategy to maximize the *average percentage of branch covered* metric (see [21]) as intermediate goal, showing that it performs worse than *additional* strategy to the ultimate goal of detecting faults.

There were previous works which exploited the combination of code coverage analysis along with change impact analysis. For example, [17] experimentally applied a procedure-level coverage regression test based on change-based test selection methods to *WebKit*,[1] an open source web browser engine project.

---

[1] https://webkit.org/.

Approaches for particular types of applications (such as for software product lines [30]) or testing strategies (e.g., model-based testing [25]) have also been introduced, as well as the use of techniques from different application domains (e.g., information retrieval ones [29]). These approaches have been employed, for example, to address coverage profiling overhead (in terms of time and space) and potential problems associated with the imprecision of static program analysis.

Several studies investigated methods to improve regression testing in Continuous Integration (CI) development environments, as analyzed in [26], which detected history-based regression test prioritization techniques as the mainly adopted approaches in CI environments. In particular, the work in [10] has introduced two regression testing techniques (for testing selection and prioritization, respectively) which use readily available test suite execution history data to determine what tests are worth executing and executing with higher priority.

3   The Proposed Prioritization Strategies

In this section, we introduce the necessary notation and concepts, and then formalize the churn-based prioritization strategy we propose.

3.1   Preliminary Definitions

In the test case prioritization problem, given a test suite $\mathcal{TS}$ over a current software version V, the goal is to find an ordering of the tests in $\mathcal{TS}$ that maximizes the regression fault-revealing capability over time of the tests on the next version of the software V' [12]. In the prioritization framework we formalize in this section, we assume that a reference *structural code unit* (e.g., statements, branches, methods), with respect to which coverage and churn metrics are evaluated, has been selected.

Given two subsequent versions V and V', the code churn between them captures the information about the amount of structural code units that were altered between the two versions. More formally, we encode the code churn between V and V' using two functions: $changed_V$, and $deleted_V$. These functions assign to each structured code unit in V a boolean value with the following semantics. For each structured code unit s in V, $changed_V(s)$ (resp., $deleted_V(s)$) is true iff s is changed (resp., deleted) in the next version V', and false otherwise.

Moreover, given a test case $t \in \mathcal{TS}$, we define $CovTest_V(t)$ as the set of structural code units that are covered by the execution of t.

To represent the coverage contribution of a test case t in a way that also takes into account churn information, we introduce the concept of *churn coverage* as follows.

For a test case t, the corresponding churn coverage $ChurnCov_V(t)$ is the triple $\langle c, d, u \rangle$, where:

- c is the number of structural code units covered by the test case t which are changed in the next version. More formally,

$$c = |\{s \in CovTest_V(t) \mid changed_V(s)\}|;$$

– d counts the number of structural code units, covered by the test case t, which have been deleted in the next version. According to our formalization,

$$d = |\{s \in CovTest_V(V) \mid deleted_V(s)\}|;$$

– u is the number of structural code units that are covered by t and remain unchanged in the next version, i.e. $u = |CovTest_V(V)| - (c + d)$.

3.2 The Proposed Ranking Strategies

By introducing suitable ordering criteria for tests in a way that takes into account churn coverage information, it is possible to define different churn-based prioritization strategies.

In what follows, we start by re-defining the total coverage prioritization strategy, which we will use as a baseline for our experiments, and then we propose three definitions of the $\preceq$ ordering relation leveraging churn coverage increments information, to instantiate different prioritization strategies.

Baseline Strategy: Total Coverage
As for the baseline strategy, we consider the *total coverage prioritization*, which is based on the definition of *total structural code unit coverage prioritization*, provided by [27]. This strategy takes into account the total coverage provided by a test case and ranks tests decreasingly according to this measure. Thus, it relies only on coverage information and does not consider churns at all.

The ordering $\preceq_{Tot}$ which realizes this strategy is defined as follows. Given two tests t and t', with $ChurnCov_V(t) = \langle c, d, u \rangle$ and $ChurnCov(t') = \langle c', d', u' \rangle$, it holds that

$$t \preceq_{Tot} t' \text{ iff } c + d + u \le c' + d' + u'.$$

Strategy 1: Prioritize Churn
The *prioritize churn* strategy prioritizes tests based on their coverage of changed and deleted structural code units. This strategy assigns a higher priority to test cases which cover little outside of the code units which have been altered (i.e. changed or deleted), and is derived from the *specific strategy* defined in [17]. The ordering $\preceq_{Churn}$ which implements the *prioritize changed* strategy is defined as follows. Given two tests t and t', with $ChurnCov(t) = \langle c, d, u \rangle$ and $ChurnCov(t') = \langle c', d', u' \rangle$, it holds that

$$t \preceq_{Churn} t' \text{ iff } \frac{d + c}{d + c + u} \le \frac{d' + c'}{d' + c' + u'}.$$

Strategy 2: Prioritize Unchanged
In a symmetric manner w.r.t. the *prioritize churn* strategy, the *prioritize unchanged* strategy aims at prioritizing tests covering more unchanged structural code units. This strategy is inspired by the *General strategy* defined in [17]. Intuitively, this ordering ranks test cases according to the ratio of unchanged statements a test case covers on the total number of its covered statements.

Using churn coverage information to formalize the principles of this strategy, we define the ordering $\preceq_{Unch}$ as follows. Given two tests t and t', with $ChurnCov_V(t) = \langle c, d, u \rangle$ and $ChurnCov_V(t) = \langle c', d', u' \rangle$, it holds that

$$t \preceq_{Unch} t' \text{ iff } \frac{u}{c + d + u} \leq \frac{u'}{c' + d' + u'}.$$

Strategy 3: Combined Approach

In the third approach, we propose a *combined* strategy, which selects first test cases covering more changed parts of the product, and then test cases guaranteeing the highest coverage of the unchanged parts.

Intuitively, this strategy first considers tests covering at least one changed structural code unit, ranking them according to the number of covered changed units, and then focuses on the remaining tests, ranking them according to their overall coverage.

More formally, given two tests t and t', with $ChurnCov_V(t) = \langle c, d, u \rangle$ and $ChurnCov_V(t') = \langle c', d', u' \rangle$ the ordering $\preceq_{Comb}$ realizing this strategy is defined as follows:

$$t \preceq_{Comb} t' \text{ iff one of the following is satisfied:}$$

1. $(c' + d') - (c + d) > 0$;
2. $\mid (c + d) - (c' + d') \mid = 0$ and $u \leq u'$.

4   Empirical Evaluation of the Proposed Strategies

In this section we present the design of the empirical study we performed to assess the effectiveness of the proposed strategies to prioritize test cases, and then discuss the results of our evaluation.

4.1   Experimental Protocol

The goal of our investigation is to assess the effectiveness of the proposed prioritization strategies (see Sect. 3), using the standard total code coverage approach as a baseline. To this aim, we first realized a toolchain implementing the three proposed strategies (plus the baseline), evaluating churns at method level. An high-level architectural representation of this solution is shown in Fig. 1.

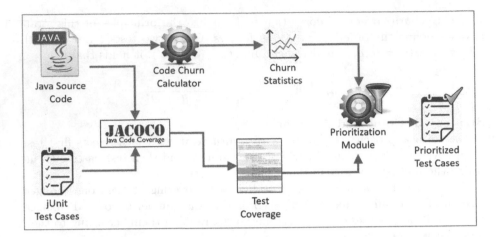

Fig. 1. Architecture of the developed solution to prioritize test cases.

The solution computes, for the various versions of a software product, statistics on code coverage of the test suites and code churn. In particular, test coverage information is obtained by JaCoCo, a widely used open source library for measuring and reporting Java code coverage.[2] Churn statistics at method level are computed by a tool we specifically developed, based on the metrics calculated by the SonarQube tool.[3] Then, a Prioritization Module takes in input the metrics obtained by Jacoco and the Code Churn Calculator, to rank test cases. We developed multiple versions of the Prioritization module, in order to implement the various strategies described in the previous section.

As *Object* of the experiments, we used a Java project often employed in software engineering empirical studies, namely *Siena* (Scalable Internet Event Notification Architecture). It is a scalable publish/subscribe event notification middleware for distributed applications [2], and is also available within the SIR repository [6], which contains software-related artifacts meant to support rigorous controlled software engineering experiments. We considered eight subsequent versions of *Siena*, the latest of which included 26 classes corresponding to 6035 lines-of-code, and 567 test cases. In Table 1, we detail, for each of the considered versions, the total number of lines-of-code, and the coverage percentage achieved by the whole test suite. Moreover, in Table 2 we report code churn information between the subsequent versions we considered.

As for the *experimental protocol*, we used our solution to prioritize test cases in the Siena test suite, for each pair of consecutive versions, and measured the relative *coverage profit* for each of the test cases. More formally, given a prioritized test suite $\langle t_1, \ldots, t_n \rangle$, and an index $i \in [1, \ldots, n]$, we define the relative coverage profit up to the i-th test in the prioritized test suite as follows:

---

[2] The JaCoCo tool can be obtained freely at http://www.eclemma.org/jacoco/.

[3] The SonarQube tool can be obtained freely at https://www.sonarqube.org/.

Table 1. Size and coverage statistics for the considered versions of Siena.

Version	Total lines of code	Covered lines of code
V_0	11384	46%
V_1	11343	30%
V_2	11349	29%
V_3	11423	29%
V_4	11471	46%
V_5	11471	47%
V_6	11426	46%

Table 2. Churn metrics for Siena.

Versions	Changed methods	Deleted methods	Unchanged methods
$V_0 \rightarrow V_1$	2	9	185
$V_1 \rightarrow V_2$	1	0	186
$V_2 \rightarrow V_3$	3	0	240
$V_3 \rightarrow V_4$	1	0	252
$V_4 \rightarrow V_5$	3	0	251
$V_5 \rightarrow V_6$	1	1	252
$V_6 \rightarrow V_7$	9	4	241

$$CovProfit(i) = \frac{\left| \bigcup_{j=1}^{i} CovTest(t_j) \right|}{\left| \bigcup_{j=1}^{n} CovTest(t_j) \right|},$$

where $CovTest(t)$ represents the set of bytecode-level instructions covered by the execution of the test case t.

4.2 Results and Discussion

The results of our experiment show that the combination of code coverage and churn metrics to prioritize test cases is leading to interesting results, especially when used between two software versions with consistent churns. In particular, for versions V_6 and V_7 of Siena, which exhibit the higher churn, with 9 changed methods and 4 deleted ones (see Table 2), the churn-based strategies remarkably outperform the baseline, as indicated by the decisively more rapidly growing relative profits curves we report in Fig. 2. In particular, the two strategies that emphasize churn coverage, namely *prioritize churn* and *combined* perform sensibly better than the others. For software versions with smaller churns, on the other hand, the differences were less remarkable, with the churn-based strategies only slightly outperforming the baseline.

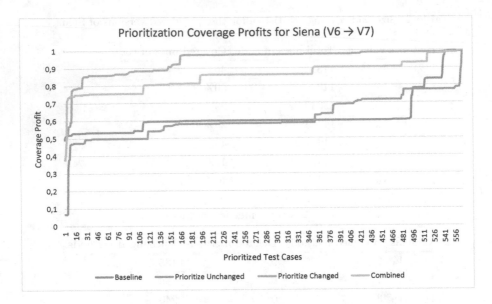

Fig. 2. Coverage profits of the considered strategies for Siena versions V_6 to V_7.

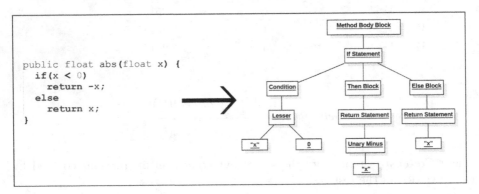

Fig. 3. A Java method and an example of the *Abstract Syntax Tree* of its body block.

Even though our churn-based strategies have proved themselves to be promising, we believe that they could be further improved by taking into account not only the fact that a given structural unit of code changed, but also the nature of said change. Indeed, it is reasonable to assume that not all the changes in source code have the same probability of introducing new faults. For example, one could argue that a refactoring operation, like a simple renaming of a local variable in a method, is less likely to introduce new faults, whereas significant control flow changes such as the update of a stopping condition in an iteration construct are more likely to introduce faults. To capture this intuition, in the next section we sketch a more refined approach we are currently investigating, that quantifies changes in a code-base at a finer grained level, discriminating between more and less significant changes. Intuitively, this new approach could allow us to prioritize tests that stress more fault-prone changes, w.r.t. those that are less likely to introduce errors.

5   A Novel Strategy to Measure Code Churns

The code churn definition we proposed in Sect. 3 quantifies the amount of changed, unchanged and deleted code between versions, at method granularity level. A more refined strategy for regression test prioritization could also take into account the *nature* of code changes, ranking test cases according to their coverage on altered code which is more likely to introduce faults.

To quantify and weight the amount of changes between two versions of a software project, we propose the evaluation of similarity between the *Abstract Syntax Trees* (*ASTs*) representation of their source code, using *Tree Kernel* functions.

*AST*s are a structured representation of source code, widely employed in many scenarios, like for example in compilers. They have also been widely and profitably used in software engineering, e.g., for *code clone detection* [3,34]. An *AST* is a tree-based representation of source code, whose inner nodes represent constructs of the programming language and leaf nodes are related to *tokens* (i.e., variable and method names, literals) appearing in a source code fragment. The topological relations between nodes establish the context of statements and expressions. A *label* is assigned to each node: inner nodes are labeled with information about the particular type of construct they model, while leaf nodes are labeled with the sequence of characters of their token. In Fig. 3, an example of an *AST* of a source code fragment in the Java language is depicted.

Tree Kernel functions are a particular family of *kernel* functions which specifically evaluate similarity between two tree objects. They have been extensively studied in tasks of *Machine Learning* and *Natural Language Processing* [22]. *Tree Kernels* assess the similarity of two tree structures taking into account both the topological information and the labels of their respective nodes, and are typically highly customizable according to a set of specific parameters, allowing them to be tailored to meet different needs in the application domain. A prior approach to evaluate similarity of source code using *AST* and *Tree Kernels* can be found in [3], where a similar technique was applied to *code clone detection*, with profitable results.

Similarity between *AST*s of source code can be used to obtain information about the amount and magnitude of changes in two subsequent versions of a software. These information can be included into code churn in order to support the ranking of test cases for regression test prioritization. To this purpose, we plan to model source code using a suitably defined *AST* representation, and to evaluate similarity between two structured code units of subsequent software versions by comparing the corresponding pair of *AST*s, by means of a specifically-designed *Tree Kernel* function, which can be normalized to produce a similarity score ξ in the range $[0, 1]$. Diversity could be evaluated as well by subtracting this similarity score from 1, i.e., $1 - \xi$.

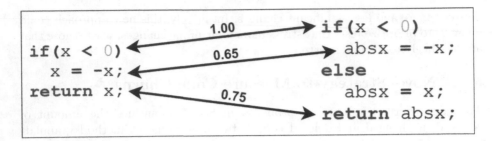

Fig. 4. An example of similarity scores evaluated by a *Tree Kernel* function at statement granularity level.

Figure 4 shows an example of normalized scores provided by a *Tree Kernel* for corresponding statements in two versions of a source code fragment.

To include similarity measures in the code churn, we extend the notation defined in Sect. 3. In particular, we characterize a code churn w.r.t. two subsequent versions V and V' not only by means of the *changed$_V$* and the *deleted$_V$* functions, but also with a new diversity function *diversity$_V$*. This function assigns to each structured code unit in V a diversity score in the range $[0, 1]$. In particular, deleted units are evaluated to 1, since there is no corresponding unit in the next version to which they can be compared. Similarly, unchanged units are evaluated to 0, as the diversity clearly is minimal in this case. In the other cases, i.e., when s changes in the next version, the score reflects the magnitude of the change.

With this new function in place, it is possible to re-define the churn coverage of a given test t, namely $ChurnCov_V(t) = \langle c, d, u \rangle$, in a way that takes into account the diversity score information. In the new churn coverage object, d and u are computed as described in Sect. 3, while c can be taken as the sum of the diversity scores in the code units covered by the test case. More formally,

$$c = \sum_{s \in Ch_V(t)} diversity_V(s),$$

with $Ch(t)$ being the set of structured code units covered by t which are changed in the next version.

6   Conclusions and Future Works

In this work, we proposed three prioritization strategies leveraging not only test coverage, but also the notion of code churn, i.e., information about which structural code units changed between two subsequent versions of a software. Intuitively, the parts of code that changed between two software versions are those that require to be tested with higher priority, w.r.t. unchanged parts which have already been tested. Indeed, code churns have been proven to be an effective indicator of defect-prone components.

We assessed the effectiveness of the proposed prioritization strategies by conducting an empirical study on a well-known open source software system, namely *Siena*. To do so, we implemented a prioritization solution consisting in both open source software and tools we specifically developed, and used this solution to prioritize the tests in the Siena test suite for 7 pairs of subsequent versions. As a baseline for our evaluation, we considered the well-known total coverage prioritization approach, which has been used in several other studies and does not take into account churn information. The promising results of our evaluation showed that the proposed strategies that prioritize the coverage of changed parts significantly outperform the baseline strategy in the version pairs in which there is a significant amount of changed parts. For prioritization tasks in which there is only a small amount of changed parts between versions, the results were inconclusive, and the churn-based strategies performed only slightly better than the baseline.

Moreover, we sketched a more refined approach to the evaluation of code churns, employing Abstract Syntax Trees to model the considered structured code units, and suitably-designed tree kernel functions to evaluate the degree of similarity between subsequent versions of a given unit. This approach is able to capture not only the fact that a given structured code unit changed or not, but also the nature of said change. Intuitively, we believe that not all changes have the same likelihood of introducing new faults, and thus this novel approach we are currently investigating could further improve the effectiveness of the proposed strategies.

In future works, we plan to extend our empirical evaluation by considering more software versions and additional coverage metrics, such as APSC [21]. Moreover, we plan to implement the novel churn quantification approach we sketched in this paper, and to conduct new empirical evaluations involving a greater number of software systems, considering evaluation metrics which measure fault-detection rate, such as the widely-used *APFD* metric [9]. Furthermore, we will explore the possibility of using our tree kernel-based approach to evaluate similarity between different graphical user interfaces (GUIs), which can also be represented with a tree-like structure (e.g.: xml layout, html documents). This could lead to the development of more advanced automatic GUI testing tools, which we could then evaluate as in [4].

References

1. Baresi, L., Pezzè, M.: An introduction to software testing. Electron. Notes Theor. Comput. Sci. **148**, 89–111 (2006). Elsevier
2. Carzaniga, A., Rosenblum, D.S., Wolf, A.L.: Achieving scalability and expressiveness in an internet-scale event notification service. In: Proceedings of ACM Symposium on Principles of Distributed Computing, PODC 2000, pp. 219–227. ACM, New York (2000)
3. Corazza, A., Di Martino, S., Maggio, V., Scanniello, G.: A tree kernel based approach for clone detection. In: 2010 IEEE International Conference on Software Maintenance, pp. 1–5. IEEE (2010)

4. Di Martino, S., Fasolino, A.R., Starace, L.L.L., Tramontana, P.: Comparing the effectiveness of capture and replay against automatic input generation for android graphical user interface testing. Softw. Test. Verif. Reliab. (2020). https://doi.org/10.1002/stvr.1754

5. Di Nardo, D., Alshahwan, N., Briand, L., Labiche, Y.: Coverage-based regression test case selection, minimization and prioritization: a case study on an industrial system. Softw. Test. Verif. Reliab. **25**, 371–396 (2015). https://doi.org/10.1002/stvr.1572. John Wiley and Sons Ltd

6. Do, H., Elbaum, S.G., Rothermel, G.: Supporting controlled experimentation with testing techniques: an infrastructure and its potential impact. Empir. Softw. Eng.: Int. J. **10**(4), 405–435 (2005)

7. Elbaum, S., Malishevsky, A.G., Rothermel, G.: Prioritizing test cases for regression testing. In: Proceedings of International Symposium on Software Testing and Analysis, ISSTA 2000, pp. 102–112. ACM (2000)

8. Elbaum, S.G., Malishevsky, A.G., Rothermel, G.: Incorporating varying test costs and fault severities into test case prioritization. In: Proceedings of ICSE, pp. 329–338. IEEE Computer Society (2001)

9. Elbaum, S.G., Malishevsky, A.G., Rothermel, G.: Test case prioritization: a family of empirical studies. IEEE Trans. Softw. Eng. **28**(2), 159–182 (2002)

10. Elbaum, S.G., Rothermel, G., Penix, J.: Techniques for improving regression testing in continuous integration development environments. In: Proceedings of FSE, pp. 235–245. ACM (2014)

11. Hao, D., Zhang, L., Zhang, L., Rothermel, G., Mei, H.: A unified test case prioritization approach. ACM Trans. Softw. Eng. Methodol. **24**(2), 10:1–10:31 (2014)

12. Hao, D., Zhang, L., Zang, L., Wang, Y., Wu, X., Xie, T.: To be optimal or not in test-case prioritization. IEEE Trans. Softw. Eng. **42**(5) (2016). https://doi.org/10.1109/TSE.2015.2496939

13. Harrold, M.J., et al.: Regression test selection for Java software. In: Proceedings of ACM SIGPLAN Conference on Object-Oriented Programming, Systems, Languages, and Applications, OOPSLA 2001, pp. 312–326. ACM (2001)

14. Harrold, M.J., Rosenblum, D.S., Rothermel, G., Weyuker, E.J.: Empirical studies of a prediction model for regression test selection. IEEE Trans. Softw. Eng. **27**(3), 248–263 (2001)

15. Hemmati, H.: Advances in techniques for test prioritization. Adv. Comput. **112**, 185–221 (2019). https://doi.org/10.1016/bs.adcom.2017.12.004

16. Huang, Y.C., Peng, K.L., Huang, C.Y.: A history-based cost-cognizant test case prioritization technique in regression testing. J. Syst. Softw. **85**(3), 626–637 (2012)

17. Jasz, J., Lango, L., Gyimothy, T., Gergely, T., Beszedes, A., Schrettner, L.: Code coverage-based regression test selection and prioritization in WebKit. In: Proceedings of International Conference on Software Maintenance, ICSM 2012, pp. 46–55. IEEE Computer Society (2012)

18. Kaushik, N., Salehie, M., Tahvildari, L., Li, S., Moore, M.: Dynamic prioritization in regression testing. In: 2011 IEEE Fourth International Conference on Software Testing, Verification and Validation Workshops (ICSTW), pp. 135–138 (2011)

19. Khatibsyarbini, M., Isa, M.A., Jawawi, D.N., Tumeng, R.: Test case prioritization approaches in regression testing: a systematic literature review. Inf. Softw. Technol. **93**, 74–93 (2018)

20. Kim, J.M., Porter, A.: A history-based test prioritization technique for regression testing in resource constrained environments. In: Proceedings of ICSE, pp. 119–129. ACM (2002)

21. Li, Z., Harman, M., Hierons, R.: Search algorithms for regression test case prioritization. IEEE Trans. Softw. Eng. **33**(4), 225–237 (2007)
22. Moschitti, A.: Efficient convolution kernels for dependency and constituent syntactic trees. In: Fürnkranz, J., Scheffer, T., Spiliopoulou, M. (eds.) ECML 2006. LNCS (LNAI), vol. 4212, pp. 318–329. Springer, Heidelberg (2006). https://doi.org/10.1007/11871842_32
23. Nagappan, N., Ball, T.: Use of relative code churn measures to predict system defect density. In: Proceedings of the 27th International Conference on Software Engineering, 2005. ICSE 2005, pp. 284–292. IEEE (2005)
24. Nanda, A., Mani, S., Sinha, S., Harrold, M., Orso, A.: Regression testing in the presence of non-code changes. In: 2011 IEEE Fourth International Conference on Software Testing, Verification and Validation (ICST), pp. 21–30 (2011)
25. Ouriques, J., Cartaxo, E., Machado, P.: On the influence of model structure and test case profile on the prioritization of test cases in the context of model-based testing. In: 2013 27th Brazilian Symposium on Software Engineering (SBES), pp. 119–128 (2013)
26. Prado Lima, J.A., Vergilio, S.R.: Test case prioritization in continuous integration environments: a systematic mapping study. Inf. Softw. Technol. **121**, 106–268 (2020). https://doi.org/10.1016/j.infsof.2020.106268
27. Rothermel, G., Untch, R., Chu, C., Harrold, M.: Test case prioritization: an empirical study. In: Proceedings of the International Conference on Software Maintenance, pp. 179–188 (1999)
28. Rothermel, G., Untch, R.H., Chu, C., Harrold, M.J.: Prioritizing test cases for regression testing. IEEE Trans. Softw. Eng. **27**(10), 929–948 (2001)
29. Saha, R.K., Zhang, L., Khurshid, S., Perry, D.E.: An information retrieval approach for regression test prioritization based on program changes. In: ICSE (2015)
30. Sánchez, A.B., Segura, S., Cortés, A.R.: A comparison of test case prioritization criteria for software product lines. In: ICST, pp. 41–50. IEEE Computer Society (2014)
31. Sarro, F., Di Martino, S., Ferrucci, F., Gravino, C.: A further analysis on the use of genetic algorithm to configure support vector machines for inter-release fault prediction. In: Proceedings of the 27th Annual ACM Symposium on Applied Computing, pp. 1215–1220. ACM (2012)
32. Shin, Y., Meneely, A., Williams, L., Osborne, J.A.: Evaluating complexity, code churn, and developer activity metrics as indicators of software vulnerabilities. IEEE Trans. Softw. Eng. **37**(6), 772–787 (2011)
33. Srikanth, H., Banerjee, S., Williams, L., Osborne, J.A.: Towards the prioritization of system test cases. Softw. Test. Verif. Reliab. **24**(4), 320–337 (2014)
34. Ul Ain, Q., Haider Butt, W., Anwar, M.W., Azam, F., Maqbool, B.: A systematic review on code clone detection. IEEE Access **7**, 86121–86144 (2019). https://doi.org/10.1109/ACCESS.2019.2918202
35. Yoo, S., Harman, M.: Regression testing minimization, selection and prioritization: a survey. Softw. Test. Verif. Reliab. **22**(2), 67–120 (2012)

Short Contributions

Using an SMT Solver for Checking
the Completeness of FSM-Based Tests

Evgenii Vinarskii[1]([⊠]) [iD], Andrey Laputenko[2], and Nina Yevtushenko[3]

[1] Lomonosov Moscow State University, 1 Leninskiye Gory Street, 119991 Moscow, Russia
vinevg2015@gmail.com
[2] National Research Tomsk State University, 36 Lenin Ave., 634050 Tomsk, Russia
laputenko.av@gmail.com
[3] Ivannikov Institute for System Programming of the Russian Academy of Sciences,
25 Alexander Solzhenitsyn Street, 109004 Moscow, Russia
evtushenko@ispras.ru

Abstract. Deriving tests with guaranteed fault coverage by FSM-based test methods is rather complex for systems with a large number of states. At the same time, formal verification methods allow to effectively process large transition systems; in particular, SMT solvers are widely used to solve analysis problems for finite transition systems. In this paper, we describe the known necessary and sufficient conditions of completeness of test suites derived by FSM-based test methods via the first-order logic formulas and use an SMT solver in order to check them. In addition, we suggest a new sufficient condition for test suite completeness and check the corresponding first-order logic formula via the SMT solver. The results of computer experiments with randomly generated finite state machines confirm the correctness and efficiency of a proposed approach.

Keywords: FSM based testing · SMT solver · Fist order logic formulas

1 Introduction

Finite state machines (FSM) based test derivation is well-known in the software testing of communication protocols and other reactive systems [2–4,10]. In this case, the behavior of the specification as well as of an implementation under test (IUT) is modeled by a corresponding FSM and testing is performed for determining whether the implementation conforms to the specification. As the number of input sequences is infinite, different limitations are imposed for an implementation under test [2,7,10,11] when deriving finite tests with guaranteed fault coverage. One of the well known limitations is to assume that the number of states of an implementation FSM is not bigger than the number of states of the specification and methods for deriving such tests are developed for various kinds of FSMs, complete and partial, deterministic and non-deterministic as well as for various kinds of conformance relations [3,9,11].

Most methods are developed for initialized complete deterministic FSMs where the conformance means the equivalence. Despite the big number of derivatives of such

This work is partly supported by RFBR project No 18-01-00854.

© IFIP International Federation for Information Processing 2020
Published by Springer Nature Switzerland AG 2020
V. Casola et al. (Eds.): ICTSS 2020, LNCS 12543, pp. 289–295, 2020.
https://doi.org/10.1007/978-3-030-64881-7_18

methods the necessary and sufficient conditions for a finite test suite to be a complete test suite are still unknown.

The main idea when deriving a complete test suite, is to establish an isomorphic relationship between state sets of the specification and an implementation under test. For this purpose, so-called state identification sequences of the specification FSM are utilized [2,3,10,11], especially, distinguishing or separating sequences. Intuitively, a distinguishing sequence is a sequence that being applied at two different states provides different output sequences and, thus, for a deterministic machine, different states can be implicitly distinguished without their direct observation. In [2,3,7,10], it is shown that the use of distinguishing sequences allows constructing a complete rather reduced test suite without explicit enumeration of all implementations of the fault domain. However, as an example in [3] demonstrates, the conditions based on distinguishing sequences are not necessary. The idea of the example is to show that two implementation states still can be implicitly distinguished without applying distinguishing sequences at these states. Such distinguishing sequences can be applied at appropriate predecessors or successors of these states. Since this fact is difficult to express as an analytical feature, we turned our attention to the formal verification that now is widely used for checking appropriate properties of different kinds of discrete event and hybrid systems [4].

In this paper, we use the following steps to verify that a test suite TS is or is not complete, i.e., whether requested fault coverage is guaranteed: (1) Given necessary or sufficient conditions for the test suite completeness and a test suite TS, we represent the conditions as a first-order logic formula. If the formula is true, then the TS satisfies the conditions, and if the formula is false then the TS does not satisfy the conditions. (2) The formula satisfiability is checked by the Z3 solver [12]. In addition, we suggest a new sufficient condition for the test suite completeness, describe this condition via a first-order logic formula and check this formula via the Z3 solver. This formula becomes true for the example in [3], i.e., a considered test suite is complete according to this formula.

This paper is organized as follows. Sections 2 and 3 briefly describe finite state machines and properties of a test suite with guaranteed fault coverage as well as include first-order logic formulas for describing some necessary and sufficient conditions for the test suite completeness. Section 4 contains the preliminary experimental results of using Z3 solver for checking the test suite completeness and Sect. 5 concludes the paper.

2   Deriving Test Suites Using Finite State Machine Based Methods

The section briefly presents the preliminary concepts that are used in the paper. Most of the definitions are taken from [3,5].

In this paper, a *Finite State Machine* (FSM) is an initialized complete deterministic machine, i.e., a 6-tuple $\mathcal{M} = \langle S, I, O, \delta_{\mathcal{M}}, \lambda_{\mathcal{M}}, s_0 \rangle$ [5], where S is a finite set of states with the designated initial state s_0, I and O are finite *input* and *output* alphabets, $\delta_{\mathcal{M}} : S \times I \to S$ is the *next state* (or *transition*) function, $\lambda_{\mathcal{M}} : S \times I \to O$ is the *output* function. In the usual way, both functions are extended to input sequences. In this paper, we consider (initially) *connected* FSMs, i.e., we assume that each state is reachable from the initial state via an appropriate input sequence.

A set *SC* of input sequences is called a *state cover set* of FSM $\mathcal{M}$ if *SC* has the empty sequence ε and for each state s_i of *S*, there is an input sequence $\alpha \in SC$ that takes FSM $\mathcal{M}$ from the initial state to state s_i. If the FSM is connected then such a state cover set always exists. As usual, $seq' = seq.i$ specifies that a sequence seq' is the concatenation of sequences *seq* and *i* and *SC.I* is the set $\{seq.i \in I \mid seq \in SC\&i \in I\}$. A set *TC* of input sequences is a *transition cover set* if for each state $s \in S$ and each input $i \in I$ there exists sequence $seq \in TC$ such that $seq = seq_1.i$ where $\delta_{\mathcal{M}}(s_0, seq_1) = s$.

Given two complete deterministic FSMs $\mathcal{M}$ and $\mathcal{P}$ over the same input and output alphabets, two states s_i of $\mathcal{M}$ and p_j of $\mathcal{P}$ are *equivalent*, written $s_i \cong p_j$, if for each input sequence $\alpha \in I^*$ it holds that $\lambda_{\mathcal{M}}(s_i, \alpha) = \lambda_{\mathcal{P}}(p_j, \alpha)$. Otherwise, we say that states s_i and p_j are *distinguishable*, written $s_i \not\cong p_j$ [5]. FSMs $\mathcal{M}$ and $\mathcal{P}$ are *equivalent*, written $\mathcal{M} \cong \mathcal{P}$, (*distinguishable*, written $\mathcal{M} \not\cong \mathcal{P}$) if their initial states are equivalent (distinguishable). Given distinguishable states s_i of $\mathcal{M}$ and p_j of $\mathcal{P}$, an input sequence $\alpha \in I^*$ such that $\lambda_{\mathcal{M}}(s_i, \alpha) \neq \lambda_{\mathcal{P}}(p_j, \alpha)$ is said to *distinguish* states s_i and p_j, written $s_i \not\cong_\alpha p_j$. An input sequence that distinguishes the initial states of distinguishable FSMs $\mathcal{M}$ and $\mathcal{P}$ *distinguishes* FSMs $\mathcal{M}$ and $\mathcal{P}$, written $\mathcal{M} \not\cong_\alpha \mathcal{P}$. FSM $\mathcal{M}$ is *reduced* if each two different states s, s' of $\mathcal{M}$ are distinguishable. For each initialized complete deterministic FSM, there exists a reduced connected equivalent FSM [5] and in this paper, we assume that all the FSMs are connected and reduced unless the contrary is explicitly stated.

Let $\mathcal{M}$ be the specification FSM with *n* states, $n > 0$; a test suite *TS* is a finite set of finite input sequences of the specification FSM $\mathcal{M}$. Given an implementation FSM $\mathcal{P}$ over alphabets *I* and *O*, the FSMs $\mathcal{M}$ and $\mathcal{P}$ are *TS-equivalent* if for each input sequence of *TS*, the output responses of both machines coincide. A test suite *TS* is *n-complete* if, for each implementation $\mathcal{P}$ with at most *n* states that is distinguishable from $\mathcal{M}$, there exists a sequence in *TS* that distinguishes $\mathcal{M}$ and $\mathcal{P}$. In other words, in this paper, we assume that the number of states of an implementation FSM is not bigger than that of the specification. We now present some conditions when a test suite is or is not *n*-complete. Let $TS = \{\alpha_1, \ldots, \alpha_k\}$ be a test suite that is checked for the *n*-completeness where $\alpha_1, \ldots, \alpha_k$ are test sequences. One of the known necessary (Proposition 1) conditions for a test suite to be *n*-complete is to contain a state/transition cover of the specification FSM. Proposition 2 gives sufficient conditions for a test suite *TS* to be *n*-complete [3].

Proposition 1. *Given the complete deterministic reduced connected specification FSM* $\mathcal{M}$ *with n states and a test suite TS, if TS does not contain the state cover set SC (the transition cover set TC) of* $\mathcal{M}$, *then TS is not n-complete.*

Proposition 2. *Given the complete deterministic reduced connected specification FSM* $\mathcal{M}$ *with n states and a state cover set SC of* $\mathcal{M}$, *let TS be a finite set of finite input sequences of* $\mathcal{M}$ *that contains the set SC.I. The test suite TS is n-complete if the following conditions hold:*

1. *For each two different states of* $\mathcal{M}$ *there exist sequences* α *and* β *in SC such that TS has sequences* α.γ *and* β.γ *where* γ *is a distinguishing sequence of the states* $\delta_M(s_0, \alpha)$ *and* $\delta_M(s_0, \beta)$.
2. *For each sequence* α.i, α ∈ SC, *that takes the specification FSM* $\mathcal{M}$ *from* s_0 *to state s, TS has sequences* α.i.γ *and* β.γ, *where* β ∈ SC, $\delta_{\mathcal{M}}(s_0, \beta) \neq s$, *and* γ *is a distinguishing sequence of states s and* $\delta_{\mathcal{M}}(s_0, \beta)$.

According to Proposition 2, given a state s of $\mathcal{M}$, different state identification sequences can be used when checking incoming transitions to state s, i.e. distinguishing sequences for the ending state of a transition can be derived on-the-fly using already a constructed part of a test suite. Based on the above proposition the algorithm has been developed for deriving an n-complete test suite, called the *improved* H-method [3]. Note that since an implementation FSM has at most n states, the fulfillment of the first condition implies that an implementation under test has exactly n different states. However, the conditions of Proposition 2 are not necessary conditions for a test suite to be n-complete and this fact is illustrated by the example of the specification FSM in Fig. 1 taken from [3].

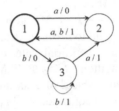

Fig. 1. The example of the specification FSM.

Consider a test suite $TS = \{raaa, rabb, rbaba, rbbab\}$. By direct inspection, one can assure that Proposition 2 does not hold, since states 2 and 3 that are reachable through sequences a and b are not distinguished with suffixes aa, bb and aba, bab. Nevertheless, if an implementation FSM $\mathcal{P}$ reaches the same state under input sequences a and b, then this machine reaches the same state under input sequences aa, ba and ab, bb. The latter means that $\mathcal{P}$ has four different responses to the set $\{a, b\}$ of input sequences and thus, the deterministic machine $\mathcal{P}$ has more than three states. This example shows that states of an IUT reached by two sequences of SC can be implicitly distinguished not only after applying a distinguishing sequence exactly at these states. This intuition leads to a new statement written as Proposition 3.

Proposition 3. *Given the reduced connected specification FSM $\mathcal{M}$ with n states and an FSM $\mathcal{P}$ with at most n states, let TS be a finite set of finite input sequences of $\mathcal{M}$ such that FSMs $\mathcal{M}$ and $\mathcal{P}$ are TS-equivalent. The FSMs $\mathcal{M}$ and $\mathcal{P}$ are equivalent if the following conditions hold:*

1. *For each state s and an input sequence α such that $\delta_{\mathcal{M}}(s_0, \alpha) = s$ there exist input sequences $\beta_1, \ldots, \beta_{n-1}$ such that all the states reached from the initial state p_0 in $\mathcal{P}$ via input sequences $\beta_1, \ldots, \beta_{n-1}$ are pair-wise different.*
2. *Given a sequence $\alpha.i, i \in I$, such that $\delta_{\mathcal{M}}(s_0, \alpha) = \delta_{\mathcal{M}}(s_0, \alpha.i) = s$, the states reached from the initial state p_0 in $\mathcal{P}$ via input sequences $\alpha, \beta_1, \ldots, \beta_{n-1}$ are pair-wise different.*
3. *Given a sequence $\alpha.i, i \in I$, such that $\delta_{\mathcal{M}}(s_0, \alpha.i) = \delta_{\mathcal{M}}(s_0, \beta_t) = s$ for $t \in \{1, \ldots, n-1\}$, the states reached from the initial state p_0 in $\mathcal{P}$ via input sequences $\alpha.i, \beta_1, \ldots, \beta_{t-1}, \beta_{t+1}, \ldots, \beta_{n-1}$ are pair-wise different.*

Sketch of the Proof. Indeed, if the condition (1) of the above proposition holds then there exists the one-to-one correspondence between sets of states of $\mathcal{M}$ and $\mathcal{P}$. The conditions (2) and (3) of the proposition show that this correspondence is valid for all transitions of $\mathcal{M}$.

Consider again the example in Fig. 1. Condition 1 of Proposition 3 holds for the state cover set ε, a, b due to the above comments. The final states of the transitions under inputs a and b from a state reached after applying input sequence a are different from states reached under input sequences of the set ε, b according to an input sequence a that distinguishes state 1 from states 2 and 3. The final states of the transitions under inputs a and b from a state reached after applying input sequence b are different from states reached under input sequences of the set ε, a according to input sequences ba and ab that distinguish state 1 from states 2 and 3, i.e., Conditions 2 and 3 of Proposition 3 also hold. Therefore, according to Proposition 3, the TS is a 3-complete test suite. We still do not know whether the conditions of Proposition 3 are necessary and sufficient conditions for the test suite completeness. However, this novel definition of determining different states of an implementation under test without using distinguishing sequences directly at these states, opens new directions to find sufficient (necessary and sufficient) conditions for the test suite completeness. In order to check the above properties, we use the Z3 solver which has already illustrated its effectiveness when solving formal verification problems.

3   First-Order Formulas and Complete Test Suites

In order to verify that appropriate properties hold for a given test suite (Propositions 1–3), we use first-order logic formulas. The notion of a first-order logic formula includes the notions of *predicate symbols*, *functional symbols* and *constants* [6]. Formally, a term $t ::= x \mid c \mid f(t, \ldots, t)$ where x ranges over a set of variables, c is a constant and f is a functional symbol. Then a first-order (quantified) logic formula is a formula $\varphi ::= P(t_1, \ldots, t_n) \mid (\neg \varphi) \mid (\varphi \wedge \varphi) \mid (\forall x \varphi) \mid (\exists x \varphi)$ where P is a predicate of arity $n \geq 1$ and t_i is a term over functional symbols and variables.

We now describe conditions for the test suite completeness of Propositions 1, 2, 3 via first-order logic formulas. Given FSM $\mathcal{M} = \langle S, I, O, \delta_{\mathcal{M}}, \lambda_{\mathcal{M}}, s_0 \rangle$, $|S| = n$, $TS = \{t_1, t_2, \ldots, t_m\}$ is a test suite for FSM $\mathcal{M}$, where t_j, $j \in \{1, 2, \ldots, m\}$, is a test sequence, with length $|t_j|$. Let $SS = \{\theta_1, \theta_2, \ldots, \theta_m\}$ ($OS = \{\zeta_1, \zeta_2, \ldots, \zeta_m\}$) be a set of sequences of states (sequences of outputs) which an FSM $\mathcal{M}$ passes when a corresponding test sequence is applied. For $j \in \{1, \ldots, m\}$ and $k \in \{1, \ldots, |t_j|\}$ we define a k-th element in a sequence t_j as t_j^k. Then the formula for Proposition 1 can be as follows: $\forall s \in S, i \in I, \exists j \in \{1, \ldots, m\}, \exists k \in \{1, \ldots, |t_j|\}((s = \theta_j^k) \wedge (i = t_j^k))$. This formula is described in python language and verified via Z3 solver. The corresponding source code is available in [8].

The formula for Proposition 2 is more complex (available in [8]) and we first describe the set of predicates for its simplification: (i) Predicate $sub\_seq(seq, TS)$ means that sequence $seq = a_1 \ldots a_k$ is a subsequence of some sequence t_j of TS; predicate $sub\_seq(seq, TS)$ can be expressed via first-order logic as follows: $\exists j \in \{1, \ldots, m\} \exists d \in \{1, \ldots, |t_j| - k\}((a_1 = t_j^d) \wedge \cdots \wedge (a_k = t_j^{d+k}))$. (ii) Predicate $reach(s_0, s, seq)$ means that state s is reached from state s_0 via sequence seq in FSM $\mathcal{M}$. (iii) Predicate $diff(s, s', seq)$ means that sequence seq is a distinguishing sequence for states s and s'. (iv) Predicate $home(s_0, s, seq, TS) = reach(s_0, s, seq) \wedge \forall s' \in S \, (s \neq s' \rightarrow \exists diff\_seq \in I^*$ $(sub\_seq(seq.diff\_seq, TS) \wedge diff(s, s', diff\_seq)))$ means that state s is reached from state s_0 via sequence seq in FSM $\mathcal{M}$ and for each state $s' \in S$, the test suite TS has a sequence which distinguishes states s and s'.

In addition, for each state s, we determine the set of all sequences of TS which take the specification FSM from the initial state to state s. If $S = \{s_0, \ldots, s_{n-1}\}$, then $SC_{s_j} = \{seq \in I^* \mid sub\_seq(seq, TS) \wedge reach(s_0, s_j, seq)\}$ for each $j \in \{0, \ldots, n-1\}$. For checking the conditions of Proposition 2 the following formula can be used: $\exists seq_0 \in SC_{s_0} \ldots \exists seq_{n-1} \in SC_{s_{n-1}} \, (home(s_0, s_0, seq_0, TS) \wedge \ldots \wedge home(s_0, s_{n-1}, seq_{s_{n-1}}, TS)) \wedge \forall j \in \{0, \ldots, n-1\} \wedge \forall i \in I \wedge \forall k \in \{0, \ldots, n-1\}((s_\ell = \delta_{\mathcal{M}}(s_0, seq_{s_j}.i) \wedge (\ell \neq k)) \rightarrow (\exists diff\_seq \in I^* \, (sub\_seq(seq_{s_j}.i.diff\_seq, TS) \wedge diff(s_\ell, s_k, diff\_seq))))$.

The formula for Proposition 3 is rather complex for the analytic description; the source code is available in [8]. The main idea of this formula is as follows. Consider the maximal subset of states $S' \subseteq S$ such that for each state $s \in S'$ there exists a sequence seq for which $home(s_0, s, seq, TS)$ is true and the non-empty subset S'' of states for which this does not hold. Let $s_\alpha \in S''$, $s_\beta \in S''$ be states reachable in $\mathcal{M}$ via sequences α and β. If the formula is satisfiable then the following holds: if an implementation under test passes the test suite TS and implementation states reachable via sequences α and β coincide, then the implementation has more than n states.

4   Experimental Results

In this section, we describe how fast the conditions of Propositions 1 and 2 can be checked when using the Z3 solver. Preliminary experiments were performed with randomly generated FSMs using FSM generator from the FSMTestOnline [1] web-service, which also allows deriving a complete test suite by various FSM-based methods. Experiments showcased that for each generated FSM and complete test suite each formula turned out to be satisfiable, as well as for an incomplete test suite the formula was unsatisfiable. For FSMs with 100 states and 8 inputs, the average time in seconds spent on checking the formula is 219.98 when the formula is satisfiable and 113.24 when the formula is unsatisfiable. The average time for checking the formula according to Proposition 2 was much bigger: for FSMs with five states and two inputs, the average time in seconds spent on checking the formula was 1203.01 when the formula is satisfiable and 18951.48 when the formula is unsatisfiable. For Proposition 3, the formula was checked only for the example of [3] where this formula was satisfiable illustrating that a considered test suite is 3-complete. To conduct experiments, a python script was developed that uses API for SMT solver Z3. The experiments were carried out using virtual machine with a AMD Ryzen 5 2500U CPU @ 2.0 GHz running OS GNU/Linux Ubuntu 16.04 with 7 GB RAM.

5 Conclusion

In this paper, we have described the known necessary or sufficient conditions for an FSM-based test suite to have guaranteed fault coverage via first-order logic formulas and checked these formulas using Z3 solver. In addition, we have suggested a new sufficient condition for the implicit distinguishability of implementation states. In the future, we are going to use this condition for deriving shorter complete test suites as well as for checking the completeness of a given test suite.

References

1. Test generation for finite state machine. http://www.fsmtestonline.ru/
2. Chow, T.S.: Test design modeled by finite-state machines. IEEE Trans. SE **4**(3), 178–187 (1978)
3. Dorofeeva, R., El-Fakih, K., Yevtushenko, N.: An improved conformance testing method. In: Wang, F. (ed.) FORTE 2005. LNCS, vol. 3731, pp. 204–218. Springer, Heidelberg (2005). https://doi.org/10.1007/11562436_16
4. Fujiwara, S., Bochmann, G., Khendek, F., Amalou, M., Ghedamsi, A.: Test selection based on finite state models. IEEE Trans. Softw. Eng. **17**, 591–603 (1991). https://doi.org/10.1109/32.87284
5. Gill, A.: Introduction to the Theory of Finite-State Machines. McGraw-Hill, New York (1962)
6. Huth, M., Ryan, M.: Logic in Computer Science: Modelling and Reasoning About Systems. Cambridge University Press, Cambridge (2004)
7. Koufareva, I., Dorofeeva, M.: A novel modification of W-method. Joint Bull. Novosibirsk Comput. **18**, 69–81 (2002)
8. Laputenko, A., Vinarskii, E.: Python scripts for z3 solver (2020). https://github.com/vinevg1996/ictss_2020
9. Petrenko, A., Yevtushenko, N., Lebedev, A., Das, A.: Nondeterministic state machines in protocol conformance testing, pp. 363–378 (1993)
10. Vasilevskii, M.P.: Failure diagnosis of automata, pp. 98–108. No. 4 (1973)
11. Yevtushenko, N., Petrenko, A.: Failure diagnosis of automata. No. 5 (1990)
12. Yurichev, D.: SAT/SMT by Example (2020)

Hacking Goals: A Goal-Centric Attack Classification Framework

Francesco Caturano, Gaetano Perrone, and Simon Pietro Romano[✉]

Department of Electrical Engineering and Information Technology,
University of Napoli Federico II, Via Claudio 21, 80125 Napoli, Italy
{francesco.caturano,gaetano.perrone,spromano}@unina.it

Abstract. Attack classification does represent a crucial activity in different security areas. During security assessment, it makes it easier to define which attacks must be performed. When conducting threat modeling activities, it simplifies the definition of attack graphs. Many works have addressed the attack taxonomy problem, by introducing different ways to classify attacks. However, these classifications are centered around vulnerabilities and have all been designed from the point of view of those defending a system. Nowadays, companies have a growing interest in Penetration Testing activities, as they have proven effective in detecting vulnerabilities. Penetration testers perform their activity by focusing on goals rather than attack types. In this paper we introduce a "goal-centric" methodology to classify attacks in terms of Hacking Goals.

1 Introduction

Attack Classification provides an important contribution in different security fields. According to [6], an attack classification approach can be leveraged to build secure systems, to identify vulnerabilities for which security defenses do not yet exist, to provide a uniform language for reporting incidents to response teams. These are all defense perspectives. There is also an offensive perspective that is used to detect vulnerabilities by simulating malicious activities. Such activities follow known methodologies, such as those mentioned in [4]. However, in the literature there are just a few contributions that try and formalize these methodologies.

This article proposes an attacker-centric methodology for attacks classification.

2 Setting the Scenario

Penetration Testing (PT) is the process of finding IT security vulnerabilities in a system, by emulating the behaviour of a malicious attacker. In black box PT, the team has no information about the target, and tries to sneak into the system by exploiting vulnerabilities. An introduction to PT tasks and tools can be found in [10]. Different phases can be identified:

© IFIP International Federation for Information Processing 2020
Published by Springer Nature Switzerland AG 2020
V. Casola et al. (Eds.): ICTSS 2020, LNCS 12543, pp. 296–301, 2020.
https://doi.org/10.1007/978-3-030-64881-7_19

- *Information Gathering*: in this phase the attacker finds publicly available information that can be used in subsequent phases, e.g., domain names, subnets owned by the target organization, systems that appear to be 'alive' in the network.
- *Scanning*: in this phase the attacker detects running TCP and UDP services exposed by the target hosts.
- *Enumeration*: in this phase the attacker enumerates running services. The goal here is to detect versions of running services and look for potential vulnerabilities;
- *Exploit*: when the attacker has detected vulnerabilities in the system, she/he tries to exploit them and get inside the target;
- *Post-Exploitation*: the attacker tries to obtain higher privileges and persistence inside hacked systems, and performs "lateral movement" activities to gain access to other internal systems.

Final deliverable of a PT activity is a detailed report, containing an executive summary, i.e., a synthesis of detected vulnerabilities, ordered by risk level.

3   Related Work

Many authors have defined methodologies to classify attacks in computer systems. Igure and Williams [6] give a formal definition of attack taxonomies and offer a complete overview of the existing ones. Authors suggest to create a layered taxonomy in order to provide an objective methodology to identify vulnerabilities. This is the most important hacking goal classification feature, as by using a goal-centric attack classification you need to focus on hacking goals dependencies. more intricate than that.

Common Attack Platform and Enumeration (CAPEC) [1] is a community resource for identifying and understanding attacks. It offers a search engine that allows users to search for specific attacks. The classification is very useful because it reports description and relationships between attacks. It describes prerequisites to perform an attack. CAPEC classifies attacks by using a target-centric approach, as some prerequisites depend on the target. When using an approach focused on hacking goals, prerequisites are instead "attacker-centric".

Kotenko and Doynikova [9] have created a generator of attack scenarios for network security evaluation. This is of interest to us, since a goal-centric classification allows simplifying the realization of attack graphs, while also defining a test result evaluation methodology.

Different authors have explored security testing by leveraging planning models. Obes et al. [7] show how is it possible to create a PDDL (Planning Domain Definition Language) representation of an attack model. PDDL contains interesting properties such as domain definition, action definition, preconditions required to perform an action and output of an action. Goal-centric classification can be used to define a hacking methodology, so it has a wider scope when compared to PDDL.

4   Hacking Goal

In this section we provide a formal definition of the proposed Hacking Goal classification, as illustrated in Fig. 1.

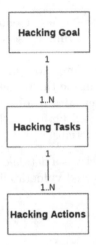

Fig. 1. Hacking Goal, Hacking Tasks and Hacking Actions relationships

A *Hacking Goal* is a macro objective that the attacker is going to achieve. An attacker performs different *Hacking Tasks* to fulfil her/his final goal. Depending on the chosen goal, the related hacking tasks metrics can change. A *Hacking Action* is a single action that an attacker executes while performing a specific hacking task. When the attacker performs Hacking Actions, she/he acquires knowledge about the target environment. For instance, when the attacker makes a TCP scan against a target, she/he "observes" which services are running on that target.

4.1   Hacking Task Properties

Table 1 summarizes the main properties of a Hacking Task, by also providing a short description for each of them.

With respect to Hacking Task metrics, they strongly depend on the specific Hacking Goal the task in question is associated with. Companies might, e.g., be interested in the effectiveness of their attack response strategies. In such a case, they carry out *Red Team* campaigns, that are an evolution of the Penetration Testing activity. While with standard Penetration Testing the target is aware of Penetration Testers attacks and purposefully disables security controls (since there's an interest in having vulnerabilities be disclosed), with Red Team scenarios the attacker needs to evade security controls and thus must necessarily

Table 1. Hacking Task properties

Property name	Property description
ID	An identifier. This can either be custom or refer to a standard Security Test classification methodology
Name	A name that helps understand what is the intent of the current hacking task
Description	A brief description of the hacking task
Prerequisites	A list of prerequisites that a hacking task must satisfy in order to be executed. Prerequisites might be the output of a previous hacking task
Dependencies	The list of hacking tasks that must be completed before the execution of the hacking task in question. For example, before trying an anonymous FTP login, the attacker should detect the presence of a running FTP service inside the system
Category	A phase of the ongoing security assessment (e.g., Enumeration, Scanning, Exploitation)
Results	Output generated upon completion of a hacking task.
Metrics	A performance indicator that describes how is it possible to evaluate the effectiveness of hacking actions with respect to performing a chosen hacking task

behave in a "stealthy" way. In this case, a Hacking Goal might include "stealthiness" requirements, and the related hacking tasks might assign a higher weight to the actions that do not trigger Intrusion Detection Systems alarms. Hacking Task metrics should in this case include such stealthiness properties.

4.2 Hacking Tasks Tree

Hacking task dependencies generate a *Hacking Tasks Tree*.

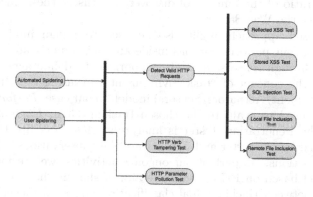

Fig. 2. Hacking Tasks Tree Example for Web Applications

Figure 2 shows Hacking Task dependencies in a Web Application Penetration Testing model. Each box is a single hacking task. A Hacking Goal in the example is "Find all injection vulnerabilities". An injection vulnerability occurs when a Web Application does not properly validate user input in an HTTP Request. In the example, the Reflected XSS Test detects Cross-Site Scripting vulnerabilities, the SQL Injection Test detects SQL Injection vulnerabilities, the Local File Inclusion Test detects LFI vulnerabilities and the Remote File Inclusion Test detects RFI vulnerabilities.

In order to find an injection vulnerability, the attacker must have chosen a valid path, a valid HTTP request and a parameter of the HTTP request that she/he wants to test. In order to choose a parameter, all forms inside HTML pages have to be found by sending valid HTTP requests to the target. In the model, the "Detect Valid HTTP Requests" hacking task is executed to the purpose. In order to send valid requests, the attacker needs to know available paths at the web server. So, before finding valid HTTP requests, she/he performs the "Automatic Spidering" and "User Spidering" tasks in order to enumerate all paths.

Hacking Goal Classification can use existing sources. As an example, in the case of Web Applications useful resources might be the OWASP [2] (Open Web Application Security Project) Testing Guide and the well-known Web Application Hackers Handbook [5].

5   Strengths and Weaknesses of Goal-Centric Classification

A goal-centric attack classification approach makes it easier to find a mapping with Penetration Testing methodologies, since Penetration Testers use hacking methodologies that are focused on goals rather than on the types of attacks they can perform. Through goal-centric classification it is possible to formalize metrics and evaluate attacks. For instance, if the goal is "Enumerate all Paths of a Web Server", a metric to estimate the effectiveness of performed actions might be the ratio of the number of discovered paths to the number of HTTP requests sent to the Web Server.

The proposed approach might also be used to design intelligent agents. An intelligent agent performs actions inside an environment, and monitors the environment through sensors. It is also important to define agent tasks. Russel [8] defines the concept of "task environment", by using the PEAS (Performance/Environment/Actuators/Sensors) model. In our case, *Performance* refers to the metric used to evaluate the chosen Hacking Goal, *Environment* is the target that the Penetration Tester is analyzing, *Actuators* are the tools and techniques used by the tester and *Sensors* are the "observations" deriving from the executed actions. As part of our ongoing activities, we are formalizing an attacker model based on PEAS, with the aim of showing how it is possible to create a link between Hacking Goal classification and an attacker's behavioral model.

On the downside, the formalization of a goal-centric attack classification model requires proficiency in the security field, as well as specific efforts to properly define metrics that might change depending on the specific hacking task to be performed.

6   Conclusion

In this paper we have proposed a switch of perspective with respect to the definition of proper taxonomies in the cybersecurity field. Namely, we have embraced an attack-centric point of view for the classification of attacks. The model we propose is a hierarchical one and helps identify macro-objectives (*Hacking Goals*) that can be further decomposed into constituent *Hacking Tasks*. For each such task, we have identified finer grained components (*Hacking Actions*), each associated with a specific attack activity.

We have formalized the above concepts as a unified taxonomy framework, illustrated ways for leveraging existing hacking goal classification approaches as sources of information and discussed strengths and weaknesses of a goal-centric attack taxonomy.

References

1. Common Attack Pattern Enumeration and Classification (CAPEC). https://capec. mitre.org
2. "OWASP", Owasp.org. (2019). https://www.owasp.org/index.php/Main_Page. Accessed 03 Nov 2019
3. RFC 4949 - Internet Security Glossary, Version 2. Tools.ietf.org (2019). https:// tools.ietf.org/html/rfc4949. Accessed 03 Nov 2019
4. The Penetration Testing Execution Standard. Pentest-standard.org (2019). http:// www.pentest-standard.org/index.php/Main_Page. Accessed 03 Nov 2019
5. Stuttard, D., Pinto, M.: The Web Application Hacker's Handbook. Wiley, Hoboken (2013)
6. Igure, V.M., Williams, R.D.: Taxonomies of attacks and vulnerabilities in computer systems. IEEE Commun. Surv. Tutor. 10(1), 6–19 (2008). https://doi.org/ 10.1109/COMST.2008.4483667. First Quarter
7. Obes, J., Sarraute, C., Richarte, G.: Attack Planning in the Real World. arXiv.org (2019). https://arxiv.org/abs/1306.4044. Accessed 04 Nov 2019
8. Artificial Intelligence: A Modern Approach. Aima.cs.berkeley.edu (2019). http:// aima.cs.berkeley.edu/. Accessed 03 Nov 2019
9. Kotenko, I., Doynikova, E.: The CAPEC based generator of attack scenarios for network security evaluation. In: 2015 IEEE 8th International Conference on Intelligent Data Acquisition and Advanced Computing Systems. Technology and Applications (IDAACS), Warsaw, 2015, pp. 436–441 (2015). https://doi.org/10.1109/ IDAACS.2015.7340774
10. Shebli, H.M.Z.A., Beheshti, B.D.: A study on penetration testing process and tools. In: IEEE Long Island Systems, Applications and Technology Conference (LISAT), Farmingdale, NY, 2018, pp. 1–7 (2018). https://doi.org/10.1109/LISAT. 2018.8378035

A Comparative Study on Combinatorial and Random Testing for Highly Configurable Systems

Hao Jin[1]([✉])(iD), Takashi Kitamura[2](iD), Eun-Hye Choi[2](iD),
and Tatsuhiro Tsuchiya[1](iD)

[1] Osaka University, Suita, Japan
{k-kou,t-tutiya}@ist.osaka-u.ac.jp
[2] AIST, Ikeda, Japan
{t.kitamura,e.choi}@aist.go.jp

Abstract. *Highly configurable systems (HCSs)*, such as software product lines, have complex configuration spaces. *Combinatorial Testing* and *Random Testing* are the main approaches to testing of HCSs. In this paper, we empirically compare their strengths with respect to scalability and diversity of sampled configurations (i.e., tests). We choose ICPL and QUICKSAMPLER to respectively represent *Combinatorial Testing* and *Random Testing*. Experiments are conducted to evaluate the *t-way coverage criterion* of generated test suites for HCS benchmarks.

Keywords: Combinatorial testing · Random testing · Software product line

1 Introduction

Highly configurable systems (HCSs), such as software product lines (SPLs), have complex configuration spaces. The configuration spaces are often determined by *features* and *constraints*, which are modeled in some logical formalism over features, such as *feature models*. Figure 1 shows a simple feature model which describes the configuration space of Eclipse IDE [9]. A *configuration* (or a *test*) specifies which features are de-/selected in a given feature model. Table 1 shows a set of configurations of the feature model of Fig. 1.

Configuration testing validates if systems run correctly at various configurations. However, testing all configurations in a given configuration space exhaustively is infeasible for any non-trivial HCS, since the number of configurations increases exponentially with the number of features (or parameters). Techniques to effectively sample configurations are needed to effectively test HCSs.

Combinatorial Testing (CT) [11] and *Random Testing (RT)* are main approaches to effective configuration sampling for testing of HCSs. Given a HCS and *strength t*, which is a small positive integer such as 2 or 3, CT requires all possible feature interactions of size t to be tested by at least one test in a test suite.

© IFIP International Federation for Information Processing 2020
Published by Springer Nature Switzerland AG 2020
V. Casola et al. (Eds.): ICTSS 2020, LNCS 12543, pp. 302–309, 2020.
https://doi.org/10.1007/978-3-030-64881-7_20

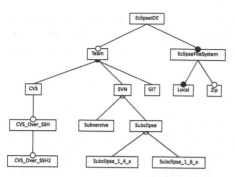

Fig. 1. A feature model of Eclipse IDE (using the notation of [9])

Table 1. Twelve configurations, sampled from Eclipse IDE feature model in Fig. 1. Each column represents a configuration, where 'X' and '-' respectively mean selected and de-selected features of corresponding features in the rows.

Feature \ Configurations	1	2	3	4	5	6	7	8	9	10	11	12
EclipseIDE	X	X	X	X	X	X	X	X	X	X	X	X
Team	X	X	-	X	X	X	X	X	X	X	-	X
CVS	X	X	-	X	X	-	X	-	X	-	-	-
CVS_Over_SSH	X	-	-	X	X	-	X	-	X	-	-	-
CVS_Over_SSH2	-	-	-	X	X	-	X	-	X	-	-	-
SVN	X	X	-	X	X	X	-	X	X	X	-	-
Subversive	X	-	-	X	-	-	-	X	-	-	-	-
Subclipse	-	X	-	-	X	X	-	-	X	X	-	-
Subclipse_1_4_x	-	X	-	-	X	-	-	-	-	X	-	-
Subclipse_1_6_x	-	-	-	-	-	X	-	-	X	-	-	-
GIT	X	-	-	-	X	X	-	X	-	-	-	X
EclipseFileSystem	X	X	X	X	X	X	X	X	X	X	X	X
Local	X	X	X	X	X	X	X	X	X	X	X	X
Zip	-	X	X	X	-	-	-	X	X	-	-	-

This condition is called the *t-way coverage criterion*. Note that the integer t is user-defined. The effectiveness of CT has been demonstrated empirically (e. g., [10,11]). Sampling algorithms for CT test suites (CT algorithms for short) are a central subject in the CT research. The 12 configurations in Table 1 meet the 2-way coverage criterion. We call such a set of test cases a *t-way test suite*.

RT for HCSs is addressed by, for example, Hirasaki et al. [8]. They developed an algorithm to randomly sample configurations from a test space specified by a logical formula. Solution sampling techniques have been actively investigated in the field of constraint solving (instead of testing), yielding several algorithms using such as SAT solvers [2,4] or Binary Decision Diagrams (BDDs) [15]. Although such sampling techniques are not originally developed for software testing, we can use them as configuration sampling algorithms because configuration spaces can be represented as Boolean formulas.

In this paper, we compare CT and RT in testing of large and complex HCSs, focusing on the following RQs:

RQ1. How scalable are CT and RT sampling techniques?
RQ2. How diverse are sampled configurations by RT in terms of t-way coverage criteria?

It is generally perceived that CT sampling is less scalable than RT sampling, since it spends computation resources to maximize t-way coverage criteria. With RQ1, we investigate scalability limits of both the approaches in the setting of HCSs in comparison. RQ2 is posed to evaluate the two approaches with respect to the quality of sampled configurations. Based on the definition of *t-way coverage criterion*, a test suite with smaller size that meets the t-way coverage criteria has better diversity as different tests in it are tending to test different t-way interactions. Hence, we choose t-way coverage criteria as the evaluation metric of the test suite diversity.

2   Related Work

Several studies have compared RT and CT from different perspectives. Arcuri and Briand [1] theoretically analyzed the fault detecting ability of RT in terms of t-way coverage, showing that any t-way interaction can be detected with a probability of 63% by an RT test suite whose size is the same as that of a theoretically-optimal CT test suite. Our work can be viewed as an empirical analogue to the theoretical analysis in the context of large HCS testing.

Wu et al. [16] empirically compared CT, RT, and Adaptive Random Testing (ART) [3] for their fault detecting abilities, in different settings concerning the proportion of parameters, constraints recognized by a tester, and fault rate (degree of injected faults in a system). They concluded, e. g., that the detecting ability of CT is high regardless of different settings and that the three techniques perform equally when a tester knows little about constraints. Contrarily, we are interested in more foundational questions about CT and RT in the context of HCS testing: e. g., scalability and diversity of sampled configurations.

3   Sampling Techniques of CT and RT

A number of CT and RT algorithms have been proposed in the literature. However, their implementations are rarely publicly available. We thus select one representative algorithm from each of the two approaches and compare implementations of the two selected algorithms in our experiments. This section briefly reviews algorithms of the two approaches and present the selected algorithms.

3.1   Sampling Techniques of CT

In this paper, we select the ICPL algorithm by Johansen et al. [9] as the representative to be compared with an RT algorithm in the next section. We explain the decision, by reviewing existing CT algorithms from three aspects.

Most of the existing CT algorithms can be characterized according to algorithm paradigms, into the two categories: *greedy* and *global optimization* algorithms. The main advantage of greedy algorithms is that they run fast while maintaining the generated test suites to be reasonably small. Algorithms/tools such as [19], including ICPL [9], belong to this algorithm paradigm. Global optimization algorithms put emphasis on minimizing test suites and use computationally costly search techniques such as constraint solving [14] or meta-heuristic search [7,12]. They generally can find smaller test suites than greedy algorithms; however, they suffer more from scalability. In this work, we do not consider global optimization algorithms hereafter, because it is already clear that these algorithms cannot compete with RT algorithms in terms of scalability.

ICPL is especially tailored to handle large and complex HCSs, i.e., HCSs with thousands of features and hundred thousands of clauses to specify complex configuration spaces. Some other greedy algorithms employ constraint handling mechanisms (e.g., [18]). The work [19] elaborates a constraint handling technique based on *Minimum Invalid Tuples (MITs)*. However, computing MITs is so costly that it cannot scale to large HCSs. Algorithm by [17] has a refined constraint handling mechanism using the notion of *un-satisfiability cores* [13]; but its implementation is not publicly available.

3.2 Sampling Techniques of RT

Random sampling techniques from configuration spaces specified by logical formulas have been studied in the field of constraint solving. Such random sampling techniques can be classified into two types: clausal-SAT-based and BDD-based. Techniques of the former approach, such as QUICKSAMPLER [4], UNIGEN [2], and SEARCHTREESAMPLER (STSAMPLER, for short) [5], take constraints in CNF as input and sample configurations. These techniques all use repetitive calls of SAT solvers to sample configurations but differ at detailed levels. The BDD-based technique by [15] performs sampling by building a BDD from the input logical formula (not necessarily in CNF) and traversing it. The technique by Hirasaki et al. [8] uses BDDs for constraint solving.

We adopt QUICKSAMPLER, a technique with the clausal-SAT-based approach, as the representative of RT sampling techniques. The clausal-SAT-based approach is superior to the BDD-based approach in terms of scalability. Among clausal-SAT-based techniques, QUICKSAMPLER is one of the most recently developed techniques, shown to be competitive with other random sampling techniques such as UNIGEN and STSAMPLER [4] in efficiency and randomness.

4 Experiments

In this section, we conduct experiments to investigate the RQs raised in Sect. 1.

4.1 Experiment Settings

Our experiments compare ICPL and QUICKSAMPLER as the representative algorithms of CT and RT generation techniques, using publicly available implementations. As benchmark data we collected models of 11 HCSs from different sources as summarized in Table 2. For the HCS benchmarks, all features have exactly two values (binary domains) and their configuration spaces are specified in CNF, which is the format both of ICPL and QUICKSAMPLER can process.

Table 2. HCS Benchmark information. The columns for '#F', '#C', '#Intr. (t = 2)', and '#Intr. (t = 3)' respectively show the number of features, of clauses, of 2-way interactions, and of 3-way interactions of features.

No.	HCS	#F	#C	#Intr. (t = 2)	#Intr. (t = 3)
1	Arcade Game Maker Pedagogical Product Line [6]	61	122	7,320	287,920
2	Berkeley DB [6]	78	151	12,012	608,608
3	Violet [6]	101	203	20,200	1,333,200
4	toybox	544	1,020	590,784	213,469,952
5	axTLS[a]	684	2,155	934,344	424,815,072
6	eCos 3.0 i386pc [6]	1,244	3,146	3,092,584	2,560,659,552
7	FreeBSD Kernel [6]	1,396	62,183	3,894,840	3,619,604,640
8	Fiasco[a]	1,638	5,228	5,362,812	5,849,040,288
9	uClinux[a]	1,850	2,468	6,841,300	8,428,481,600
10	BusyBox[b]	6,796	17,836	92,357,640	418,318,537,440
11	X86 Linux Kernel 2.6.28.6[c]	6,888	343,944	94,875,312	435,540,932,288

[a] https://zenodo.org/record/265808#.X08JB9P7RGA
[b] http://www.busybox.net/
[c] https://www.kernel.org

We measure the computation time (for RQ1), and sizes of generated t-way test suites by ICPL for $t = 2$ and $t = 3$ (for RQ2) for the HCS benchmarks. We also let QUICKSAMPLER sample as many configurations as those generated by ICPL to meet the 2-way and 3-way coverage criteria. We measure the computation time of QUICKSAMPLER and the t-way coverage of the sampled configurations. We set timeout for sampling to 1 h and timeout for measuring coverage of sampled configurations to 4 h. For benchmarks for which ICPL failed to generate test suites within the time limit, we let QUICKSAMPLER sample 1000 and 2000 configurations for 2-way and 3-way coverage, respectively, as a enough large number to confirm its scalability.

All the experiments are conducted on a machine 3 GHz 8 Core Intel Xeon E5 1680v2 CPU and 64 GB memory, running MacOS Sierra. QUICKSAMPLER can only run on a single thread, while ICPL internally runs on eight threads in the experiments. Both are allowed to use 64 GB memory.

4.2 Experimental Results, and Answers for RQs

Table 3 shows the experimental results, based on which we answer the RQs.

Table 3. Experimental results. The columns for 'time' and 'size' in 'ICPL (2-way)' respectively show the generation times (in seconds in wall time) and sizes of generated 2-way test suites, where 'T.O.' means ICPL failed in generation within the time limit. The columns for in 'ICPL (3-way)' show the same for 3-way test suites. The columns for 'QUICKSAMPLER' show (1) the computation time ('time') to sample configurations of the specified sizes ('size'), where 'T.O.' means measuring coverages does not finish within the time limit, and (2) the coverage scores of the sampled configurations for the 2-way coverage criterion ('cov. (%)'). The columns for 'QUICKSAMPLER' show the same items but include columns 't = 2 cov. (%)' and 't = 3 cov. (%)' for the scores of 2-way and 3-way coverage criteria.

No.	ICPL (2-way)		ICPL (3-way)		QUICKSAMPLER			QUICKSAMPLER			
	Size	Time(s)	Size	Time(s)	Size	Time(s)	cov. (%)	Size	Time(s)	t = 2 cov.(%)	T = 3 cov.(%)
1	22	0.33	75	7.10	22	0.01	42.33	75	0.04	44.85	30.80
2	26	0.35	122	7.03	26	0.02	35.55	122	0.05	51.42	37.78
3	31	0.49	153	593.03	31	0.02	30.10	153	0.05	32.93	19.67
4	23	2.89	T.O.		23	0.09	61.43	(2000)	0.66	70.39	T.O
5	25	7.99	T.O.		25	0.26	57.14	(2000)	1.04	59.32	T.O
6	72	107.04	T.O.		72	0.73	30.71	(2000)	3.15	31.85	T.O
7	82	134.73	T.O.		82	3.20	28.71	(2000)	9.24	31.79	T.O
8	155	124.31	T.O.		155	1.96	77.76	(2000)	3.37	80.22	T.O
9	32	91.23	T.O.		32	0.18	57.49	(2000)	1.55	58.24	T.O
10	T.O.		T.O.		(1000)	8.92*	T.O	(2000)	13.25*	T.O	T.O
11	T.O.		T.O.		(1000)	47.83*	T.O	(2000)	78.24*	T.O	T.O
Avg.							46.80			51.22	29.41

Answer to RQ1: "How scalable are CT and RT sampling techniques?" Observing Table 3, we can conclude the answer as follows: ICPL can scale for 2-way test suites for HCSs to up to 1850 features, and for 3-way test suites to up to 101 features. Considering also Table 2, several billions of interactions may be scalability limit of CT in our computing environment. On the other hand, QUICKSAMPLER can sample (even 2000 configurations) for all the HCSs including those with 6888 features and hundred thousands clauses.

Answer to RQ2: "How diverse are sampled configurations by RT in terms of t-way coverage criteria?" Table 3 shows that when the number of sampled configurations is equal to the 2-way and 3-way test suites generated by ICPL, QUICKSAMPLER achieves only 46.8% and 29.4% for 2-way and 3-way coverage respectively. We thus conclude that *the diversity of configurations sampled by CT is 2 to 3 times higher than those sampled by RT*. It is also interesting to see the following: (1) Even sampled configurations are as many as the 3-way test suite generated by ICPL, QUICKSAMPLER achieves only 51.22% with respect to 2-way coverage. (2) The measured t-way coverages of RT test suites are much less than the theoretical bound (63%) provided by [1]; this can be explained by that the theoretical analysis assumes unconstrained configuration spaces, though.

5   Threats to Validity

A possible threat to the validity of this comparative study is the representativeness of the HCS benchmarks used in the experiments. In the HCS models, all features are modeled as binary values. Coverage results might be qualitatively different, when features are modeled with more than two values. Such models can be handled by many CT algorithms such as [17,18]. It is, however, worth noting that recent CT algorithms, including ICPL, are optimized to deal with binary features for acceleration [9,19]. To reflect such recent advances of CT algorithms, our experiments focused on HCSs with binary features.

The validity may also be threatened by the selection for representative algorithms of CT and RT, i.e., ICPL and QUICKSAMPLER. Although we have explained rationale of the selection, experiments using different algorithms may show different results. This paper reports the first step toward comparison of CT and RT in the setting of HCSs, and thus we plan to extend the study to include other algorithms from both CT and RT in experiments in our future work.

6   Conclusion and Future Work

Sampling techniques from logical formula have been an active research subject in the fields of system testing and constraint solving, and various algorithms have been proposed recently from the fields. On the other hand, relatively little attention has been paid to comparing their strengths. This situation causes a problem in testing practice such as testers have difficulty choosing right testing techniques. In this paper, we took the first step toward this problem, investigating strengths of CT and RT in testing of large HCSs.

We consider several directions for future work. First, we plan to extend this comparative study to include other representative algorithms from CT, RT, and constraint solving techniques. In addition to QUICKSAMPLER and ICPL, we plan to include other clausal-SAT-based sampling techniques (e. g., UNIGEN [2] and STSAMPLER [5]), BDD-based techniques (e. g., [8,15]), and other CT greedy algorithms (e. g., [17]) in the comparative study. We also plan to extend the study to investigate fault detection capabilities of CT and RT, as done by [16].

References

1. Arcuri, A., Briand, L.C.: Formal analysis of the probability of interaction fault detection using random testing. IEEE Trans. Softw. Eng. **38**(5), 1088–1099 (2012)
2. Chakraborty, S., Fremont, D.J., Meel, K.S., Seshia, S.A., Vardi, M.Y.: On parallel scalable uniform sat witness generation. In: Baier, C., Tinelli, C. (eds.) TACAS 2015. LNCS, vol. 9035, pp. 304–319. Springer, Heidelberg (2015). https://doi.org/10.1007/978-3-662-46681-0_25
3. Chen, T.Y., Leung, H., Mak, I.K.: Adaptive random testing. In: Maher, M.J. (ed.) ASIAN 2004. LNCS, vol. 3321, pp. 320–329. Springer, Heidelberg (2004). https://doi.org/10.1007/978-3-540-30502-6_23

4. Dutra, R., Laeufer, K., Bachrach, J., Sen, K.: Efficient sampling of SAT solutions for testing. In: Proceedings of ICSE 2018, pp. 549–559 (2018)
5. Ermon, S., Gomes, C., Selman, B.: Uniform solution sampling using a constraint solver as an oracle. In: Proceedings of UAI 2012, pp. 255–264 (2012)
6. Gargantini, A., Radavelli, M.: Migrating combinatorial interaction test modeling and generation to the web. In: 2018 IEEE International Conference on Software Testing, Verification and Validation Workshops (ICSTW), pp. 308–317, April 2018. https://doi.org/10.1109/ICSTW.2018.00066
7. Garvin, B.J., Cohen, M.B., Dwyer, M.B.: Evaluating improvements to a meta-heuristic search for constrained interaction testing. Empirical Softw. Eng. **16**(1), 61–102 (2011)
8. Hirasaki, Y., Kojima, H., Tsuchiya, T.: Applying random testing to constrained interaction testing. In: Proceedings of SEKE 2013, pp. 193–198 (2014)
9. Johansen, M.F., Haugen, O., Fleurey, F.: An algorithm for generating t-wise covering arrays from large feature models. In: Proceedings of SPLC 2012, pp. 46–55 (2012)
10. Kuhn, D.R., Bryce, R., Duan, F., Ghandehari, L.S., Lei, Y., Kacker, R.N.: Chapter one - combinatorial testing: theory and practice. In: Advances in Computers, vol. 99, pp. 1–66. Elsevier (2015)
11. Kuhn, D.R., Kacker, R.N., Lei, Y.: Introduction to Combinatorial Testing. CRC Press, Boca Raton (2013)
12. Lin, J., Cai, S., Luo, C., Lin, Q., Zhang, H.: Towards more efficient meta-heuristic algorithms for combinatorial test generation. In: Proceedings of ESEC/FSE 2019, pp. 212–222 (2019)
13. Lynce, I., Silva, J.P.M.: On computing minimum unsatisfiable cores. In: Proceedings of SAT 2004 (2004)
14. Nanba, T., Tsuchiya, T., Kikuno, T.: Using satisfiability solving for pairwise testing in the presence of constraints. IEICE Trans. **95-A**(9), 1501–1505 (2012)
15. Oh, J., Batory, D.S., Myers, M., Siegmund, N.: Finding near-optimal configurations in product lines by random sampling. In: Proceedings of ESEC/FSE 2017, pp. 61–71 (2017)
16. Wu, H., Nie, C., Petke, J., Jia, Y., Harman, M.: An empirical comparison of combinatorial testing, random testing and adaptive random testing. IEEE Trans. Softw. Eng. (2018)
17. Yamada, A., Biere, A., Artho, C., Kitamura, T., Choi, E.: Greedy combinatorial test case generation using unsatisfiable cores. In: Proceedings of ASE 2016, pp. 614–624 (2016)
18. Yu, L., Lei, Y., Kacker, R.N., Kuhn, D.R.: ACTS: a combinatorial test generation tool. In: Proceedings of ICST 2013, pp. 370–375 (2013)
19. Yu, L., Duan, F., Lei, Y., Kacker, R., Kuhn, D.R.: Combinatorial test generation for software product lines using minimum invalid tuples. In: Proceedings of HASE 2014, pp. 65–72 (2014)

Architecture Based on Keyword Driven Testing with Domain Specific Language for a Testing System

Ricardo B. Pereira[✉], Miguel A. Brito, and Ricardo J. Machado

Centro ALGORITMI, Dep de Sistemas de Informação, University of Minho, Guimarães, Portugal
ricardo-97-pereira@hotmail.com, {mab,rmac}@dsi.uminho.pt

Abstract. For Cyber-physical systems (CPSs), whose task is to test industrial products, to carry out these tests, highly qualified engineers are always needed to design the tests, since the computational part of the tests is programmed in low-level languages. To optimize this process, it is necessary to create an abstraction of current methods so that tests can be created and executed more efficiently. Although this problem has arisen within the CPS, the architecture we propose will be generic enough to solve the problem in any testing system. We intend to do this by automating some of the current processes to minimize human error. In this paper, we present a novel architecture for a testing system that abstracts single low-level programming and coding of tests, based on two main concepts: the use of Keyword Driven Testing (KDT) that will abstract tests to the person responsible for the machine; the creation of a Domain Specific Language (DSL) to help configure and design new tests without requiring the experience of a highly qualified engineer.

Keywords: Cyber-physical systems · Test automation · Keyword Driven Testing · Domain Specific Language · Architecture

1 Introduction

Cyber-physical systems (CPSs) are integrations of computing, network, and physical processes. Embedded computers and networks monitor and control physical processes. A CPS integrates the dynamics of physical processes with software and the network, providing abstractions and modeling, design, and analysis techniques for the integrated whole [4]. According to the state-of-the-art, the CPSs provide the necessary technology to improve the realization and automation corresponding to a complex system on a large scale. Currently, CPSs require solutions that support it at the system level. This is a challenge that includes an engineering approach and a fusion of information and automation technologies [1–3]. Traditional testing systems are adapted to each case, requiring a very expensive and time-consuming effort to develop, maintain, or reconfigure. The current challenge is to develop innovative, and reconfigurable architectures for

© IFIP International Federation for Information Processing 2020
Published by Springer Nature Switzerland AG 2020
V. Casola et al. (Eds.): ICTSS 2020, LNCS 12543, pp. 310–316, 2020.
https://doi.org/10.1007/978-3-030-64881-7_21

testing systems, using emerging technologies and paradigms that can provide the answer to these requirements [5]. The challenge is to automate the maximum number of tasks in this process and get the most out of the testing system, be it a CPS or just software.

What we intend with this research is to optimize the process of creating and executing the tests. Although this problem has arisen within the CPS, the architecture we propose will be generic enough to solve the problem in any testing system that supports the use of the software. We intend to do this by automating some of the current processes to minimize human error. In this paper, we present a novel architecture for a testing system that abstracts single low-level programming and coding of tests, based on two main concepts: the use of Keyword Driven Testing (KDT) that will abstract tests to the person responsible for the machine; the creation of a Domain Specific Language (DSL) to help configure and design new tests without requiring the experience of a highly qualified engineer.

Section 2 provides a background on KDT and DSL, as these are two important concepts to understand the architecture presented. Section 3 describes and presents the proposed architecture. Finally, Sect. 4 concludes and identifies future work.

2 Background

Keyword-Driven Testing is a type of functional automation testing framework which is also known as table-driven testing or action word based testing. In KDT, we use a table format, usually a spreadsheet, to define keywords or action words for each function that we would like to execute. It allows novice or non-technical users to write tests more abstractly and it has a high degree of reusability. The industrial control software has been having an enormous increase in complexity as technology has developed and requires a systematic testing approach to enable efficient and effective testing in the event of changes. KDT has been proving that it is a valuable test method to support these test requirements [6]. Recent results from other researchers have shown that the design of the KDT test is complex with several levels of abstraction and that this design favors reuse, which has the potential to reduce necessary changes during evolution. Besides, keywords change at a relatively low rate, indicating that after creating a keyword, only localized and refined changes are made. However, the same results also showed that KDT techniques require tools to support keyword selection, refactoring, and test repair [7].

Domain-Specific Language is a language meant for use in the context of a particular domain. A domain could be a business context or an application context. A DSL does not attempt to please all. Instead, it is created for a limited sphere of applicability and use, but it's powerful enough to represent and address the problems and solutions in that sphere. A DSL can be used to generate source code from a keyword. However, code generation from a DSL is not considered mandatory, as its primary purpose is knowledge. However, when it is used, code generation is a serious advantage in engineering. DSLs will never be a solution to all software engineering problems, but their application is currently unduly limited by the lack of knowledge available to DSL developers, so further exploration of this area is needed [8]. Other researchers used DSL in CPSs and left their testimony of how the specification language hides the details of the implementation. The specifications are automatically enriched with the implementation through reusable mapping rules. These rules are implemented by the developers and specify the order of execution of the modules and how the input/output variables are implemented [9].

3   Architecture

The architecture that we propose in this paper aims to automate and facilitate the process of creating new tests. To have a complete understanding of the architecture and how its components interconnect, it will be explained first how to use KDT and DSL and only after how they work together.

3.1   KDT

We will use KDT to abstract low-level code scripts, associating each script with a keyword that will represent it most descriptively and explicitly possible. This way the user will not need to know the details of the script implementation, but only what it does. We will also associate each keyword with metadata related to the corresponding test, which will be stored in a database. Figure 1 shows the approach taken in using KDT. Note that the names given to the tests in the figure are only fictitious names to demonstrate that the names given to the keywords must be as descriptive as possible.

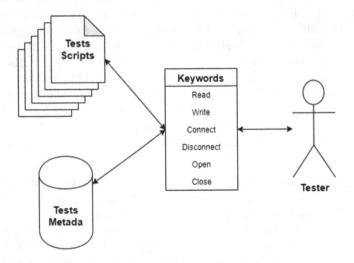

Fig. 1. Keyword Driven Testing approach

In Fig. 1 we see a stack of sheets that represent the test scripts already existing in the system, in this case, they should be primitive tests that focus only on testing a feature or a set of features as long as they can be well-identified only by a word that can serve to be a keyword. We also see the representation of a database that will be where all the information and metadata about the tests existing in the system will be stored, that is, the same ones that are represented in the stack of sheets previously explained. Connected to the database and the stack of sheets, we have a table with keywords in which each keyword represents all the information related to a test. This table is the most important element in the figure because it is where we can relate all the information in the stack of sheets and the database, and this is achieved with just one word which makes it possible for users/testers with little programming knowledge to be able to interpret what each test does or means. Finally, we have the connection between the Tester and the table of keywords that demonstrates that the Tester will only have access to the keywords without needing to know any details of implementation.

3.2 DSL

This use of KDT alone does not bring great advantages because we still need someone to design a test execution flow according to their purpose. This is where the importance of DSL comes in, as it allows us to define a friendly language for workers, without the need for very sophisticated programming knowledge. The proposed language is extremely simple, but it allows the creation of new scripts with new execution flows and logical rules applied, only with the use of keywords defined by the use of KDT and some symbols previously defined in the DSL. Table 1 shows the terminal symbols of the defined DSL and what they represent.

Table 1. DSL symbols description

Symbol	Description
keyword	Catches the keywords in the script
->	Catches the "next" symbol, which means that after that symbol the next block to be executed arrives
?	Catches the conditional expressions from the script
(	Catches the opening parenthesis
)	Catches the closing parenthesis
:	Catches the next block of code to be executed when a condition is false
;	Catches the end of the script
&	Catches the logical operator that means intersection
|	Catches the logical operator that means union

3.3 Proposed Architecture

To achieve the full potential of this architecture, a final abstraction of all these processes is necessary. In Fig. 2 we can see the diagram of the final architecture that ensures to abstract the whole complex process of creating new tests for the system, thus giving the possibility to users less endowed with programming knowledge to be able to build new tests.

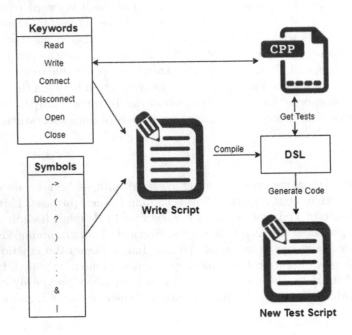

Fig. 2. Architecture

The two tables that are illustrated in Fig. 2, "Keywords" and "Symbols" represent the elements that can be used to form scripts in a lexically correct manner. The syntactically correct way of writing scripts will be explained in the next section where we show an application example. The elements of the "Keywords" table contain the keywords that correspond to the tests that are defined and available in the system to be used as part of new tests. It is also possible to check the connection between this table and the existing tests programmed in lower-level languages, such as C++. The elements of the "Symbols" table contain the terminal symbols of the defined DSL and are what allow to give logic and organization to the new tests of the system. Therefore, the Tester will be able to write the script with the elements available in these two tables and that is exactly what is represented with the connections between the tables and the "Write Script" element of the figure.

Subsequently, the DSL will analyze the script written by Tester using a Lexer and a Parser and will check if it is syntactically and lexically well written.

The "Compile" connection represents this step of analyzing and verifying the script. If the script is correct according to the defined rules, the DSL will compile that script and generate the code for a new test. The DSL needs to access the code of the test scripts that were used through the keywords and it does so as can be seen in the "Get Tests" connection. The DSL will form a new test based on the tests that Tester specified using the keywords. This is only possible because the DSL can match the tests to the keywords that identify them. At the end of this process, we have the connection that shows us that the DSL generates the code for the new test and from that moment it is available for execution.

3.4   Example of Application

In this chapter, we will present a complete example of creating a new test with this architecture to demonstrate its simplicity and efficiency. In this example, we consider that our scope of tests will be the same shown in the "Keywords" table represented in Fig. 2. The symbols that we can use will be those shown in Table 1, as they are the symbols that the developed DSL recognizes. The first step is to write the script with the available keywords and symbols. In this example we will use this script:

```
( Connect & Open ) ? ( Read -> Write -> Close ) : ( Disconnect ) ;
```

Here the scripts corresponding to "Connect" and "Open" will be executed and if both return a positive result (a positive or negative result will be defined by those who create these test primitives) the execution will follow to the block just after "?". If any of the scripts return a negative result, the next block of execution will be the one after the ":" symbol. The block after "?" will execute the three scripts corresponding to "Read", "Write" and "Close" sequentially in the order they are specified in the script. The block after ":" will execute only the script corresponding to "Disconnect".

Now that the script has been written, it will pass through the Lexer defined on the DSL, which will analyze whether all elements that are in the script are part of the language dictionary. In this case, all symbols will be recognized successfully and then it is the DSL Parser's turn to continue with its parsing and check that all the sentence formation rules are respected. Once verified, as this script is correct it will be compiled by the DSL and the source code of the new test script will be generated at that moment. The way the new script is created is by using the existing source code of the tests that are referenced in the script by the keywords and adding to it the logic applied by the DSL symbols used in the script.

4   Conclusions and Future Work

In this paper, we presented a novel architecture for a testing system that will allow cyber test components to have a much simpler and more efficient way to create new tests.

This architecture demonstrates how we can use KDT and DSL to achieve great abstractions and automate the process of creating new tests. This type of architecture gives a boost to the world of CPS research, but also to the general context of testing systems, since it is generic and can be applied both in the context of CPS and in any other context that allows the use of software.

The future work will be to continue the evolution of this new architecture, implementing a functional prototype and a system to be integrated into the CPS industry. And with that to be able to contribute even more to the investigation bringing real results of the application of the architecture.

Acknowledgments. This paper is a result of the project POCI-01-0247-FEDER-040130, supported by Operational Program for Competitiveness and Internationalization (COMPETE 2020), under the PORTUGAL 2020 Partnership Agreement, through the European Regional Development Fund (ERDF).

References

1. Leitão, P., Colombo, A.W., Karnouskos, S.: Industrial automation based on cyber-physical systems technologies: Prototype implementations and challenges. Comput. Ind. (2016). https://doi.org/10.1016/j.compind.2015.08.004
2. Liu, Y., Peng, Y., Wang, B., Yao, S., Liu, Z.: Review on cyber-physical systems. IEEE/CAA J. Autom. Sin. (2017). https://doi.org/10.1109/JAS.2017.7510349
3. Seshia, S.A., Hu, S., Li, W., Zhu, Q.: Design automation of cyber-physical systems: challenges, advances, and opportunities. IEEE Trans. Comput. Aid. Des. Integr. Circuits Syst. (2017). https://doi.org/10.1109/TCAD.2016.2633961
4. Lee, E.A.: Cyber physical systems: design challenges. In: Proceedings - 11th IEEE Symposium on Object/Component/Service-Oriented Real-Time Distributed Computing, ISORC 2008 (2008). https://doi.org/10.1109/ISORC.2008.25
5. Leitão, P.: Agent-based distributed manufacturing control: a state-of-the-art survey. Eng. Appl. Artif. Intell. (2009). https://doi.org/10.1016/j.engappai.2008.09.005
6. Hametner, R., Winkler, D., Zoitl, A.: Agile testing concepts based on keyword-driven testing for industrial automation systems. In: IECON Proceedings (Industrial Electronics Conference) (2009). https://doi.org/10.1109/IECON.2012.6389298
7. Rwemalika, R., Kintis, M., Papadakis, M., Le Traon, Y., Lorrach, P.: On the evolution of keyword-driven test suites. In: 2019 12th IEEE Conference on Software Testing, Validation and Verification (ICST), Xi'an, China, pp. 335–345 (2019)
8. Mernik, M., Heering, J., Sloane, A.M.: When and how to develop domain-specific languages. ACM Comput. Surv. (2005). https://doi.org/10.1145/1118890.1118892
9. Ciraci, S., Fuller, J.C., Daily, J., Makhmalbaf, A., Callahan, D.: A runtime verification framework for control system simulation. In: IEEE 38th Annual Computer Software and Applications Conference. Vasteras 2014, pp. 75–84 (2014)

Author Index

Printed in the United States
By Bookmasters

Printed in the United States
By Bookmasters